THE MASTER MUSICIANS

D0733069

ROSSINI

Series edited by Stanley Sadie

The Master Musicians

Titles available in paperback

Berlioz *Hugh Macdonald*
Brahms *Malcolm MacDonald*
Britten *Michael Kennedy*
Bruckner *Derek Watson*
Chopin *Jim Samson*
Grieg *John Horton*
Handel *Donald Burrows*
Liszt *Derek Watson*
Mahler *Michael Kennedy*
Mendelssohn *Philip Radcliffe*
Monteverdi *Denis Arnold*
Purcell *J.A. Westrup*

Rachmaninoff *Geoffrey Norris*
Rossini *Richard Osborne*
Schoenberg *Malcolm MacDonald*
Schubert *John Reed*
Sibelius *Robert Layton*
Richard Strauss *Michael Kennedy*
Tchaikovsky *Edward Garden*
Vaughan Williams *James Day*
Verdi *Julian Budden*
Vivaldi *Michael Talbot*
Wagner *Barry Millington*

Titles available in hardback

Bach *Malcolm Boyd*
Beethoven *Barry Cooper*
Chopin *Jim Samson*
Elgar *Robert Anderson*
Handel *Donald Burrows*

Schubert *John Reed*
Schumann *Eric Frederick Jensen*
Schütz *Basil Smallman*
Richard Strauss *Michael Kennedy*
Stravinsky *Paul Griffiths*

In preparation

Bartók *Malcolm Gillies*
Dvořák *Jan Smaczny*

Musorgsky *David Brown*
Puccini *Julian Budden*

THE MASTER MUSICIANS

ROSSINI

Richard Osborne

OXFORD
UNIVERSITY PRESS

OXFORD
UNIVERSITY PRESS
Great Clarendon Street, Oxford OX2 6DP

Oxford University Press is a department of the University of Oxford.
It furthers the University's objective of excellence in research, scholarship,
and education by publishing worldwide in

Oxford New York

Athens Auckland Bangkok Bogotá Buenos Aires Cape Town
Chennai Dar es Salaam Delhi Florence Hong Kong Istanbul Karachi
Kolkata Kuala Lumpur Madrid Melbourne Mexico City Mumbai Nairobi
Paris São Paulo Singapore Taipei Tokyo Toronto Warsaw

and associated companies in Berlin Ibadan

Oxford is a registered trade mark of Oxford University Press
in the UK and in certain other countries

Published in the United States
by Oxford University Press Inc., New York

First published 1986
First paperback edition 1987
Revised 1993 by J.M. Dent & Sons Ltd

First published as an Oxford University Press paperback edition 2001

The moral rights of the author have been asserted

Database right Oxford University Press (maker)

British Library Cataloguing in Publication Data

Data available

Library of Congress Cataloging in Publication Data

Osborne, Richard, 1943–
Rossini / Richard Osborne.
p. cm.—(The master musicians)
Includes bibliographical references (p.) and index.
1. Rossini, Gioacchino, 1792–1868. 2. Composers—Biography.
I. Title. II. Master musicians series.
ML410.R8 O9 2001 782.1′092—dc21 00–057106
ISBN 0–19–816490–4

Printed in Great Britain
by Biddles Ltd.,
Guildford & King's Lynn

Contents

Illustrations

Key to sigla

The following works are referred to in abbreviated form in footnotes

BdCRdS   *Bollettino del Centro rossiniano di studi* (Pesaro, 1955–60, 1967–)

Gossett   Philip Gossett, *The operas of Rossini: problems of textual criticism in Nineteenth-Century Opera* (Dissertation, Princeton University, 1970)

LdR   *Lettere di G. Rossini*, ed. G. Mazzatinti with F. and G. Manis (Imola, 3/1902)

Hiller   Ferdinand Hiller, 'Plaudereien mit Rossini' (1856), *Aus dem Tonleben unserer Zeit*, ii (Leipzig, 2/1871)

Michotte   Edmond Michotte, *Richard Wagner's Visit to Rossini* and *An Evening at Rossini's in Beau-Sejour*, translated and annotated with an introduction and appendix by Herbert Weinstock (Chicago, 1968)

Radiciotti   G. Radiciotti, *Gioacchino Rossini: vita documentata, opere ed influenza su l'arte*, 3 vols (Tivoli, 1927–9)

Rognoni   Luigi Rognoni, *Gioacchino Rossini* (Turin, 3/1977)

Roncaglia   Gino Roncaglia, *Rossini l'olimpico* (Milan, 1946)

VdR   Stendhal, *Vie de Rossini* (Paris, 1824 translated into English and annotated by Richard N. Coe, London, 2/1970)

MMR   Frank Walker, 'Rossiniana in the Piancastelli Collection', *Monthly Musical Record*, xc (1960), p.138ff, p.203ff

Weinstock   Herbert Weinstock, *Rossini: a biography* (New York, 1968)

To Hailz-Emily

Preface

Despite the widespread popularity of a handful of his works, Rossini has some claim to being the most neglected and generally misunderstood of all the great nineteenth-century composers. Indeed, it is a measure of this neglect that no full-length study of his life and works has appeared in English for over fifty years.

The reasons for the decline in Rossini's reputation in the years following his death will be touched on later; but it can be said at the outset that his art and personality have always been something of an enigma, naturally resistant to the quick and easy solutions readily on offer. The grounds for the popularity of his better known work are not difficult to find. Rossini's most characteristic music is rhythmically vital, sensuous, and brilliant; 'full of the finest animal spirits', wrote Leigh Hunt in his *Autobiography* of 1850, 'yet capable of the noblest gravity'. It might also be agreed that Rossini's natural stance is a detached one, detached enough for his admirers to think him a fine ironist and for his detractors to dub him cynical. But the image which devolves from this – Rossini as a gifted but feckless amateur who at an early age abandoned his career to the otiose pleasures of the table – bears no relation to the facts of the career as we have them. The man, who in his lifetime was happy to cultivate a mask of casual unconcern, was in reality an odd mixture of affability and reserve, industry and indolence, wit and melancholy. And there were other paradoxes, too. A classicist by training and a conservative by inclination, Rossini none the less broke the mould of the old Italian operatic order and laid the foundations for a new generation of romantically inspired music-dramatists. The persona foisted on the young Rossini by an adoring public was, in fact, little more than an agreeable fiction. Yet it was a fiction which provided Rossini with the protection he needed: both as a creative artist anxious to make his mark in a rumbustious and changing world and as a man increasingly prey in his later years to debilitating bouts of physical and mental illness. The truth is, Rossini was not only one of the most influential, he was also one of the most industrious and at the same time one of the most emotionally complex of nineteenth-century composers.

To understand this, it is necessary to look afresh at Rossini's life and at the conditions which existed in Italy and France during his long career; for without an informed knowledge of the context in which Rossini wrote it is impossible to arrive at a secure idea of how the works themselves might best be assessed and revived. And unfashionable as it now is to separate out life and works, the works themselves merit separate, and chronological, treatment: for ease of reference and in order to avoid the kind of damaging generalisations which have bedevilled some earlier Rossini criticism. Only by considering each of Rossini's thirty-nine operas, his principal choral works, and the substantial body of late piano and vocal music can we properly prepare the ground for more informed, general discussion of his art and influence.

In adopting this approach, I have not, I hope, neglected some larger issues. The principal facets of Rossini's art – his mastery of the comic medium, the nature of his treatment of the *seria* and *semiseria* genres and, above all, his evolution of those new and far-reaching forms which were to dominate Italian operatic procedures for the next fifty years – are dealt with in the context of the work-by-work guide to his output. Thus the chapters on such pivotal works as *Tancredi*, *L'italiana in Algeri*, *Il barbiere di Siviglia*, *La Cenerentola*, *La gazza ladra*, *Armida*, *Mosè in Egitto*, *Ermione*, *Maometto II*, and *Guillaume Tell* serve a double purpose: surveying the work in question, whilst at the same time examining issues central to any proper assessment of Rossini's style and method. I have included a separate chapter on Rossini's use of the overture, and another (Chapter 18) setting out some of the problems we need to bear in mind as we approach the works.

Assessment of the operas continues to be hampered, of course, by the fact that none of us has seen the entire opus in the theatre, let alone the entire opus sympathetically produced and sung, with the right kind of orchestra in the right size of auditorium. As Rossini himself affirmed in conversation with Wagner in 1860: 'It is only in the theatre that it is possible to bring equitable judgement to bear on music meant for the stage'. Nor do we have the benefit of a complete set of scholarly texts. Reading nineteenth-century vocal scores is no substitute for the detailed examination of the mass of materials –

including the important variants sanctioned by Rossini himself – which goes to make up a critical edition. Happily, an edition is underway; and though it will be many decades before its seventy or so volumes are complete, the initiative, begun at the Fondazione Rossini, Pesaro, in the early 1970s, has already yielded a mass of materials germane to a fresh understanding of Rossini and his music. This Rossini Edition, under the joint editorship of Bruno Cagli, Philip Gossett, and Alberto Zedda, is one of the great musicological enterprises of our time; without its example and without the detailed findings it has thrown up in the last ten years, this book could not have been written.

As to performances of Rossini's works, the situation is improving by the year and there is the added promise of significant bicentenary celebrations in 1992. In the 1950s and 1960s a number of Rossini's finest comic operas, including such rarities at the time as *Le Comte Ory* and *Il turco in Italia*, underwent stylish revival at Glyndebourne, an ideal Rossini theatre, and elsewhere. Nowadays we can, if we are so minded, travel to Pesaro itself, Rossini's birthplace, where each year the beautifully restored small Teatro Rossini becomes the focal point for a summer festival in which distinguished singers, players, and conductors, backed by the formidable scholarly resources of the Fondazione Rossini, come together to revive works which fifty years ago were written off as failures on no stronger ground than that of contemporary neglect. Meanwhile, the gramophone continues to provide inestimable help in bringing these productions to a wider audience.

The prospects, then, are bright for a just and sustained reappraisal of Rossini's music. In such circumstances enthusiasm for the Rossini cause should no doubt be tempered by a measure of Rossinian scepticism; but if the book which follows veers towards the former, I make no apology. The detractors have had their way with Rossini for far too long.

Bradfield, Berkshire   R.O.
August, 1985

Preface to the paperback edition

A paperback edition has allowed me to make some minor corrections and to update the text in one or two places. The Rossini revival continues apace. In August 1986, the Pesaro Festival restored to the stage *Bianca e Falliero*, which has enabled me to redraft my comments on that opera. The new edition also gives me an opportunity to thank a number of people for their helpful scrutiny of the text at various junctures, notably William Mann, Rodney Milnes, Jerrold Northrop Moore, whose advice on a number of matters was invaluable from the first, and my editor, Julia Kellerman.

1987   R.O.

'I love Italian opera – it's so reckless. Damn Wagner, and his bellowings at Fate and death. Damn Debussy, and his averted face. I like the Italians who run all on impulse, and don't care about their immortal souls, and don't worry about the ultimate.'

> D.H. Lawrence, letter to Louie Burrows, 1 April 1911.

Tous les genres sont bons,
Hors le genre ennuyeux.

> Gioachino[1] Rossini, letter to Filippo Filippi, 26 August 1868.

[1] Though 'Gioacchino' is the familiar spelling of the name, Rossini himself more usually adopted the spelling 'Gioachino'. This is now the accepted spelling of his first name and is used throughout the present volume except where the alternative spelling has been adopted in the titles of books and articles on Rossini.

1

The formative years (1792–1810)

Pesaro and Lugo

Like most popular seaside resorts, Pesaro has succumbed in recent years to a certain amount of commercialization and concrete; but the delectable small township evoked by Stendhal in the first chapter of his *Vie de Rossini* is still recognizably there, snug at the mouth of the River Foglia with a pleasing hinterland of woods and hills, and Urbino not far distant. In a house in the narrow, bustling main street of the old town Gioachino Rossini was born on 29 February, 1792.

His mother was a native of Pesaro, but his father, Giuseppe Rossini, an itinerant trumpeter and horn player, came from Lugo, a small town to the north, 28 kilometres from Ravenna. In 1789, Giuseppe had successfully sought an option on the post of Town Trumpeter in Pesaro. After some backstairs dealing with the incumbent, Luigi Ricci, the post was vacated early in 1790 on terms favourable to Ricci. Giuseppe applied for release from his temporary position with the garrison band in Ferrara, but was refused. Infuriated, and perhaps already a little drunk with revolutionary fervour, Giuseppe remonstrated with the authorities and, not for the last time in his life, was imprisoned for insubordination. The subsequent imbroglio, a fit subject for one of his son's later *farse*, ended in his release, his confession and apology to the Pesaro authorities, Ricci's dismissal for attempting to barter a public office, and Giuseppe's appointment to the post. In this, as in some later incidents, Giuseppe emerges as a splendidly robust character: earthy and energetic, a shade naif perhaps, querulous at times, but a natural improvisor, an honest schemer.

His first lodgings in Pesaro were in the Via del Fallo, in a house shared by the Guidarini family. Domenico Guidarini, a baker by trade, had married Lucia Romagnoli whose family came from Urbino. There were four children: a son and three daughters. The second daughter appears to have been known to the Pesaro police as a local harlot, and the pretty eldest daughter, Anna, was certainly flirtatious. We can only speculate on Giuseppe's reasons for taking up lodgings in the Guidarini house; what is certain is that Anna became pregnant in the summer of 1791. She was nineteen, Giuseppe was thirty-two. On 26 September, the lovers were married in the old cathedral in Pesaro. Five months later, Anna gave birth to her only child. He was baptized Gioachino Antonio in the cathedral on the day of his birth; two members of the local nobility stood as god-parents. In Pesaro there appears to have been an easy commerce between the classes; added to which, Anna was exceptionally pretty and Giuseppe's energy and charm – he was nicknamed 'Vivazza' – clearly endeared him to the local community.

As a child and young man, Rossini appears to have inherited something of his mother's charm, grace, and feminine good looks; in later years, he came more and more to resemble his father.[1] The photographs of the 1850s show us a heavier, sturdier, more resilient figure, thinner-lipped but still with a lively, enquiring, ironic gaze.[2] Rossini's relationship with his parents was a close one. The grief he exhibited at the time of his mother's death in 1827 and his father's in 1839 is sufficient testimony to the depth and warmth of the rela-tionship. When Wagner praised William Tell's aria 'Sois immobile' during the conversation he had with Rossini in Paris in 1860, Rossini commented: 'I'll tell you that the feeling which moved me most in my life was the love I had for my mother and my father, and they repaid it at a userer's rate of interest, I'm happy to tell you. It was there, I think, that I found the note that I needed for this scene of the apple in *Guillaume Tell*.'[3]

Giuseppe's exuberance and zeal for the new Republican cause which was sweeping Europe in the wake of the French Revolution was far from unpopular in a town which was thoroughly disen-chanted with Papal rule, though it was to land him and his family in trouble in the winter and spring of 1799 and 1800. The French, who had first entered northern Italy in 1792, made further advances in 1796 under Napoleon Bonaparte, the new commander-in-chief of the army in Italy. In October 1796 Bologna and Ferrara were taken; and French troops met minimal resistance when they marched into

[1] See plate 2.
[2] See plate 18.
[3] Michotte, pp.69–70

Pesaro on 5 February, 1797. In December 1797 Guiseppe's zeal in a situation which was still politically fluid lost him his post as town *trombetta*, but in the heady pro-Republican atmosphere so fervent a patriot was not long denied office. The establishing of the Cisalpine Republic and, in 1798, the French invasion of the Papal States, raised hopes of an Italian republic on French lines. In 1797–9 the ideals of the *Risorgimento* were taking root. They were, none the less, uncertain times. In 1799 Papal forces rallied and the French suffered temporary set-backs at the hands of the Austro-Russian armies. With the Austrians back in power, activists were rounded up by the spies and gendarmes of the old regime. 'The war of the gendarmes against thought', Stendhal called it, in a phrase prophetic of Orwell. One such victim was Giuseppe Rossini. He was arrested in Bologna, detained for questioning, and eventually imprisoned. Only when the Austrians were defeated at Marengo in June 1800 was his position secure, his freedom guaranteed.

What effect these political events had on the growing boy is difficult to determine. 'Without the French invasion of Italy', Rossini later told Azevedo, attributing to events a providential role, 'I would probably have been an apothecary or olive-oil merchant.'[4] In his middle years Rossini became ultra-conservative. The revolutions of 1830 and 1848, coming in the wake of the long-drawn-out Napoleonic wars, his own exacerbated nerves, and the drift to conservatism that often comes naturally with age must be held largely responsible for Rossini's not unreasonable loathing of those who would seek endlessly to disorder the world. Yet, as a child, Rossini probably enjoyed the general excitement and noise (in 1798 he appears to have played a percussion instrument in the band of the Civil Guard of Pesaro) and as a growing boy he may have begun to share his father's political enthusiasms. The 21-year-old composer of *L'italiana in Algeri* who hid a reference to the 'Marseillaise' in the chorus which precedes the politically inflammatory 'Pensa alla patria' cannot be thought wholly reactionary, as Rossini himself pointed out in a letter to Filippo Santocanale in June 1864.[5]

At some point between Gioachino's birth and the end of the decade, Anna Rossini decided to put her own musical talents to use.

[4] A. Azevedo, *G. Rossini: sa vie et ses œuvres*, Paris, 1824, p.21.
[5] LdR pp.270–2; Rognoni pp.315–16.

She had received little if any formal training, but she had a sharp ear, a pleasing voice, and an attractive stage manner. Not surprisingly, she was soon in demand as a *seconda* or even *prima donna soprano* in several local houses. Many stories are extant about her brief career, not least that of her son allegedly rushing from the wings to revive her when she fainted during a stormy performance of Nasolini's revised version of *La morte di Semiramide* in Trieste in 1802. Not all such stories are verifiable, but we know that Anna Rossini was in regular demand from about 1799 onwards; with her husband in prison, her own capacity to earn money would have seemed doubly important. In the early years of the new century Anna sang regularly in Imola and Ravenna in operas by Mosca, Weigl, Fioravanti, and Gazzaniga. From 1802 the family was based, not in Pesaro, but in a rather bleak-looking house in Giuseppe's native Lugo. How regularly Gioachino travelled with his mother is not certain, yet it is clear that he saw and heard a good deal of opera in these formative years. By the time of his precocious entry to Bologna's Accademia Filarmonica at the age of 14 in 1806, he must have had the same kind of family experience of opera houses which a boy brought up in a circus would have of that not dissimilar world.

In spite of a partially itinerant life in these years, the Rossinis saw to it that their son received a basic education. If the reminiscences of Francesco Genari in a letter to Rossini in 1865 are to be believed, the young Rossini was a high-spirited scamp, much given to stone-throwing and the raiding of cruets in the cathedral sanctuary; but he was put to school and given a basic grounding in reading and writing (like many famous men, he remained an erratic speller throughout his life), as well as mathematics, Latin, and decorative handwriting. And there was an evolving musical training. In 1801 Giuseppe Rossini was appointed by the Bologna Accademia as a 'professore di corno di caccia', and the young Rossini is known to have taken lessons from his father at this time. In addition, there was a steady flow of outside help for the Rossinis' handsome, musically-gifted young son. An early teacher in Bologna where Gioachino was briefly boarded out was Giuseppe Prinetti, around whom Rossini later wound several tales for the benefit of Ferdinand Hiller and others. According to Rossini, Prinetti slept upright among the colonnades of Bologna and made ends meet by brandy distilling and cembalo lessons. No doubt Rossini's childhood world was partly peopled by real-life *buffo* types; but there were serious influences, too: first, Padre Giovanni Sassoli and later, whilst the Rossinis were still living in Lugo, Canon Giuseppe Malerbi.

Under Malerbi's guidance Rossini laid some of the foundations of his compositional style. He also sang (he later developed a fine baritonal tenor), played the cembalo, and read and played through a collection of music, much of it by Mozart and Haydn, which was to leave a permanent mark on his musical style. At the Palazzo Malerbi he also met Giuseppe's brother, Luigi, a lively, caustic man whose musical compositions are said to have reflected his original and mordant view of the world. The Rossinis no doubt glimpsed the good life here. They often dined at the Palazzo, occasions which may have helped alert the young Rossini to the pleasures of the table.

By 1803/4, with Malerbi's help, Rossini was beginning to write music of his own, in addition to performing and acting as helper to his mother. In Imola in 1804 an *avviso pubblico* was posted, in Gioachino's name, announcing a concert at the Teatro Comunale on the evening of 22 April. The notice features arias to be sung by 'Cittad. Anna Rossini', a 'Duetto eseguito dalla Cittadina Rossini, e Figlio', fully costumed, and a 'Cavatina cantata dal Citt. Gioachino Rossini', also costumed and in the *buffo* style. This is significant enough; yet it is a slender achievement when set beside the six *sonate a quattro* for two violins, cello and double-bass which Rossini wrote for the 23-year-old landowner and merchant Agostino Triossi at his holiday home in the village of Conventello near Ravenna in the summer of 1804. Later in his life Rossini was fond of writing ironically affectionate attestations on his old autograph manuscripts. His attestation of these youthful sonatas is one of the most charming, even if the note about an absence of lessons in thorough-bass is, perhaps, a shade disingenuous.

> First violin, second violin, violoncello, and contrabass parts for six *horrendous* sonatas composed by me at the country house (near Ravenna) of my friend and patron, Agostino Triossi, at the most youthful age, having not even had a lesson in thorough-bass. They were all composed and copied in three days and performed in a doggish way by Triossi, contrabass; Morini (his cousin), first violin; the latter's brother, violoncello; and the second violin by myself, who was, to tell the truth, the least doggish.[6]

[6] Reprinted in facsimile by Alfredo Casella in *Rossiniana*, Bologna, 1942, pp. 37–9. Weinstock's variant reading of the final sentence (p.13) is a mistranslation.

Triossi was to commission a good deal from Rossini, much of it unearthed in recent times by the Italian scholar, Paolo Fabbri. To judge by these works, the hours spent with Malerbi and the resources of the Palazzo Malerbi were well used. The sonatas reveal an instinctive feel for speed and economy of gesture. A mordant wit goes hand in hand with a certain sensuous lyricism, short-breathed but sweet. There is an easy mastery of simple forms, including the implied structuring of tonal contrasts, and an acute ear for the interplay of instruments of disparate tonal volume (in this case, the double-bass and the two violins). Above all, the twelve-year-old Rossini declares himself to be a composer of energy and resource, quick-witted, assimilative, but with a manner and voice which is distinctly his own.

Bologna

Bologna is one of Italy's oldest and most distinguished cities. Stendhal called it 'the headquarters of music in Italy'[7] and Charles Dickens, walking its red arcaded streets in the 1840s during Rossini's final period of residence there, commended 'the grave and learned air' of this 'ancient sombre town'.[8] The Rossinis moved there in the latter part of 1804 to be nearer the centre of musical life. Anna Rossini's voice, never properly trained, was more and more afflicted by strain and by a debilitating infection of the tonsils. Increasingly, Gioachino was looked to for modest contributions towards the family budget, singing in local churches and, more important, acting as *répétiteur* and continuo player in local opera houses. Playing for Weigl's *L'amor marinaro* (part of whose text, Rossini himself briefly set), he was announced with full honours as '*Maestro al cembalo* sig. Giovacchino Rossini Accademico Filarmonico di Bologna'. The next year, in 1807, he is recorded as playing in Guglielmi's *La serva astuta* in Faenza; in Bologna in 1809 he played in operas by Paër, Sarti, and Cimarosa. He was, it seems, good at his job; but an intelligent teenager with a highly developed sense of humour can easily cause offence. In Senigallia Rossini was rebuked for laughing during a performance at a harmonically implausible cadenza being essayed,

[7] VdR, p.110.
[8] *Pictures from Italy*, Oxford Illustrated Dickens, London, 1957, p.324.

not for the first time, by Adelaide Carpano. The audience approved the joke but neither the *prima donna* nor her protector, the Marchese Cavalli, were much amused. Not that the incident did Rossini much harm. It was Cavalli who was to give Rossini his first fully-fledged commission, a setting of the *farsa Il cambiale di matrimonio*, in Venice in the winter of 1810.

In the autumn of 1805 Rossini appeared in a stage role at Bologna's Teatro del Corso. The work was Paër's *opera semiseria, Camilla*. He sang the role of the Adolfo, Camilla's son, and is said to have shown greater ardour in rushing into the arms of the ampler of the two *prime donne* engaged for the production's popular and taxing run. During this first full year in Bologna Rossini studied privately with the excellent Padre Angelo Tesei before being admitted to the Liceo Musicale in April 1806 where he was to study singing, cello, piano, and counterpoint under the director of the Liceo, Padre Stanislao Mattei. It was here that the 14-year-old Mozart had studied briefly with Mattei's legendary predecessor, Padre Martini, who had done as much as anyone to turn Bologna into an internationally famous centre of musical scholarship. The libraries alone were goldmines of ancient and modern music (Martini had left a collection of over 17,000 volumes). Rossini was able to read widely, furthering his knowledge of the music of Haydn and Mozart. Indeed, more than one commentator has alleged that it was they who were Rossini's real teachers in Bologna, not the somewhat conservative Mattei.

Clearly, there is an element of truth in this. Rossini's nature was both practical and instinctive. In a deeply characteristic utterance he once referred to Mozart as 'the admiration of my youth, the desperation of my mature years, and the consolation of my old age'. To the 14-year-old Rossini, Mozart and Haydn, too little noted by conservative and chauvinistic taste in early nineteenth century Italy, were a true source for admiration. Their forms provided Rossini with lively and lucid models, whilst the music itself was rich in felicitous melody and orchestration. Haydn, in particular, seems to have been a kindred spirit in the string quartets, *The Creation* and *The Seasons*, echoes of which abound in Rossini's own compositions. Here was a man of energy and wit, a 'natural' composer – in Schiller's formulation a true *naïf* – with whom Rossini could identify. The teachers at the Liceo Musicale did much to direct Rossini's enthusiasms. He learnt from them what he needed to learn: simple though not necessarily conservative harmonic procedures, clear part-writing, and how to develop still further his already acute ear for instrumental sonorities. But esoteric theorizing passed him by. Ever the sensitive barometer of impending tension, he became increasingly nervous of the training he was being offered. Too much theory threatened his natural instinct for composition. What's more, personal relationships were never easy. Even the kindly Mattei appears to have become impatient with the young man, though it must be said in Rossini's defence that Mattei was probably not the best of teachers. Later in life, he told the musicologist, François-Joseph Fétis: 'I would have had greater interest in cultivating stricter, more serious types of music if my counterpoint teacher had been someone who explained the purpose of the rules to me; but when I asked Mattei for explanations. he always replied: "This is the way it has been done" '.[9]

Such teaching, though common enough in all disciplines and ages, can be stultifying. When, in 1810, Mattei suggested a two-year course in plainsong and canon, Rossini decided to call it a day; though the parting was, according to Rossini, amicable and not without subsequent regrets on both sides.

Nothing Rossini wrote between 1806 and 1810 has achieved the popularity of the six *sonate a quattro* of 1804. It was a period of re-adjustment, the way ahead temporarily obfuscated by pedagogic restraints, Rossini's own fascination with the German tradition, and, no doubt, a certain adolescent self-consciousness. From this period we have a small quantity of choral music, commissions from Bologna, Rimini, and Ravenna. The Cantata for tenor, chorus, and orchestra, *Il pianto d'Armonia sulla morte d'Orfeo* won an academic prize and was performed at convocation in Bologna on 11 August, 1808. Much of the part-writing for chorus is wooden and the writing for tenor solo lacks Rossini's later melodic fluency. Perhaps he was striving too hard for a certain 'German' cut to the phrasing and harmony. There is, though, some characterful orchestral writing, with lovely wind solos and a glimpse of Rossini's new-found love, the solo cello.

The best vocal writing from this period is to be found in some of the numbers which Rossini wrote, on a piecemeal basis, for the opera

---

[9] Fétis, *Biographie universelle des musiciens;* quoted *Grove* 6, Vol.11, p.828.

Demetrio e Polibio. In 1805 he became acquainted with the distinguished old tenor, Domenico Mombelli. Mombelli, then in his
mid-50s, was well-connected musically. His first wife, Luisa Laschi,
had created the role of the Countess Almaviva in Mozart's *Le nozze
di Figaro* (and was Mozart's Zerlina in the Vienna revival of *Don
Giovanni*); his second wife, Vincenza Viganò, was a niece of
Boccherini and sister of the celebrated choreographer, Salvatore
Viganò, creator of Beethoven's *Prometheus* ballet. Two of their ten
children were adept singers and the Mombellis had formed themselves
into a touring opera group, in which capacity they arrived in Bologna
in 1805. Years later, Rossini described to Ferdinand Hiller how a
rich patroness and lady-friend (even at the age of 13 Rossini appears
to have been a sexual *galant*) requested from him a copy of an aria by
Portogallo currently being performed by the Mombellis. The copyist
declined to provide Rossini with the material, as did Mombelli who
probably resented a pert teenager as much as he feared a commercial
rival. Nothing daunted, Rossini announced to a sceptical Mombelli
his intention of returning to the opera and writing out the piece from
memory. At first, Mombelli suspected collusion with the copyist; but
Rossini rapidly convinced him of his quick ear and sound technique.
A friendship was struck and Rossini was informally launched on his
career as opera composer when stray numbers from a libretto by
Signora Mombelli were offered to him. Stendhal's account of *Demetrio e Polibio*, which was not staged until 1812, is a dizzying blend
of fact and fantasy. But whether or not he saw the opera on a flawless
summer's day in Como, his judgment of the celebrated duet 'Questo
cor ti giura amore' accurately denotes an aspect of Rossini's appeal
to a widening public in the years up to and including the *prima* of
Tancredi in February 1813.

> A factor which strongly contributed to the charm of these perfect
> *cantilenas* was the unobstrusiveness and, if I may use the term, the
> *modesty* of the accompaniments. These songs were the first fragile
> blossoms of Rossini's genius; the dawn of his life had left the dew
> still fresh upon them[10]

The Bologna period produced a number of overtures and sets of
instrumental variations. The Variations in C for Clarinet and
Orchestra have survived and are sometimes played, though it needs a

[10] VdR, p.143.

certain transforming wit on the performer's part if the music is to avoid sounding vapid. Far more revealing are the five overtures: bright, engaging music, inventive but lacking, as yet, proper formal control. Some of the music has entered the repertoire in covert form: the first theme of the Overture in D *al Conventello* (1806 or 1807, another Triossi commission) recurs in the overture to *Il Signor Bruschino*, and the entirely characteristic second theme from the D major Overture (1808) crops up again in the overture to *L'inganno felice*. Even without the yet-to-be-invented *crescendo*, the somewhat misleadingly titled *Gran' Overture, obbligato a contrabasso*[11] is memorable for its imaginative use of instrumental blends and contrasts: the crepuscular colouring of cellos, basses, and bassoons or the charming exchanges of clarinet and flute in the second subject group. There are also hints of *buffo* comedy in the contrapuntal writing for the basses. Yet, to achieve these effects Rossini often seems to be putting the music into a strait-jacket; melodically and harmonically it is undistinguished. Throughout these pieces we sense Rossini's uncertainty about form. The spirited Overture *al Conventello* is all at sea in the matter of tonic/dominant relationships; a boy who begins his second subject group with a solo cello in the wrong key is likely to be the toast of his friends and the despair of his teachers.

These were passing and predictable uncertainties. Contemporary operatic procedures were, however, unhelpfully inert. Though composers like Mayr and Paër had enriched the orchestral resources, Italian opera of the time lacked the basic structures to take *opera seria* into a post-Metastasian romantic age or to take *opera buffa* forward into the hurly-burly of post-revolutionary times. We may smile at the charming ineptitude of the teenage Rossini in his attempts to master the rudiments of classical form, but we should remember that within a decade he had invented and stabilised a series of formal procedures which were to change the face of nineteenth-century Italian opera. Compare nodal moments in Mosca's *L'italiana in Algeri* (1808) with Rossini's, set to an identical text in 1813, and it will be seen how in a mere five years the apprentice had become the master builder. Rossini's defection from the

---

[11] The contrabass part is less adventurous than the title suggests. For comments on the dating and authenticity of this overture see Gossett, 'The Overtures of Rossini', *19th Century Music*, iii, (1979–80), pp.25–7.

academic world not unnaturally made him enemies in later years. Academics are always likely to take a dim view of the worldly success of those who, in their view, are academically unsound. Yet it is difficult to see how Rossini would have been a better composer had he enjoyed a more thorough grounding. As P.G. Wodehouse has demonstrated, where the comic muse is concerned a little learning can be a disarmingly useful thing.

The Bologna years were important in one further respect: the chances they afforded Rossini to hear some of Europe's leading singers, more especially the last of the great *castrati*, Giovanni Battista Velluti, and a rising star of the operatic scene, the prodigously gifted Isabella Colbran who was destined to play a far greater part in Rossini's life than he can have imagined when he first saw and heard her in Bologna in 1807. Velluti and Colbran: it was a revealing contrast. The old order, now doomed to extinction but leaving in its wake a sense of the brilliance, tonal homogeneity and stylistic address of the old *bel canto* style; the new order of singing actresses with brilliantly developed coloratura techniques stretching across several registers of the voice. Years later, Rossini was to recall his impressions of the *castrati*.

> I have never forgotten them. The purity, the miraculous flexibility of those voices and, above all, their profoundly penetrating accent – all that moved and fascinated me more than I can tell. I should add that I myself wrote a role for one of them, one of the last but not of the least – Velluti. That was in my opera *Aureliano in Palmira* . . .[12]

For Rossini *bel canto* skills rested on three elements: the instrument, what he called 'the Stradivarius', elaborate technical skills, and 'taste and feeling', the style with which the technique was deployed. The acquisition of the first element, the effortless emission of finely equalised tone, was for the finest singers the work of years. Incidentally, Rossini himself was briefly threatened with the possibility of joining the dwindling ranks of the *castrati*. One of his uncles, a butcher by trade, was much taken with the idea but, as Rossini later told Michotte 'my brave mother would not consent at any price'.

By 1810, Rossini's 18th year, he was widely versed in the practices and procedures of music-making in Bologna and the

---

[12] Michotte, p.109.

surrounding towns. Emancipated from Mattei and the Liceo, no longer a prodigy, and clearly ready for more substantial challenges, he was fortunate in the arrival in Bologna in 1810 of old friends of his parents, the composer and conductor, Giovanni Morandi, and his wife, the singer Rosa Morolli. The Morandis were on their way to Venice to join the small and enterprising company of the Marchese Cavalli for a season of *farse* at the Teatro San Moisè. The news that Gioachino was looking for an opening as a stage composer probably came as no surprise; nor did they forget his request. When the Cavalli season ran into difficulties – we must recall that in those days impresarios were obliged to stage a preponderance of new works each season[13] – he was persuaded by the Morandis to commission a one-acter from the cheeky but talented cembalo player whom Cavalli had encountered in Senigallia. It was an ideal opening. A small theatre, run on a shoe-string, with a good company and only the most basic needs was the perfect place for an unostentatious debut. As he said, a young composer could show off his natural fantasy (if Heaven had granted him any) and his technical skill (if he had any). The text Rossini was given, a one-act farrago with a Canadian and a predictable pair of temporarily thwarted lovers, was no better and no worse than scores of comparable scenarios extant at the time. What was different was Rossini's music which astounded the unsuspecting Venetians with its pace, energy, and dispassionate wit. In manner, matter, and impact the early success of Rossini's operas distantly resembles the success of the comic masters of early silent film. With characteristic aplomb the 18-year-old Rossini scored a hit with his first attempt.

[13] The advantage of a leasing system which obliged impresarios to commission two or three new works a season, with a guaranteed run of three performances, was well put by Stendhal when he observed that 'academically venerated dead masters are kept in Italy from strangling new ones at birth'.

2

Venice and Milan (1810–14)

Venice, where Rossini now found himself, had become, politically, something of a backwater. A kind of unabashed hedonism had sapped the political will of the once indomitable Republic. In May 1797 its demoralized citizens allowed over three thousand French troops to sail through the Porto di Lido and occupy the Piazza San Marco. Thereafter the French and Austrians played musical chairs with the city until the time of Daniele Manin. But it's an ill wind: the Venetians loved their music – 'Of all the lands of Italy', wrote Stendhal 'Venetia stands supreme in the sureness of its taste and the keenness of its appreciation of music written for the human voice' and they were clearly happy to be diverted from a somewhat grim and ignominious present by Rossini's ebullient music. Their taste for it remained unabated throughout Rossini's Italian career from *La cambiale di matrimonio* in 1810 to *Semiramide* in 1823. Despite fiascos in Bologna and Ferrara during 1812, Rossini was able to thrive on a steady flow of Venetian commissions, no less than six in fifteen months, taking him from *L'inganno felice* in January 1812 to the twin peaks of *Tancredi* and *L'italiana in Algeri* in the spring of 1813.

Though the two fiascos – *L'equivoco stravagante* (Bologna, 26 October, 1811) and *Ciro in Babilonia* (Ferrara,? 14 March, 1812) – are of interest musically, we know too little about the circumstances of their failure to assess them biographically. In the case of the earlier opera, it appears that the plot gave offence and that the opera was withdrawn on police instructions after the statutory three performances. As for *Ciro in Babilonia*, it has become best known through the marzipan ship which Rossini ordered on his return to Bologna. 'On the pennant,' he later told Hiller 'there was the name *Ciro*. The ship's mast was broken, its sails were in tatters, and the whole thing lay shipwrecked in an ocean of cream. Amid great hilarity, the happy gathering devoured my shattered vessel.'

Rossini's fortunes remained afloat, however, thanks to the

successes enjoyed in Venice in January and May 1812 by *L'inganno felice*, a story previously set by Paisiello, and *La scala di seta*. *L'inganno felice* became popular in other places, too. We read much about censorship, volatile audiences, lack of social mobility in a time of economic recession, and the absence of a critical tradition binding together like-minded people in disparate communities; but it is an earnest of the essential vitality of Italian operatic life at this time that within a year of its *prima L'inganno felice* had been staged, according to Radiciotti's listings, in Bologna, Florence, Verona, Venice (the Teatro San Benedetto), and Trieste.

Rossini's own energy at this time seems to have been boundless. Characteristically, Stendhal puts it down to the stimulus of passion; above all, Rossini's passion for Maria Marcolini, the most important *prima donna* in Rossini's life before Colbran. She was dazzled by him and he, according to Stendhal, turned her into 'the finest musician you might hope to find in all Italy'. He adds: 'It was at *her* side, upon *her* piano, and within the walls of *her* country-house at Bologna' that he wrote some of his finest pages.[1] Sceptical though one might be about the Freudian idea that artists are stimulated by a desire for 'power, wealth, fame, and the love of women',[2] it would be idle to pretend that Rossini's liaison with Marcolini was not a stimulus, though musicians will inevitably be more curious about the effect of Marcolini's singing – her technique and style – on Rossini's own writing. Like so many subjects close to Rossini, this is one which awaits editorially sound textual evidence as a basis for systematic exploration. Rodolfo Celletti's comments on an aspect of the vocal writing in *L'italiana in Algeri*[3] is an interesting example of what might be achieved here.

The first great joint success of Rossini and Marcolini came in September 1812 in Milan with the *prima* of *La pietra del paragone*, Rossini's first fully-fledged masterpiece. The commission was won in a mixture of circumstances, prime among which were Rossini's own soaring reputation and the personal interventions of Marcolini and the bass, Filippo Galli, who had sung with Rossini in *L'inganno felice* and who was to become one of the finest Rossini interpreters of his age.

[1] VdR, p.97.
[2] Sigmund Freud, *Introductory Lectures on Psycho-Analysis*, London, 1963, Vol. XVI, p.376.
[3] Rodolfo Celletti, *Storia dell'Opera*, Turin, 1977, Vol.III, Tome 1, p.119n.

This is not the place to discuss *La pietra del paragone* in any detail but it is worth noting that the opera ran for fifty-three performances in its first season. Rossini received a satisfactory initial payment and exemption from military service, a useful concession in 1812.[4] From now on, he could think himself a *maestro di cartello*, a composer whose name alone guarantees a public. The libretto, by Luigi Romanelli, one of La Scala's resident writers, is no masterpiece but it allowed Rossini to show off his paces to Italy's smartest audience as a wit, as a romantic tone-painter, and as a skilled purveyor of the atmosphere of the bustling, vituperative worlds of the press and the theatre. It also gave his public a first substantial glimpse of Rossini's genius for setting jangling verbal nonsense. Pacuvio's aria 'Ombretta sdegnosa' with its 'Missipípí, pípí, pípí' refrain, embryonic Offenbach, became a popular smash hit overnight, as did the word 'Sigillara' – 'let the seals be affixed!' – repeated to great comic effect in the scene in which the Count, Galli's part, appears in Turkish garb and affects to take over his own possessions. For many weeks the Milanese had only one desire: to secure a seat for 'Sigillara'.

The La Scala triumph did not, however, stop Rossini – prudent, ambitious, and with parents to whom he remained indebted – from returning to the humbler context of the San Moisè in Venice for two new commissions, *L'occasione fa il ladro*, first heard on 24 November, 1812, and *Il signor Bruschino*, a small treasure-trove of comic devices, first heard in January 1813 and an auspicious start to a yet more remarkable year ahead.

In the latter part of 1812 Rossini received a commission from Venice's leading house, La Fenice. Though opera at this time was considered to be above such meaner art forms as spoken theatre, music-hall, and circuses, the stratifications within the form were clear enough, with major differences in status, cost, and venue between *opera seria*, the more middlebrow *opera semiseria*, and *opera buffa*, which required neither a large chorus nor historically accurate sets and costumes.[5] The subject suggested to Rossini by La Fenice was a *melodramma eroico* based on Voltaire's *Tancrède*

---

[4] By 1812 there were over 90,000 Italian conscripts. Losses in the Peninsular War and in the Russian Campaign of 1812 were especially heavy.

[5] See John Rosselli, *The Opera Industry in Italy from Cimarosa to Verdi*, London, 1984, p.40. Until 1838 it would, in general, have cost more to see an *opera seria* at La Scala, Milan, than an *opera buffa*.

(1760). The play, rather crudely transcribed for Rossini by Gaetano Rossi, was one of many eighteenth century derivatives from Tasso's *Gerusalemme liberata*. (James Thomson's *Tancred and Sigismunda* had been in Garrick's repertoire.) Those who suspected Rossini of liberal tendencies would have done well to note that he was currently depicting, not some moody outcast like Schiller's Karl von Moor, but a figure – noble, rational, public-spirited – of whom even the most conservative taste might approve. In spirit and style *Tancredi* is an idyllic work, a late flowering of that serene, neoclassical tradition which Winckelmann had promulgated fifty years before. As an opera, *Tancredi* breaks new ground for Rossini, formally and musically, but its immense popularity rested from the first on its sensuous vocal writing, its limpid instrumentation, its moments of patriotic sentiment, at once stirring and nostalgic and, of course, on 'Di tanti palpiti', the subversively charming *cabaletta* to Tancredi's entrance aria. As harmonically guileful as a Venetian street song, 'the rice aria' as it was popularly known,[6] became the rage of Europe, as wonderfully and wearisomely popular in its day as Verdi's 'La donna è mobile' was to be forty years later.

After the triumphant *prima* of *Tancredi* in Venice, Rossini travelled to Ferrara in the company of Luigi Lechi to prepare a new production and, as it turned out, a new version of the opera. Lechi, six years Rossini's senior and the *inamorato* of Adelaide Malanotte, the first Tancredi, came from a famous Brescian family. His academic career in medicine, literature, and philosophy had been a distinguished one and he had become a respected member of a group of northern Italian writers with special interest in neoclassical art and literature. For the Ferrara production, Lechi re-drafted the end of *Tancredi*, keeping close to the sense and texture of Voltaire's verses and restoring the play's so-called 'tragic' ending. It was a remarkable act of literary intervention, the implications of which will be discussed in a later chapter.[7] In the event, the revised ending did not please. Rossini withdrew it and, as was his habit, redistributed some of the music in a later work. Meanwhile *Tancredi* began

---

[6] The story was put about that Rossini composed the piece while supervising a pan of lightly boiled rice: about four minutes, according to Stendhal's closely worked calculation.

[7] See Chapter 21.

its triumphal progress through Europe and beyond. Lechi and Malanotte remained together until her death in 1832, hosts, in their Lake Garda home, to many distinguished musicians, including Giuditta Pasta whose musico-dramatic assumption of the role of Tancredi was one of the most completely chronicled operatic performances of its day.[8]

The Ferrara *prima* of *Tancredi* was in late March. By late April, Rossini was back in Venice, almost certainly at the behest of Gallo, the crisis-laden impresario of the Teatro San Benedetto. During April Rossini's music had been continuously before the Venetian public. *L'inganno felice* had been revived and the Venetian *prima* of *La pietra del paragone* was promised, alongside a new opera by Carlo Coccia. It was at this point that things began to go wrong for Gallo. Unaccountably, *La pietra del paragone* flopped. It was taken off, replaced by Pavesi's *Ser Marcantonio*, and then partially reinstated with Act 1 of the Pavesi playing in nightly tandem with Act 2 of the Rossini, one of those odd accommodations to which impresarios were driven and audiences accustomed. With Gallo's fortunes sinking fast, and no sign of Coccia's new opera (it finally reached the stage on 26 June as *La donna selvaggia*), Rossini was summoned to help bail out the vessel.

In the circumstances, it was hardly surprising that an existing libretto was called back into service: Angelo Anelli's *L'italiana in Algeri*, first set to music by Luigi Mosca for La Scala, Milan in 1808. Who revised the libretto is not entirely clear. Was it Anelli himself, Giuseppe Foppa, or Gaetano Rossi, the *Tancredi* librettist and the candidate most confidently advanced by Azio Corghi in his Critical Edition? The additions to and deletions from Anelli's text are of special interest, evidence of Rossini's own predilections and his sharp eye for essentials in an eleventh-hour crisis. The contract was signed and the music composed within twenty-seven days, an astonishing early example both of Rossini's musical fertility and his ability to make practical and creative use of his own evolving musical and structural procedures. In *L'Italiana in Algeri* these procedures not only helped speed the compositional process; they helped give to the music a wit, pace, and point which is often lacking in Mosca's more free-wheeling setting of Anelli's text.

---

[8] For Stendhal's analysis of Pasta's close yet always spontaneous attention to the detail of the role, see VdR, pp.379–82.

Though Marcolini, the Isabella, was said to be unwell, the opera had its *prima* on Saturday, 22 May. It had been cast from strength. Apart from Marcolini, the cast included Galli as Mustafà, Serafino Gentili in the semi-serious tenor role of Lindoro, and Paolo Rosich, a skilful actor as well as a reputable *primo basso*, as Isabella's aged, hangdog admirer, Taddeo. The splendidly informative *Giornale dipartimentale dell'Adriatico* reported 'deafening, continous general applause' for a work which had 'greatly enthused a demanding, intelligent public'. Marcolini's singing of 'Pensa alla patria' was especially praised, though her indisposition forced the suspension of performances until 1 June when the reception was even more enthusiastic, the *Giornale* now declaring, with admirable prescience, that the opera 'will find a place among the finest works of genius and art'.

The Venetians were, none the less, watchful. In its review of 24 May, the *Giornale* notes talk of plagiarization among the audience, a charge the paper refutes. If there are echoes of extant works, it argues, then they are merely echoes; what was perhaps hinted at in some earlier compositions is now brought to a pitch of formal excellence in the newest work. It is a sophisticated and perceptive defence; but the rumours persisted and during the charity perform-ance of 21 June, a performance which would automatically include a number of additions and encores, Marcolini took the unusual step of attempting to include Mosca's earlier setting of 'Pensa all patria'. The differences between the Mosca and the Rossini were so clear that the Mosca was drowned out before it was half finished. Marcolini had demonstrated in practice what the correspondent of the *Gior-nale* had proposed in theory.

A few weeks later principals, chorus, dancers, and stage-sets moved to Vicenza, the home town of Palladio midway between Padua and Verona and much enhanced by him in the sixteenth century. There is no evidence that Rossini travelled with the com-pany (which also lost Galli and Gentili) though at some stage after the Venetian *prima* he wrote an alternative cavatina for Marcolini which is extant but which has not supplanted the original 'Cruda sorte!'. Celletti has suggested that the original *cavatina* did not lie well for Marcolini's voice; this is almost certainly true, though, like many of her tribe, Marcolini was a creature of whim, switching in and out of plausible *cavatinas* (not all of them by Rossini) through-out her career.

After *Tancredi* and *L'italiana in Algeri*, Rossini appears to have settled into a period which, by contrast with what had preceded it, seems positively comatose. Between June 1813 and December 1814 he wrote three new operas none of which was an immediate success. *Sigismondo*, written for La Fenice, Venice, in late 1814, had a reception which was as polite as it was cool. Legend has it that Rossini was touched and not a little annoyed by the audience's chivalrous treatment of so tedious a piece. 'Whistle!' he is alleged to have hissed to the unaccountably sympathetic audience. *Sigismondo* is a dull and difficult piece but we should beware of dismissing it too abruptly; there is a good deal of reconstituted *Sigismondo* in some of the successful operas which followed it.

The other two operas, *Aureliano in Palmira* and *Il turco in Italia*, were both written for La Scala, a house which was probably too big for either piece. *Aureliano in Palmira* is full of exquisite things: some tender pastoral writing, a tiny chorus, rich in pathos, taken over from the ill-fated Ferrara revision of *Tancredi*, and several winning inventions which, like the overture, were soon to find their way into *Elisabetta, regina d'Inghilterra* and, even more importantly, into *Il barbiere di Siviglia*. The overriding interest of the piece at the time was almost certainly the presence in the original cast of the castrato Velluti; it was his first Rossini role and his last, though he was to sing in Rossini's Cantata *Il vero omaggio* in Verona in 1822. As Celletti has demonstrated, stories about Velluti's embellishment of Rossini's music have been much exaggerated. But embellished or not, Velluti's singing did little to enhance the fortunes of the opera.

During this Milanese period, Rossini was probably as preoccupied with the staging of older works as with the composition of new ones. In December 1813, shortly before the *prima* of *Aureliano in Palmira*, a new theatre, the Teatro Rè, was inaugurated with a production of *Tancredi* supervised by Rossini. The following April he almost certainly oversaw the Milanese *prima* of *L'italiana in Algeri*, also at the Teatro Rè. The opera was not received with the enthusiasm which had greeted it in Venice, but its success was sufficient to cast a cloud over the La Scala *prima* of *Il turco in Italia* in August, 1814. In our own times, *Il turco in Italia* has been well regarded, a success at Glyndebourne and at La Scala itself, with Callas giving the character of Fiorilla added presence and point. It is, in fact, one of Rossini's most succinct and sophisticated essays in *opera buffa*. To the Milanese, though, it was merely an impertinent inversion of *L'italiana in Algeri*. Disappointed but not demoralized, Rossini bided his time before trying out some of the music on the unsuspecting Neapolitans in September 1816 in the guise of a two-act *dramma, La gazzetta*.

Whilst in Milan Rossini wrote a short Cantata for soprano, mezzo soprano, and piano, entitled *Egle ed Irene*, for the Princess Belgiojoso, one of a growing band of wealthy female admirers. The work is an extended three-part duet, with lengthy recitatives and lyric sections which are graciously if at times rather woodenly written. It is the cantata's closing section, though, which will intrigue modern audiences familiar with *Il barbiere di Siviglia*, for here are the very phrases which Rosina and Count Almaviva will utter, and Figaro ironically echo, in Act 2 of the opera's nocturnal Trio. What is charming in the cantata becomes both charming and scathing in the opera, such is music's chameleon character.

Another work, very different in concept, which may have been conceived during this period is Rossini's incidental music for a translation by Giambattista Giusti of Sophocles's *Oedipus at Colonus*. Rossini had studied classical and renaissance texts with Giusti in Bologna in 1808 and the music, written for a private performance of Giusti's *Edipo a Colono*, clearly derives from early interests in classical and neo-classical literature, interests deepened, perhaps, by Rossini's knowledge of Sacchini's *Oedipe à Colone* (Paris, 1787), a work of considerable importance to composers interested in the Franco-Italian tradition of lyric drama. Rossini's setting consists of an overture and thirteen episodes drawn from four of the work's principal choruses[9] (the *parados*, the chorus's formal entry, is unaccountably omitted). Given the music's unusual and fragmented forms – bass recitative and arioso, choruses – it is difficult to match it stylistically with the main body of Rossini's work at this time. The concept seems early; the writing seems late. The bass's realization of the Chorus's meditation on the vanity of all earthily things is powerfully, flexibly shaped, with a dark, sardonic end worthy of Verdi's Sparafucile. And the choruses, the best of which were recast as *La foi* and *L'espérance* as part of the Parisian choral triptych of November 1844, are also powerfully fashioned. Melodic spans are

[9] Sophocles, *Oedipus at Colonus* trans. E.F. Watling, London, 1947, 11.667 ff., 1041 ff., 1211 ff. and 1559 ff.

generous but carefully shaped, rhythms are unobtrusive. There is little polyphonic writing; instead, Rossini achieves his effects through richly blocked harmonies and a very full and effective use of antiphonal effects for the divided male chorus. The music is pre-1817, but the magnificent 'O Giove, egioco' with its eloquent address to 'the august Athena' ('O tu, Dea virgine') seems to anticipate the manner of *Ermione*, a work which powerfully reappropriates the classical tradition for romantic-melodramatic ends, rather than looking back to anything we might hear in *Tancredi* or *Aureliano in Palmira*.

Europe, too, was nearing a crossroads in 1814 with Napoleon's abdication and exile to Elba in April following Castlereagh's Chaumont initiative the previous month. Back in Bologna early in 1815, Rossini gave music lessons to Napoleon's niece, the daughter of Elisa Bacchiocchi; but his involvement with the failing Republican cause was closer still in April 1815 when Joachim Murat, Napoleon's brother-in-law and *de facto* King of Naples since 1808, launched upon a series of political initiatives all too typical of this Ruritanian adventurist. On 5 April, in Rimini, Murat declared Italian independence from Austrian rule. Bologna responded with enthusiasm. Verses were penned by Rossini's old mentor, the revered translator of *Edipo a Colono*, and set by Rossini. Murat was present in the Teatro Contavalli when the *Inno dell'Indipendenza*, 'Sorgi, Italia, venuta è già l'ora', was given its rousing *prima* on 15 April. Unhappily for all concerned, the Austrians re-took Bologna the next day. Years later, it was put about by Eugène de Mirecourt in his shamelessly vituperative *Rossini*[10] that Rossini had promptly altered the words and returned the music to the Austrian general tied with a ribbon in the national colours of Austria. The story would not be worth repeating but for the fact that Rossini attempted on several occasions strenuously to deny it, thus proving the wisdom of Dr Johnson's dictum that 'few attacks of either ridicule or invective make much noise but by the help of those they provoke'. Rossini's claim that he was in Naples in April 1815 is one which, in the absence of air travel at the time, is difficult to substantiate.

Whatever the truth, or otherwise, of the incident, Rossini was in Naples by the mid-summer of 1815. It was precisely the new

---

[10] Mirecourt, *Rossini*, Paris 1855, reprinted in fascimile, Paris 1981, pp. 31–4.

environment and the new challenge which, to judge by *Sigismondo*, he urgently needed. Stimulated by a beautiful and exuberant city, a remarkable impresario, and an equally remarkable singer, Rossini was about to enter into what was, creatively, the heartland of his musical career.

3

Arrival in Naples

1815 was the year in which the old order was substantially restored.
French rule had left an indelible mark on Italy, and the seeds of
republicanism had been sown, but there was a sense in which
post-revolutionary Europe reverted under Metternich's watchful eye
to the *status quo ante*: Habsburgs ruled again in the north, Pius
VII governed in Rome and the Papal States, and in June Ferdinand
IV, with Austrian and British backing, re-established Bourbon rule in
Naples. Naples had been ruled by the Bourbons since 1734 and by
Ferdinand, the interregnums of 1799 and 1806–15 excepted, since
1759. Like Fielding's Squire Western, he seems to have been robust,
amiable, and delightfully uncouth, a hunting man who also enjoyed
the rough-and-tumble of water-sports in the famous bay; a man
polite enough to sit through an *opera seria* but more at home with
opera buffa or the scabrous stage comedies which were a Neapolitan
specialty. His first wife, the politically active Queen Caroline,
daughter of Maria Theresa and sister of Marie-Antoinette, was a less
attractive personality, rumoured to have been responsible, among
other things, for Cimarosa's imprisonment and subsequent death
after the Parthenopean revolt of 1799. As Cimarosa's crime had been
the writing of a Republican hymn shortly before Ferdinand's troops
re-entered the city in June 1799, Rossini – after his not dissimilar
Bologna experience – might have been as relieved as many Neapolitans were that Caroline was dead and her place taken by the King's
former mistress, a woman described by Acton as 'pretty, placid, and
practical'.[1]
    Whatever the Bourbons' failings, they were generous patrons of
music. The San Carlo theatre, built in 1737, was one of the most
handsome and lavishly equipped in Europe, with boxes like miniature drawing-rooms. A traveller in Italy in the 1760s noted:

---

[1] Harold Acton, *The Bourbons of Naples (1734–1825)*, London, 1956,
p.632.

> Music is the triumph of the Neapolitans. It seems that in this
> country the fibres of the ears are more sensitive, more harmo-
> nious, more sonorous than in the rest of Europe. The whole
> nation sings. Gestures, the inflection of the voice, the cadence of
> syllables, conversation: everything there expresses and exhales
> music.[2]

The Neapolitans were conscious of the glories of the *settecento*, that
theirs was the city of Alessandro Scarlatti, Pergolesi, Cimarosa, and
Paisiello. During Ferdinand's final years, the Indian Summer which
lasted from 1815 to his death in 1825, the San Carlo continued to be
the most lavishly underwritten opera house in Europe.[3] Stendhal
judged it to be less useful than La Scala as a place of general
rendezvous but 'infinitely better suited for listening to music'.[4] Its
orchestra was thought the best in Italy by Stendhal, by Berlioz, by the
generality of informed opinion. The wealth of the San Carlo was
founded, like that of La Scala, Milan, on a mixture of patronage and
gaming; and in 1815 it had as its impresario one of the most
remarkable figures in the history of opera administration, the self-
made millionaire gaming magnate, huckster, and theatrical entrepreneur, Domenico Barbaia.[5] To Barbaia, Rossini was a property
with super-star status, and it was Barbaia and the complex administration which stretched through theatre boards and ministers to
Ferdinand himself who defended their new investment against the
spoiling tactics of conservative academics and the animadversions of
Naples's sophisticated but parochial theatre-going public.

Born in 1778, Barbaia had begun his working life as a waiter.
Legend has it that he made his money out of a patent concoction of
chocolate or coffee and whipped cream. In reality, it was his wheeler-
dealing during the French wars in Italy and his exploitation of the
new game of roulette which made him his money. With the spacious
foyers of the big opera houses, natural gathering places of the
wealthy, leased as gaming parlours as part of complex arrangements
with courts, governments, and private theatre owners, it was inevitable that Barbaia would buy himself into opera-house management.
His first pitch had been La Scala; then, in 1809, he moved to Naples,

[2] J.J. De La Lande, *Voyage d'un français dans l'Italie,* Venice, 1769, p.33.
[3] See Rosselli, op. cit., pp.72–3, fig.1.
[4] VdR, p.439.
[5] See plate 4.

where he was to stay for the best part of thirty years. To judge by his lifestyle, his letters, and his artistic achievements, he must have been a remarkable man. His letters, at times barely literate and often obscene, are full of cajolery, abuse, hectoring, and self-pity; yet they are the letters of a personality one can't help liking. He made enemies, but the abiding impression is of a man of flair and acumen with an instinct for 'the best' even if he himself was singularly lacking in what we might choose to call good taste.

His artistic achievements were formidable. As manager of the San Carlo and, for briefer periods, La Scala, Milan and the Kärntner-tortheater in Vienna, he encouraged, and in some instances launched, the careers of Carafa, Mercadante, Weber, Pacini, Donizetti, Bellini, and Rossini himself. Within three years of his arrival in Naples he had brought a new weight and seriousness to the Neapolitans' grasp of *opera seria*. Productions were mounted of Spontini's *La vestale* and Gluck's *Iphigénie en Aulide*. And his roster of singers was, predictably, a strong one, a little top heavy in great tenors, perhaps, but including David, Garcia, Nozzari, Benedetti, and Isabella Colbran, Barbaia's mistress and, as it later turned out, the first Mrs Rossini.

As we have seen, Rossini first encountered Colbran in Bologna in 1807. She was then near the start of her career, astounding audiences with a voice that is said to have ranged from G below the stave to E flat *in alt* and with a compelling stage presence. Portraits of her are difficult to find;[6] out of costume she has the air of a rather determined housewife, with short hair, a roundish face, and a certain ironic twist to the mouth; on stage, though, she seems to have been totally transformed:

> It was a beauty in the most queenly tradition: noble features which, on stage, radiated majesty; an eye like that of a Circassian maiden, darting fire; and to crown it all, a true and deep instinct for tragedy. Off-stage, she possessed about as much dignity as the average milliner's assistant; but the moment she stepped on to the boards, her brow encircled with a royal diadem, she inspired involuntary respect, even among those who, a minute or two earlier, had been chatting intimately with her in the foyer of the theatre.[7]

[6] See plate 6.
[7] VdR, p.157.

So wrote Stendhal: a striking tribute from a man whose loathing of the Bourbons and all those who served them often led him to write dyspeptically of her. Like Pasta, whom Stendhal did venerate, Colbran alienated the canary-fanciers, those for whom Angelica Catalani – the brilliant exponent of coloratura titbits especially written for her by men like Pucitta and Portogallo – was the contemporary ideal. Ten of the eighteen operas written by Rossini between *Elisabetta, regina d'Inghilterra* (1815) and *Semiramide* (1823) were written with Colbran's voice – its colours, its declamatory and decorative powers, the tessitura best suited to it – very much in mind. That the voice went into decline towards the end of this period is not open to question; but study of the texts written for her would indicate that the decline was more gradual and accompanied by more fascinating shifts and gradations of tone and technique than Stendhal's writings allow. A more substantial charge that might be levelled at Colbran and Barbaia, a charge which Beethoven ('Above all, make more *Barbers*!') seems to have endorsed in one of the most back-handed compliments ever made to a fellow-composer, is that they drew Rossini away from his natural habitat, *opera buffa*: 'A great comic poet forced against his will and judgement into the paths of erudition', as Stendhal put it.[8] It is a plausible prejudice which still has wide currency; but it is only substantial ignorance of the nature of Rossini's Neapolitan achievement, and its subsequent fruits in his work and in the work of composers as various as Donizetti, Bellini, Meyerbeer, and Verdi, which can sustain the prejudice.

Rossini's contract with the San Carlo and del Fondo theatres was worth between 8,000 and 12,000 francs a year. Unpaid leave to undertake truant commissions elsewhere was permitted, but the Neapolitan work schedules were strenuous, involving composition, administration, and the musical preparation of his own and other people's music. 'If he had been able to,' Rossini later remarked, 'Barbaia would have put me in charge of the kitchen as well.' The fact that the Neapolitans had hitherto largely ignored the Rossini phenomenon allowed Rossini to play himself in with some old numbers, the partially self-derived *Elisabetta* acting as a skilfully made bridge between Rossini's old and new worlds. As a subject, it was well chosen. The title role suited Colbran, and an imperial English subject

[8] VdR, p.171.

– albeit one poorly derived by Federici and Schmidt from a pseudo-historical English novel of the 1780s – was apt to the year of Waterloo. Naples had long been popular with the English (the influential ambassadorship of Sir William and, latterly, Lady Hamilton in the years 1764–1800 had seen to that) and with the wars over they began to return in numbers. 'All London is here', Stendhal gloomily remarked a year or two later.

The Neapolitan press treated Rossini's arrival in Naples and his promised new opera (first seen at the San Carlo on 4 October) with predictable coolness. 'A certain Signor Rossini, a choirmaster, who has come, we've been told, to present an *Elisabetta, regina d'Inghilterra* of his . . .' adequately conveys the languidly partisan tone of the *Giornale delle Due Sicilie*. Rossini was astute enough, however, to consolidate his Neapolitan debut with a new production of *L'italiana in Algeri* at the Teatro dei Fiorentini later the same month. With *Elisabetta* successfully launched and *L'italiana* evidently popular, the *Giornale* published a grudging acknowledgement of Rossini's successes at the end of October. Even here, though, the writer seems more preoccupied with Naples's glorious past, with 'the imaginative Cimarosa and the tender and passionate Paisiello', than with its vivacious present.

Significantly, *L'italiana in Algeri* was staged in a modified edition. 'Pensa alla patria', with its inflammatory nationalist sentiments, was replaced by a new aria 'Sullo stil de' viaggiatori'. Despite its great popularity (Ricordi had published it in a separate full-score edition shortly after the Milanese *prima*), its sentiments were not ones which the Bourbon monarch would favour, nor ones which a newly prudent Rossini would wish to promulgate at this particular time; but even without 'Pensa alla patria', *L'italiana in Algeri* rapidly became a favourite with Neapolitans from the King downwards. And whilst Naples was rocking to the madcap rhythms of his first fully-fledged comic masterpiece, Rossini was about to write a pair of operas, one of which would render him unignorable by contemporaries and posterity alike.

4

Rome and Il barbiere di Siviglia (1816)

Rossini arrived in Rome in November 1815. The immediate task in hand was the preparation of a revival of *Il turco in Italia*; that, and the writing of a new opera for the Teatro Valle, *Torvaldo e Dorliska*. The text was by Sterbini and the opera had its *prima* on 26 December. The work, a *dramma semiserio*, was a sentimental 'rescue' opera, and it failed to please, in spite of a strong cast which included Donzelli, Galli, and Raniero Remorini in the semi-comic role of Giorgio.

As *Torvaldo e Dorliska* was going into final rehearsals, Rossini signed a contract for another opera, to be performed at the Teatro Argentina the following February. The date of the contract is 15 December, 1815 and the date is worth noting; for though *Il barbiere di Siviglia*, as it later came to be called,[1] was written, according to Rossini, in thirteen days, the project was in train for the better part of two months. The Teatro Argentina, Rome's most handsome theatre, had been built in 1732 by Duke Francesco Sforza-Cesarini and had remained in the family. Rossini's contract was with Francesco Sforza-Cesarini who had continued to lavish the family fortune on the theatre, though, sadly, he did not live to hear the masterpiece he had commisioned. He died on the night of 6 February, 1816, aged 44, just two weeks before the rowdy *prima* of his *Almaviva*.

The contract for *Almaviva*, which is fairly representative of opera contracts at this time, commissioned Rossini to write an opera to a libretto provided by the impresario. Dates were laid down for the completion of the first act and for the *prima* itself. The composer must agree to carry out any modifications to his score requested by the singers; he should be available during rehearsals; and he should direct the first three performances from the keyboard. (In the event, Rossini did not comply with this last point, feigning illness after the

---

[1] In deference to Paisiello's *Il barbiere di Siviglia* (St. Petersburg, 1782), Rossini's opera was announced as *Almaviva, ossia L'inutile precauzione*. It reverted to *Il barbiere di Siviglia* in Bologna in the summer of 1816.

first-night débâcle.) Apprized, no doubt, of Rossini's socializing and gourmandizing, the Duke also stipulated that he should lodge with Luigi Zamboni, the man who would sing Figaro at the first performances. Financially, the terms were comparatively generous, a fee the equivalent of several hundred pounds and a hazel-coloured jacket with gold buttons; though it should be noted that Manuel García was paid more to sing in *Almaviva* than Rossini was to write it. Singers' fees had always been a scandal; as one contemporary wag put it: 'For a *cavatina* a city; for a *Rondo* an entire province'.

How much conviviality there was in the Zamboni household, we can't say; though it is not difficult to imagine the kind of roisterings which might have accompanied the composition and first play-throughs of Figaro's famous 'Largo al factotum'. It is clear, though, that *Il barbiere di Siviglia* must have been, in some degree, a premeditated work. The assumption is made that Rossini wrote the piece from a standing start, setting Sterbini's text as it arrived day by day. This latter point is probably true, allowing Rossini somewhere between thirteen days (his own story) and nineteen days (Radiciotti's estimate) for the completion of the autograph. What's more, as we have already seen in the case of *L'italiana in Algeri*, Rossini had evolved formal procedures which allowed both for speed of composition and the cleanest kind of comic pointing. Yet germinal ideas which are here brought to full flower can be traced back through a number of Rossini's earlier compositions and it is undoubtedly the case that Rossini might have long pondered Beaumarchais's play, if only through the refracting medium of Paisiello's own widely popular *Il barbiere di Siviglia*.

Indeed, Paisiello's opera presented Rossini with a problem which was a good deal more ticklish than the one which later faced Verdi when he began work on his *Otello*. Not only was Paisiello's work extant, but so was the composer,[2] vigorously backed by a vociferous claque of supporters urged on, no doubt, by rival managements and the general riff-raff which invariably attaches itself to any kind of mob activity. In later years, Rossini gave details of a letter which he wrote to Paisiello; in addition to Rossini's own letter, the management of the Argentina published a lengthy *Avvertimento al pubblico* in the printed libretto of *Almaviva*. The notice pointed out that the title of the work had been changed, that it had been newly

[2] He died on 5 June, 1816.

versified and adapted and that such efforts had been made out of 'respect and veneration' for the 'greatly celebrated Paisiello'. In the next paragraph a somewhat tactless reference to the fact that times had changed since Paisiello wrote his opera is wrapped round with more obsequious references to 'the immortal composer', 'the renowned Paisiello'. Finally, there is an abject apology to the Comédie-Francaise for the use of a chorus in the new setting. It was, if we may borrow the opera's famous sub-title, a futile precaution. Such a harvest of compliments to Paisiello and so much deference on the management's part, can only have been grist to the mill of *paisiellisti* who proceded to do what factions invariably do when they are shown deference: they spotted the uncertainty and they determined to pounce.

A good deal has been written about the fiasco of the opera's first night on 20 February, 1816, and a good deal of it is probably true: the factional animosity, the jeering and catcalls (including the tasteless 'Here we are at the funeral of Duke Cesarini'[3]), the numerous stage mishaps, the mockery of Rossini in his new jacket, and Rossini's own attempts calmly to encourage the singers. At the end of the performance, Righetti-Giorgi tells us, he left 'like an indifferent onlooker'.[4]

The second performance, from which Rossini absented himself, was a success. According to one source,[5] Rossini spent the evening pacing his rooms, watch in hand, imagining the performance's progress scene by scene. When he heard a noisy rabble approaching later that evening, he concluded that the opera had again failed and went to bed. By the other account,[6] he was roused from his bed, and fearing a lynch-mob, slipped through to a stable at the back of the courtyard. After a few minutes he heard Garcia summoning him to acknowledge cries of 'Bravo, bravissimo Figaro' from a streetful of eager people. 'F*** their bravos, I'm not coming out', was Rossini's blunt rejoinder. The hotel manager pleaded with him lest the mob turned violent; but Rossini was adamant. A few windows were

[3] G. Righetti-Giorgi, *Cenni di una donna già cantante sopra il maestro Rossini*, Bologna, 1823; repr. Rognoni, p.358.
[4] Righetti-Giorgi, op. cit. p.359.
[5] Salvatore Marchesi di Castrone, quoted Weinstock p.61.
[6] Michotte, pp.124–5

broken and Rossini tells us that he slept through the January (*sic*) night with an icy blast penetrating his room.

What is interesting about these anecdotes is the impression they provide of a Rossini who is consciously acting out his unconcern. The mythologized Rossini, the agreeable *bon viveur* who boasted that he could set even a laundry list to music is, we know, some way from the truth. It was, though, a useful protective mask; the public required an image of Rossini, and the image they gave him, which he often so obligingly authenticated, was both plausible and flattering. At the time of *Il barbiere di Siviglia*, he was a few days short of his 24th birthday. As far as we know, his health was still unimpaired, though at some stage in his operatic career he must have experienced the onset of the gonorrhoea which, in its more chronic manifestations, caused him so much illness and pain in the 1830s and 40s. Outwardly, his star was still rising in 1816; like Figaro, he was a man of ingenuity and irrepressible energy. But for a man whose later life provides evidence of obsessive and manic-depressive elements in his make-up, the shock of the public response to his Beaumarchais opera must have been unnerving. At one point in Beaumarchais's play, in lines omitted in Sterbini's text, Figaro remarks 'I force myself to laugh at everything, for fear of having to weep'. Though he would not admit it in public, Rossini probably shared the sentiment. Certainly, it was not long before word was abroad that Rossini was talking to friends about the possibility of retiring from the theatre at the age of thirty.

5

Naples, Rome, and Milan (1816–17)

Having celebrated his 24th birthday by signing a contract with Rome's Teatro Valle for a new opera to be performed on Boxing Day, 1816,[1] Rossini returned to Naples to find that the 78-year-old San Carlo theatre had been gutted by fire on the night of 13 February. Within a year it had been lavishly rebuilt, with Barbaia's own building firm (the man's business acumen seemed to know no bounds) advancing the entire cost against an exceptionally generous government concession to Barbaia on future gambling revenues.

Rossini's first task upon returning to Naples in 1816 was the writing of a wedding cantata for the marriage of Princess Maria Carolina, Ferdinand's granddaughter, and the Duc de Berry, the second son of the future Charles X of France whose own coronation in 1825 was to occasion one of Rossini's most extraordinary works, *Il viaggio a Reims*. The subject for the Neapolitan pageant was based on the story of Thetis, the Nereid fated to bear a son mightier than his father, and Peleus to whom the gods married her, a legend memorably treated in a painting by Poussin. Taking its place within a long history of Italian court pastoral cantatas, *Le nozze di Teti e di Peleo* was staged; but in the absence of anything which might reasonably be called a plot, dramatic interest was sustained by scenic splendours and allegorizing gestures. The text of this royal epithalamium, which was performed for the one and only time at the Teatro del Fondo on 24 April 1816, was by Angelo Maria Ricci. Ricci confines the action to Peleus's honouring of Thetis, a love duet ('Costante al tuo fianco'), and several symbolic tableaux in which the gods – Jove, Juno, and Ceres – bless the nuptials and speculate about events which may one day derive from this auspicious linking of royal houses. The Naples cast was as predictable as it was distinguished: Thetis and Peleus were sung by Margarita Chabrand and Giovanni David, Jove by

---

[1] *La Cenerentola*. It did not reach the stage until 25 January, 1817.

Andrea Nozzari, Juno by Girolama Dardanelli, and Ceres by Isabella Colbran.

As far as I am aware, the work has never been revived; however, the autograph score, which is now in the Naples Conservatoire, has been examined by Philip Gossett.[2] What is fascinating about the piece, apart from some new writing of great limpidity and charm – 'Rossini's art at its most appealingly naive', as Gossett puts it – is the extent of the self-borrowing. With eight of the eleven principal numbers partially or wholly borrowed and subjected to several modes of musical adaptation, *Le nozze di Teti e di Peleo* emerges as a brilliant patchwork of Rossiniana. It is a work which on grounds of curiosity alone merits resuscitation.[3]

A fortnight after the performance of this nuptial cantata, Rossini's paternal grandmother, Antonia Olivieri Rossini, died in Pesaro aged eighty-one; she had looked after young Gioachino during some of his parents' absences in the 1790s and he must have mourned her passing. Naples, though, was proving a stern taskmaster; there was a revival of *Tancredi* to supervise and new works to be written for the Teatro Fondo and the Teatro dei Fiorentini. Had Rossini been entirely self-confident, he might have attempted to bring *Il barbiere di Siviglia* to Naples. Instead, he met buzzing expectation with *La gazzetta*, a deft, busy piece about what happens when a pompous old father advertises in the local *gazzetta* for a suitable son-in-law. Writing for the Teatro dei Fiorentini, the home of Naples's own hallowed brand of *opera buffa*, Rossini must have felt like a visiting chef trying his hand at some famous local dish. In the event, he was helped by Palomba's libretto which puts the part of the father, Don Pomponio Storione, into Neapolitan dialect, and by the local *buffo* who created the role, Carlo Casaccia. 'Casacciello', as he was known

[2] Philip Gossett, 'Rossini in Naples: some major works recovered', *Musical Quarterly*, Vol.LIV No.3 (July 1968), pp.316–25.

[3] A complete list of borrowings, as identified by Gossett, appears in the above article, pp.321–2. They include the following from *Il barbiere di Siviglia*: 'Cessa di più resistere', re-written for soprano; the theme of 'Zitti, zitti, piano, piano' from the Act 2 Trio transcribed for Chorus; and five bars from the Largo of the Act 1 finale, 'Freddo ed immobile' used in the Finale 'Sacro ad Ausonia'. The following works are also drawn upon: a tenor concert aria, 'Dolci aurette che spirate', 1809; *L'equivoco stravagante, Ciro in Babilonia; La scala di seta; Aureliano in Palmira; Il turco in Italia; Sigismondo; Torvaldo e Dorliska*.

by admiring locals, was, it seems, a comic genius, a huge hill of a man with a whining voice and a great facility for falling off chairs. As for Rossini himself, he played safe, serving up some pre-cooked dishes: a trio from *La pietra del paragone* and a couple of numbers from *Il turco in Italia*, substantial numbers, which give body to this frothy and eminently enjoyable two-acter.

The second commission for the autumn season, this time for Barbaia's company in their temporary home, the Teatro del Fondo, was to be a version of Shakespeare's *Othello*. It was a bold choice and might have made compelling music-drama had not the Marchese Francesco Maria Berio di Salsa so neutered Shakespeare's play, turning all but the final movement into arid melodrama. Byron saw the opera at the San Benedetto in Venice in 1818:

> They have been crucifying Othello into an opera (*Otello* by Rossini) – Music good but lugubrious – but as for the words! – all the real scenes with Iago cut out – & the greatest nonsense instead – the handkerchief turned into a *billet doux*, and the first Singer would not *black* his face – for some exquisite reasons assigned in the preface. – Scenery – dresses – & Music very good.[4]

Berio (1767–1820) was a literary dilettante who had flitted elegantly around the Neapolitan cultural scene since the 1780s and it was perhaps inevitable that Rossini would be encouraged to work with him. Writers like Lady Morgan[5] were much taken with the Palazzo Berio and its 'congregation of elegant and refined spirits' but professionals were less impressed. Stendhal calls him an 'unmentionable literary hack' and Goethe, who was visited by Berio in 1787, thought him enthusiastic but feckless. None the less, Act 3 of *Otello* is a notable distillation, with a little help from Dante, of Shakespeare's concluding scenes, in particular the scene of Desdemona's Willow Song. Meyerbeer spoke for a whole generation (*Otello* was to be one of Rossini's most frequently played scores) when he wrote:

> The third act of *Otello* established its reputation so firmly that a thousand errors couldn't shake it. This third act is really godlike, and what is so extraordinary is that its beauties are quite un-Rossini-like. First-rate declamation, continuously impassioned

---

[4] *Byron's Letters and Journals*, ed. Marchand, London, 1976, Vol.6, p.18.

[5] *See* Lady Morgan, *Italy*, London, 1821, 3vv., *passim*. Lady Morgan (*née* Sidney Owenson, c.1776–1859) is best known for her novel *The Wild Irish Girl* (1806). Byron thought her books on Italy 'fearless'.

recitative, mysterious accompaniments full of local colour, and, in particular, the style of the old romances brought to the highest perfection.[6]

Otello had its *prima* in Naples on 4 December, 1816, leaving Rossini precious little time to get to Rome, let alone write a new opera, by Christmas. When he arrived in Rome in mid- or late-December there was the further complication of the ecclesiastical censor's having rejected the libretto proposed by the impresario of the Teatro Valle, Pietro Cartoni. At this stage, Cartoni must have settled for a postponement of the new Rossini. What followed is chronicled by the librettist, Jacopo Ferretti, in a memoir later reproduced by Alberto Cametti.[7] According to Ferretti, he was summoned to Cartoni's house two days before Christmas. For several hours they sat, chilled to the marrow and drinking 'Jamaica tea', turning over 'twenty or thirty subjects for a *melodramma*'. Some were too serious for the Carnival season, others too costly; some were too complex, others ill-suited to the available singers. With Ferretti half asleep and Rossini having climbed into a bed in the room 'the better to concentrate', the following exchange is reported.

> FERRETTI: (murmuring) Cinderella?
> ROSSINI: (sitting bolt upright in bed) Would you have the courage to write me a Cinderella?
> FERRETTI: Would you have the courage to set it to music?
> ROSSINI: And the outline . . .?
> FERRETTI: You can have it in the morning if I go without sleep tonight.
> ROSSINI: Good night! (Wrapping himself in the bedclothes and falling 'like Homer's gods' into a blessed sleep.)

The exchange is, of course, an agreeable fiction; like all acts of reminiscence it gives to events a shape and a pattern which at the time they did not necessarily possess. It helps in the mythologizing of Rossini – the Olympian unconcern is central to the popular view of the man; and yet the alacrity of Rossini's response to the suggestion of Cinderella is of more direct interest. As we shall see,[8] the substance

[6] *Giacomo Meyerbeer: Briefwechsel und Tagebücher*, ed. Heinz Becker, Berlin, 1960, I, p.359.

[7] A. Cametti, *Un poeto melodrammatico romano*, Milan, 1898.

[8] Chapter 26, pp.192ff.

of the Cinderella story in the form Rossini received it drew from him music in which the tragi-comic rhythm of the fairy-tale is tellingly, at times movingly, pointed. Where Ferretti is downright disingenuous is in his suggestion that he conceived and sketched the libretto in a flash of nocturnal inspiration. Two texts, apt to Rossini's style and interests were extant: Charles-Guillaume Etienne's libretto for Nicolò Isouard's *Cendrillon* (Paris, February 1810), which preceded and directly influenced Felice Romani's libretto for Stefano Pavesi's *Agatina, o La virtù premiata* (Milan, April 1814). Not for the first time, Rossini's librettist is not creating a new text but revising and re-shaping an existing one, as had been the case with *L'italiana in Algeri*, *Il turco in Italia*, and *Il barbiere di Siviglia*. Where musical precedents also existed, Rossini was provided at the start of his own rapid compositional process with a valuable set of perspectives, literary and musical, with which to work. Most of *La Cenerentola* is new. Three of the original numbers were the work of Luca Agolini, who also wrote much of the recitative,[9] and there are two significant self-borrowings: the overture, which is taken directly from *La gazzetta*, and the music for Cenerentola's concluding Rondo and variations in Act 2, which is based on the Count Almaviva's Act 2 aria, 'Cessa di più resistere', in *Il barbiere di Siviglia*. This latter borrowing is the more curious. As it is unthinkable that Rossini had written off *Il barbiere di Siviglia* in its entirety, we must assume that he was unhappy with the aria in its original context. In Bologna in the summer of 1816 the aria was sung by Rosina (again Righetti-Giorgi) in the upward transposition of F major. There is no evidence that Rossini was in Bologna at the time, but he may have sanctioned the change, and, as we have seen, he himself adapted the aria for soprano voice as part of *Le nozze di Teti e di Peleo*. Righetti-Giorgi also created the role of Cenerentola, from which we can reasonably assume that she liked the music and that Rossini was happy to accord to it, at last, a proper resting-place, a decision which posterity has reciprocated by persistently ignoring 'Cessa di più resistere' in its original context.

The cast, headed by Righetti-Giorgi, was a strong one and included two singers – Andrea Verni as Don Magnifico and Giuseppe de Begnis as Dandini – who had sung the equivalent roles in

---

[9] Agolini's contributions are: Alidoro's Act 1 aria 'Vasto teatro è il mondo', the Act 2 Chorus 'Ah questa bella incognita', and Clorinda's Act 2 aria 'Sventurata! me credea'.

Pavesi's opera in 1814. The *prima* on 25 January 1817 was full of mishaps and was noisily received; but Rossini was by now inured against the Roman mob and, it seems, more confident of what he had written. And rightly so: *La Cenerentola* quickly won wide acclaim and was for many years much more popular than *Il barbiere di Siviglia*. It is certainly the most humane of Rossini's great comedies.

Rossini left Rome for Bologna with the Marchese Francesco Sampieri on 11 February. Pleasant as a break with his parents in Bologna must have been, his real purpose in travelling north was to complete a major new commission from La Scala, Milan. The La Scala audience, it will be recalled, had not been happy with Rossini's last effort for them, *Il turco in Italia*. The new commission was thus an important one and there is every evidence that Rossini, lodging with his old Fiorilla, Francesca Maffei-Festa, worked assiduously on the new opera in the late winter and early spring of 1817. There were distractions, no doubt, one of them being the presence in Milan of Peter Winter whose *Maometto II* to a libretto by Romani had opened at La Scala on 28 January. Legend has it that Winter was a dirty eater, something which did not commend him to the over-fastidious Rossini. More germane was the opening of an opera on a subject Rossini himself would return to no less than three times in his subsequent career.

The libretto which Rossini was handed in Milan, *La gazza ladra*, was a happy imposition. Rossini had long been fascinated by the *semiseria* form: but it was not a genre, by and large, which the Barbaia-Colbran regime in Naples was likely to favour. *La gazza ladra* was to be staged in Naples in 1819 with a star-studded cast, but the original commission owes everything to Rossini's desire to write for houses other than the San Carlo, to Barbaia's willingness to let him travel, and to Rossini's own continuing willingness to cross and re-cross Italy on bad roads in draughty coaches with recalcitrant mules. ('Bestie buggierone', he calls them in an undated letter describing one such journey 'tragico-buffo'.) The variety of commissions Rossini was afforded helped broaden his experience and enrich his style, something to which the best works of the years which follow powerfully testify.

Writing to his mother in March 1817 about the *La gazza ladra* libretto, Rossini noted: 'il soggetto è bellissimo'. The subject – the story of a French peasant girl condemned to death for allegedly stealing silver cutlery which later proves to have been taken by a light-beaked magpie – had been submitted to a Milan theatres libretto contest on the subject *Avviso ai giudici* by a philologist, poet, and medical man, Giovanni Gherardini (1778–1861). Letters have come to light which reveal the reasons why at least one member of the prize jury thought so well of Gherardini's work. Some minor caveats apart, the libretto was commended for the naturalness and clarity with which this rather elaborate tragic-comic subject had been handled. Looking at the text, one might think Gherardini rather too sparing with words in places, but it is a fault in the right direction. In its variety, clarity, and poise, the text suited Rossini admirably. Paër's loss (he turned the libretto down in 1816) was Rossini's immeasurable gain. The *prima* on 31 May, 1817, with a strong cast headed by Filippo Galli as the girl's deserter-father, Fernando, was a triumph. What's more, some brief echoes apart, the music was entirely new, further evidence of the thought and care Rossini had put into the composition.

After what we must assume was a well-earned rest in Bologna, Rossini returned to Naples, to a re-built Teatro San Carlo, and to yet another musical, aesthetic, and dramatic challenge: a libretto, drawn from Tasso's *Gerusalemme liberata*, on the subject of Armida. Tasso's fabulous temptress had not only cast her spell over the knight, Rinaldo. A dozen composers, including Lully, Handel, Gluck, and Haydn had been tempted by the tale; so had Goethe whose verse adaptation was to lure Brahms into writing a surprisingly frank and erotic cantata on the subject. Rossini's approach, to the first act in particular, was remarkably clear-sighted; yet the subject could not be adequately tackled without radical innovations – innovations which go beyond the inclusion of ballet music and an extended chorus role – in Rossini's method. It was, as Weinstock rightly suggests, a very singular piece, so singular that it was not, in its day, much liked; yet it is hardly an exaggeration to claim that without *Armida*, and the dramatic and musical implications the work raises, many later works up to and including *Guillaume Tell* could not have been written as they were.

After the comparatively fallow years 1814–15, Rossini was once again working at an extraordinary rate. With *La Cenerentola*, *La gazza ladra*, and *Armida* written within the space of ten months – a phenomenal achievement which must itself explode once and for all the myth that Rossini was a lazy man – he travelled to Rome to write a new opera for Cartoni who after Sforza-Cesarini's death had taken over the management of the Teatro Argentina. The libretto, another of Giovanni Federico Schmidt's efforts, told of military confrontation in medieval Italy. Radiciotti thought *Adelaide di Borgogna* 'the worst of Rossini's *opere serie*', though experience of the work in performance would suggest otherwise. It was not well received by the Roman audience in December 1817 but it is an opera which merits an occasional airing.

6

Mosè in Egitto and return to Pesaro (1818)

Rossini wrote three new operas in 1818: *Mosè in Egitto, Adina*, which remained unstaged until 1826, and *Ricciardo e Zoraide*. It is also a year in which we can note Rossini's evolving responsibilities towards the expanding body of successful operas he had written since 1812. In April 1818 there was a Neapolitan revival of *La Cenerentola* with the role of Don Magnifico cast in Neapolitan dialect; Rossini would not have undertaken such work, but he perhaps sanctioned it. Later, in June, Rossini supervised a new production of *La gazza ladra* in his native town of Pesaro. Meanwhile, there was a new opera to be written for the San Carlo. Lenten regulations governing the theatres demanded something, in outward appearance at least, chaster and more scriptural in subject and tone. By designation, *Mosè in Egitto*, a tolerable libretto derived by Tottola from Francesco Ringhieri's *L'Osiride* (Padua, 1760), is an *oratorio* or *azione tragico-sacra* but there was a strong operatic cast on hand for which to write: Moses would be sung by the popular and accomplished bass, Michele Benedetti, Nozzari would sing the tenor role of the Pharaoh's son, Osiride, Colbran the role of the Aida-like heroine, Elcia. Assigning the title role to a bass was unconventional at the time.

Stendhal tells us how he attended the San Carlo with 'a marked lack of enthusiasm for the plagues of Egypt'. Libretti based on holy scripture, he suggests, are more to the taste of the Bible-reading English. He also confesses to a predisposition to mock the stage effects in the opera's first scene, prematurely as it turned out:

> When the curtain went up, I am afraid that I simply burst out laughing at the sight of all those wretched little groups of Egyptians, plunged into Stygian darkness by the Plague of Dimmers, lost in the wilderness of an apparently boundless stage, and praying like fury. Yet before I had heard twenty bars of this

superb *introduzione* I could see nothing less profoundly moving than a whole population plunged into deep misery.[1]

Certainly, the first act of *Mosè in Egitto* (Act 2 in the inflated and re-drafted Parisian re-write) ranks with the third act of *Otello* in musical, theatrical, and imaginative skills memorably sustained. Stendhal was also much impressed by Benedetti's Moses:

> [he] entered, wearing a costume which was sublime in its very simplicity, and had been copied from Michelangelo's statue in the church of San Pietro in Vincoli, in Rome . . . Moses was no longer a shoddy conjuror turning his rod into a serpent and playing cheap tricks on a primitive simpleton, but a great Minister of the All-Powerful, who could cause a vile tyrant to shake upon his throne. I can still recall the overwhelming impression produced by the first hearing of the words: 'Eterno, immenso, incomprensibil Dio!'.[2]

No doubt, in the phrase 'vile tyrant', we catch an echo of Stendhal's anti-Bourbon views. Lady Morgan contests this Stendhalian hyperbole by noting how the potentially unsympathetic King of Egypt was shown 'every possible delicacy' in the San Carlo production. One of the triumphs of *Mosè in Egitto*, something entirely lost in the Paris re-write, is the electrifying climax to Act 2. By contrast, Act 3 was not, in the 1818 version, a success. The crossing of the Red Sea was badly staged and Rossini, whose finales can be perfunctory, had not written music of sufficient quality to sustain this short but important final act; by March 1819 he had completely redrafted it. The story of how he went about this, including the composition of the famous prayer, 'Dal tuo stellato soglio', is one of Stendhal's more outrageous fictions, but his account of the impact of the revised Act 3 is worth quoting if only because it communicates the emotions which this famous scene was to arouse in the breasts of his contemporaries. After the stage-management's disasters of the previous year, many in the audience had turned up to enjoy another fiasco.

> the laughter was already bursting forth audible from the pit, when the audience suddenly became aware that Moses was starting an unfamiliar aria – a prayer which all the people echo in chorus after Moses.

[1] VdR, p.319.
[2] ibid., p.320.

The effect of the new aria and chorus was a powerful one:

> People stood up in their boxes and leaned over the balconies, shouting to crack the vault of heaven . . . I have never known such a triumph – which was all the more tremendous since everyone had come expecting to laugh or jeer . . . Who will deny, in the light of such an experience, that music can provoke an immediate and physical nervous reaction?[3]

Though *Mosè in Egitto* was, until very recently, eclipsed by Rossini's own inflated and in some respects unsatisfactory revision for the Paris Opéra in 1827, it won for itself a considerable international reputation and was framed in fiction by Balzac in his story *Massimilla Doni* (1839). Only the 'Bible-reading English' were less than enthusiastic. Covent Garden staged a shortened concert version on 30 January 1822 and later that year it was staged in surrogate secular form as *Pietro l'eremita*. No wonder the English thought Rossini's treatment of the subject inferior to Handel's.

In May, 1818 Ester Mombelli gave the first public performance of a short cantata for soprano, chorus, and orchestra, *La morte di Didone*, which Rossini had written in 1811. Savaged by the Venetian press, it sank more or less without trace, thought parts of it were published in Milan two years later.

The most pleasurable event of 1818 for Rossini was probably the gala opening on 10 June of the new opera house in Pesaro, time-consuming though the arrangements proved to be. Rossini had first heard from two prominent Pesaresì, Giulio Perticari and Antaldo Antaldi, in January 1818. What followed is of considerable interest, for nowhere else do we get so well documented a picture of how Rossini set about staging a revival of one of his own works.[4] His immediate concern was the engagement of singers, after which an appropriate opera would be selected. On 27 January he wrote to Antaldi to confirm that he was trying to engage the services of Colbran and Nozzari. The negotiations dragged on for two months during which time it became clear that Pesaro could not afford, or

---

[3] ibid., pp.324–5.
[4] See LdR, pp.15–17.

would not specify how much they would pay, such celebrities.[5] Eventually, he managed to engage the bass Raniero Remorini, the tenor Alberico Curioni and, after more wheeler-dealing, the soprano Giuseppina Ronzi De Begnis. The opera was to be *La gazza ladra*, staged with sets by Landriani and Sanquirico. The letters which are extant show an almost obsessive attention to detail on Rossini's part. The layout of the orchestra, the space between players and the lighting, are all specified; the co-ordination of stage designers and stage managers is set in train; even the toy magpie is ordered. Rehearsals for the soloists began in Bologna around 20 May; by 1 June an orchestra, an *ad hoc* group of the best local players, and chorus were assembled and in rehearsal. Remorini appears to have given Rossini a good deal of trouble, demanding and getting an entrance aria for Fernando, an aria taken directly from *Torvaldo e Dorliska*, one of Galli's arias which Remorini, who sang Giorgio in the opera's Rome *prima*, clearly coveted. In the preface to the printed libretto, the impresario, Giovanni Massei, announced that the opera had been 'revised and expanded'. It was certainly expanded; not only did Remorini have his entrance aria, there was also an extra movement for Ninetta and Giannetto: the sumptuous love duet 'Amor, possente nome' from *Armida*. Dramatically indefensible (it would be difficult to find two heroines more different than Ninetta and Armida), the decision is defensible within the context of a gala evening the like of which Pesaro has probably not seen since. The extended performance began on the evening of the 10th, but it was not until dawn on the 11th that the official and unofficial junketings were over. This Rossini Festival, which later included some indifferent performances of *Il barbiere di Siviglia*, nearly had a tragic outcome when Rossini was struck down with 'severe inflammation of the throat'. His death was rumoured as far afield as Naples and Paris. But he survived, nursed back to good health at the Villa Perticari and honoured with another banquet before travelling to Bologna and one of his strangest commissions at this time, the one act opera, *Adina*.

[5] According to Rosselli, op.cit., p.62, Table 4, Colbran commanded a monthly fee of 909 ducats at the San Carlo. At a slightly later date, Nozzari's fee was 600 ducats a month. At these rates a San Carlo-derived cast would have cost about 3400 ducats. From what Rossini's letters reveal, the cost of his Pesaro cast was in the region of 1850 scudi or app. 2390 ducats.

The opera was written at the behest of a Portuguese patron in Lisbon. The subject was a popular one which had already been treated by Boieldieu and Manuel García, but neither the subject nor Rossini's name ensured prompt staging. Some say there was pique in Lisbon at Rossini's refusal to provide an overture (none having being stipulated in the contract). The opera was not staged until 1826 and not published until 1859. Why did Rossini bother with the piece? Was it for amusement, or money, or simply to please the Marchese Gherardo Bevilacqua-Aldobrandini, an amateur librettist and patron of Bologna's Liceo Musicale, who adapted the text from a libretto by Romani? All we can be certain of is that it is a winning reminder that he had not lost his old skill as a composer of *farse*.

In Naples Berio had come up with another libretto for the San Carlo, *Ricciardo e Zoraide*, a tale of high passion and knightly daring with an array of Asian potentates, African warriors, and Christian Crusaders which even Marlowe might have wondered at. The opera had its *prima* on 3 December 1818 and was to be seen again, to some acclaim, in the spring of the following year. In *Ricciardo e Zoraide* we hear a further consolidation and enriching of Rossini's *opera seria* style. Meanwhile, in Milan, Meyerbeer was hearing of other matters to do with Rossini: rumours of problems with the Italian Opera in Paris, of approaches to Rossini, of his terms (said to be 'oltremodo stravagante e forte'), of possibilities of Rossini writing for the Opéra itself.[6] It would take nearly eight years for all these predictions to be proved correct but there is a prescient quality about the latter which suggests a keen ear, excellent sources, and a shrewd instinct. Rossini's Italian career was already moving into its final phase.

[6] Meyerbeer, op. cit., p.360.

7

1819–21

In late 1818 or early 1819, whilst preparing a revised re-staging of *Armida*, Rossini appears to have written two short cantatas for use on state occasions at the San Carlo. The first, *Omaggio umiliato* to a text by Niccolini, was eventually performed on 20 February 1819 as a celebration to mark King Ferdinand's recovery from illness. The drama briefly enacts the solicitations of a people troubled about their sovereign's health and their joy at the news of his recovery. The *Giornale delle due Sicilie* praised the drama as spectacle and went on:

> The highest praise for this festival is due to the famous Cavalier Niccolini who designed it and directed all its parts. He also was capable of interpreting the feeling of the public, writing the poem set beautifully to music by maestro Rossini and sung by the *prima attrice* of the Royal Theatres, Signora Colbran. Delightful were the dances invented and directed by Signor Taglioni, and marvellous the effect produced by one hundred and twenty wind instruments directed on the stage by the valorous Signor Caligari.[1]

The extant music consists of an orchestral introduction, an aria, 'Deh al tuo popolo perdona', and an orchestral dance movement in theme and variation form, not unlike some of the ballet music written the previous autumn for *Armida*. Some music which is missing was evidently common to *Omaggio umiliato* and the Cantata which was performed at the San Carlo on 9 May in honour of a state visit by the Austrian Emperor, Francis I. As Rossini was *en route* from Venice to Naples at the time, he did not attend the performance on 9 May but he provided music for it, including a Trio, sung by Colbran, David, and Rubini, and an array of short dance movements in the Italian and Austro-Hungarian styles, as well as a

---

[1] Quoted by Gossett, 'Rossini in Naples: some major works recovered', p.325.

three-part harmonization of Haydn's celebrated Emperor's Hymn.
The Cantata ended spectacularly:

> At the end of the performance, while the chorus directed prayers
> to Felicity, and sang:
> Serba AUGUSTO ai prodi suoi
> E a noi serba il PADRE e il RE.
> a beautiful transparency appeared at the back of the stage, in
> which the KING our Lord was seen in the act of greeting his
> august nephew, relation, and friend, the EMPEROR.[2]

In addition to revising Act 3 of *Mosè in Egitto*, Rossini also
produced a new work for the San Carlo, *Ermione*, first seen there on
27 March. The choice of play – Racine's first great tragedy, the swift
and impassioned *Andromaque* – was an inspired one. As for the
music, it is – *pace* Toye, Derwent, and even Radiciotti – exceptional
in its power and declamatory force, and not merely in the penultimate scene to which references are invariably made. The central
character, Pyrrhus, the warrior-king who is loved by Hermione but
who dotes on the widowed Andromache, is written in a manner
which makes one lament the fact that Rossini's *Otello* was not
written three years later and to a better libretto. For here, at last, we
glimpse writing for heroic tenor which is awful in its power. Andromache, a more shadowy figure, is a grieving heroine with one superb
aria of melancholy in the Bellini style; but at the centre of the drama
is Hermione herself, beloved by Orestes but doting on the vain and
unworthy Pyrrhus. It was Colbran's role – sung to David's Orestes
and Nozzari's Pyrrhus – and is powerfully written: a romantic,
melodramatic paraphrase of the French classical style executed in the
grand manner, by turns expansive and restrained. It is a pity that
Maria Callas – a striking Armida and a superb Médée in Cherubini's
opera of that name – never studied this role. But with the opera being
written off by every Rossini biographer – in criticisms which often
seem merely to rationalize the writers' lack of access to the music –
there was little chance of such an initiative being taken. Even Rossini
rationalized the work's lack of success in his conversations with
Hiller some years later, though his clear attempt to use some of its

[2] ibid, p.328.

finest pages for *Ugo, re d'Italia* in London six years later,[3] suggests that at the time he was loathe to let the music vanish from public view.

With *Ermione* on the stage and barely enough time to reach Venice in time for his next commission, Rossini was obliged to piece together a do-it-yourself opera on a libretto taken from Pavesi's *Odoardo e Cristina* (Naples, 1810). Several new numbers were written; the rest was plundered from operas unfamiliar in Venice: *Adelaide di Borgogna, Ricciardo e Zoraide*, and *Ermione*. Here, perhaps we do see the cynical Rossini of unsympathetic popular legend; Rossini the improviser, the entertainer of a fickle public, basking in his new-won status as a cult figure of the post-war world. Byron was in Venice in May 1819 and wrote in a letter: 'There has been a splendid Opera lately at San Benedetto – by Rossini – who came in person to play the Harpsichord – the People followed him about – crowned him – cut off his hair 'for memory'; he was Shouted and Sonnetted and feasted – and immortalized much more than either of the Emperors.'[4] There can be little doubt that by now Rossini was, indeed, a cult figure, more and more subject to the inequalities of popular judgement (pastiche, like *Eduardo e Cristina* acclaimed, *Il barbiere* shouted down, the original *Ermione* soon to be neglected). When Shelley, enthusing over Peacock's *Rhododaphne* published in 1818, writes: 'There is here, as in the songs of ancient times, music and dancing and the luxury of voluptuous delight', he is commending in Peacock many of the qualities which Rossini was heard to be conveying to his public. Byron may have tired of 'Di tanti palpiti' but many fellow writers and artists had turned veneration of latin, mediterranean culture – a culture characterized by its elegance, harmony, and devotion to the comic muse – into a new aesthetic imperative which was to last into the 1820s. And whilst sophisticated spirits revelled in the subtler colours of Rossini's art, the artisans whistled his tunes. Rossini's tunes, an English traveller of the period tells us,[5] were 'warbled with as much passion as the most tolerolol tunes are bawled about in England'.

---

[3] See G. Carli Ballola, 'Lettura dell' *Ermoine*', BdCRdS, 1972, No.3, pp.33–5.

[4] Byron, op. cit., p.132.

[5] W.S. Rose, *Letters from the North of Italy*, 1819, II, p.123.

From Venice Rossini travelled via Pesaro to Naples where a new production of *La gazza ladra* was in hand and where *La donna del lago* would shortly be written, Rossini now directly engaging the newly fashionable literature of the age. His return to Pesaro on 24 May should have been a happy one after the triumphs of the previous year. In the event, it was an ill-fated one, poisoned by the animosity of Caroline of Brunswick, the estranged wife of the English Prince Regent, and the sleek and sinister Bartolomeo Bergami who, to the outrage of conservative Pesarese society, had become the lover of this future Queen of England. Whether Rossini had really snubbed the woman the previous year with such ill-judged witticisms as 'certain rheumatic afflictions, having deprived him of elasticity in his spine, do not permit him to make the accustomed bows prescribed by court etiquette' is uncertain. What is certain is that on 24 May Bergami's henchmen seriously disrupted the evening's performance. Rossini's appearance was greeted with jeers and catcalls so threatening that he had to be spirited to the comparative safety of a box and, later, out of the theatre and town altogether. The local council made valiant attempts to retrieve the situation, but the aggravation continued and Rossini left Pesaro, agitated and angry, much as he was to leave Bologna thirty years later. Rossini was 27, and though he survived into his 76th year, he was never again to set foot in Pesaro.

During the summer and autumn of 1819 Rossini returned to the familiar routine: a new opera for the Teatro San Carlo in late October, and another journey north to Milan for a further commission, Romani's *Bianca e Falliero*, in December. The Neapolitan opera was *La donna del lago*. It was noisily received on the first night, as Stendhal, who was not there, vividly reports; but it was to be one of Rossini's most frequently revived operas in the nineteenth century.

A glance at the list of Rossini's compositions during 1820 might suggest that it was a fallow year, albeit a year which arrived at an imposing resting point with the *prima*, at the San Carlo on 3 December, of *Maometto II*. The year was not, however, uneventful. If his thoughts were increasingly turning to the idea of a career outside Italy, then there were events in 1820 – personal, political, and musical – which may have brought him closer to such a decision. Unusually, the year began with Rossini devoting a great deal of his time, not to his own music, but to the preparation of the Italian *prima* of Spontini's revision of his *tragédie lyrique*, *Fernand Cortez*

(Paris Opéra, 28 November, 1809; 2nd ed. Paris Opéra, 8 May, 1817). Its influence on *Maometto II*, which was received by the Neapolitans almost as coolly as they received the Spontini, is perhaps more marginal than central, stimulating existing elements in Rossini's own evolving style, especially in matters relating to writing for chorus and the use of the orchestral brass, rather than setting in train new methods.

The Lenten season did draw from Rossini a major new work, but it was not an opera. (An opera had been promised to mark the wedding of the son of the Duchess of Lucca, but despite disingenuous notes of encouragement by Rossini it never materialized.) It was, in fact, a Mass, his *Messa di Gloria* or 'Messa a 4 Voci e più strumenti Obligati' as it is described in a manuscript version held by Ricordi. As the title suggests, it is a work which confines itself to the Kyrie and the Gloria. It is made up of ten movements and has over the years been the subject of a great deal of misleading comment, most of it stemming from a review – a mischievous farrago of half-truths, lies, and libels – by a minor German composer, Carl von Miltitz. Miltitz's comments first appeared in the annotations to Amadeus Wendt's German edition of Stendhal's *Vie de Rossini* and have been reproduced in English by Weinstock as an apparently valid source and by Philip Gossett as part of a properly researched survey of the Mass's compositional history.[6] Contrary to Miltitz's allegations, the *Messa di Gloria* is not a ragout of Rossini's own operatic phrases themselves largely stolen from the works of the great German masters, but a newly written work of great accomplishment and character which has rightly, albeit tentatively, entered the mainstream of the nineteenth-century choral repertoire.

The *Messa di Gloria* was first performed, in a concert which also included a performance of Pergolesi's *Stabat Mater*, on 24 March, 1820. A few weeks later Isabella Colbran's father died, leaving her heiress to a considerable estate, including the large family home at Castenaso near Bologna.[7] Rossini, who was almost certainly Colbran's lover by this time, commissioned a monument for the tomb of the man who, had he survived a further two years, would have become his father-in-law. If Colbran's and Rossini's fortunes

---

[6] Weinstock, pp.100–1; Gossett, 'Rossini in Naples: some major works recovered', pp.331–9.

[7] See Plate 5.

were changing, so were those of the King. In the summer of 1820 there was a rising against the Bourbon regime. The demand was a new constitution on the lines of that granted to Spain in 1812. The rising was led by a motley group of disaffected army officers, priests, and some better-heeled members of the middle class. Ferdinand took the matter rather lightly and the new constitution was quickly promulgated, a move which sent shock-waves through the Holy Alliance. With Naples in a disorderly state throughout the summer and early autumn, a British frigate was dispatched to the city and Ferdinand summoned by the Tsar and Metternich to a council-of-war at Laibach in January 1821. Metternich had never placed much trust in Ferdinand ('He still thinks that the throne is an easy chair to sprawl and sleep in', he is reported to have said) though he was not unwilling to provide an 'Austrian solution' to the Neapolitan problem. In March 1821 General Pepe and the Carbonari were roundly beaten by the Austrian army and, after a suitable interval, Ferdinand returned to Naples.

Despite the political upheavals, Rossini had remained in Naples to complete work on *Maometto II*; but by mid-December he abandoned the city in order to spend another Christmas in Rome with his old friend Pietro Cartoni. The story of the making of the libretto for *Matilde di Shabran*, the opera which Rossini was about to write for a Carnival season *prima* at Rome's Teatro Apollo, is complex even by Rossini's standards.[8] The result, though, if not perhaps an opera of the scope and quality of *La gazza ladra*, is another substantial essay in the *semiseria* style: *melodramma giocoso* is its official designation. The first performance was directed not by the music-director of the Apollo, who had died of apoplexy during rehearsals, but by Niccolò Paganini. The two men had met before, during Paganini's Italian tours of 1816 onwards, and Paganini had direct experience of conducting from his period as leader of the Court Orchestra in Lucca, domain of the enterprising and clever sister of Napoleon Bonaparte, the Princess Elisa Bacchiocchi. During the Carnival itself Rossini and Paganini dressed as beggars and sang a quasi-mournful ditty in the Roman thoroughfares: 'Siamo ciechi; siamo nati/Per

---

[8] See M. Tartak, 'Matilde and her Cousins', BdCRds, 1973, No.3, p.13.

campar di cortesia./ In giornata d'allegria/Non si nega carità.'[9] Rossini, we are told, filled out his already ample frame with bundles of straw, whilst Paganini remained 'as thin as a door with a face which resembled the neck of a violin'.[10] Laurel and Hardy could not have provided a more engaging show. Rather less engaging, in that it was an artistically questionable act for which Rossini received the by no means inconsiderable sum of 150 zecchini, was the edition of *Otello* which he had prepared for Cartoni in the autumn of 1819 for the 1820 Roman Carnival. We should not, I suppose, be unduly exercised about the imposition of happy endings on the plots of Shakespearian operatic transcriptions when the English themselves were playing *King Lear* in the Nahum Tate version until Macready's restoration of the tragic ending in 1838. None the less, Act 3 of *Otello* was self-evidently one of Rossini's finest early achievements: to delete the Gondolier's Song, insert the famous love duet from *Armida* in place of the murder scene and end with a festive ensemble from *Ricciardo e Zoraide* smacks of commercial opportunism of the worst kind.

After the Roman carnival Rossini returned to Naples in the wake of the Austrian army. In April 1821 he conducted a performance of a favourite work whose influence on him is evident in the first act of *Mosè in Egitto:* Haydn's *The Creation*. By now, Rossini was negotiating freely with managements abroad, eager, among other things, to make official visits to both London and Paris. In December, 1821 Barbaia signed a contract which would take the Naples company to Vienna's Kärntnertortheater as part of the Habsburg's policy of leasing to enterprising impresarios this old and distinguished theatre, forerunner of the Hofoper and present-day Staatsoper whose site is now adjacent to that of the older building. At the same time, a new contract was negotiated with Rossini, allowing for visits to Vienna, Paris, and London, but envisaging, wrongly as it turned out, his eventual return to Naples.

The opera which the San Carlo would take to Vienna was *Zelmira*, scheduled for a trial *prima* in Naples in February. In the

[9] 'We are blind; we were born/To survive on favours./On this joyful day /Don't refuse us charity.' Rossini turned this into a *buffo* ensemble for vocal quartet and piano, the whining opening nicely preserved, in *Carnevale di Venezia*, Milan, 1847; reproduced in facsimile by G. Monaldi, *Noi e il mondo*, August, 1925. The piece has been recorded.

[10] Massimo d'Azeglio, *I miei ricordi*, II, p.146.

meantime, Rossini had another, smaller commission to complete, a cantata, to be performed at a gala concert in his own honour, at the San Carlo on 27 December, 1821. It was a valediction, an expression of royal thanks designed, no doubt, to hasten his return to so generous a city. The King, court, and ministers attended. With all takings made over to Rossini, it was for him a lucrative evening. The cantata was entitled *La riconoscenza*, 'Gratitude'. The text was again the work of Giulio Genoino and was another elaborately staged, dramatically static neo-classical entertainment in which the principal characters, swathed in the trappings of Arcadia, contemplate the source of all beneficence and harmony. The solo vocal writing, which occasionally evolves into elegantly turned ensemble writing for two and three voices, is in Rossini's suavest pastoral vein, a conscious re-affirmation of the lyric-idyllic aesthetic of *Tancredi* and parts of *La donna del lago*. The male characters, the philosopher and priest, Fileno and Elpino, also draw from Rossini harp and horn accompaniments in that romantic, ossianic style which would remain popular for several decades to come in both Italy and Germany (one thinks of Brahms's choral songs Op.17). The soloists on 27 December were G. B. Rubini, his wife, Adelaide Comelli (*née* Chaumel), Girolama Dardanelli, and Michele Benedetti: further evidence of Rubini's long apprenticeship in Naples under Barbaia's rule. (His debut had been in the 1815 revival of *L'italiana in Algeri* at the Teatro dei Fiorentini.) *La riconoscenza* was to be revived and revised on several occasions, in Naples in 1822, in Verona later the same year as *Il vero omaggio*, and in Bologna in 1829.

    Zelmira itself was staged on 16 February, 1822. It was no more than a *succès d'estime*, the audience not unreasonably sensing a chilly, rather petrified quality in the score. The press, which was now as enthusiastic about Rossini as it had once been cool, was generally favourable, criticizing the dingy costumes but praising the lavish sets, questioning Ambrosi's playing of the old King Polidoro as a figure from a *comédie larmoyante* and Giovanni David's preoccupation with *bel canto* at the expense of dramatic verisimilitude, but praising in fulsome terms both Nozzari and Colbran: Nozzari for his familiar command of both the music and the stage and Colbran for a performance which one pro-Colbran (and Stendhal would say pro-Bourbon) writer termed 'sublime, admirable, inimitable'.

    Before the company left for Vienna, Rossini conducted a performance of Mayr's oratorio *Atalia*, a performance complicated by

Colbran's refusal (or inability) to sing the title role and the conse-
quent need for Rossini to adjust parts of the role for the darker-
voiced and not wholly adequate substitute, Giuseppina Fabré. Towards the end of February, the 24-year-old Donizetti had arrived in
Naples. In a letter written to Mayr at the time he claims to have
'stayed out of sight', yet he complains vigorously about Colbran's
defection, about the cuts which are being made in the music, about
Rossini's 'jesuitical' complaints about the singers, and about his
habit of gossiping with prima donnas during rehearsal when he
would have been better employed conducting.[11] By contrast, a
report, quoted by Radiciotti, sent to the *Journal des Débats* of 11
March, 1822 gives a rather different picture of Rossini's rehearsal
methods during the preparations for the first night of *Zelmira*:

> Rossini has a way of rehearsing which is entirely his own. He
> never gets ruffled; he hardly says two or three words, and trusts
> the work of Festa [his conductor and répétiteur] completely. His
> principle is not to upset the orchestra and, above all, not to
> humiliate the singers. His prodigious memory allows him to make
> his observations to each one in particular after the rehearsal.
> Leaving the San Carlo, I accompanied him to the house of the
> copyist to whom he pointed out some fifty mistakes without
> looking at the score! The more one observes this man at close
> quarters, the more one finds him a superior being.[12]

---

[11] Guido Zavadini, *Donizetti: vita, musiche, epistolario*, Bergamo, 1948,
pp.231–2.

[12] Radiciotti, I, pp.432–4.

8

Vienna, Verona, Venice (1822–3)

Rossini and Colbran left Naples after the final performance of *Zelmira* on 6 March. Accompanied by Nozzari, David, and Ambrosi, they travelled north to Vienna, breaking their journey at Bologna. Near there, on 16 March, Rossini and Colbran were married in the small church of San Giovanni Battista in Castenaso. Anna and Giuseppe Rossini were both present. Many years later, Rossini told the painter Guglielmo De Sanctis that it was his mother who had urged him to marry, perhaps on grounds of propriety. Left to his own devices, he told De Sanctis with the benefit of hindsight, he would have remained single. Certainly, he had no need at this stage in his life of a powerful protectress, nor was Isabella temperamentally suited to such a role. Money may have been a consideration. Isabella had inherited lands in Sicily and the villa at Castenaso. Rossini's legal entitlement under the terms of the marriage dowry have been estimated at 40,000 Roman scudi.[1] Inevitably, tongues wagged on this and other matters. The disparity in their ages was exaggerated. (In fact, Colbran was 37, Rossini was 30.) Yet, unhappily, the gossips were to be proved right. The marriage was not a success and it would have been a surprise if it had been. Rossini's star was rising and ahead lay extensive travel abroad. He was still composing (and, contrary to popular belief, was to go on doing so until the end of his life) whereas Colbran's career was all but finished. In the 1830s, whilst Rossini was involved in protracted litigation in Paris and already living with Olympe Pélissier whom he was to marry after Isabella's death in 1845, it was his widowed father, back in Bologna, who had to put up with Isabella's gambling, tantrums, and general disaffection.

Shortly after the marriage and the Rossinis' arrival in Vienna we have a clear record of Rossini's growing determination to effect a

[1] Approximately £50,000.

break with Naples and to secure work elsewhere. On 22 March he wrote the following letter from Vienna to the impresario Benelli in London:

> I don't wish to go back to Naples nor do I wish my wife to go back there. If you have no prima donna for next year and if you can offer me an advantageous contract I would come to London and undertake to write an opera in the course of the contract and to stage all the others you wish. Make me an offer for the pair of us. Let me know in detail the obstacles and the advantages. All that in secret for the present because I have other negotiations in hand, and you will understand that it wouldn't do to fall, as they say, between two stools. I would have my wife make her début in *Zelmira*, the opera which I gave recently at Naples, which I am now giving in Vienna, and which is my property. Very well then: we shall see what you can do for me. I await with impatience the results of your deliberations.[2]

There are a number of things which need to be said about this letter. First, though Rossini did visit London and did begin work on an opera for London none reached the stage. Secondly, what rights did Rossini have over *Zelmira* which he claims in his letter to be his own property? It was Rossini's belief that though propagation and printing rights were often devolved via managements to theatre copyists (e.g. Ricordi in Milan and Girard in Naples) the composer's own right to the autograph manuscript was inalienable. Clearly, Barbaia did not share Rossini's view. From a letter written by Rossini to Carlo de Chiaro on 17 April, 1823,[3] we must deduce that Rossini's holding of the *Zelmira* autograph had resulted in Barbaia withholding from Rossini the capital and interest he had invested in Barbaia's gaming empire, money which Rossini should have been paid at the time of his departure from Naples the previous year. There is no space here to explore in the kind of detail it deserves the subject of Rossini's managerial skills or his fascination with business dealings, legal conundrums, and litigation. Suffice it to say that in this jungle where only the fittest survived, Rossini's record was a combative one. He was an apt pupil of Barbaia; indeed, in the mid-1820s we often glimpse him manoeuvering against his old mentor in the hiring and firing of singers for Paris's Théâtre-Italien. From now on we are

[2] MMR, pp.141–2.
[3] LdR, pp.27–9.

dealing with a man who is increasingly responsible for his own and other people's careers, further evidence that though Rossini might at times be accused of behaviour which is obsessive and even aggressive, charges of laziness are almost impossible to substantiate.

Meanwhile, with his usual acumen, Barbaia had launched his Viennese tenure with a letter to Weber asking for a new opera,[4] whilst offering in the meantime to stage *Der Freischütz* (Berlin, 18 June, 1821) which had already made a deep impression on the German-speaking musical world. By all accounts, Weber disliked the production and was sufficiently ill to find conducting a burden; but he was much impressed, as Rossini was to be, by the Agathe of Wilhelmine Schröder-Devrient. The two men did not meet in 1822 though Weber, by now a dying man, called on Rossini in Paris in 1826, a visit Rossini later movingly recounted to Wagner: 'Not having foreseen his visit, I must admit that when I found myself unexpectedly facing that composer of genius, I felt an emotion not too unlike the one that I had felt earlier upon finding myself in the presence of Beethoven.'[5]

To Rossini's embarrassment, Weber had come to lay the ghost of his criticisms of Rossini's music. It is clear that at the time of Rossini's visit to Vienna Weber's defensiveness towards him bordered on paranoia; no one was safe from what Wagner called 'the natural intolerance of the man of genius'. Even Beethoven's music was subject to Weber's excoriations. In fact, Weber had been far from unresponsive to Rossini's music. He had conducted *La donna del lago* and is said to have fled from a performance of *La Cenerentola* muttering, 'I'm going; I'm beginning to like the stuff!'. According to his son, Max von Weber, he feared that *Euryanthe* would be no more than 'dreamy moonlight' compared to the 'bright day' of Rossini's writing.

Meanwhile, Vienna was about to succumb to Rossini fever during the three-month season which began on 13 April and ended on 8 July. In addition to *Zelmira*, the season included *La Cenerentola*, *Elisabetta, regina d'Inghilterra*, *Matilde di Shabran*, *La gazza ladra*, and *Ricciardo e Zoraide*. Beethoven's amanuensis, Anton Schindler, quotes the response to a performance of *Matilde di Shabran* published in the *Allgemeine musikalische Zeitung*: 'It was

[4] *Euryanthe*, Kärntnertortheater, Vienna, 25 October, 1823.
[5] Michotte, p.34.

really enough, more than enough. The entire performance was like an idolatrous orgy; everyone acted there as if he had been bitten by a tarantula; the shouting, crying, yelling of 'viva' and 'fora' went on and on.'[6] Schindler's own comments are rational and cool. Although Colbran did not come up to expectation, the exceptional quality of the Barbaia company was, he suggests, sufficient reason for Viennese enthusiasm, even if 'a less hedonistic audience' would have assumed 'a more moderate attitude after the first surprise'. Two years later, when Vienna was still in the grip of Rossini fever, the German philosopher Hegel (an admirer of Rossini's music, as were Schopenhauer, Heine, and other German intellectuals mesmerized by the cult of the South) made the memorable remark that Italian music is made for Italian throats as surely as Strasbourg pâtés are made for the throats of gourmets.[7]

As Rossini was wined and dined by the Viennese he must have been aware that this was the city of Haydn and Mozart. It was also Beethoven's home. Rossini knew some of Beethoven's music and heard more of it, including the *Eroica* Symphony, whilst in Vienna. Schindler flatly states that Beethoven declined to see Rossini,[8] but this is, at best, a half-truth. Overtures through the publisher Artaria did, it seems, come to nothing. It was left to Salieri and Rossini's principal publicist in Vienna, Giuseppe Carpani, to arrange the meeting which Rossini was later to recount in detail to Hiller, Wagner, Hanslick, and many others. In his *Life of Beethoven*,[9] Thayer quotes Hanslick's re-iteration of Schindler's story and Rossini's response that, on the contrary, he was received promptly and politely, albeit briefly given the fact that conversation with Beethoven was nothing less than painful. If Rossini did meet Beethoven, he met him at one of the most absorbing moments in his career. Litigation, hard work, and illness had borne down upon him; yet only weeks before he had finished the benedictory Op.110 Piano Sonata, the *Missa Solemnis* was nearing completion, and the Ninth Symphony would be begun within a few months. In his conversation

[6] Anton Schindler, *Beethoven as I knew him*, ed. Donald W. MacArdle, trs. Constance S. Jolly, London, 1966, p.271.

[7] *Briefe von und an Hegel*, Leipzig, 1887, p.154.

[8] Schindler, op. cit. pp.376–7.

[9] See Thayer, *Life of Beethoven*, rev. and ed. Elliot Forbes, Princeton 1967, pp.804–5.

with Wagner, Rossini talked of the 'undefinable sadness' which spread across Beethoven's features, 'so that from under heavy eyebrows there shone, as if from the depths of caverns, two eyes which, though small, seemed to pierce you'.[10] Elsewhere, Beethoven had expressed the view that Rossini was a talented and melodious composer, and a good scene painter, apt to the sensuous and frivolous spirit of the times. He was, above all, the composer of *Il barbiere di Siviglia*, a work which Beethoven appears to have read with more immediate pleasure than some of his contemporaries. According to Rossini, Beethoven was sceptical about the ability of any Italian composer to treat serious subjects. Despite Carpani's pressing upon him the merits of *Tancredi, Otello,* and *Mosè in Egitto*, his parting remark to Rossini was 'Above all, make lots of *Barbers!*'.

The juxtaposition of this visit – the fastidious Rossini more than usually shocked by the disorder and apparent poverty in which Beethoven lived – with the glitter of a gala dinner presided over by Metternich, moved Rossini to speak of the need to find Beethoven better lodgings and greater recognition from Viennese society. He even contemplated launching a subscription, but the idea was poorly supported. To the Viennese, Beethoven was an odd bird, an outsider. Give him a house, they said, and he will sell it. He is always on the move and is no more capable of looking after a house than he is of keeping servants. The two men never met again, though 'Di tanti palpiti' was sung by David between the 'Kyrie' of the *Missa Solemnis* and the finale of the Ninth Symphony at a concert in Vienna on 23 May, 1824. As Schumann observed when he heard of Rossini's meeting with Beethoven: 'The butterfly crossed the path of the eagle, but the latter turned aside in order not to crush it with the beating of his wings'.

Rossini's earnings from his Viennese tour were considerable, a foretaste of the large sums he would later earn in London. At parting, he wrote a song, 'Addio ai viennesi', which he was to re-use, with emendations to the name of the river in the final stanza, as his farewell to several cities, his 'Addio di Rossini'. The first stanza, in the minor, speaks of leave-taking, whilst the second pays tribute to the people, 'nobile e sincero', from whom he is reluctantly departing. The third stanza with its gentle elaborations and talk of murmurous

[10] Michotte, p.44.

air and the song of the nightingales is perhaps a covert recommendation of the sensual allure of Italian singing and Italian vocal writing. Think of this, he says finally, as Rossini expressing his feeling with 'a crescendo of sighs': the famous crescendo punningly alluded to before being subsumed in a grand, elaborate, yet perfectly scaled peroration with which he makes the Danube (Thames, Seine, or whichever) resound to the applause of the adoring multitude. The song is quintessential Rossini: affecting yet ironic, propelled and coloured by harmonies which are as unobtrusive as they are ingenious, gloriously laid out for the voice, grand but never pompous, and not a moment too long. No wonder they were charmed by him.

The Rossinis left Vienna at the end of July and spent the summer at Castenaso whilst Rossini busied himself with property renovation in Bologna. By the autumn he had begun work on a new opera for the 1823 carnival season in Venice. The subject, much used by earlier composers and one rich in dramatic archetypes, was the legend of Queen Semiramide. The immediate source was Voltaire's *Sémiramis* (1748). As with *Tancredi*, Rossini's previous Voltaire setting, the libretto was to be the work of Gaetano Rossi. In many ways, *Semiramide* is an enriched, formally stabilised, and dramatically more potent re-run of a type of music-drama first fully essayed by Rossini in *Tancredi*. This time, however, Rossini was taking no risks; there would be nothing slipshod about the plotting. The dramatically implausible sequences he was landed with in *Tancredi* would not be repeated. This much may be deduced from the work itself and from the fact that Rossi was closeted in Rossini's palatial country residence throughout October 1822 working in detail on the *Semiramide* text.[11]

On 5 November, and not earlier in the year as Radiciotti, Weinstock and others suggest, plans were put in train to invite Rossini to contribute to the official junketings at the Congress of Verona which had been convened by the great powers to contemplate, among other things, the developing saga of the war of Greek Independence. In mid-November Rossi must have run up the texts of two official cantatas, *La Santa Alleanza* and *Il vero ommagio*, the latter, as has already been noted, based on the music written in

---

[11] Meyerbeer, op.cit., pp.443–50. Rossi was in regular correspondence with Meyerbeer at this time.

Naples in 1821 for *La riconoscenza*. Both works are now lost, though Rossini certainly owned the autograph of *Il vero ommagio* since it provided a further example of his fierce defence of his rights of ownership when representatives of Verona's Royal Chamber of Commerce tried to seize it. Whilst in Verona, Rossini attended a performance of *L'inganno felice* but he cannot have supervised the production as some have suggested nor would he have supervised or even seen *La donna del lago*. Similarly, there is no evidence that he supervised the autumn revival of *La donna del lago* in Bologna in which Teresa Melas sang Elena and Rosamunda Pisaroni sang Malcolm.[12]

Of greater musical significance than Rossini's brief and over-publicized part in the show-biz of the Verona Congress, was his Venetian visit of December 1822 to March 1823 during which he effected a major revision of *Maometto II*, newly staged at La Fenice on 26 December, and completed work on *Semiramide* which had its *prima* at La Fenice on 3 February. Both are substantial achievements to which we must return. The Rossinis left Venice in mid-March. On 1 April, 1823 a memorial bust to the sculptor Antonio Canova was unveiled in Treviso to the accompaniment of another of Rossini's occasional cantatas, *Omaggio pastorale*. Otherwise, it was a quiet spring and summer spent exclusively in Bologna and Castenaso. Consciously or otherwise, Rossini was gathering his resources for the journeys which lay ahead.

[12] ibid. pp.445–6.

9

Paris and London (1823–4)

The Rossinis arrived at the rue Rameau in Paris on 9 November, 1823 as guests of the Genoese writer, Nicola Bagioli. They stayed for a month during which time Rossini had vivid foretastes of Parisian salon society and the socializing, gourmandizing, and musical in-fighting which was to come. The grandest event of his stay took place at the Restaurant du Veau Qui Tette on Sunday, 16 November. There were over 150 guests drawn from the cream of Parisian society. Among those present was the painter Horace Vernet whose mistress at the time was Olympe Pélissier, Rossini's future, second wife. Auber, Boieldieu, and Hérold were present as were Pasta, García, and the soprano Laure Cinti-Damoreau[1] who was to play a leading part in Rossini's Parisian career. It was, according to one newspaper, 'a colossal picnic' dominated by all manner of visual, gastronomic, and musical manifestations of Rossiniana. The event was brilliantly mocked a fortnight later by a one-act vaudeville performed at the Théâtre du Gymnase-Dramatique to a text by Scribe and Mazères.[2] Later in his visit, Rossini attended a charity

---

[1] See plate 15.

[2] August-Eugène Scribe and Edmond Mazères, *Rossini à Paris, ou Le grand dîner*, Paris, 1823. Scribe was to be Rossini's librettist for *Le Comte Ory* but this earlier vaudeville slyly points both the charm and the absurdity of the Rossini craze which was sweeping Europe. In a plot which predicts Gogol's *The Government Inspector*, Rossini is expected in town at any moment though no one knows what he looks like. A landlord by the name of Biffteakini plans a grand dinner. It will bring him large profits and will unite his two great passions, food and music, though he and his cronies are in a state of some consternation: all Italians are rogues but Rossini is a god (the epithets are lavish, 'le grand Rossini', 'le divin Rossini', 'Amphion Rossini', 'Apollon Rossini'). Biffteakini has a daughter who has been unsuccessfully put to music; after three months at the academy she still lacks a voice ('Faites donc une omelette sans oeufs', she languidly rejoins). She does, however, have an eye for the boys and when a young student, Giraud, turns up at the inn she takes to him at once. Giraud is a penniless

performance of *Otello* in honour of García,[3] with Pasta as Desdemona, a performance which encouraged Stendhal in the fond belief that under the influence of this remarkable singer Rossini might return to the sublime simplicities of his *Tancredi* style.

By the time of Rossini's arrival in Paris his music was already well known. Many of his operas had been staged by the Théâtre-Italien, albeit in fractured and juggled versions. The theatre's director at the time was Ferdinando Paër, the composer of *Camilla* in which Rossini had made a precocious debut in Bologna in 1805. Paër had won favour with Napoleon and had succeeded Spontini as director in 1812. By 1823, the Théâtre-Italien in general and Paër in particular were surrounded by controversy, the butt of pamphleteers, including Stendhal himself, whose motives were a confusion of political, personal, and musical beliefs and prejudices. Paër was characterized as an implacable opponent of Rossini who had delayed the staging of Rossini's operas, promoted the weaker scores, and mutilated the finer ones. This seems improbable, whatever Paër's private feelings about his young rival. Indeed, there is evidence that Paër sought and received Rossini's own co-operation in planning the various shortenings and adaptations of his pieces for the Paris stage. If, as is the case, French theatres and French publishers ended up mangling works like *Il turco in Italia* it was probably as much to do with muddle, inadvertance, and a kind of unruly artistic pragmatism as it was to do with deliberate malice.

Conservatoire student with an ambition to produce a great edition of French operas by subscription (a satire directed as much against the current state of French music as against the Rossini cult.) News that Rossini has reached Paris leads Biffteakini and his friends to mistake Giraud for Rossini, a plausible device given Rossini's age at the time. Like Gogol's hero, Giraud is lavishly treated. A special soup is concocted in his honour, though whilst it is being prepared Biffteakini is much exercised as to which Rossini air he should sing during the cooking; wryly, Scribe settles for 'Di tanti palpiti'. Toasts are proposed to great composers: Paisiello (a nice touch), Mozart, and Gluck. Grétry is proposed but dismissed as a purveyor of 'petite musique'. Finally, there is the grand dinner, the apostrophizing of Giraud, and the revelation of his true identity. The choruses designed for musical setting include the spirited: 'Rossini, Rossini/Toi que j'implore aujourd'hui/Rossini/Pourquoi n'es-tu pas ici?', verses admirably suited to some early form of *cancan*.
[3] See plate 13.

After a channel crossing from which it took Rossini a week to recover, he arrived in London with Isabella on 13 December, 1823. Their base until 24 July, 1824 was No.90 Regent Street in rooms which boasted both a view and a parrot of particular splendour. Invitations were immediately issued to him from the court of George IV. If Rossini harboured any ill-feelings over the king's former wife, now disgraced and dead, who had helped drive him from his native Pesaro, he kept them to himself. On 29 December he arrived in Brighton, where the court was in session, with a large enough wallet of letters of introduction (some provided in Milan by the Duke of Devonshire) and enough good will to keep at bay the more snobbish and xenophobic members of the court and press. Those who were determined to dislike Rossini thought him casual before the king and were scandalized by his singing Desdemona's 'Willow Song' in falsetto. The admirably judicious *Quarterly Musical Magazine and Review* thought otherwise,[4] though it took the liberty of observing that English humanity and English decorum had long since banished the castrato from the stage. Rossini also sang the mandatory 'Largo al factotum' from *Il barbiere di Siviglia*, and the band played the overture to *La gazza ladra* in an arrangement by Franz Kramer.

Those who met Rossini at this time found him genial and rather bland. The *Quarterly Musical Magazine* wrote: 'He certainly looks more like a sturdy beef-eating Englishman than a sensitive, fiery-spirited native of the soft climate of Italy. His countenance when at rest is intelligent yet serious, but bears no marks of the animation which pervades and indeed forms the principal feature of his compositions.'[5] In his journal of 7 March, 1824, Thomas Moore was to note that Rossini seemed 'a fat, jolly-looking person, with a sort of vague archness in his eye, but nothing further'. He added: 'His mastery over the pianoforte is miraculous', a judgement which such expert witnesses as Saint-Saëns would again endorse in later years.

Opinion on Rossini's music was divided. Old-timers like the influential amateur musician and one-time composer, the Earl of Mount-Edgcumbe (1764–1839), a Paisiello man if ever there was one, were sceptical about the new phenomenon, in terms which even today might be endorsed by some English musical

4 QMMR, vi, 1824, p.50.
5 ibid., pp.49–50.

opinion. Certainly, Edgcumbe's criticisms touch some potentially sensitive areas. He complains of a similarity between Rossini's compositions, mentions the self-borrowings, and suggests that music which is the product of formula and mannerism is difficult to lodge in the memory. He also suggests that Rossini's imagination 'seems already to be nearly drained'.[6] Others, less musically informed than Edgcumbe, simply opposed the Rossini cult on principle. Chorley tells us that when the name of Rossini was mentioned to the poet and dilettante Samuel Rogers (1763–1855) he would merely 'raise his eyebrows and speak of Paisiello'. The most balanced view of Rossini's music by a contemporary English writer is probably that of Leigh Hunt (1784–1859). Like so many people, Hunt had given *Il barbiere di Siviglia* a dusty reception when he first encountered it in London in 1818. By 1819 he appears to have recovered sufficiently from the shock of the impact of the Rossini style to write a constructive piece on *L'italiana in Algeri*:

> The author seems to delight in expressing a precipitate and multitudinous mirth; and sometimes works up and torments a passage, and pours in instrument upon instrument, till orchestra and singers all appear drunk with uproariousness, and ready to die on the spot. He carries this feeling, we think, to a pitch of genius, and even to something exclusive and peculiar to himself – nor does it hurt perhaps the general effect and character of this species of talent, that nothing seems to come amiss to him when he gives way to it, old or new, masterly or indifferent. He is like a wit, fond of punning and intoxicated with social enjoyment. Old jokes and new, his neighbours' and his own, all run merrily through his hands. His good things exalt the occasion; the occasion, in return, does as much for his bad.[7]

By 1824 Hunt had come to the conclusion that a man who failed to be fired by Rossini's music must be lacking in animal spirits, though like many writers he felt compelled to compare Rossini with Mozart: the smart schoolboy, Hunt suggests, alongside the true man of sentiment.

Apart from supposedly working on a new opera for presentation in London, Rossini's most immediate responsibility was the

[6] Mount-Edgcumbe, *Musical Reminiscences of an old Amateur*, London 1825, 2/1827, p.126.
[7] *The Examiner*, 31 January, 1819, p.77.

musical direction of the season of his operas which was about to play in the partially refurbished King's Theatre, Haymarket. Since 1821, the theatre had been under the management of John Ebers who had introduced *La gazza ladra* and *Il turco in Italia* in his very first season. For the 1824 Rossini season the theatre was sub-let to the profligate Benelli, the man with whom Rossini had corresponded from Vienna in 1822.[8] Eight Rossini operas were scheduled for the season, as well as works by Mozart, Mayr, and Zingarelli, and guest performances by the biggest box-office draw of her day, Angelica Catalani, now at the end of her career and also something of a financial liability. Neither *Zelmira* with the failing Colbran, nor *Il barbiere di Siviglia* with Vestris, a singer English audiences appear to have treated harshly at the time, were much liked, an expensive mistake when Colbran's fee was £1500. *Otello* and *Semiramide*, with Pasta and García, were equally costly with fees of £1400 and £1000 respectively,[9] but they won a larger measure of public approval. In an absorbing brief comment, the *Quarterly Musical Magazine* noted that Rossini's were operas 'which not only task the execution of the singer but which, by identifying ornament with expression, stimulate [García] to new experiments'.[10] According to Chorley,[11] Rossini was less enamoured of Pasta – 'she always sang false' – than he was of Colbran or Malibran, though he must have coached her for her London Semiramide which was her début in the role. Hunt thought her 'a great tragic actress; and her singing, in point of tone, tenderness, and expression, was equal to her acting'. He considered that she wanted height and was possessed of 'somewhat too much flesh', but he judged her Otello (*sic*) to be 'fierce, masterful, oriental' and, in a memorable vignette, he notes that 'when she measures her enemy from head to foot, in *Tancredi*, you really feel for the man, at seeing him so reduced to nothingness'.[12]

The vast sums of money Rossini made in London, sums estimated to have run into tens of thousands, were largely derived from

---

[8] See p.55.

[9] John Ebers, *Seven Years of the King's Theatre*, London, 1828, p.229.

[10] *QMMR*, p.58.

[11] Henry Chorley, *Thirty Years' Musical Recollections*, London, 1862, rev. Newman, 2/1926, p.27.

[12] Leigh Hunt, *Autobiography*, World Classics edition, London, 1928, p.159.

numerous public and private appearances for which he made handsome charges. Two concerts were given at Almack's, the first on 14 May, the second on 9 June. They were star-studded programmes at properly inflated prices devoted to extracts from Rossini's operas expertly interlarded with items by Cimarosa, Zingarelli, Guglielmi, and others. The roster of singers was dazzling: Pasta, Catalani, García, and Remorini, as well as Colbran and Rossini himself. At the second concert Rossini sang the short tenor part in the first performance of his *canzone* in memory of Lord Byron who had died of fever in Greece on 19 April. *Il pianto delle muse in morte di Lord Byron* is written for tenor, a chorus of six solo voices (three sopranos, two tenors, and a bass) and orchestra: music made up of solemn drum rolls, sudden grieving exclamations, and broken repeated lamentations all coaxed by Rossini into a song of mourning as gracious as it is brief. Years later Rossini would write another short funeral lament, more original and yet more touching, for the dead Meyerbeer. During his stay, Rossini travelled to take part in the Cambridge University Music Festival, but it was in the drawing-rooms of the wealthy and the influential from the Duke of Wellington downwards that he spent a great deal of his time. Smart society and the daughters of smart society were all too eager to take a lesson from Rossini, and his name in the family song album was much sought after. At a time when the best music teachers were charging one guinea an hour, Rossini was being offered one hundred guineas. The Rossinis' appearance fee at an evening occasion was fifty guineas. One such occasion at the house of the banker David Salomons resulted in a commission of new music from Rossini, the *Duetto* for cello and double-bass written for Salomons and the great double-bass virtuoso, Domenico Dragonetti, a long-standing London resident and a man as keen on good food and high fees as Rossini himself. Rossini's ear for the colours of the old three-string bass and his sense of its capacity for expressing a kind of grumbling good humour is as evident in the work's finale as it was in his *sonate a quattro* of 1804. Another distinctive feature of the entire three movement work is Rossini's success in distinguishing between the sombre colours, the black and several rich purples, of the two instruments in their various registers.

None of which helped Rossini with his appointed task of completing *Ugo, re d'Italia*. As the *Quarterly Musical Magazine* elegantly put it, 'his public obligations have been postponed to his private engagements'. Benelli's bankruptcy and Rossini's departure to official positions in Paris effectively sealed the fate of the partially completed opera which Rossini deposited with Ransoms bank, along with a bond of £400 which would be forfeit in the event of his failing to complete the commission.[13] The opera was never finished, nor did Rossini return to London. In the autumn of 1826 Ebers went to Paris at the time of the *première* of *Le siège de Corinthe* to try to secure the future of the King's Theatre in a triple alliance between Barbaia, Rossini, and himself. He secured Filippo Galli's services for London, but not those of 'the director and *bon vivant*' himself. The death of Rossini's mother in February, 1827 was blamed by Ebers for the subsequent breakdown in negotiations; and he himself died soon afterwards.

[13] For details of the manuscript's subsequently tangled history and eventual disappearance, see Andrew Porter's, 'A Lost Opera by Rossini', *Music and Letters*, xlv, 1964, p.39.

10

Paris (1824–9)

During the autumn of 1824, the Rossinis moved to No.10, boulevard Montmartre. Since the end of the Napoleonic wars Paris had been inundated with *arrivistes* from the provinces and abroad, swelling the ranks of an increasingly influential bourgeoisie; by 1830, fifty-five per cent of the registered electors of Paris were immigrants to the city. Rossini's first sustained residence in Paris thus coincided with a buoyant period in the city's history. To some extent he thrived on this, presiding over a famous chapter in the history of the Théâtre-Italien, making a good deal of money for himself (there was something of the *arriviste* in Rossini, too) and cautiously proceeding to establish a base from which he would be able to make a significant contribution to nineteenth-century French opera and operatic procedures. Between 1825 and 1829 he was to write three new operas and renovate two others. In retrospect it is a formidable output; but expectations ran ahead of Rossini's own performance; by 1826 and early 1827 his affairs were sufficiently entangled and his resources sufficiently stretched to make some kind of early retirement from operatic composition a distinct possibility.

During the period of Rossini's directorship of the Théâtre-Italien the music of composers other than himself was frequently heard; one of his most striking initiatives was the staging of the Paris *première* of Meyerbeer's *Il crociato in Egitto* in September, 1825. But it was the staging of Rossini's own operas with some incomparable casts which created the greatest interest. Pasta was the principal lure for many Parisians, though by the late 1820s it was García's daughter, Maria Malibran, whom Rossini most revered; 'the greatest was Colbran,' Rossini later told Michotte, 'but unique was Malibran.'[1] Parisians also heard Sontag, Pisaroni, and the hapless

---

[1] Michotte, pp.121–2. Rossini added: 'Ah, that marvellous creature! She surpassed all her imitators by her truly disconcerting musical genius, and all the women I have known, by the superiority of her intelligence, the variety of her knowledge, and her flashing temperament, of which it is

Joséphine Fodor-Mainvielle whose career went into a sudden decline after the Paris *première* of *Semiramide* on 8 December, 1825. Having wrested the title-role from Pasta, Fodor-Mainvielle sang whilst indisposed and did irreversible damage to her voice. Of the French-born sopranos, it was Laure Cinti[2] whom Rossini most favoured. She created important roles in each of the five operas Rossini either wrote or adapted for Paris. Chorley thought her a delectable singer, though he judged the very finish and playfulness of her art better suited to smaller houses. The Rossini years also saw the rise to pre-eminence of three tenors: Domenico Donzelli, Adolphe Nourrit, and Giovanni Battista Rubini, of whom Chorley later wrote 'Never was there an artist who seemed so thoroughly and intensely to enjoy his own singing.[3] It was with such singers that Rossini was able to mount productions of *La Cenerentola*, *La donna del lago*, *Otello*, and *Semiramide* within a year or two of arriving in Paris.

The staging of existing operas was part of Rossini's contract with the Departement des Beaux-Arts and the Maison du Roi. Negotiations with Paris had begun as far back as 1818; but it was the contract, signed in London in February 1824 and revised and ratified the following November after the death of Louis XVIII, which provided the artistic and financial basis of Rossini's Paris career. The contract was principally concerned with new works. Within the year, it was hoped, Rossini would provide for the Paris stage a new *grand opéra* and a shorter *opera buffa*, an obligation he did not meet until – after much delay and under a new contract – the years 1828/29. There were sound artistic reasons for Rossini's prevarication: his French, and his command of French prosody and the French

impossible to give an idea ... she sang in Spanish (her native tongue), Italian, French, German, and after eight days of study, she sang *Fidelio* in English in London. She sketched, painted, embroidered, sometimes made her own costumes; above all, she wrote. Her letters are masterpieces of subtle intelligence, verve, of good humour, and they display unparalleled originality of expression.' See plate 14.

[2] After her marriage to the tenor, V.C. Damoreau, in 1827 she took the name Cinti-Damoreau. Her cadenzas and variations for 'Pensa alla patria' from *L'italiana in Algeri* are reproduced in the definitive critical edition of the opera, ed. Azio Corghi (Pesaro, 1981). See bibliography for two important essays by Austin Caswell on Cinti-Damoreau's vocal embellishments in Rossini's Paris operas. See also plate 15.

[3] Chorley, *op.cit.*, p.22.

declamatory style had to be worked on; his own compositional style was in need of modification; and singers needed re-schooling as part of the process of re-aligning French and Italian traditions and methods. It is here, too, that we see Rossini's own mature personality at work: a prudent and conservative man, disinclined to take risks, astute and personable in private relationships and financial dealings though at times obliged to behave in a way which can only be described as disingenuous. For the most part, the French authorities, in the person of the Vicomte de la Rochefoucauld, were both efficient and accommodating, though Rossini's prevarication landed them in more than one example of what the paper *La Quotidienne* called in October 1825 'un fracas administratif'. An early cause of friction between Rossini, the government, the Administrateur of the Académie Royale de Musique, and the press was his persistent coolness towards Étienne de Jouy's *Le Vieux de la montagne*, the libretto with which he had been all too promptly provided in late 1824. Even as late as November 1827 La Rochefoucauld was laying plans for the opera's *première*; but the opera, like the still more mysterious *La figlia dell'aria*, never came to production.

Rossini's first unavoidable duty came with the coronation of Charles X in Reims Cathedral in June, 1825. The coronation itself was an elaborate affair after the manner of the rulers of the *ancien régime* and it spawned a score of official entertainments, vaudevilles, comedies, divertissements, and other *pièces de circonstance* in late May and the first fortnight in June. That Rossini's new opera was intended as a special event, a serious offering amid all the ephemeræ is confirmed by the fact that the *première* of *Il viaggio a Reims* took place a fortnight after the coronation at a special royal gala in the Théâtre-Italien's Salle Louvois. The opera was an immediate success and although Rossini attempted to withdraw the piece after three performances he was prevailed upon to allow a fourth performance on 12 September, 1825 as part of a benefit in aid of the victims of a fire in east central France.[4] Why Rossini wished to withdraw the

---

[4] An important insight into Rossini's ideas about the staging of his works arises from his firm refusal to allow *Il viaggio a Reims* to transfer to the Opéra's larger, 1954-seat Salle Le Peletier for the performance on 9 September. *La donna del lago* had already suffered from an inadequate production in the larger theatre. Rossini's preference brought with it serious financial implications but he was not prepared to let them override his sense of the artistic necessity of the smaller theatre.

opera – a move which has led most biographers to conclude that *Il viaggio a Reims* was a failure – is not entirely clear. Some of the music would re-appear in intriguing new configurations in *Le Comte Ory* in August 1828; but perhaps Rossini had other, earlier plans for parts of the opera. Janet Johnson[5] has pointed to a moment in Mme De Staël's *Corinne*, an important source-work for *Il viaggio a Reims*, in which the heroine takes part in an *opéra-comique* based on Gozzi's *La fille de l'air, ou Sémiramis dans sa jeunesse*. The link between *Corinne* and *La figlia dell'aria*, the new Italian opera planned for Pasta in Paris in the autumn of 1826, is temptingly established. As we shall later see, *Il viaggio a Reims* was clearly designed to work at several levels: as an act of homage to Charles X, as a piece of international musical razzmatazz, and as a showcase for a troupe of star singers led by Pasta, Cinti, Donzelli, Pellegrini (replaced by Galli in the September benefit performance), and Levasseur. It was also an entertainment, and an elaborate appropriation of and partial satire on De Staël's highly romantic novel, travelogue, and fantasy autobiography, *Corinne*.

Rossini's need to secure the right singers for particular productions and projects necessarily involved him in time-consuming negotiations. There were many such negotiations in the Paris years, though one is of special interest, revealing as it does the kind of tasks he was undertaking in the years 1826–7 and his working relations with his former boss, Domenico Barbaia. On 7 February, 1826 Rossini wrote the following letter to Domenico Donzelli advising him how he might best break his contract with Barbaia in Italy:

> The day you leave Florence you must write a letter to B. telling him that your advancing years and the impossibility of making your fortune with him oblige you to leave Italy, and that you are going to France and to England, where you are certain to become very rich in a few years. You must try to touch his heart, so that he doesn't make you pay the whole fine, but rather himself suggests a compromise ... In short, you must write to him in a loving manner, so that he is not too bitter about it. He will certainly want the whole fine and M. La Rochefoucauld will pay it, as I've told you.[6]

[5] Janet Johnson, 'A lost Rossini opera recovered: *Il viaggio a Reims*', *BdCRdS*, 1983, pp.55–7 and 110–12.

[6] LdR, pp.35–6; MMR, p.142.

Donzelli came to Paris, and so did an infuriated Barbaia. Eighteen months later Rossini was still attempting to mend fences, making full use of those professional business ploys – the rhetoric, the appeals to friendship, self-interest, and so on – which Rossini had almost certainly learned from their greatest exponent, Barbaia himself:

> You are going to leave Paris, then, without having settled anything! What will they say in Italy? They will say that you have wasted time and money. To avenge yourself for that, what will you do? You will seek, during these five years, to bring actions, will incur expenses in order to ruin the Father of a Family . . . Donzelli has no funds in hand: do you think he will be such a fool as to have any on his return to Italy? . . . In proving to singers that they can break their contracts, you will make possible many things that could be more harmful to you than the loss of Donzelli. You will engage in a contest with the financial resources of a Government!   Has my friendly and disinterested mediation, then, not touched your heart at all? With immense regret I see that you are still bitter about the Donzelli affair. He has certainly been guilty of an oversight, but what he did was for the good of his family. Do you, yourself a most loving Father, wish to regard Donzelli as an Assassin, and contemplate blows which will fall on the heads of the innocent? No: this is not worthy of you, and allow me to say that it is unworthy of a Man of Honour, with a Heart like yours. I don't mean by this letter of mine to be anyone's advocate, but I do mean to speak to a friend of fifteen years in the language of probity and of the heart.[7]

Radiciotti quotes only the final sentence from the above extract as evidence of Rossini's continued friendship with Barbaia; Frank Walker, quoting the full text, calls the letter disingenuous, which it undoubtedly is. Yet, in a sense, moral judgements must be partially suspended. As an example of a theatre director's letter of the early *ottocento* it is both representative and a *tour de force*.

In 1826 Rossini added to speculation about this willingness to write fresh material for Paris when he gave his blessing to a pastiche based on Scott's *Ivanhoe*. The text was the work of Emile Deschamps and Gabriel-Gustave de Wailly; the music was selected from an array of Rossini operas by Antonio Pacini, the Neapolitan-born composer who had established himself as one of Paris's leading

[7] MMR, pp.142–3.

music publishers. Scott saw the pastiche and thought it 'superbly got up'; the fact that his plot was barely recognisable he put down to the inevitable vagaries of the lyric stage. Shortly after the appearance of *Ivanhoé* at the Théâtre de l'Odéon on 15 September, Rossini produced the first of two of his own full-scale revisions of earlier works. *Le siège de Corinthe*, the second revision Rossini had made of *Maometto II*, was seen at the Paris Opéra on 9 October, 1826. The following March, *Mosè in Egitto* was staged at the Opéra in its new guise as *Moïse et Pharaon*. In both instances Rossini was to benefit from popularity of plots which could be directly or indirectly linked with the most fashionable of all the political causes of the 1820s: that of Greek independence. Pro-Greek and anti-Turkish sentiments had already been inflamed by romantic preoccupations with classical antiquity, and by Byron's death in Greece in 1824. In France, where the government had temporarily and pragmatically adopted the Turkish cause, the writings of Lamartine, Hugo, and Chateaubriand gave imaginative and intellectual support to the Greeks. Rossini, who was not always on the right side of the revolutionary tide, was fortunate on this occasion. On 3 April, 1826 – the day before the signing of the Anglo-Russian agreement on the Balkans, and three months before the French endorsed the agreement – he conducted a charity concert organised on behalf of the Greeks. With 20-franc tickets changing hands at over 100 francs, substantial sums were raised. The *première* of *Le siège de Corinthe* later the same year was thus doubly timely. In revising *Maometto II*, Rossini and his librettists redefined the background, making the drama unequivocally a tragedy of the Greek people. (One of the opera's few wholly new numbers is Hiéros's blessing of the Greek banners before the final catastrophe.) They also tautened the drama, giving it a ferocity and pace which the more spacious *Maometto II* rarely achieves. The staging by the Paris Opéra was itself especially lavish. Where the Milan production of 1828 was to look magnificent in Sanquirico's noblest classical manner, the Opéra provided sets which were both exotic and intrinsically dramatic. The final tableau depicting the sacked and burning Corinth must have horrified contemporary audiences as pictures of Dresden or Hiroshima were to shock and stir people in our own century.

In theatrical terms, *Le siège de Corinthe* is an advance on *Maometto II*, but it would be wrong to assume, as many critics have done, that the Paris revisions are necessarily, and in most respects, superior to the earlier Neapolitan versions. Indeed, the revision of *Mosè in Egitto* by Balocchi and de Jouy shows scant regard for the integrity and simplicity of the original music-drama. Its shape is lost, scenes are indiscriminately re-ordered, arias are re-allocated, and newer, grander ideas liberally imported. We are moving in *Moïse et Pharaon* into the age of the operatic blockbuster. A celebrated clerihew has it that:

> Cecil B. De Mille
> Rather against his will
> Was persuaded to leave Moses
> Out of the Wars of the Roses.

De Mille, we can assume, would have approved of Balocchi and de Jouy, more especially of their decision to import into the Paris revision the episode of the handing down of the Ten Command-ments. In the Exodus story, Moses brings the tablets down from Sinai *after* the departure from Egypt; placed within the drama of *Mosè in Egitto* the episode is as theatrically inept as it is Biblically awry. The revision also relegates the Scene of the Shadows, one of the finest opening movements in opera, to Act 2, upsetting the formal balance of the drama as well as its simple harmonic patterning.

During the rehearsals for *Moïse et Pharaon*, Rossini had been alerted to the fact that his mother was gravely ill. He immediately planned to leave for Bologna, but Dr Conti, who had seen Anna Rossini in Bologna and who brought news of her condition to Paris, advised against it. On an earlier occasion, Anna had been so excited and overwrought by one of Rossini's visits that she had made herself ill. It was, however, unavailing advice. The painful aneurism took its baleful course. On 20 February, 1827 Anna Rossini died. She was 55. Grief-stricken, Rossini ordered masses to be said for the repose of his mother's soul, though he was unable to return to Bologna for the funeral. Instead, he urged his father to join him in Paris, something Giuseppe was reluctant to do. The recent shock, the late-winter weather, a touch of constipation: such were the impediments to his leaving Bologna. But staying there must have come to seem the grimmer alternative for within a fortnight he had agreed to make the journey in the company of one of Isabella's servants.

Once in Paris, Giuseppe found himself at the centre of things, for there can be no doubt that Rossini's career was moving to a climax with all its old rapidity. With a new contract partially negotiated, public opinion temporarily assuaged, and the rudiments of the French style mastered, Rossini was soon to produce *Le Comte Ory*, an elegant swan-song to his career as a master of *opera buffa*, and *Guillaume Tell*, the long-awaited *grand opéra*. Perhaps it was as well that he was busy, that bereavements come, as T.S. Eliot's Becket has it, when we are engrossed with matters of other urgency. His mother's death and his father's restlessness were evidently unsettling. Writing from Dieppe in November 1827, Rossini expresses himself disaffected and bored – could it be otherwise, one wonders, in Dieppe in November? – but is interested to learn of the renovation of his *palazzo* in Bologna. By the spring of 1828 the Paris newspapers were speculating about a possible end to Rossini's career as an opera composer.

Meanwhile, Rossini continued working. During this period he often lived and worked in the country villa of his banker-friend Alexandre-Marie Aguado. It was the kind of congenial environment which suited him (in later years he would build his own villa in Passy), a reminder perhaps of his earliest days as a composer in Triossi's country house at Conventello. Certainly, *Le Comte Ory* looks back with a mixture of irony and affection to an earlier idyllic world of romance and knightly endeavour whilst, at the same time, anticipating the piquancy, grace, and guile of the language Rossini will later develop for the works of his final Paris period, 1857–68. There was also some occasional music written in 1827 and 1828: a cantata for six solo voices and piano written for the baptism of Aguado's son in July (Rossini's fee was a Sèvres dinner service) and a splendid *Rendez-vous de chasse* for four horns and orchestra which Weber or Schumann might have been pleased to sketch. With its romantic, picturesque, *al fresco* mood, the *Rendez-vous de chasse* acts as a kind of one-line epigraph to the mighty *Guillaume Tell* which was soon to follow.

The background to the writing of *Guillaume Tell* is complicated but can be rapidly re-stated: the rejection of two librettos by Scribe (one of which later became Auber's *Gustave III* and Verdi's *Un ballo in maschera*, the other Halévy's *La juive*), the acceptance of a lengthy four-act version of Schiller's *Wilhelm Tell* by Étienne de Jouy, the partial re-writing of Jouy's text by H.-L.-F. Bis, and additional emendations by Rossini himself and by Aguado's young secretary, Armand Marrast. Whatever the problems of the making of the libretto, the subject was an ideal one for Rossini at this juncture.

Elements of his art which had been developed over the past seventeen years could come together in a new and satisfying ensemble. Musically, we are aware of a classical sense of melody and a natural Italianate lyricism offset by a highly developed skill in the writing of rhetorically charged arioso and accompanied recitative. Pastoral and folk elements, and an instinctive feel for the style of the picturesque, are also present, as is Rossini's interest in the psychology of a drama of paternity and in the politics of a people who seek independence with peace. Schiller's play is neither revolutionary nor tragic. In an important essay to which we must return in connection with the so-called tragic finale of *Tancredi*, Susanne Langer assesses *Wilhelm Tell* as 'a species of serious heroic comedy'. As such, it is heir to a tradition which Rossini had closely engaged in his *opere serie* of the years 1812–23. Langer says of Schiller's play:

> Tell appears as an exemplary personage in the beginning of the play, as citizen, husband, father, friend, and patriot; when an extreme political and social crisis develops, he rises to the occasion, overcomes the enemy, frees his country, and returns to the peace, dignity and harmonious joy of his home. The balance of life is restored. As a personage he is impressive; as a personality he is very simple. He has the standard emotions – righteous indignation, paternal love, patriotic fervour, pride, anxiety, etc. – under their obvious conditions. Nothing in the action requires him to be more than a man of high courage, independent spirit, and such other virtues as the mountaineers of Switzerland boasted, to oppose the arrogance and vanity of foreign oppressors. . . . Such are the serious products of comic art; they are also its rarer examples. The natural vein of comedy is humorous – so much so that 'comic' has become synonymous with 'funny'.[8]

Rossini had become a master of the comic style in both its aspects: comedy as humour and comedy as a vehicle for expressing vitality, continuity, and harmony in human affairs however strong the potential for disorder in those affairs may be.

The final preparations for the completion and staging of *Guillaume Tell* were hedged round with difficulties. With the government fearful of another 'fracas administratif' over the new opera, Rossini chose to foreclose the unresolved details of his contract. In April 1827 he had written a long and courteous letter to La Roche-

---

[8] Susanne K. Langer, *Feeling and Form*, London, 1953, p.338.

foucauld, its carefully shaped paragraphs and decorous phrasing leading from political overtures, through at least one shrewdly placed maxim ('Men do not always remain in the same position; other men may neither think nor act like them') to an unvarnished demand for a pension of 6000 francs a year for life. The age of patronage was not quite dead and if Rossini is more polite than Dr Johnson in his famous letter to Lord Chesterfield, he is none the less playing the same game with comparable tenacity. The letter of 1827 got him nowhere and in April 1829 he renewed his petition, pointing out that other cities were seeking his services and implying that he no longer needed to continue his career as a composer. He was, how-ever, prepared to commit himself to a series of new operas, to be written over the next ten years, given the right terms and the confirmation of the life annuity. To bolster the impact of this letter, he also informed the management of the Opéra that unless he had satisfaction from the royal household rehearsals of *Guillaume Tell* would be called off and the third and fourth acts withheld from the copyists. With the management already beset with problems (among them, the pregnancy of Cinti-Damoreau which had occasioned additional delays in rehearsal schedules) the pressures were such that on 8 May, 1829 Charles X signed the contract. It secured *Guillaume Tell* for the Opéra but was to cost Rossini further time and effort in the 1830s.

Guillaume Tell was eventually seen and heard on 3 August, 1829, conducted by Habeneck. Apart from Cinti-Damoreau, the cast included Henri-Bernard Dabadie as Tell, and Adolphe Nourrit as Arnold. The public was polite, the press generous, and Troupenas paid Rossini 24,000 francs for the publishing rights. But this great opera was to have a chequered history. It was soon cut, and from the outset Nourrit experienced difficulties with the role of Arnold. By and large, tenors have fought shy of the part on stage. 'The role would have ruined my voice,' said Pavarotti, explaining his refusal to make his La Scala debut as Arnold. It was not until the fearless Gilbert-Louis Duprez made his Paris debut in the role in 1837 that the opera's fortunes underwent a powerful temporary resurgence.

Within ten days of the *première* of *Guillaume Tell*, the Rossinis left Paris for Italy. Isabella was never to return, though Rossini himself, alone or with his second wife, would spend another twenty years there. On the way to Bologna, Rossini stopped in Milan where he met Bellini and attended a performance of Bellini's *Il pirata* at the

Teatro della Canobbiana. According to the Milanese, Rossini noted in *Il pirata* a 'finish' and organization worthy of a fully mature man, and a depth of feeling won, perhaps, at some cost to the music's brilliance. They were judgements, directly attributable or not, which Bellini was only too happy to broadcast to the world at large.

11

Retirement from operatic composition

Guillaume Tell was Rossini's thirty-ninth opera. Rossini had often talked of retirement and after Anna Rossini's death it was certainly his father's wish that he might do so. 'He has toiled long and wearily enough', wrote Giuseppe to a friend in 1827. There seem, though, to have been no clear plans. Rossini's own natural prudence in financial and artistic matters had been both a spur and a hindrance to his work during the 1820s and there is every possibility that a similar pattern would have continued into the 1830s if the political events described in the next chapter had not intervened.

Rossini was also at an age which has often proved critical in the lives of musicians, painters, and writers. 'It is the age when the most fluent composer begins to lose the ease of inspiration he once possessed,' notes Charles Rosen in an otherwise unhelpful aside on Rossini's retirement, 'when even Mozart had to make sketches and to revise.'[1] It is well put. Creative failures, lapses into silences far more complete than Rossini's, suicides, and unanticipated deaths are all too common at this stage in the lives of many creative artists. But although poor health, both physical and mental, would later inhibit and incapacitate Rossini, reducing his creative flow to a trickle during the years 1836–57, there is no evidence that these were primary causes of what Toye misleadingly and melodramatically calls 'the great renunciation' of 1830. It will be necessary in due course to address directly Rossini's mental condition: the manic-depressive illness and the far from debilitating obsessive traits which writers like Riboli[2] and Storr[3] have diagnosed. But we must reject as idle speculation less well researched psychological theories about the retirement from operatic composition, notably Schwartz's idea that

[1] Charles Rosen, *The Classical Style*, London, 1971, p.386.
[2] B. Riboli, 'Profilo medico psicologico di G. Rossini', *La rassegna musicale* 7–9, Rome, 1954, p.292.
[3] Anthony Storr, *The Dynamics of Creation*, London, 1972, p.92.

Rossini's retirement was a manifestation of an oedipal condition triggered by his mother's death in 1827.[4] It would also be wise to treat with some circumspection the idea widely held and encouraged by Rossini himself in his later years, that the retirement was a cynical gesture by an idle and venal *bon viveur*. Restored to a semblance of health in the late 1850s and early 1860s, Rossini was happy to play the role of the *vieux rococo*, the *bon viveur*, the exemplar of a vanished age; but many of his stories were either paraphrases of the truth or convenient fictions, amusing acts of self-deprecation, designed to satisfy the curious and keep them at bay.

In 1830 it was a complex web of circumstances which turned the possibility of retirement to a probability and, by 1836, into a certainty. Tiredness, family concerns, political, artistic, and social changes during the period in question, and the achieving of a natural cadence in his own creative life are all relevant to the issue. In some ways, the last point is the most interesting. Two things stand out in Rossini's Paris operas: a degree of self-parody, evident in *Il viaggio a Reims* and, by devolution, in *Le Comte Ory*, and the implications for opera in general of Rossini's grandiose transformations of works as individual, as local, and as finely proportioned as *Mosè in Egitto* and *Maometto II*. The self-parody, the wry recollection of procedures established in *Tancredi*'s heyday, implies the existence of a musical code complete and stable enough to merit ironic appraisal. Indeed, it is a measure of the extent of Rossini's achievement and a token of his intelligent self-awareness that he should view the achievement with so amused and objective a gaze. But if Rossini was in some sense aware of a natural rounding out in his career as an opera composer, he must also have been conscious of his own complicity in helping shape a style of *grand opéra* which was paradoxically alien to his own background and instincts. Rossini was less hard on Meyerbeer, both as a man and a musician, than many of his critics have subsequently been, but it was Meyerbeer who, in Peter Conrad's word, 'mechanized' the epic.[5] *Robert le diable* appeared in 1831, *Les Huguenots* in 1836. Robbed of Rossini's authority and his classical breeding, *grand opéra* became in lesser hands both lavish and impersonal.

---

[4] D.W. Schwartz, 'A psychoanalytic approach to the great renunciation', *Journal of the American Psychoanalytic Association*, 1965, 13, p.551.

[5] Peter Conrad, *Romantic Opera and Literary Form*, London, 1977, p.16.

Those who would have had Rossini pursue two careers rather than one might argue, as Winton Dean has done,[6] that Rossini should have faced the challenge of the new age, taking his style and his public with him. Circumstances, though, were unpropitious. Artistically and politically the Paris Opéra was more or less closed to him. Berlioz's star was rising, and despite often execrable performances the influence of Beethoven's music on audiences and fellow-musicians was being increasingly felt. Rossini had made his mark and established his line. In his years with the Théâtre-Italien between 1830 and 1835 he was able to observe and encourage the continuation and renewal of that line in the works of Donizetti and Bellini. Significantly, his grief at Bellini's early death in 1835 was marked; difficult though Bellini was, he had become one of the first of Rossini's surrogate sons, the exemplary bearer of the torch which Rossini himself had lit.

The wisest of all remarks on Rossini's retirement from operatic composition, the one which most fundamentally agrees with the personal and musical facts of the case, was written by Rossini himself in a letter to Giovanni Pacini in 1866:

> This art, which has its sole basis in 'idealism' and 'sentiment', cannot separate itself from the times in which we live; and idealism and sentiment have nowadays been exclusively turned over to 'steam', 'robbery', and the 'barricades' . . . Dear Giovanni, be calm; remind yourself of my decision to abandon my Italian career in 1822, and my French career in 1829; such a presentiment is not given to everyone; God granted it to me and I bless him for it every hour.[7]

Rossini's life after 1829 was rich in incident and he was yet to write some of his most moving, diverting, and influential music; but his withdrawal from operatic composition was both naturally felt and shrewdly judged. In its way *Guillaume Tell* is as exemplary a resting-point as *The Tempest* or *Falstaff*. As Hamlet notes in the 37-year-old Shakespeare's most famous play, 'the readiness is all'.

---

[6] *The New Oxford History of Music*, VIII, ed. Abraham, London, 1982, p.406.

[7] LdR, pp. 295–6; Rognoni pp.321–2.

12

Bologna, Paris, Madrid (1829–35)
Stabat mater, Balzac, and Olympe Pélissier

Rossini returned to Bologna on 6 September, staying first at Castenaso and moving back into his renovated palazzo in Bologna's Strada Maggiore at the start of the winter season. Three Rossini operas, *Tancredi*, *Otello*, and *Semiramide* were to be staged at Bologna's Teatro Comunale with Pasta as the principal draw but, contrary to the suppositions of earlier biographers, there is no evidence that Rossini attended any of these performances or helped in their preparation, though some private advice to Pasta on points of ornamentation and smaller musical details may well have been forthcoming. After Paris, Bologna's winter season must have presented Rossini with what Lord Derwent has called 'a whirl of mundanities'. He was among old cronies again. When Édouard Robert, co-director of the Théâtre-Italien, arrived in Bologna he found it difficult to lure Rossini away from endless cloistered conversations in Bologna's arcaded thoroughfares. In the spring of 1830 Rossini, apparently eager to resume composition, wrote to La Rochefoucauld in Paris to enquire about a promised libretto. Rossini had sketched out a scenario based on Goethe's *Faust*, an operatic subject which might have magnificently rounded out a movement in Rossini's operatic development which had begun in 1817 with the San Carlo production of *Armida*. But nothing came of it. In early June, Rossini made the short journey to Florence, attended the Teatro della Pergola, and sat for the sculptor, Bartolini. The remainder of the spring and early summer was spent at Castenaso.

In early August news reached Bologna of the July revolt in Paris. The rule of Charles X which had begun so propitiously had become increasingly troubled. In August 1829, as Rossini was leaving Paris, Charles was reforming his cabinet, strengthening it with hard-liners of his own persuasion, principal among them the Prince de Polignac. The new cabinet antagonised opinion at home and abroad; and with a hard winter following a poor harvest in 1829 there were signs in the spring of 1830 of a powerful confluence of hitherto disparate opposition factions. The elections of July 1830 strengthened the hand of the liberals, prompting Polignac to attempt a virtual *coup d'état*, calling for renewed elections with a reduced electorate and a strictly circumscribed press. These were draconian measures. After their imposition Charles, with characteristic Bourbon insouciance, rode off to Rambouillet to hunt, leaving the army unprepared for the groundswell of revolt which followed. By 30 July when Charles was sufficiently alerted to the dangers of the situation to dismiss Polignac, it was too late. He was driven into exile and the Restoration, a not entirely unsuccessful chapter in post-Napoleonic French history, came to an abrupt end. The loss to the arts was substantial. For whatever reasons, the Restoration years had seen a surge of artistic activity in Paris to which the government had been tolerably responsive. Under Louis-Philippe, the new 57-year-old 'citizen king', belts were tightened. More accountable to the Chamber of Deputies than its predecessor, the new government moved promptly to cut the Civil List from 40 million francs a year to a mere 12 million; and it was under this Civil List that Rossini's contract and lifelong annuity had been registered.

Only vaguely aware of the political and economic problems facing the new French government, Rossini set out for Paris on 4 September, 1830 to lay claim to his contracted rights. In the event, it took six years of waiting, lobbying, and litigation to secure the pension, though in the end the pension was not only confirmed but paid retrospectively from its point of suspension in 1830. It is said that the presence of the late King's signature on the contract was a determining factor in Rossini's favour, a detail which reflects credit on the advice Rossini received from Aguado and others during the negotiations of 1827–9.

Rossini's lengthy periods away from Bologna during the 1830s give the lie to his statement made to Hiller some years later that his retirement from opera was prompted by a desire to live in the country and the need to be with his father in his last years. Though Rossini's visit to Bologna in the summer of 1834 was evidently therapeutic, he seemed unwilling or unable to settle there for any length of time. Meanwhile, his father, who spoke no French and who had no desire to move to Paris, was left in Bologna to cope as best he could with his increasingly irritable daughter-in-law. In a famous letter, written in August 1833, Giuseppe expressed his feelings in tones 'less like those of a father, more like those of an upright steward, an old domestic, devoted and grumbling':[1]

> When your wife left for the country, she had everything locked up, so that I had to buy plates, glasses, and bottles, a thing they don't do even in Turkey. And how one has to behave to live and get along with a proud and disgraceful woman, a spendthrift who looks only for ways to show spite, simply because one does not want to give way to her affectations and insanities; and she does not remember her birth, that she too was the daughter of a poor trumpet player like me and that she has a sister in Midrit [Madrid] who bombards her with letters ... All I say is, 'Evviva' the Venetians for the time when they hissed her to death, it would have been better if they had done away with her as they intended, and then my poor wife would not have died of distress, and if things go on in this way I too shall go crazy. You are lucky to be far away, and may God always keep you thus so that you can always be tranquil and enjoy your peace which you probably could not enjoy near her; she thanks the Heavens a thousand times for having taken you as husband; for if she had married a man who thought as she thinks by now they would both be in the poorhouse.

Perhaps Isabella did not deserve Giuseppe's sympathy, though her own letters at the time are sufficiently disturbing. Shut up in provincial obscurity, bored and depressed, she had taken to gambling with consequences which she explained to the sculptor Bartolini:

> When Fortune frowns everything conspires against one. I have need of a friend and my mind turns to you. You know that my health is always poor, that my affairs go from bad to worse. To distract myself I turned to gambling, with such misfortune that I cannot pick up a card that is not beaten. The idea that my luck would change has caused me to go too far and to get into difficulties.[2]

She goes on to explain that she has a valued portrait in miniature from her Naples years which she fancies may fetch a handsome sum:

> There are so many English people at Florence who collect fine things. Couldn't you try to sell it for me? Believe me, dear Bartolini, I am in a most horrible situation. You have shown me friendship, in all circumstances, – don't abandon me.

[1] Romain Rolland, 'Rossini', *La revue musicale*, Paris, 1902, ix, p.374.
[2] MMR, p.144.

In Paris, Rossini stayed first with Aguado, later in rooms above the Théâtre-Italien which was thriving again despite the prevailing mood of political uncertainty. His remaining there is understandable; he had lived among theatre people most of his life and the company available to the Théâtre-Italien at this time was exceptional: Pasta, Malibran, the young Giulia Grisi, Rubini, Tamburini, and Lablache, a singer, according to Leigh Hunt, of 'might and mirth'. Distinguished revivals from this period included Donizetti's newest masterpiece, *Anna Bolena*, with Pasta, Rubini, and Lablache aptly cast as Enrico VIII; Bellini's *Il pirata* with Schroeder-Devrient and Rubini, and revivals, equally notably cast, of two further Bellini operas, *La straniera* and *I Capuleti e i Montecchi*. In 1835 the Théâtre-Italien staged two notable *prime*: Bellini's *I puritani* and Donizetti's *Marin[o] Faliero* in which the part of the Gondoliere was sung by Rossini's youthful protégé, the young Russian tenor, Nicholas Ivanoff.[3]

For both operas Rossini acted as a kind of musical midwife, advising Bellini extensively on *I puritani* and, according to Bellini, offering comparable help to Donizetti on *Marino Faliero*, a work about which Bellini expressed typically acerbic opinions shortly after its *prima*. Certainly, Bellini was disingenuous in his dealing with fellow musicians. He was also a rabid socializer, quick to exploit Rossini's liaison with Olympe Pélissier, ingratiating himself with her, and taking evident delight in her public approval of *La sonnambula*. Bellini's death of a recurrent intestinal disorder on 23 September, 1835 came as a great blow to Rossini. The funeral service in Les Invalides was a grand one; the honorary pallbearers included Carafa, Cherubini, Paër, and Rossini himself. Later, Rossini braved the mud and the rain and the slow march to the Père-Lachaise cemetery, where he himself was later to be buried, in order to be at the graveside. As he wrote to Filippo Santocanale on 3 October, 1835:

> a military band of one hundred and twenty musicians escorted the procession, every ten minutes a blow on the tam-tam resounded; and I assure you that the throng of people and the sorrow reflected in their faces made an inexpressible effect; I cannot tell you how great the affection was which this poor friend of ours had inspired. I am in bed, half dead, for I won't hide from you that I

[3] See plate 17.

wanted to be present when the last word was pronounced over Bellini's grave.[4]

Donizetti was to survive Bellini by a further thirteen years. Rossini's ability to help him, after 1835, was more limited, though he would later engage Donizetti to conduct the Italian *prima* of the all-Rossini *Stabat mater* in Bologna in 1842.

In its original form the *Stabat mater* was far from being all-Rossini. The work was commissioned in Spain in 1831 during one of several excursions from the cold, cholera, and politics of Paris which his old friend Aguado arranged for Rossini during these years. Rossini was warmly received in Madrid by the King, the court, and the public. Indeed, his reception was so warm and his general indebtedness to Aguado so great that it was difficult for him to decline a request for an original Rossini composition from Aguado's friend, the priest and state counsellor, Fernández Varela. A *Stabat mater* was suggested, an added burden for Rossini in view of the existence of Pergolesi's widely respected setting. None the less, by March 1832 Rossini had completed six of the proposed twelve movements (Nos.1, and 5–9) before an attack of lumbago, actual or imagined, overtook him, obliging him to delegate the completion of the work to Giovanni Tadolini. Tadolini was born in Bologna in 1789. Like Rossini, he had been a pupil of the city's Liceo Musicale. During the years of Rossini's meteoric rise to fame, he had worked in Bologna and at the Théâtre-Italien in Paris where he had returned as music director in 1829. Eight of his operas are extant, including a *dramma giocoso* to a text by Sterbini and a *melodramma eroico* to a text by Rossi. So Rossini's ghost-writer was not without experience. It is not known what Rossini paid Tadolini; Rossini received from a delighted Varlea a gold snuff box studded with diamonds. The Rossini-Tadolini *Stabat mater* was first heard in the chapel of S. Filippo El Real in Madrid on Good Friday, 1833. When Varela died in 1837, leaving his considerable fortune to charitable causes, the manuscript, which Rossini had stipulated should not be sold or published, was purchased for 5000 reales and eventually acquired by the Parisian publisher Aulagnier. Given its value and its dual-authorship, this was an alarming prospect which was to stir an ailing Rossini to swift and effective acts of reclamation, and, in 1841, to fresh composition.

[4] LdR, pp.62–4; Rognoni, pp.291–2.

Amid these journeyings to Madrid and elsewhere, Rossini's affairs were undergoing a sea-change occasioned by his own deteriorating health and by the development of a relationship with the very remarkable woman who was to be his loyal companion for over thirty-five years until his death in 1868, Olympe Pélissier.

We do not know precisely when and where Rossini first met Olympe or what occasioned their growing familiarity. She was born on 9 May, 1797, the illegitimate daughter of a woman who later married Joseph Pélissier whose name she assumed. She had become a fashionable courtesan at an early age and although her career is obscured by rumour and innuendo, it is fairly certain that she was for a time the mistress of the painter Horace Vernet.[5] Rossini probably knew her in the 1820s but a form of attachment becomes clear only in 1832; it was in this year that Rossini wrote his *Giovanna d'Arco*, a far from insignificant cantata for soprano and piano, composed 'expressly for Mademoiselle Olimpia Pélessier'. Earlier the same year, Rossini dined with Olympe in the company of the rising star of the French literary scene, Honoré de Balzac, whose *La peau de chagrin* (Paris, 1831) is of some interest to students of Olympe Pélissier and, in a more general way, of Rossini himself. Like Rossini, Balzac was a stocky, short-necked, full-bellied man, a classic example of the pyknic type; he was also immensely productive and, like Rossini, subject to some form of cyclothymic illness. They seem to have dined together a good deal in the years 1832–5 and clearly had more in common than the friendship of Olympe and some passing physical similarities. Both moved in well-to-do society which they observed at a distance, both distrusted public opinion ('that perverted trollop' as Balzac called it) and the new liberal-democratic ideals, and both loathed the new regime in France. ('You may tell as many lies as a newly crowned king', observes a character in *La peau de chagrin*.)

In a celebrated incident in *La peau de chagrin* the hero of the novel, Raphael, conceals himself in the bedroom of the alluring and influential Foedora, an incident based on one of Balzac's own adventures in Mlle Pélissier's rooms. In the novel, Foedora is seen as

---

[5] Vernet is said to have used her as model for Judith in his painting *Judith et Holopherne*. Berlioz judged Vernet to be 'austere, caustic, straightforward. Fond of Gluck and Mozart. Hates the Academy. A good man.' (*Correspondance générale*, I, p.447.)

the embodiment of some of the essential characteristics of Society itself and it would be an over-simplification to suggest that we have in Foedora a full-length portrait of Olympe. Yet it is difficult to ignore the impression Balzac gives us of this woman: physically opulent, sexually chilly, snobbish and insecure, yet possessed of a strange inner warmth, a private serenity, which manifests itself to Raphael's astonishment in her solitary rendition of an air from Cimarosa's *Il matrimonio segreto* in a voice of 'true pitch and liquid clarity'.

Music, and in particular Rossini's music, is also important to the texture of ideas in the novel. Seen from one perspective, Rossini is an urbane figure from a bygone age, a composer devolved from the school of Cimarosa and Paisiello, an emblem of a kind of classical sweetness and classical decorum which the besotted wretches of Parisian society yearn for in the their morning-after moods. Seen from another perspective, Rossini's music, judged by staid bourgeois taste to be merely noisy, is itself kin to a clamorous, dissipated world of high living and heightened sensation. It is as though Balzac is seeking not only the truth about the enigmatic Foedora but also the truth about this most enigmatic of composers who seems to feed classical and romantic sensibilities with equal ease. Rossini's own contacts with Balzac were necessarily short-lived; by the time of his return to Paris in 1855 Balzac was dead.

It seems to have been Rossini's fate to inherit other men's women: Colbran from Barbaia and Olympe Pélessier from Vernet, Balzac, and others; but the relationship between Rossini and Olympe which began as a discreet liaison among the drawing-rooms and at the dinner tables of fashionable Paris, grew into something altogether deeper, stabilizing two unstable lives. Olympe found security of a kind in Rossini's reputation and in his continuing trust, even though marriage was impossible whilst Isabella was alive and even though the duties demanded of her were formidable. For over twenty, often bleak, years she encouraged, comforted, and nursed Rossini through many periods of physical and mental illness, more a second mother than a would-be wife. Indeed, after the death of Anna Rossini in 1827, it is Olympe Pélissier who emerges as the only wholly reassuring presence in Rossini's often troubled world.

13

Paris, the Rhineland, and return to Italy (1835–46)

Whilst Rossini remained in Paris awaiting the pronouncements of legal experts on his government annuity, his relationship with Olympe could flourish unhindered. It was not until 1837, after his return to Italy, that more formal procedures needed to be put in hand. Meanwhile, Rossini continued to write occasional items for singers and social gatherings, the music a very Rossinian blend of salon, folk, and operatic styles in which the composer's acute ear for the possibilities of the voice and his own considerable sophistication as a pianist are everywhere apparent. In 1835 Troupenas persuaded Rossini to publish these as a group of eight chamber arias and four duets under the title *Les soirées musicales*, music which Respighi and Britten did much to popularize but which merits consideration in its original form for voice and piano, rather than as orchestral pastiche, however brilliant.

On Christmas Eve 1835, after a year of backtracking and appeals against a judgement in Rossini's favour, the Committee on Finance finally agreed that his claim to a life annuity was valid. A swift return to Bologna seemed in order. Whilst Rossini was tidying up his Paris affairs he received an offer from the Kärntnertortheater in Vienna to write an opera on a libretto of his own choice. He declined. It is at this point, one senses, that his career as an operatic composer was definitely over. By contrast, the proposal of a trip to Belgium and the Rhineland in the company of his banker friend, Lionel de Rothschild, was more agreeably received.

The northern European's veneration for the mediterranean countries has not always been reciprocated by artists of Latin extraction; but Rossini was generous in his enthusiasm for the landscapes, towns, churches, cathedrals, and paintings of the Flemings and Rhinelanders. Only the railway from Antwerp to Brussels unnerved and displeased him. Many years later, he composed a not altogether amusing piano piece, 'Un petit train de plaisir comico-imitatif'[1] in which genial mimicry of the train's progress is overtaken by a fatal derailment, the contemplation of the heavenward flight of the victims' souls, and a sardonic coda in which the heirs of the more well-to-do victims cut a few celebratory capers.

During the tour Rossini met the 27-year-old Felix Mendelssohn. In his book on Mendelssohn published in 1874, Ferdinand Hiller wrote:

> Rossini had lost the enormous corpulence of former years: his figure was still full but not disproportioned, and his splendid countenance, which displayed both the power of the thinker and the wit of the humourist, beamed with health and happiness. He spoke French quite as well as Italian, and with the most melodic voice; his long residence in Paris, and intercourse with people there, had transformed him from a haughty young Italian into a man of the world, dignified, graceful and charming, and enchanting everyone with his irresistible amiability.[2]

Away from the social throng – men and women 'ready to faint with fear and surprise when he appeared'[3] – Rossini was able to be his witty and amiable self. His admiration for the economy, sensitivity, and vivacity of Mendelssohn's music was instinctive and deep-seated and he treated him as an equal. Mendelssohn, by contrast, appears to have shown some initial nervousness of the great man. Rossini's amused and by no means uncomplimentary remark that a caprice by Mendelssohn had the smell of Scarlatti about it was not well received. But this was not typical of their relationship. Not only did Mendelssohn find Rossini infinitely amusing, he was also touched by his surprising and sincere veneration of the music of Bach, a veneration, shared by Mendelssohn, which finds many a direct echo in the piano music Rossini was to write in Paris in the 1860s, a decade or more after his brilliant young Frankfurt acquaintance was dead and gone.

After a brief visit to the spa town of Kissingen in Bavaria, Rossini returned to Paris to prepare for the journey back to Italy. After a stately progress through Turin, Milan, and Mantua, he

[1] *Péchés de Vieillesse*, vi, *Album pour les enfants dégourdis*, No.10; QR ii, 42.
[2] Hiller, *Felix Mendelssohn-Bartholdy: Briefe und Erinnerungen*, Cologne, 1874; trs. M.E. von Glahn, London, 1874, p.56.
[3] ibid., p.59.

90

arrived in Bologna in late November. He missed Olympe but he was able to keep in touch with her through his friend Severini. More important, plans were afoot to bring Olympe to Bologna after what seem to have been tolerably amicable plans for a formal separation between Rossini and Isabella. Early in 1837 Olympe made her will, piled her possessions into a rickety carriage and set off for Bologna which she reached, after a dangerous and uncomfortable winter's journey, in late February. It is clear that Olympe was nervous of her position in Bologna. There was no question of her living with Rossini; on the other hand, the relationship, sincere and firmly-rooted though it was, required discreet handling. Above all, it was vital that Isabella should accept her and it was no doubt a relief to all the parties when a luncheon at Mme Rossini's winter residence in Bologna went off without incident. Resorting to diplomatic jargon, Rossini described their meeting as 'friendly'.

At the end of 1837 Rossini and Olympe travelled to Milan where they passed the winter season. As ever, Rossini was the centre of social and musical attention and in the soirées which he and Olympe gave in Milan there are foretastes of the famous *samedi soirs* of the Paris years. Writing to Antonio Zoboli in Bologna on 29 November, 1837, Olympe noted:

> We stayed five days with la Pasta and on our return Rossini opened up our house and all Milan wants to visit us. On Fridays we have soirées which Rossini calls musical evenings; next Friday our amateurs will perform *The Creation*, and the celebrated pianist Litz [Liszt], with his rare talent, will for the second time play some new pieces. In short, the Milanese musical world is enchanted.[4]

On 10 December, 1837 Liszt gave a solo recital at La Scala, Milan, somewhat to the bemusement of the Milanese. 'Vengo al teatro per divertirmi e non per studiare!' bawled one listener.[5] Liszt and Rossini were to meet and correspond on several occasions over the next thirty years. Liszt thought Rossini 'rich, idle, and illustrious' when he first encountered him; Rossini, who later wrote at least one informed

---

[4] MMR, p.145.
[5] 'I come to the theatre for enjoyment, not for study!' Alan Walker, *Franz Liszt, The Virtuoso Years 1801–1847*, London, 1983, p.250.

and witty parody of the Liszt style,[6] was diverted and impressed by him, though Liszt's mistress, the Countess Marie d'Agoult, appears to have been chilly towards Olympe. A fortnight after Liszt's Milan recital, the Countess gave birth to Liszt's second daughter, Cosima. In essence, her relationship with Liszt was no different from Rossini's with Olympe. Liszt, however, showed no such aristocratic condescension towards Rossini and as an earnest of his goodwill (and no doubt to ingratiate himself with the Italian public) he made piano transcriptions of the complete set of Rossini's *Les soirées musicales*.

1838 began ominously for Rossini. On the night of 14–15 January the Salle Favart, home of the Théâtre-Italien in Paris, went up in flames. Sets, costumes, manuscripts, and some of Rossini's own music were lost in the conflagration. Even worse, Rossini's friend and colleague, Carlo Severini, died jumping from the fire. (The jump was not from a great height, but he had landed on stones, breaking his back and dying instantly.) News of Severini's death, which reached Italy via the newspapers, was a terrible blow both to Isabella, with whom he had loyally corresponded during difficult times, and to Rossini. Not only had the hypersensitive Rossini lost a close friend (who had recently bought a house near Bologna), he was also all too easily haunted by the horror of being caught in a fire in a building he himself had occupied during his days in Paris. Severini's death was only one of many which was to affect Rossini in the grim decade which lay ahead. The following year he was prostrated by the death of his father; Barbaia died assisting building workers at his villa near Naples in 1841; Aguado died in Spain in 1842 after a strenuous walk following the blocking by snow of the road on which he was travelling; Isabella died in 1845. By 1850 others in the musical world had gone, too; minor figures like Rossini's friend Gabussi and giants such as Chopin, Donizetti, and Mendelssohn. Like so many artists, they had not survived the critical period of their mid- and late 30s, a transition during which Rossini himself had faltered but not fallen.

The first indication that Giuseppe Rossini was ailing came in the spring of 1838 when Rossini and Olympe were forced to return from Milan to Bologna. Happily, Giuseppe recovered sufficiently to be able to celebrate his 80th birthday the following October. Rossini

---

[6] *Péchés de vieillesse*, viii, *Album de château*, No.12, 'Spécimen de l'avenir'; QR x, 104.

later returned to Milan at Metternich's invitation but, by his own admission, was now caught up in one of his increasingly frequent depressive cycles. Explaining an absence to the Princess Hercolani, he wrote:

> As for desertion, I must tell you that my poor father was ill all the summer and autumn and part of the winter. I too am in a poor state of health, oppressed in spirit as I am. I see no one. I go nowhere and I live unhappily, waiting and waiting for a better future. I hope that suffices to excuse me.[7]

Giuseppe Rossini died on 29 April, 1839. Although not unexpected, his death was a grievous blow to Rossini whose 'filial piety', Fétis's phrase, was a watchword to all who knew him. Clearly seriously depressed, Rossini wrote to a friend:

> I have lost all I possessed that was most precious to me on earth. Without illusions, without a future, imagine how I spend my days! My doctor wants me to go to Naples to take mud-baths, sea-baths and another medicinal cure. I endured a winter so cruel that I shall have to make up my mind to this trip, which in other circumstances would have been delightful, but which, in the grief of my present life, will be a matter of utter indifference to me. If only I could get over my glandular troubles and the pains in the joints that transfixed me all last winter.[8]

Ever thoughtful and hospitable, Aguado wrote from Paris commiserating and offering Rossini rest and quiet in his Paris home. Rossini did not accept the invitation. The doctors prevailed and it was left to Olympe to supervise the summer's journey to Naples. Neither the change nor the so-called cures appear to have done Rossini's health much good; but Olympe was greatly amused by Barbaia with whom they stayed, and it is difficult to imagine that Rossini was not cheered by the company of his old friend.

It would have been easy for Rossini to have lost himself completely in morbid introspection, and nothing would have accelerated the process more certainly than his being housebound in Bologna. Happily, the Liceo Musicale had begun to harbour the hope that Rossini might busy himself again with their affairs. In January 1839 he was

[7] MMR, p.145.
[8] ibid.

offered an honorary consultancy. In a letter dictated during his father's final illness, Rossini gratefully accepted the proposal as a token of his own debt to his former teachers and to the city of Bologna itself. Although he attended the Liceo only once before setting out for Naples in June 1839, he was soon to set in train a bold if ill-fated attempt to attract Mercadante to the position of professor of counterpoint and composition at the Liceo, a post which carried with it the executive directorship of the school. The plan foundered,[9] but Rossini continued conscientiously to carry out his duties at the Liceo. Fétis, who visited Bologna in 1841,[10] noted that Rossini attended the Liceo almost daily, supervising teaching, presiding over rehearsals, and generally lavishing on the students and teachers a wealth of care and experience. Not a great deal took place operatically. In the autumn of 1840, *Guillaume Tell* underwent a bizarre transformation as *Rudolfo di Sterlinga*. It can hardly have excited Rossini but the production had for him the merit of featuring his protégé, the tenor Ivanoff. Acting on Ivanoff's behalf Rossini tried, but failed, to interest Venice's La Fenice in the project. Another lost cause espoused by Rossini at this time was Vincenzo Gabussi's new opera, *Clemenza di Valois* a three act *melodramma* derived by Rossi from Scribe's *Gustave III*. Olympe travelled with Rossini to the *prima* at La Fenice on 20 February, 1841, but to little avail. The opera rose and fell with barely a trace.

Meanwhile, medication appears to have worsened Rossini's physical condition in ways which must have been both painful and humiliating. The gonorrhoea continued to produce secretions and blockages. A catheter was regularly inserted and the urethra dosed with a bewildering variety of concoctions: sweet almond, mallow, gum, and flower of sulphur mixed with cream of tartar. There were warm baths, salts, castor oil and purgative broths. Leeches were applied to haemorrhoids and to the perineum; there were rashes and infections of the scrotum; and, on top of all this, debilitating bouts of diarrhoea after the Venetian trip in February 1841. Much of this is detailed in a doctor's report compiled in Bologna in 1842 and sent by Olympe to her friend, Hector Couvert.[11] Using terminology which

---

[9] Mercadante accepted the post but promptly decamped to Naples. Rossini made subsequent unsuccessful approaches to Pacini and Donizetti.

[10] *Gazette et revue musicale*, Paris, 1841, No.61.

[11] Reprinted in English translation in Weinstock, Appendix B, pp. 379–81.

Petrarch or Chaucer would have understood, the doctor described Rossini as being of the lymphatic or sluggish temperament rather than, as superficial appearances might suggest, sanguine. His nervous system was said to be highly sensitive. In a notable euphemism we are told that Rossini 'abused Venus' in his earliest youth from whence the gonorrhoeal condition had derived. The doctor – on whose evidence it is not made clear – confidently states that the patient began to moderate his sexual activity at the age of 44 (i.e. in 1836) and that the present condition had become marked in the late 1830s, serious by 1840, and critical in the two years which had followed. The end of the report indicates that many of the treatments had merely irritated Rossini's, mercifully robust, system. As any man might under such circumstances, Rossini became prey to morbid speculation about the precise nature and extent of the disease. Weakness, tiredness, and irritation were, it seems, nothing alongside Rossini's terror of the consequences of untreated or untreatable retention of urine.

During 1841, at the height of these medical problems, the case of the *Stabat mater* swam back into view. In his conversations with Rossini in 1841 Fétis had raised the question of Rossini's potential skills as a composer of church music. Rossini demurred. He was not, he argued, a learned musician; besides, he added, 'I no longer concern myself with composition'. He did, however, still concern himself with litigation. In September 1841, Oller Chetard, the original purchaser of the Varela manuscript of the *Stabat mater*, sold it to the Paris music publisher Antoine Aulagnier. Acting with due propriety, Aulagnier wrote to Rossini to seek formal permission to publish. Rossini's reply was a swift and combative one in which he argued that the work had merely been dedicated to Varela and that all rights remained with the composer. Furthermore, the work was incomplete, as would be evident to any competent musician who took the trouble to examine the manuscript. Events moved quickly. By the end of September Rossini had drawn up a contract making over the rights of an all-Rossini *Stabat mater* to Troupenas. He was also busily composing. A letter of 24 September mentions three fully scored numbers which are being forwarded to Paris; it also confronts Aulagnier's shrewd counter-claim that the gift of the gold snuff box constituted a contract of sale, one of several claims and counter-claims which were subsequently rejected in law.

By late October, Troupenas had both the work and the rights to it and extracts were prepared for a series of private previews. It was the brothers Léon and Marie Escudier, though, who masterminded the work's *première* at the Théâtre-Italien in Paris on 7 January, 1842. Whilst still in their teens those enterprising young men had founded *La France musicale* as a rival of Italianate orientation to Schlésinger's *Gazette et revue musicale*. Adam, who wrote glowingly of private previews of the *Stabat mater*, Balzac, Castil-Blaze, Gautier, and Schumann were among the journal's early contributors. In the Aulagnier-Troupenas dispute, the Escudiers were on the side of Troupenas to whom – with all the brimming confidence of youth – they now made an offer of 8,000 francs for an exclusive three-month option on the performing rights of the new work. As Troupenas had paid only 6,000 francs for the work itself, he was happy to oblige. The managements of both the Opéra and the Théâtre-Italien were less co-operative. Nothing daunted, the Escudiers hired the Théâtre-Italien at their own expense and set about assembling the finest available quartet of soloists. According to their own reminiscences,[12] it was the bass, Tamburini, who was so taken with his own solo, the 'Pro peccatis', that he persuaded Grisi, Albertazzi, and Mario to accept the Escudiers' offer. Rehearsals were strictly private. Dormoy, the unimaginative manager of the Théâtre-Italien, was instructed to turn away hundreds of requests to attend, heightening still further the sense of anticipation which existed before the *première*. In such an atmosphere the work might easily have failed; in fact, it was a triumph. The next day, the Escudiers tell us, Dormoy was at their door begging permission to bolster up the Théâtre-Italien's flagging finances with further performances. The Escudiers took a 12,000 franc profit and in a gesture of extraordinary generosity, ceded their rights to the theatre. By the end of the season the Théâtre-Italien was wealthier to the tune of 150,000 francs.

In the meantime, plans were afoot for a Bologna *prima* of the work. As part of his eventually unsuccessful strategy to tempt Donizetti into accepting the directorship of the Liceo, Rossini invited him to conduct the performance. For Bologna and the Liceo the *prima* was an important event, even if they were unable to command the kind of vocal resources available in Paris. Ivanoff and Clara Novello were natural choices. Rossini had known and admired

[12] M. and L. Escudier, *Rossini: sa vie et ses oeuvres*, Paris, 1854.

Clara Novello since, as an 11-year-old child, she had been brought by her parents to the Institution de Musique Religieuse in Paris in 1829. Subsequently, she had sung for Mendelssohn in Germany and had made her Bologna debut as Semiramide in 1841. As a token of his affection for her, Rossini wrote a charming cadenza to be inserted at the end of the 'Sancta Mater' in the Bologna *prima*. The contralto and bass solos were sung by talented amateurs. For the rest, Rossini urged, cajoled, and flattered able singers and instrumentalists to serve in the specially assembled orchestra and chorus. He even persuaded the temperamental Stefano Golinelli[13] to act as *répétiteur*. The performances on 18, 19, and 20 March were a further triumph, though Zanolini tells how Rossini was reduced to 'a trembling and copious sweat' by an abusive newspaper article on the work.[14]

Donizetti was embraced in public by Rossini and given a set of diamond studs. Rossini continued to negotiate with him about the Bologna posts but Donizetti's eye was on Vienna. To extricate himself he made unrealistic demands which Rossini countered with a firm, fair, and generous letter offering terms as liberal as local resources permitted. He offered Donizetti help with the investment of capital and pointed out that in Bologna one could live like a lord on a few *scudi*. But it was to no avail. Donizetti had success with *Linda di Chamounix* at the Kärntnertortheater in May 1842, and, ironically, with Rossini's *Stabat mater*. Shortly afterwards the position of Kapellmeister to the Austrian court was offered to him. It was a more prestigious post than anything Bologna could offer and gave him generous leave in which to write the handful of operas which he was able to complete before the serious onset in 1844 of the illness which was to bring his career to a swift and premature close.

Rossini continued to busy himself with Liceo affairs, with the propagation of 'new' music (Beethoven's *Egmont* Overture was

[13] Golinelli, who was head of the piano school at the Liceo, was a typical appointment of the Rossini years. Young and greatly gifted, with a marked predilection for music of the classical era, his playing was admired by Schumann and by Hiller who was not alone in thinking him the finest Italian pianist of his generation.

[14] There is no indication of who wrote the review. Wagner's malicious, *ad hominem* article on the legal manoeuvrings surrounding the revised *Stabat mater* had appeared in the *Neue Zeitschrift für Musik* on 28 December, 1841.

programmed) and with fund-raising. Olympe, meanwhile, was concerned with medical matters. The Bologna physician's report on Rossini had been forwarded by Couvert to the Parisian surgeon, Jean Civiale and in May 1843 Rossini set out with Olympe for consultations and treatment in Paris. His arrival in Paris created an inevitable and unwelcome furore. His apartments, the Escudier brothers tell us, had the air of a busy theatre foyer, people queuing to call on him. They were to be disappointed. Rossini was put onto a strict regime which proscribed all socializing. Some business was carried out: Léon Pillet, the director of the Opéra, importuned Rossini on the subject of a new opera but Rossini declined, adding that *La donna del lago*, an opera which in his view was highly suitable for the French stage, still awaited a satisfactory production. Though Pillet took Rossini at his word and later visited him in Bologna with the librettist Gustave Vaëz and the composer and arranger, L.-A. Niedermeyer, the result was neither a new opera nor *La donna del lago* but an elaborate *pasticcio*, based on *La donna del lago*, entitled *Robert Bruce*. The production, which was a moderate commercial success, opened in Paris on 30 December, 1846 and aroused a long and bitter controversy to which contributions were made by the leading musical journals, Heller, Berlioz, and even Olympe herself who, in her new role as music critic and polemicist, announced that she was sending ass's ears to the editor of the *Journal des Débats*, François-Édouard Bertin, and to Berlioz. The critics were right, of course; unfortunately, justifiable criticism of *Robert Bruce* was used as a basis for wider-ranging attacks on Rossini's personal and artistic integrity at a time when his stock was already falling in informed musical circles. In assisting with the preparation of this *pasticcio*, he was surrendering a number of hostages to fortune.

Rossini returned to Italy in the autumn of 1843 none the better for his visit. In March 1844 he contributed a cantata, 'Santo Genio dell'Italia terra' to a text by Marchetti, as part of the tercentenary celebrations of the birth of Tasso which were being held in Turin. The cantata, for chorus and orchestra, is an elaboration of the famous 'Chorus of the Bards' from *La donna del lago*. Later the same year he also completed another small commission for his old friend Troupenas. In June 1843 Rossini had made over to Gabussi the publishing rights of the incidental music to *Edipo a Colono* which Gabussi had curiously unearthed. During a visit to Rossini in Bologna Troupenas successfully persuaded Rossini to create a choral triptych by adding a third chorus to two from *Edipo a Colono* which might usefully be transcribed. The new work would take as its title and subject St Paul's famous trinity of moral imperatives: faith, hope, and charity. Once more Rossini's disinclination to compose had to be weighed against his instinct for keeping faith with friends and his charitable regard for Gabussi who stood to benefit financially from any such initiative. French texts were quickly assembled. 'Dall'alma celeste' from *Edipo a Colono* furnished music for 'La foi', and 'O Giove, egioco' became 'L'espérance'. The transcriptions were for piano and a dozen female voices, one of which has a small solo role. It is an ensemble that distantly predicts the forces Rossini would one day assemble for his *Petite messe solennelle*. The chorus which Rossini added to complete the triptych might sound well in any musical soirée; yet it is full of distinctive touches, notably in the harmonization of the piano part which keeps sentimentality at bay. The pieces were first heard in the Salle Troupenas in Paris on 20 November, 1844. Adam enthused and Berlioz bitched: M. Rossini's alms-giving will not ruin him, he uncharitably observed.[15] Liszt was more impressed; in 1847 he made a transcription of 'La charité' for voice and organ which he occasionally performed in later years.

During 1844 Rossini continued to busy himself in minor ways with operatic matters. In May he journeyed to Ferrara to hear Donzelli, now nearing the end of his career, in Mercadante's *Il bravo* (Milan, 1839). He also continued to promote Ivanoff's career by commissioning and funding a new grand aria to be written by Verdi for Ivanoff's exclusive[16] use in Act 2 of *Ernani*. What Rossini thought of the piece and what Ivanoff made of it must be matters for speculation; Rossini's letters to Verdi at this time are strangely obsequious in tone. One imagines that the gracious *andante* suited Ivanoff better than the strenuous *cabaletta*. According to Chorley, who greatly admired Ivanoff's Rodrigo in Rossini's *Otello*, his strengths were neatness of execution and a 'delicious' tone, sweet and gentle. Chorley was less impressed by his presence on stage; 'like an automaton not wound up', is how he put it.[17]

[15] *Journal des Débats*, Paris, 6 December, 1844.

[16] According to Julian Budden, *The Operas of Verdi*, London, 1973, Vol.1, p.169n., the tenor Gaetano Fraschini somehow obtained a copy of the aria which he sang at Sinigallia in the summer of 1846.

[17] Chorley, *op. cit.*, p.54.

In October 1845 Isabella died. She was 60. Rossini had seen little of her since their formal separation eight years earlier but when news reached him that Isabella was gravely ill he drove at once to Castenaso. He spent half an hour at her bedside and was, we are told, much moved by the occasion. As Ernest Newman was to write in another context: 'the severance of a long tie . . . must inevitably mean much bitterness and suffering, much dwelling in the past and self-reproach. We always seem heavy debtors to the dead: we feel that they have not had their chance and that life has given us an unfair advantage over them'.[18] Such thoughts must have crossed Rossini's already troubled consciousness as the woman whom he had in some sense abandoned lay dying. For a month he received daily reports on Isabella's condition. She died on 7 October, allegedly murmuring Rossini's name. With both parents, and now Isabella, dead he was even more an exile in his own country. His remaining tie was with the French-born Olympe whom he married, after a decent interval, in the summer of 1846. The date was 16 August and it coincided with the unofficial *prima* of the second of two cantatas which Rossini was persuaded to write in honour of the newly elected Pope Pius IX.

[18] Vera Newman, *Ernest Newman: a memoir by his wife*, London, 1963, p.18. Newman was referring to the death of Lady Elgar.

14

Times of Barricades and Assassinations: Bologna, Florence, and departure from Italy (1847–55)

Given Rossini's essentially conservative temperament, his involvement in the popular enthusiasm surrounding the election of Pius IX must be seen as a further example of his being inadvertently caught up in events he could neither predict nor influence. With hard-line activists urging popular uprising, the abolition of the Papacy's temporal powers, and the setting up of a united democratic Italian republic, the initiatives of more tentative liberalisers like Pius IX and Charles Albert of Piedmont were treated as cues for far more radical reforms. The Sicilian revolt of 12 January, 1848 helped set in train the revolutionary uprisings which were to sweep through Europe in the weeks and months which followed. Bologna was quickly involved and, as inevitably happens at such times, matters quickly got out of hand. Hot-headed republicans, fellow-travellers, and marauding soldiery, some of it Sicilian in origin, were suspicious of 'rich reactionaries' among whose number Rossini was unhappily counted. Rossini had, in fact, signed a liberal, pro-nationalist petition to Cardinal Riario Sforza and had made some modest contributions towards nationalist funds; but it was no secret that he was disturbed by much of the political violence, particularly by the several arbitrary and unchecked killings which had taken place in Bologna. After a disturbance outside their house on 27 April, Rossini and Olympe beat a hasty retreat to Florence the following day. His departure caused consternation in Bologna. Pro-Rossini demonstrations were put in hand and amiable, windy speeches made at torch-lit meetings. From his Florentine fastness, Rossini replied decorously and at length to a humble request for his return to Bologna by Padre Ugo Bassi. Not unreasonably, Rossini pleaded ill-health as the cause of his being unable to return to his 'second home'; but as a palliative he accepted Bassi's suggestion that he should compose music for a nationalistic hymn. Bassi was wounded in fighting soon afterwards and the words for the hymn were drafted by Filippo Martinelli. Rossini sketched a choral march and left the writing of the band accompaniment to his friend, the clarinettist Domenico Liverani. A succession of euphuistic letters flowed between Bologna and Florence as arrangements were put in hand for the first performance of the piece in Bologna's Piazza Maggiore on 21 June, 1848; but this was one *prima* at which Rossini would be conspicuous by his absence.

During the period 1848–50, Rossini appears to have been generally unwell, worrying about the minutiae of domestic and legal matters he had left unattended in Bologna and dictating or initiating an endless stream of enquiries about everything, as Frank Walker puts it, from ink pots to horses. They are concerns which were no doubt rooted in the realities of his situation but which were almost certainly magnified and exacerbated by his depressive condition and his obsessive concern for detail. That there were, however, periods of remission and a return to casual good humour is confirmed by his writing the extraordinarily jaunty 'Inno alla pace' ('È foriera la Pace ai mortali' for baritone, male chorus, and piano) as a gift for the painter Vincenzo Rasori in the summer of 1850.

By September 1850 the political situation was sufficiently stable and Rossini himself sufficiently fit for him to return to oversee his affairs in Bologna, though he was prudent enough to request a police escort for the latter stages of the journey. He found Bologna tense and inward-looking. He also found the feeling of hostility towards the Austrians – and to the governor, Count Nobili, in particular – too much to stomach. In Florence when he had learned that an Austrian officer was living in his Bologna apartment, he expressed himself honoured but asked that the linen should be looked to. It was a characteristic response. Like Richard Strauss's in Germany eighty or more years later, Rossini's attitude to the political events which surrounded him was one of public compliance and private disdain, matched with a keen sense of self-preservation and an instinctive skill for relegating political concerns below social and aesthetic ones.

During the winter of 1850–1 Rossini supervised the packing of his most valuable household effects and sold the villa at Castenaso which had been rented out since Isabella's death in 1845. He left Bologna in May 1851 and never returned. Indeed, in later years he developed a morbid dislike of the city. Looking back to these 'times of Barricades and Assassinations' in a letter to Ivanoff written from Paris on 11 November, 1862, he notes: 'You inhabit a city [Bologna], the sons of which, great and small, live by their Wits, by Fraud and by Lies. I still feel remorse for having induced you and the good Donzelli to establish yourselves in that Sewer. May God forgive me!!!'[1]

Rossini's four years in Florence seem to have coincided with some of the deepest troughs in his depressive cycles. Many who visited him during this time report extreme nervousness or morbid excitability. He suffered from insomnia, from loss of appetite and from a series of physical disabilities which often reduced him to a child-like dependence on Olympe and their servants. Writing to Santocanale on 3 February, 1855,[2] he admits that he is incapable of dressing without help. Conversation became difficult and visitors were often burdened with elaborate details of his illnesses. In the summer of 1854 Rossini visited the baths at Lucca, to no avail. Despairing of doctors, he submitted to a number of new patent treatments including a bogus 'magnetic' cure. He contemplated suicide, but said he was too much of a coward to take the decisive final step. Gossips as far afield as Paris and Milan reported him incurably insane.

Yet he remained physically robust. The earliest known photograph of Rossini, a rare daguerreotype dating from about 1850,[3] shows a substantial, corpulent figure and an alert albeit pensive expression. Evidence from letters written during the years of illness suggest that during periods of remission Rossini could be characteristically hyperactive. Commending the clarinettist Liverani to Michael Costa in London in 1842, Rossini wrote:

'Tis Liverani, my sweet friend, who will hand you this. He has done his duty in coming to put himself *at your service* in the Great Capital. Now you have a duty to fulfil, and that is to put him in the way of earning some Guineas, of which he has a great need!!! I demand of your Omnipotence and Friendship that you secure for him all necessary means of giving a Magnificent Concert in the High Season. I demand further that you impose him on those

[1] MMR, p.147.
[2] Rognoni, p.309.
[3] See plate 18.

Noble Milords, for their Private Musical Entertainments, called Concerts, in the style of Puzzi and Dragonetti.[4]

In December 1853 he wrote a similar letter to a sausage and pasta specialist in Modena, full of high-flown praise, amusing musico-gastronomic references and an almost manic *joie de vivre*. In these years Rossini undoubtedly became master of what Frank Walker has called the epistolary *buffo* style, even if at times the humour can seem strained and unnaturally ebullient. At other times, he is rationality itself. In a famous letter written to Luigi Ferrucci in 1852 or early 1853, Rossini dwells on the special beauties of the contralto voice, that lower, darker female voice for which he had written so much of his finest music. In the same letter he also warns against the domination of the voice by the new instrumental forces which contemporary composers are deploying: 'The head will conquer the heart, science will lead art to its ruin under a deluge of notes; what is called "instrumental" will be the sepulchre of voices and of feeling. May it not come to pass!!!'[5] Clarity, elegance, and balance – the classical virtues – are what Rossini continued to commend to friends and students. More aware than he cared to admit of what composers like Liszt and Wagner were about, Rossini took refuge in the new Bach-Gesellschaft edition (Leipzig 1851 ff.) and in the music of Palestrina, Haydn, and Mozart.[6]

Occasionally, he made music, usually among friends, after dinner, with the lights subdued. He could rarely be induced to play, and when he did he was often left in a distressed and tearful state. Yet the old mastery had not left him. Emilia Branca Romani who was present on such an evening in Florence in 1854 noted the brilliance of his improvised accompaniment for Matilde Juva in 'Bel raggio lusinghier' from *Semiramide* and notes that his own improvisations around Desdemona's famous *romanza* – 'a *fantasia alla Thalberg*' – were 'magnificent, astonishing, dumbfounding'.[7]

Florence was, however, only a temporary home. Olympe hankered after Paris: its society and its doctors. By April 1855 preparations had been completed for the move to Paris. It was a bold

---

[4] MMR, p.204.

[5] LdR, pp.336–7; Rognoni, pp.306–7.

[6] In 1856 Rossini attempted unsuccessfully to buy the autograph manuscript of *Die Zauberflöte*.

[7] Weinstock, pp.257–9.

decision and for whatever cause – a new environment, new medication, or simply the moderating processes of age as Rossini passed his 60th year – it proved to be an efficacious one.

15

Return to Paris

After the long and exhausting journey from Florence, the Rossinis took temporary accommodation in Montmartre, though in 1856 they were to rent a small villa in Passy which so delighted Rossini that negotiations were put in hand about the possibility of his acquiring – or as it later turned out, building – a residence of his own there. In July 1855 he travelled to the Normandy resort of Trouville where he met Ferdinand Hiller. Their conversations helped recall many figures from Rossini's younger days: Mayr, Paisiello (unflattering remarks about his general cultural awareness, and his spelling, hardly Rossini's own strong point to judge from his letters), Cimarosa ('a fine, educated mind') and Weber whose overtures are praised but not, significantly, the integral use within the overtures of themes which will be of importance later in the work. The interrelationships cannot be judged at the outset, Rossini argues, and their charm and novelty is dissipated in the process.[1]

Slowly Rossini's health began to improve. The change of environment was clearly working wonders. Not only was there the salubrious atmosphere of French and German spas, there was also the invigorating atmosphere of Paris itself. Rossini's arrival there in 1823 had coincided with a period of optimism and renewal and now, despite unstable and repressive aspects of the Second Empire, economic growth was again formidable and the new spirit – symbolized by Offenbach and the Bouffes-Parisiens – decidedly lively. In the summer of 1856 Rossini made a stately progress through Strasbourg to the spa town of Wildblad where one observer noted an elderly man, 'a little tremulous in his motions but with an open face and a lively eye'. Rossini appears to have been reconciled to – perhaps, in some sense,

---

[1] Rossini had occasionally failed to follow his own precept – the overture to *Semiramide* is an example – but his own concept of the form and function of the operatic overture was essentially different from that of Weber, Wagner and others. See Chapter 20.

enjoyed – the role of what he called 'un vieux rococo'. Enclosing a photograph of himself for a friend in 1864, he wrote: 'It represents a certain vigour which is only apparent since my weakness increases by reason of my years, so that I can no longer make use of my legs, and *Memory, Acumen, Wit, etc., etc.,* are similarly wasting away. There's a death penalty for not attaining these miseries. Let us live, then, and be patient!'[2] Written so soon after the successful first performances of the *Petite messe solennelle* this charmingly wry letter needs to be taken with a pinch of salt.

By early 1857 Rossini was beginning to compose again. The first substantial sin of his old age, as he liked ironically to call these late pieces, was a set of six different settings of favourite lines by Metastasio, 'Mi lagnerò tacendo della mia sorte amara', tragic-sounding sentiments but a marvellous gift for Olympe on her name-day, 15 April, 1857. Over the music, with its sad, Satie-like title, 'Musique anodine', Rossini wrote:

I offer these modest songs to my dear wife Olympe
    as a simple testimonial of gratitude for the
affectionate, intelligent care of which she was prodigal
    during my overlong and terrible illness
        (Shame of the [medical] faculty)

With Rossini in generally improved spirits, and composing again, the Rossinis' social life began to flourish. A spacious second-floor apartment was found in the rue de la Chaussée d'Antin and was to remain the Rossinis' winter residence for the remaining years of his life. The apartment was admirably suited to its dual purpose as private home and social meeting-place. There was a spacious entrance hall and grand salon, complemented by a private sitting room and a series of separate bedrooms. Rossini's own bedroom, where he often received visitors, either bewigged or with his magnificent domed head swathed in a huge coloured handkerchief, was filled with bric-à-brac, private icons, and general memorabilia: signed photographs, a clock topped with the bust of Mozart, numerous insignia and decorations, Isabella's jewelry, a small collection of musical instruments, some firearms, and a tobacco jar from Scotland with silvered goat's horns.

[2] MMR, p.147.

Reports vary on the state of the room. Pauline Viardot noted that all round the room Rossini's wigs hung on long poles, alongside musical instruments, and — bizarre touch — the catheter which Rossini termed 'the best of instruments'. An American visitor in 1864 professed to find a mess of items on one of Rossini's tables: brushes, combs, toothpicks, and a tube for making macaroni. The overall impression, though, is one of orderliness. Guglielmo De Sanctis, the Italian painter for whom Rossini sat in 1862, observed Rossini at work in his rooms in Passy with painter's eye for detail and a shrewd sense of the personality which the scene reflected:

> Rossini takes the greatest pains when copying out his writings, never wearying of perfecting them, often going back to read them over and alter notes, which he is in the habit of erasing with a scraper with truly singular patience. One never would say that a man of such fervent imagination could lend himself to such minutiae. Another thing that I observed about him was the regularity of his habits, not to mention the symmetrical order in which he placed the furniture and objects around him. The room that he habitually occupied for many hours each day, both for receiving and for working, was his bedroom. There, the writing table was in the centre, and on it set out in perfect order were the papers, his indispensable scrapers, the pens, the inkstand, and whatever else he needed for his writing. Three or four wigs were placed in a row on the mantel, evenly spaced. On the white walls hung some Japanese miniatures on rice paper, and some Oriental objects had been placed like a trophy on the chest of drawers; the bed, against the wall, always neat; a few simple chairs around the room . . . When, struck by that perfect orderliness, I showed my surprise to the Maestro, he said to me: 'Eh, my dear fellow, order is wealth.'[3]

In *The Dynamics of Creation*, Storr productively juxtaposes De Sanctis's description with similar descriptions by Nabokov and Ramuz of Stravinsky's study in Hollywood where the careful ordering of furniture, books, scores and the like was complemented by a writing desk on which inks, erasers, rulers, and knives were laid out in an elaborate hierarchy, each item, Ramuz suggests, playing its part in the ordering of Stravinsky's art. Although De Sanctis seems to have been mildly surprised, as many people are, to find so much

---

[3] Weinstock, pp.317–8, translated from G. De Sanctis *Gioacchino Rossini: appunti di viaggio*, Rome, 1878.

order in the room of an artist, especially an artist as allegedly casual as Rossini, creativity and obsessional behaviour are not incompatible. There is no evidence that Rossini's tidiness was pathological; that he merely tidied and never wrote. His productivity in his last years was remarkable, as was the productivity of other obsessionals listed by Storr: Beethoven, Dickens, Ibsen, Dr Johnson, Swift. Certainly, the ordering process can itself help generate the conditions in which creative work is possible; it may also become what Storr calls an outward and visible sign of that very order which the creative artist aims to perfect in his finished composition.[4]

Just as his rooms and working conditions were meticulously ordered, so was Rossini's daily routine. Though he was often seen setting out to Passy to supervise the building of his villa during 1859 (the cornerstone was laid on 10 March, 1859) as early as 7.00 a.m., he normally rose at 8.00 and breakfasted on a roll dipped in coffee or, in later years, on two soft-boiled eggs and a glass of claret. After breakfast his mail would be read to him by Olympe and if the weather and he were well suited, he would walk or drive, doing some gentle shopping and very occasionally calling on a select circle of well-to-do friends, the Rothschilds or the Countess Pillet-Will. He rarely ate lunch; but as his health improved he ate handsomely enough at 6.00 p.m. His knowledge of French and, more especially, Italian food was legendary. According to Michotte he shocked an expatriate Italian grocer by returning to him some 'Neapolitan' macaroni on the eminently justifiable ground that it clearly came from Genoa. After dinner, Rossini would take a nap and sometimes smoke a cigar. At 8.30 p.m. he would hear the papers read and might receive a small number of guests who were required to depart on the stroke of 10.00, what Rossini called 'the canonical hour'. Though he occasionally visited private musical gatherings in the daytime in the early 1860s, he dined away from home as rarely as he attended the opera or concerts. It was a sensible regime and clearly did much to promote and sustain the period of comparative good health during the late '50s and early '60s.

In March 1860, Rossini was visited by Wagner.[5] On the face of

---

[4] Storr, op. cit., p.134.

[5] Michotte, pp.1–90; French text, Rognoni, pp.385–426. Though Michotte's text, first published in 1906 from notes assembled in 1860, is a revised and edited version of the conversation, there is no reason to doubt its general accuracy.

it, this was an odd meeting, a musical summit between the leaders of
the old order and the new. In the event, mutual curiosity, good
manners, and a shared absorption in the business of music-making in
general and opera in particular ensured that the meeting was both
keen and affable. From the outset Rossini is at his most disarming,
pleading ignorance of Wagner's music in the theatre (the only
context for proper judgement, Rossini avers) and trying to lay the
dust of some of his own alleged witticisms at Wagner's expense.
Though Wagner is clearly fascinated by Rossini's reminiscences of
Beethoven and Weber, he is less tactful about those operas which
rely on the very formulas Rossini has done so much to develop and
extend. He is scathing about bravura arias, insipid duets, vocal *hors
d'oeuvres* which hold up the stage action, and banal end-of-act
septets. 'The row of artichokes,' is Rossini's tolerant rejoinder. 'I
assure you I was perfectly aware of the silliness of the thing. It always
gave me the impression of a line of porters who had come to sing in
order to earn a tip.' On the question of libretti there seems to be no
common ground, with Rossini genuinely surprised by the suggestion
that a composer should write his own text. Wagner's response is
robust. Whilst studying counterpoint, why should a composer not
study literature and history and read mythology? Wagner goes on
to argue that at nodal points in the drama composers necessarily
involve themselves in shaping the text. He cites the oath-swearing
scene in *Guillaume Tell*, an observation as shrewd as it must have
been flattering. Emboldened by evidence of Wagner's detailed knowledge of *Guillaume Tell*, Rossini turns to the subject of 'mélopée
déclamatoire'. Wagner's defence of the flexible, personally involving, declamatory style is full and impassioned. 'The funeral oration
of melody', Rossini rejoins, but Wagner merely re-states his case,
attacking 'symmetrical periods, persistent rhythms, predictable harmonic progressions, and obligatory cadences'. Melody, he argues,
must be free, independent, unfettered; and he goes on, curiously but
with a measure of relevance, to cite Tell's 'Sois immobile' with its
freely singing line and the breathing strokes of the cello's accompaniment. Rossini's reply – 'So I made music of the future without
knowing it' – is as agreeable and misleading as is his line on the rapid
composition of *Il barbiere di Siviglia*, 'I had facility and lots of
instinct'. Rossini's genius for wittily defensive verbal sword-play
disguises the real extent of the effort involved in the creation of *Il
barbiere di Siviglia*, just as the quip about the funeral oration of

melody disguises the part played by the new, declamatory writing in his own later Neapolitan works in shaping an operatic tradition to which Wagner was substantially indebted. None the less, it is clear that Wagner recognised in *Guillaume Tell, Mosè in Egitto,* and parts of *Otello,* works cited during the conversation, important elements which his own and subsequent generations were blithely to ignore. In retrospect, Wagner is said to have found Rossini simple, natural, and serious, a genius led astray by his Italian scepticism and the Latin's natural reluctance to treat art as religion. As for Rossini, he followed Wagner's career with renewed interest after their encounter. In the end, their aesthetic positions were irreconcilable. Wagner thought Rossini unserious and Rossini thought Wagner 'lacked sun'. Rossini was also to be credited, for better or for worse, with that most famous of all aphorisms directed against Wagner: 'Monsieur Wagner a de beaux moments, mais de mauvais quart-d'heures!'.[6]

There were other visitors the same summer who were less demanding. Both the music and the conversation of Ignaz Moscheles with their fluency, guile, and grace were more to Rossini's taste than the music of the future. Rossini praised Palestrina and Marcello; Moscheles was wise enough to praise Clementi, much of whose music Rossini knew by heart. Eduard Hanslick also came in Wagner's wake, a nice juxtaposition. As he sat in Rossini's new villa overlooking the sun-drenched garden with its flowerbeds laid out in the shapes of musical instruments – Rossini now unmistakably the *bourgeois gentilhomme* – Hanslick fantasized about his host, a man of ease, 'an epicurean sage' who had spent thirty years of his life in a 'soft, smooth tide of secure leisure'. As a picture of Rossini's life it is cruelly inaccurate, but Hanslick was on safer ground when he saw Rossini as 'the disinterested spectator, a man who watches without envy or bitterness, though not always without irony'.[7]

[6] Michotte, pp.135–6.
[7] Hanslick, *Aus dem Concert-Saal,* Vienna, 1870; 2/1897.

16

Saturday soirées and a new Mass

The first of the *samedi soirs* was held on 18 December, 1858. Over the next ten years (the last soirée was on 26 September, 1868) artists, politicians, diplomats, and the well-to-do attended the Rossinis' salon in the rue de la Chaussée d'Antin to mingle with and hear a galaxy of musical talent. Invitations were much prized and the list of those who attended is both long and distinguished. Weinstock lists over seventy names.[1] Composers who attended and sometimes performed included Auber, Boito, Gounod, Liszt, Anton Rubinstein, Meyerbeer, Saint-Saëns, Thomas, and, as Louis Diémer put it, 'the taciturn Verdi'. Foremost among the singers were Alboni, Jean-Baptiste Faure, Grisi, the Marchisio sisters, Nilsson, Patti, Tamberlik, and Tamburini. Pianists, all of whom appear to have marvelled at Rossini's own playing, included Diémer and Thalberg, as well as Liszt and Saint-Saëns. Violinists included Joachim and Sarasate. Many of the artists were young and on the threshold of their careers. Patti was 21 when she made her Paris debut and Diémer was still a teenager when Rossini entrusted to him the task of playing through and memorizing newly written pieces during preparations for each soirée. Like Patti, Diémer survived into the next century and made gramophone recordings. He also taught: Cortot was a pupil, and so was Robert Casadesus.

Though the Rossinis would entertain up to a dozen guests privately on a Saturday evening, the 'gala soirées' as Michotte calls them, began later, at between 8.30 and 9.00 p.m., leaving the fashionable hordes to pick their way through unappetizing tit-bits, many of them from Olympe's hoard of gifts and samples of pasta, cheese, olives, and wine with which they were inundated from all corners of Europe. Socially, the evenings were overseen by Olympe who held court in the grand salon; and woe betide anyone who did not make proper obeisance to her. Rossini tended to distance himself

[1] Weinstock, pp.467–8.

1 Rossini's birthplace, Pesaro.

2 Giuseppe Rossini

3 Anna Rossini

4 Domenico Barbaia. In the background are smaller portraits of
Rubini, Rossini, and Pasta.

5 Isabella Colbran's villa at Castenaso, near Bologna.

6 Isabella Colbran, for whom Rossini created ten major roles between 1815 and 1823. Rossini married Colbran in Castenaso on 16 March 1822.

7 Alessandro Sanquirico's design for the Tribunal Scene in La Scala, Milan's production of *La gazza ladra*, 1817.

8 Alessandro Sanquirico's design for La Scala, Milan's production of *Semiramide*, 1824.

9 Part of the autograph manuscript of the 'Eja Mater' from the movements composed for the *Stabat mater* in 1832.

10 Part of the autograph manuscript of the final movement of the *Stabat mater* added during the completion of the work by Rossini in 1841.

11 Filippo Galli, for whom Rossini created many important bass roles.

12 Giuditta Pasta
as Tancredi.

13 Manuel García, father of
Maria Malibran, as Otello.

14 Maria Malibran. 'The greatest was Colbran', Rossini once said, 'but unique was Malibran'.

15 Laure Cinti-Damoreau, who created leading soprano roles in all five of Rossini's operas for Paris.

16 Olympe Pélissier,
Rossini's second wife.

17 The tenor Nicholas
Ivanoff, Rossini's protégé
and friend.

18 Rossini *c.* 1850

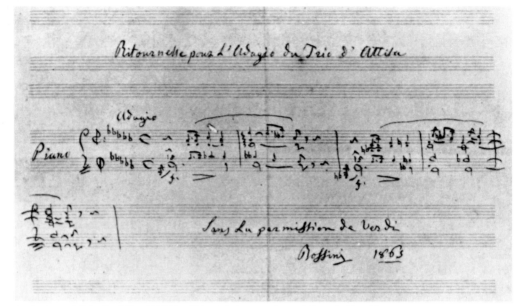

19 Bars written by Rossini for one of his Saturday soirées in Paris in 1863 as preface to the Trio from Verdi's *Attila*. The purpose of the preface is to stop conversation. Though Verdi was present, Rossini added a humorous subscription: 'Sans la permission de Verdi'.

20 Rossini's apartment in the rue de la Chaussée d'Antin where the Saturday soirées were held from December 1858 to September 1868. The apartment is marked with a star.

21 Carlotta Marchisio

22 Barbara Marchisio

23 Adelina Patti

The Marchisio sisters,
for whom Rossini wrote the
soprano and contralto parts in
the *Petite messe solennelle*,
regularly sang at Rossini's
Saturday soirées, as did the
young Adelina Patti.

24 Rossini on his deathbed. An engraving by Gustave Doré
from sketches made on 14 November 1868.

from the social hubbub, closeted in an adjacent room with special guests and what Pauline Viardot called the 'second-rate hangers-on' who enjoyed his witticisms and coarse jokes. Principal among these was his old friend, Michele Carafa. Carafa, who was four years older than Rossini, had known him since his Naples days when he had occasionally made contributions – recitatives, an aria or two – to Rossini's operas. Blaze de Bury, who observed Carafa in Paris, suggested that he resembled one of 'those chamberlains in attendance on exiled royalty who are unwilling to resign themselves to their lot and who continue the observance of court etiquette towards their sovereign'.[2] Rossini is alleged to have said to him, 'Carafa made the mistake of being born my contemporary'. Yet he was generous to him in practical ways. The rights for the French edition of *Semiramide* were ceded to Carafa who adapted the work, added ballet music, and supervised a lavish new production which opened at the Paris Opéra on 9 July, 1860. The production also marked the Paris debut of the Marchisio sisters[3] whose singing recalled for Rossini a vanished age. In a presentation copy of the French edition, he wrote: 'To my beloved friends and incomparable interpreters, Carlotta and Barbara Marchisio, possessors of that song which is sensed in the soul'.

The programmes for the soirées, many of which were formally printed, were assembled by Rossini himself with special care. A good deal of the music was his own, some of it newly written: a substantial body of work which must be looked at later in more detail.[4] In addition to this, the music of Pergolesi, Haydn, Mozart, Gounod, and Verdi was often featured. On one occasion, Rossini added a preface to a piece by Verdi, the Trio from *Attila*, 'to stop conversation and draw attention to Verdi's music', signed by Rossini 'without the permission of Verdi'.[5] Occasionally new music by other composers would be heard: a short chamber opera by Weckerlin and the first public hearing of Liszt's two *Légendes*, 'St François d'Assise: la prédication aux oiseaux' and 'St François de Paule marchant sur les flots'. A new Duo for flute and clarinet by Saint-Saëns was passed off by Rossini as his own work, to the great consternation of Rossini's

---

[2] Quoted by Julian Budden, *Grove 6*, Vol.3, p.768.
[3] See plates 21 and 22
[4] Chapter 37.
[5] See plate 19.

simpering admirers when the ruse was revealed.[6] Longer items were rarely included, though Rossini did programme his cantata *Giovanna d'Arco*, an ideal piece for such a gathering, the more so as it was a work written for Olympe. The most striking exception to this rule came in 1861. Occasionally, soirées would be held on a Friday; thus it came about that on Good Friday, 1861 Rossini devoted the entire evening's music-making to his *Stabat mater* sung by a quartet which included Carlotta and Barbara Marchisio, and accompanied by a double string quartet. Two years later Rossini varied the idea, interleaving some piano pieces and an aria by Haydn with extracts from his own and Pergolesi's settings of the *Stabat mater*.

Sometimes there would be skits and music-hall *chansons* arranged by Gustav Doré; and always, for those who could catch them, there were Rossini's own wry asides on the proceedings. Singers, in particular were closely scrutinized by their host who allowed no loose, ugly, or unstylish effect to go unremarked. In the most quoted of all interventions, the young Adelina Patti was brought down to earth with a bump when her over-decorated account of Rosina's 'Una voce poco fa' met with the rejoinder: 'Very nice, my dear, and who wrote the piece you have just performed for us?'[7] A soprano Rosina would not have been entirely to Rossini's taste but it was the rococo ornamentation, almost certainly the work of Patti's mentor, Maurice Strakosch, which undoubtedly irked him. 'Strakoschonné!' – 'Strakoschonized!' – was the expletive Rossini invented to describe the horror. Young as she was, Patti appears to have taken offence at the time; but Saint-Saëns tells us that she had the good sense to return to Rossini for advice. He was to invite her to many subsequent soirées when she was often accompanied by Rossini himself or, as was the case on 9 March, 1866, by the distinguished Belgian harpist and pianist, Félix Godefroid. The entire programme for that date was as follows:

Première Partie

1. PRELUDE DE MON TEMPS .... ROSSINI
   Exécuté par Mr. Diémer

[6] Saint-Saëns, *Ecole buissonnière*, Paris, 1913, pp.261–7.
[7] ibid.

2. *Quatuor de* MOÏSE .... ROSS'NI
   Mlles. A. Patti et Zeiss
   Mrs. Fraschini et Gardoni

3. *Duo de* CENERENTOLA.. ROSSINI
   Mrs. Delle-Sedie et Zucchini

4. CANZONE .... ROSSINI
   Mr. Fraschini

5. *Trio dell'* ITALIANA IN ALGERI .... ROSSINI
   Mrs. Tamburini, Gardoni et Zucchini

6. Romance d'OTELLO .... ROSSINI
   Mlle. A. Patti
   Avec accompangement par Mr. Félix Godefroid

Deuxième Partie

1. *Duo 'Mira mi bianca luna'* .... ROSSINI
   Mlle. A. Patti, Mr. Gardoni

2. *Romance del* BALLO IN MASCHERA .... VERDI
   Mr. Delle Sedie

3. *Duo d'*OTELLO.. ROSSINI
   Mrs. Fraschini et Verger

4. CANZONE .... ROSSINI
   Mr. Gardoni

5. *Duo del* BARBIERE DI SIVIGLIA .... ROSSINI
   Mlle. A. Patti, Mr. Tamburini

6. *Trio del* CRISPINO E LA COMARE .... RICCI
   Mrs. Agnesi, Zucchini et Mercuriali

Impromptu, composé et exécuté par Mr. F. Godefroid.
   Piano: Mr. A. Peruzzi

It was Patti, too, who led a memorable performance of the Quartet from *Rigoletto* with Alboni, Gardoni, and Delle-Sedie; Giulio Ricordi noted that only Verdi could have accompanied as expertly and as sympathetically as Rossini did on this occasion.

The gap between Rossini's private music-making and his more official public musical utterances remained as wide at this period as it had been before. Though he followed closely the fate of Verdi's *Inno delle nazioni* at the London Exhibition in 1862, he declined to contribute himself; he had, however, accepted a commission from the Société des Concerts du Conservatoire on behalf of a committee appointed by the Florentines to erect a monument in honour of Cherubini. It was his *Chant des Titans*, first heard in full-dress orchestral and choral garb, at the Paris Opéra on 22 December, 1861. The text, a rather violent affair, was by Émilien Pacini, to be sung by four basses in unison, with chorus and orchestra.[8] The piece is curiously empty. The opening figure on the violas, cellos, and basses sounds like a leitmotif associated with a sprightlier version of Wagner's Hunding, but what follows is far from Wagnerian: busy ostinato rhythms, four-square declamation, and melodramatic harmonies as part of Rossini's rather half-hearted attempt to suggest the piling of Pelion on Ossa. Under the final C major chord are written the words 'Laus Deo', an odd subscription at the end of so brutal and pagan a piece. One wonders to what extent Rossini believed in works like this.

There can, however, be no doubting the sincerity of the *Petite messe solennelle* which Rossini worked on during 1863 and the early part of 1864. Part mass, part cantata, the work is quintessential Rossini, a serious, beautifully ordered, at times strikingly novel work whose immediate public face is ironic and relaxed. The irony is evident in the Credo's joky tempo indication, *Allegro cristiano*, and is persistently deployed in the famous epigraph in which the number of singers – 'twelve singers and three sexes: men, women, and eunuchs' – is justified in terms of the twelve apostles and the Last Supper. It is, Rossini tells his Maker, 'the last mortal sin of my old age'. He continues, in his quipping, punning style:

> Dear God, here it is finished, this poor little Mass. Is this sacred music which I have written or music of the devil? [Est-ce bien de la musique sacrée que je viens de faire ou bien de la sacrée musique?] I was born for *opera buffa*, as you well know. A little science, a little heart, that's all. Be blessed, then, and admit me to Paradise. G. Rossini. Passy 1863.

It is a witty preface but a defensive one, as though Rossini is reluctant to appear in public without his cap and bells, his jester's garb. And

---

[8] In his letter of 15 October, 1861, Rognoni p.310, Rossini nominates the 'four fellows' who will sing in the *première* and wryly notes that the music is innocent of roulades, chromatic scales, trills, and arpeggios. The Titans listed in the full score are Encelade, Hypérion, Coelus, and Poliphème.

yet, as anyone who is attentive to the music – to the 'Kyrie' or the concluding 'Agnus Dei' – will quickly recognize, this is a work which is as anxious as it is serene, as melancholy as it is jocund. It is said that Rossini brooded over it for a long time and was unsettled by it during composition.

To all outward appearance, Rossini was not a religious man. Even on his deathbed he prevaricated, though the Abbé Gallet de St.-Roch reports him meeting the ritual question on belief with the words: 'Would I have been able to write the *Stabat* and the *Messe* if I had not had faith?'.[9] Rossini's faith was certainly not a formal or institutionalized one and may have been criss-crossed with uncertainty; but as the poet Tennyson writes in *In Memoriam*: 'There lives more faith in honest doubt/Believe me, than in half the creeds'. Rossini would almost certainly have endorsed such a sentiment. He was, none the less, a man in whom the primary affections and loyalties were strong; and it is often primary forms of belief which inspire and sustain the finest religious art. Though the Mass's language is of its time, and even in some senses a forerunner of a French tradition of sacred music which runs from Fauré to Poulenc, the work is also the product of an old man's vision of the past, of the methods and ideals of an age which was seemingly simpler and less cluttered than the one in which he now found himself. The Mass's title, which is not a joke, indicates an economy of scale – the orchestra banished[10] and the voices accorded their old primacy – as well as an intrinsic seriousness and formality. 'Solennelle' not only indicates that this is a sung Mass, a *missa solemnis* as opposed to a *missa lecta*, it also suggests the order and propriety of ritual observance, all qualities which are central not only to Rossini's psychology but to his art and craft, and nowhere more so than in the pristine

---

[9] Abbé Gallet, *Le Figaro*, Paris, 27 February, 1892.

[10] In 1867 Rossini orchestrated the piece, omitting the 'Prélude religieux', in order to prevent others attempting to do so. The original accompanying instruments – two pianos, harmonium – are, however, crucial to the work's character and colour. After Rossini's death, Olympe sold the rights of the orchestral version to Maurice Strakosch who toured it, lavishly and profitably, for a number of years. The work's immediate international success was considerable. The Marchisio singers sang it in Moscow under the direction of Anton Rubinstein; it even reached Australia within a year of the Paris *première* of the orchestral version which took place at the Théâtre-Italien on 24 February, 1869.

masterpieces of his earliest years: *Tancredi, L'italiana in Algeri, Il barbiere di siviglia* prime among them.

A key factor in drawing Rossini back to the old world state was the presence in Paris of the two Marchisio sisters whose art, as we have already seen, was a reminder to Rossini of the vocal glories of a vanished age. It is also worth noting that the *Petite messe solennelle* is patently unsuited to the concert hall. As it was also barred from performance in Catholic churches because of the ban on female singers, its first performances were in the private chapel of the Countess Louise Pillet-Will: aptly so, for the *Petite messe solennelle* is a courtly work conceived and written in an age when the court composer was a thing of the past. Given that the Mass's true provenance is that of a private salon or chapel, to be performed by hand-picked singers before a select and discriminating audience, there is little wonder that it has met with only moderate success in more recent times: a comment as much on changed social priorities as on the music itself.

The Mass was first heard on 14 March, 1864 at a private dedication of the Pillet-Will chapel. The four soloists, supplemented by eight singers from the Conservatoire hand-picked by Auber, were the Marchisio sisters, Italo Gardoni and the Belgian bass, Louis Agniez. Rossini stood by one of the pianists, Georges Mathias, giving the tempi and turning the pages. The audience was small and select: Auber, the inevitable Carafa, Meyerbeer, and Thomas were among those present. The second performance, which Rossini appears not to have attended, drew a larger and even more socially desirable audience. Meyerbeer came a second time and was again so effusive that Rossini was all solicitation: 'Will his health permit these emotions?' he worriedly asked when he heard of Meyerbeer's state. It was a prudent enquiry; seven weeks later Meyerbeer was dead.

The death of Meyerbeer on 2 May, 1864 moved Rossini to write what is in some ways a poignant coda to the Mass, his 'Quelques mesures de chant funèbre: à mon pauvre ami Meyerbeer'.[11] It is written for four-part male chorus accompanied by nothing more than a series of sombre taps and rolls on a drum. The light march rhythm, the text's gentle rhetoric which might sound trite in another language but which is lofty enough in French ('Pleure, pleure, muse sublime'), the simple declamation, the fine part-writing, the limpid

[11] In *Morceaux réservés;* QR vii, 84.

modulations, and the hieratic calm of the twice-uttered closing 'Requiem', pitching lower, all make for something which is exquisite, touching, perfectly judged. Meyerbeer's nephew is also said to have written a funeral march in his uncle's honour. 'Excellent', observed Rossini, inspecting the piece, 'but wouldn't it have been better if you had died and your uncle had written the march?'. True or not, it is a story Verdi enjoyed recounting.

The Mass had added yet more lustre to Rossini's name and he was increasingly honoured at home and abroad. In the summer of 1864 he was made a *grand officier* of the Légion d'honneur by Napoleon III; at the same time there were junketings at Pasy in honour of his name-day. Pesaro, too, was *en fête*, but by now wild horses could not have dragged Rossini back to his native land.

17

Last years (1865–8)

Apart from some smaller pieces quietly crafted for the *samedi soirs*, the *Petite messe solennelle* was indeed the last substantial sin of Rossini's old age. His desire to have the work sung in church led him into correspondence with Liszt, who had taken minor orders of the Catholic church in 1864, and, via Ferrucci, with Pope Pius IX. Rossini's request was the revocation of the Papal bull forbidding mixed choirs in church, a tradition deriving not so much from St Paul (1 *Corinthians* xiv.34 is concerned with woman in charismatic assemblies) as from St Jerome and other influential anti-feminists in and fourth and fifth centuries. A lover of castrato purity and women's voices, Rossini found boys' voices 'sour and out of tune'. The Pope's reply, when it came, was full of gracious platitudes but disobligingly failed to mention the question of the bull. The idea of the Swan of Pesaro taking on the Vatican had the international press by the ears; but though he promised further initiatives, Rossini never saw the matter through to a satisfactory conclusion.

By and large, Rossini was unsuccessful in the initiatives of his later life. In earlier years he had been disingenuous but shrewd in his dealings with governments, impresarios, and singers. Now he was either inept or too fond and sentimental. The notorious Broglio affair, a sad episode in the last months of Rossini's life, arose from his all too enthusiastic response to a letter from Florence's Minister of Public Education, Emilio Broglio. Ostensibly the letter proposed the setting up of a Rossini Society; but in so doing it also proposed that the new Society would be responsible for what we would now call the privatization of some of Italy's leading musical conservatories whose funds would be henceforward directed through non-government channels. Broglio's letter, rambling and obsequious, was to be brilliantly parodied by Boito,[1] who at least injected a degree of humour into a controversy which fired many, Verdi among

[1] *Il Pungolo*, 2 May, 1868.

them, to extreme anger. When Rossini realised what he had done, he wrote to Rossi (a letter subsequently released to the press)[2] affirming his support for the conservatories, as well as re-stating some of his old preoccupations, 'Simple Melody – clear Rhythm', and his distrust of the 'new philosophers' whose music lacked 'ideas, inspiration'.

Rossini's fondness, his touching concern for one or two musicians to whom he became a kind of surrogate father, is best seen in his long and buoyant correspondence with Michael (later Sir Michael) Costa who ruled the London musical roost for well over forty years. In 1865, Rossini gave Costa unavailing support and encouragement for his oratorio *Naaman*:

> My dearest Son,
> Just a few lines to convey my Joy at being able to embrace your good Brother and at his bringing me the oratorio (which has so augmented your Fame), together with your letter. The promises that you make me in it are true Balsam to my Paternal Heart. Continue then in this Oratorical Speciality of yours and write a third one, in the certainty that *Trinum est perfectum*. Choose a good subject, work on it without a word to anyone, and if you are satisfied with your work, in three years' time, and *not before*, let it see the light. Three years are needed to confirm the fame of your *Naaman*, otherwise, as proverb says, one will smash the other! It is not given to us to change the nature of Swinish Humanity! I have a friend who knows English well and who will help me to read your *Naaman*. As you can well believe, the feeling that predominates in such reading is not mere Curiosity but rather true Joy, for him who will always be glad to be able to call himself
> Your affectionate Father,
> ROSSINI.[3]

A plan to tie in the French *première* of *Naaman* with the opening of a new concert hall in the rue Scribe came to nothing, though Rossini's letters on the subject are long, detailed, and enthusiastic. Rossini had more success with Costa's gifts of English cheeses, *lo Stilton* as well as Cheddar:

---

[2] LdR, pp.325–7; Rognoni pp.329–31. Lauro Rossi (1812–85) was Director of the Milan Conservatory.
[3] MMR, p.208.

The cheese sent me would be worthy of a Bach, a Handel, a Cimarosa, let alone the old man of Pesaro! For three consecutive days I tasted it and moistened it with the best wines in my cellar . . . and I swear I never ate better food than your Chedor Chiese (cursed be the Brittanic Spelling!)[4]

In December 1866 Rossini had some kind of stroke or thrombosis but he survived well enough to be able to receive the many greetings and honours lavished on him the following February, his 75th birthday. A year later, on 10 February, 1868 he was similarly fêted on the occasion of what the management of the Paris Opéra claimed to be the 500th performance of *Guillaume Tell*. The soirées continued, and Olympe went on masterminding his life with her usual rigour. When Ricordi appeared one day with some royalties secured under a new legal agreement, Rossini dropped the money into a drawer. 'Pocket money,' he murmured, conspiratorially. His last official public compositions were no more distinguished than earlier ones had been; the hymn 'Dieu tout puissant'[5] first heard at the Palais de l'Industrie on 1 July, 1867 drew criticism and another highly partial defence by Olympe. Rossini was less sanguine, claiming that the piece was written to be sung *en famille* (*sic*) in his garden in Passy. 'What could I do?' he asked. 'I was asked to write it and couldn't refuse.' It was not his last official offering. In 1868 King Victor Emanuel II nominated Rossini as a Grand Knight of the Order of the Crown of Italy; Rossini's response was a fanfare for military band, including saxophones. As things turned out, the piece was not played until ten years after Rossini's death; its first performance took place in Rome on 25 November, 1878 played by seven massed bands and a contingent of thirty additional drummers, an act of musical supererogation if ever there was one.

In the early part of 1868 Rossini was unwell with severe catarrh and a general malaise brought upon him by the winter weather; but the summer had greatly cheered him. In early August he was able to write a generous and witty letter to a young man, Costantino Dall'Argine, who proposed to dedicate to Rossini his new setting of Sterbini's libretto for *Il barbiere di Siviglia*![6] Later the same month he wrote a long and wide-ranging letter on music and musical aesthetics

[4] ibid.
[5] *Hymne à Napoléon III et à son vaillant peuple*; QR xii, 21.
[6] LdR, pp.328–9.

to the critic and Wagner apologist, Filippo Filippi,[7] in which for the last time Rossini reaffirmed the classical virtues of the early *ottocento* style, adding for good measure a famous maxim:

Tous les genres sont bons,
Hors le genre ennuyeux.

All genres are good,
Except the boring one.

At the start of the winter season, he was well enough to attend a soirée on 26 September, but within a month he was seriously ill. A rectal fistula was identified and an operation deemed necessary, problematic for a man of Rossini's age. The first of what were to be two operations took place on 3 November. It was cancer. Nowadays doctors would no doubt administer a massive sedative and wait for the end; for poor Rossini, though, whose life had been bedevilled by the incompetence and inexperience of doctors, it was a matter of lingering for over a week in the most abject circumstances. Reluctant to agree to the administration of the last rites, he was eventually prevailed upon to receive a visit from the Abbé Gallet. 'If I had dealt only with French priests,' he murmured diplomatically, 'I would have been a practising Christian.' But he was Catholic enough to call out to the Blessed Virgin in the seemingly endless watches of the night, and shortly before his death he received extreme unction. Alboni, Tamburini, and Patti were at Passy at the time; Patti was said to have been more than usually distressed. Rossini's last recorded utterance was the name of the woman who had cared unstintingly for him over a period of more than thirty years, though he was also heard to murmur the names of Santa Maria and Sant'Anna, a last fleeting thought, perhaps, for his beloved mother. He died at 11.15 p.m. on Friday, 13 November, 1868.

The obsequies were predictably lavish. Over four thousand mourners attended his funeral in Paris and his works, sacred and profane, were revived in a host of memorial concerts throughout the world. Verdi proposed that the leading Italian composers of the day should contribute movements to a Requiem Mass in honour of their great predecessor and that it should have its *prima* in Bologna, 'Rossini's

[7] ibid., pp.329–33; Rognoni pp.333–6.

real musical homeland', in the church of San Petronio. But the powers-that-be in Bologna would have none of it; Rossini's 'city of assassins' had the last word.

Rossini left an estate which would today be valued in hundreds of thousands, distributed according to his will of 5 July, 1858 to which numerous codicils had been added. After small bequests to members of his family in Pesaro and Bologna, the bulk of the estate was left, for the perpetuity of her life, to Olympe 'to whose merit every praise would be inferior'. In a codicil of 15 June, 1865 Olympe was also entrusted with all Rossini's unpublished music (including most of the *Péchés de vieillesse*) and his autograph manuscripts. After Olympe's death the estate was to pass to the Commune of Pesaro for the founding and endowing of a Liceo Musicale. This was duly done and the new Liceo opened on 5 November, 1882. Rossini also left enough money for the building of a home for retired operatic performers in Paris, the Maison de Retraite Rossini.

Initially, Rossini was buried in the Père-Lachaise cemetery in Paris but it was inevitable that plans would be set in train for a re-burial in the church of Santa Croce in Florence. At first, Olympe insisted that she, too, should be interred in the same place. The suggestion scandalized the Italians, not least Verdi, and she later relented with a melancholy grace. 'After the removal of my husband's mortal remains to Florence,' she wrote 'I shall remain there [in the cemetery of Père-Lachaise] alone. I make this sacrifice in all humility; I have been glorified enough by the name I bear. My faith and my religious feelings give me the hope of a reunion which escapes earth.'

Though she suffered considerable privations in the Paris Commune of 1870, Olympe survived in all her mingled grandeur and oddity until 1878. A letter survives in which she writes to Romanina Castellani:

> My dear,
> I expect all three of you to dine with me tomorrow, the 9th. It is hot; I am stupid as a goose but my heart is as warm as a duck for you and for my Castellani.
> Your old,
> O. Rossini[8]

[8] MMR, p.147.

She died on 22 March, 1878. Nine years later, on 2 May, 1887, Rossini's body was ceremonially laid to rest in Santa Croce, though it was not until June 1902 that the famous memorial was erected. On the cartouches at the foot of the memorial are the words 'Pesaro – Firenze – Parigi', a slight to Bologna and to Naples and another of those pieces of misinformation which have done so much to obscure a proper assessment of the life and achievement of this complex, generous, and prodigiously talented man.

18

Entr'acte: some problems of approach to the works

The decline in the popularity of Rossini's operas which Chorley had noted as early as the 1840s was followed after Rossini's death by a decline in his overall reputation and in the care shown by musicians and critics for his work. Though the reputation of *Il barbiere di Siviglia* continued to soar, much else of quality was lost to the general view. One of the first to notice the change was Wagner, whose own work had done much to bring about the new aesthetic priorities of the 1870s. Having met Rossini in Paris in 1860 and, years earlier, studied his music with evident interest, Wagner was intelligently aware of the gap between the real Rossini and the careless, sceptical fellow characterized by what Wagner called 'the gaping herd of parasites and punsters' who surrounded him in his later years. In a fine posthumous tribute,[1] Wagner notes that Rossini was as important to his age, the Italian *ottocento*, as Palestrina, Bach, and Mozart were to theirs; yet Rossini's star will remain obscured, he suggests, until historical and musical perspectives on the early years of the nineteenth century are properly re-established. 'Our age boasts progress in the arts', Wagner observed, 'but neglects to note the downfall of an earlier refinement'.

It has taken the best part of a hundred years for those historical and musical perspectives to be restored; and even now general awareness of what Rossini was about remains limited. The low-point in the understanding of Rossini can be traced from the 1880s to the outbreak of World War I. Fed on a diet of Victorian performances of the *Stabat mater* and pier-end renditions of the more popular overtures, George Bernard Shaw was able to declare on the occasion of the centenary of Rossini's birth that he was 'one of the greatest masters of claptrap that ever lived';[2] and Ernest Newman

[1] R. Wagner *Eine Erinnerung an Rossini*, 1868; *Richard Wagner's Prose Works*, ed. and trans. W.A. Ellis, London, 1895, iv, pp.269–74.
[2] *Illustrated London News*, 5 Mar, 1892.

was later to write in a similar vein, unworthily so given his position as editor of Chorley's works. In the 1920s, partially helped perhaps by the emergence of a new neo-classical school, Rossini's reputation took a turn for the better and was immeasurably enhanced by the publication between 1927 and 1929 of Radiciotti's great three-volume study of his life and works. A milestone in Rossini scholarship, though sadly a limited edition and never translated, it generated some useful literature: in England, Lord Derwent's *Rossini and some Forgotten Nightingales*, in Italy Roncaglia's *Rossini l'olimpico*. Radiciotti's work was also drawn upon by Francis Toye for his affable *Rossini: a study in tragi-comedy*, a less good book than Derwent's but one which has been in print for sufficiently long periods to take on the air of a standard work despite its cavalier dismissal of a significant portion of Rossini's output. Rossini's cause was also taken up, though in a damagingly equivocal way, by the English critic, Edward J. Dent. Dent had a larger scholarly reputation than Toye and had taken the trouble to inspect editions of some of Rossini's lesser known works. Generous to *Guillaume Tell*, bound to acknowledge the merits of *Il barbiere di Siviglia* and *La Cenerentola*, and shrewd enough to see possibilities in *La gazza ladra*, Dent was none the less happy to dismiss *Mosè in Egitto* and *Semiramide* as 'hopelessly artificial and unreal'. As for earlier Rossini 'it may be dismissed as dead and buried', Dent averred in lectures delivered at Cornell University in 1937–8 and reprinted by the Cambridge University Press in 1976.[3] Such superficially informed half-truths, authoritatively stated, did as much to poison Rossini's reputation with the wider public as did the increasing scarcity of singers capable of coping with Rossini's more elaborate vocal writing.

A good deal of anti-Rossini rhetoric is based on premises which are clearly questionable. Let us take, for instance, the question of self-borrowing. In Anglo-Saxon countries self-borrowing is often represented as something intrinsically dishonest, when the real issue is not the fact of the self-borrowing (raw material is not *per se* good or bad, proper or improper) but the manner of the re-working and the efficacy, or otherwise, of the result. Like many of his seventeenth- and eighteenth-century predecessors, Rossini was a regular

---

[3] Edward J. Dent, *The Rise of Romantic Opera*, Cambridge, 1976, p.118; his point is refuted by Winton Dean in an editorial footnote.

self-borrower, the cues for which are not difficult to trace: a sudden, urgent commission, or an understandable desire to rescue from probable obscurity a particularly promising idea. Only when the Critical Edition is further advanced than is currently the case will we be able to examine the full range of techniques used by Rossini in the self-borrowing process. Some of his self-borrowings and substitutions are cynically done; but what can be already deduced from available examples, some of which will be cited in the chapters which follow, is the care with which he invariably applied himself to matching old formulas to new compositions. His adaptive skills, like his harmonic skills, are as extensive as they are unassuming: fine examples, as often as not, of the art which disguises art.

But the old assumptions – that self-borrowing is a sign of congenital laziness, that speed of composition implies glibness of spirit – die hard; as does the use of terminology which is misleadingly loose. Musical and literary terminology needs to be clarified if we are to achieve a proper understanding of Rossini's formal mastery or his skills in handling the complex array of theatrical genres – *buffa, seria, semiseria* – available to him. Above all, knowledge needs to be extended. Problems inevitably arise and issues become blurred – Rossini's treatment of texts, his relationship to his immediate predecessors – when it is learned that so successful a piece as *L'italiana in Algeri* is a musical setting of a second-hand libretto previously set by Luigi Mosca in 1808. In fact, several of Rossini's most successful works adapt or appropriate known texts: not only *L'italiana in Algeri* but *Il barbiere di Siviglia* and *La Cenerentola* as well. The advantages of such an approach are manifold. With the text known in advance or already actively contemplated, Rossini was able to concentrate his attention on formulating specifically musical answers to the problems and opportunities afforded by the text. The difference between Rossini's *L'italiana in Algeri* and Mosca's is the superior quality of the internal musical organization of Rossini's score. Working under pressure but thinking in an intelligent and original way, Rossini was able to emulate Mozart in making form a potent force in the comic method. As we shall see in Chapter 22, Rossini's attention to word-pointing, rhythmic characterization, and orchestration, as well as the new formal ordering undreamt of by Mosca, are central to the work's success. (A success which producers would do well to note; the best jokes in Rossini are the musical ones.) It is also clear that Rossini's need – in the case of *L'italiana in Algeri* –

to use an extant text allowed him to approach it with a degree of detachment which, in turn, helps to explain the persistent play of irony in the music, not least in those passages where the librettist's characters assume heroic or sentimental postures.

Much more work needs to be done on Rossini's librettos and his librettists, if only to get us away from the erroneous idea that Rossini 'lacked literary taste and was a poor judge of a dramatic text'.[4] True, there is no partnership in Rossini's career to compare with that of Da Ponte and Mozart, Boito and Verdi, or Hofmannsthal and Strauss. (The relationship with Luigi Lechi promised well but was short-lived.) On the other hand, we know that Rossini himself invariably chose, advised on, or emended the texts which he set. The evidence we have suggests an alert and engaged mind, whilst the range of subjects he essayed is striking: librettos derived from Racine, Voltaire, Beaumarchais, Schiller, and Scott, alongside some skilful appropriation of fairy-tale and Biblical mythology. Occasionally bold initiatives seriously misfired; the first two acts of *Otello* are a disgrace, though the third is a thing of genius, the act's shape and some of its content certainly determined by Rossini himself. It would be wrong, of course, to claim intrinsic literary merit in the work of such Rossini regulars as Rossi and Tottola. But the true test of a musical text is its appropriateness to musical setting; and here Rossini's judgement was far from flawed.

On the matter of 'comic' and 'tragic' modes in Rossini's music, and his seemingly indiscriminate stylistic commuting between the two, a major misunderstanding has arisen. Those who would argue as Dent has done that Rossini 'makes no attempt to distinguish between the serious style and the comic'[5] have a problem on their hands; for, as the late Professor Joad would have said, it all depends on what you mean by 'comic' and 'serious'. In the chapters which follow, and more particularly in the chapters on *Tancredi* and *Guillaume Tell*, it will be one of my concerns to define the nature of Rossini's 'serious' art – its heroic, idyllic character – whilst at the same time stressing the importance of those stylistic features which the *seria, semiseria,* and *buffa* genres have in common. Rossini's natural medium was comedy and though there is some veering away from the mode in the late Neapolitan works – in *Ermione* and in

[4] *The New Oxford History of Music,* London, VIII, 1982, p.406.
[5] Dent, op. cit., p.117.

Maometto II as well as in the earlier *Otello* – his prevailing image is
what Susanne Langer has called the image of 'human vitality holding
its own in the world amid the surprises of unplanned coincidence'.[6]
Communal, invigorating, concerned with continuity rather than
with change and thus precluding the need to search out the inner lives
of individual characters, the comic spirit, which embraces *Guillaume
Tell* as surely as it embraces *Il barbiere di Siviglia*, is the one which is
most consistently explored by Rossini in his work. Indeed, there is a
measure of wholeness about his work, a degree of inner consistency,
previously unperceived by those whose approach to his music has
been either partial or piecemeal. With that in mind we can now
examine the opus as a whole.

[6] Langer, op. cit., p.331.

19

The early operas

Demetrio e Polibio – La cambiale di matrimonio – L'equivoco stravagante – L'inganno felice – Ciro in Babilonia

Rossini's graceful, vivacious manner and his acute ear for idiosyncratic phrasing and movement are everywhere apparent in his six *sonate a quattro* of 1804. We do not know precisely when he first attempted to translate these precocious skills into operatic form, taking them into his mother's world of stage-play and song, but there is evidence that he might have done so as early as 1803. It was a piecemeal process at first and remained so two or three years later when the Mombelli family commissioned settings which would emerge in the fulness of time as *Demetrio e Polibio*, Rossini's first complete opera, though not his first to be staged. It is doubtful whether Padre Mattei would have approved of much of the music. The overture, which has some accomplished solo woodwind writing, is so badly assembled that when the publisher Diabelli, greedy for anything Rossinian, published it in piano reduction in Vienna in the 1820s, he restructured parts of it, tidying up the second subject group and writing a more formally correct recapitulation.[1]

Though unsatisfactory in most respects, the piecemeal commissioning of items for *Demetrio e Polibio* must have alerted Rossini to the fact that contemporary Italian operas could be little more than an inert procession of bespoke set-piece compositions lacking any real sense of the need for that dramatic tension and dramatic continuity which larger forms confer. Rossini would continue to write set-piece arias in later years, but under his innovative genius forms would become more dynamic, longer-breathed, more richly elaborated. *Demetrio e Polibio* is not, however, all loss. Flawed though the libretto is, it has the merit of drawing on that general stock of tales in which royalty, parenthood, and young love are suggestively present.

---

[1] See Philip Gossett, 'The Overtures of Rossini', *19th-Century Music*, iii (1979–80), p.16.

The opera's title refers not to the young lovers but to their fathers, the kings of Syria and Parthia. As is often the case in fairy-tale, they are radically opposed in temperament. The kindlier Polibio is a father twice over: father to his daughter, Lisinga, and adopted father to her lover, Siveno, the estranged son of Demetrio now living in the Parthian court. Demetrio, by contrast, is very much the villain of the piece. Turning up in disguise, he demands Siveno's return to Syria and becomes aggressive when Siveno is reluctant to obey. Demetrio's seizing of Lisinga and Polibio's tit for tat arrest of Siveno precipitates the opera's one moment of genuine confrontation and the famous quartet 'Donami ormai Siveno' which is notable not only for the melodic charm of Lisinga's *Andante giusto* 'Padre, qual gioia prova' but for the urgent chromatic writing Rossini provides for her in the quartet's opening movement. Generally speaking, the opera's set pieces are undistinguished, with Rossini understandably tentative about characterization and motivation in the drama. The highlight of the score is the duet 'Questo cor ti giura amore' during which the lovers pledge themselves before the high altar. It is a classic Rossini melody (Ex.1) announced in thirds after a rapt, horn-led introduction.

Ex.1

He was to redeploy the melody on several subsequent occasions. And no wonder, for it is an early example of Rossini at his most sensuously beguiling, a touchstone for those hedonists and ur-romantics who see Rossini, in Peter Conrad's formulation, ministering to 'the delicious idleness of private life, the dreamy connoisseurship of sensation'.[2]

There are some comparable moments in *La cambiale di matrimonio* – the *Andante* of Fanny's 'Vorrei spiegarvi il giubilo' is a case in point – but in his first fully-fledged public commission Rossini is more the bright schoolboy than the man of sentiment. Like many libretti provided for Rossini or knowingly chosen by him, this one had a previous record. Carlo Coccia, a Paisiello pupil, had set a

[2] Conrad, op.cit., p.12.

similar version of Federici's original play in Rome in 1807.[3] The story is an early attempt to make sport of the American in Europe, in this instance the egregious Slook who comes to purchase a wife from Tobias Mill, the English merchant whose hard-headed commitment to the law of supply and demand allows him to trade his daughter, Fanny, on much the same terms as he trades his other merchandise. The libretto makes nothing of the international theme. Slook, who turns out to have a heart of gold, is merely outwitted by Fanny, her penniless lover, Edoardo (*sic*) Milfort, and their far from intimidating servants, Norton and Clarina.

Throughout the score we are aware of Rossini's extraordinary energy, something which manifests itself in the overture, a somewhat disingenuous revision of the E flat overture written in Bologna in 1809, and in the many motivating rhythmic figures and soaring wind solos. 'Rather faceless' is Gossett's judgement on some of the motifs, and it is true that they turn up, in person or in mutated forms, in all the early operas. Rognoni's 'gossiping themelets' is perhaps a more engaging way of describing them. Whatever the terminology, it is worth noting the care with which Rossini handles his material at nodal points in the comedy. As portraits of American businessmen go, Slook is no Lambert Strether, but Rossini shades and shapes the musical portrait with intelligence and delight. Slook's entry into the Mill household is rich in new world decorum, something which Rossini reciprocates (Ex.2) with an orchestral accompaniment which is both witty and generous. But it is an altogether cheekier Slook (Ex.3) who announces to an astonished Tobias Mill that the long-suffering Fanny is to be made over to Edoardo as part of a generous deed of gift.

We recognize in such moments the inventiveness and fantasy which Rossini was already bringing to the task of revitalizing and refurbishing the *buffo* traditions of the *settecento*. And there is sentiment, too. The duet 'Tornami a dir che m'ami' is eloquently launched by Edoardo and met by Fanny with an elaborate web of vocal sound which in no way clogs or obscures the limpidity of the original idea. Her 'Vorrei spiegarvi il giubilo' is also crammed with invention, not least in the quicker outer movements which predict Rosina in *Il*

---

[3] See Francesco Cacaci, '*La cambiale di matrimonio* da Federici a Rossi', BdCRdS, 1975, 1–2, p.22.

EX.2

Ex 3

barbiere di Siviglia. Newly emancipated from academic study, Rossini was clearly determined to make his mark.

La cambiale di matrimonio will be seen as a characteristic beginning by those who regard Rossini primarily as a composer of *opera buffa*. His next three operas, though, take us swiftly into genres which were no less central to his development, not least the mixed *semiseria* genre to which *L'equivoco stravagante* and *L'inganno felice* – precursors of works like *La gazza ladra, Matilde di Shabran*, and, in parts, *La Cenerentola* – clearly belong.

L'equivoco stravagante, a two act *dramma giocoso*, is a remarkably ambitious piece. Its length (nearly 300 pages in the Ricordi vocal score of *c.*1850), the importance given to ensemble writing over solos and *secco recitative*, the stylistic range, and the musical acumen all suggest that Rossini was determined to do something of note for his first professional engagement in Bologna. Sadly, the libretto was *risqué* enough to offend the Bologna police. The opera was taken off after three performances and though three numbers, somewhat ironically, were later to have religious texts added to them, the opera has been more or less forgotten ever since. The story, hardly shocking to modern taste, concerns the young, impoverished Ermanno and his clandestine love for Ernestina, the literature-loving daughter of a *nouveau riche* farmer called Gamberotto. Unhappily for Ermanno, both Gamberotto and his daughter are much taken with a poseur called Buralicchio, described in the cast list as 'young, rich, and stupid'. To scare off the fop, Ermanno and a pair of unusually astute servants dream up the idea of telling him that Ernestina is a boy: a castrato and, a problem in 1812, an army deserter. On the strength of these ingenious slanders and some improbable dramatic developments, Ernestina is eventually arrested, only to be freed by Ermanno who ceases to be her tutor and becomes her husband.

From the outset, we are aware of the scope of Rossini's invention in this opera. Pastoral, burlesque, buffo, and romantic elements are disarmingly mixed. The opera's opening is charmingly pastoral. Ermanno's 'Si cela in quelle mura' occupies musical ground which years later will be appropriated by Mascagni in the cherry duet from *L'amico Fritz*. Typically, 'Si cela in quelle mura' is not a closed *cavatina* but a stalking horse for a brilliant Trio for Ermanno and the two servants, a *buffo* ensemble with quicksilver string writing whose phrase ends curl upwards in a characteristically Rossinian ironic grimace. The opening scenes thus establish the pastoral-comic mood. The formal *cavatinas* for Gamberotto and Buralicchio are not so interesting, but the duet between the two men with its preface of fanfaring horns, is a fine piece of musical burlesque, full of absurd syllabic and melismatic stutterings. Provided a full text is played, Ernestina has several sides to her personality: the charming *ingénue* of her *cavatina*, the shrewish heroine (her Act 2 duet with Buralicchio), and the glittering warrior in *marziale* mood. What is also striking about the opera is the frequency and length of the ensembles, notably 'Ti presento a un tempo istesso' in Act 1 and the Act 2 Quintet 'Spera se vuoi, ma taci', with its long and impassioned tenor line. Some of the *stretti* have a rhythmic virulence which anticipates later, better known Rossini. There is no extant overture to *L'equivoco stravagante*. The nineteenth-century Ricordi edition unblushingly prints the overture to *Il barbiere di Siviglia*, a stylistic impossibility given the state of development of the Rossini overture in 1811. If a curtain-raiser is needed for this opera, the overture to *La cambiale di matrimonio* is as good as any from the period before 1812–13.

If *L'equivoco stravagante* was compromised by official interference and public indifference, *L'inganno felice*, first performed in Venice on 8 January, 1812, was an instant success. Within a year of the *prima* it had been revived in Venice and given new productions in Bologna, Florence (twice), Verona, and Trieste. It would feature in Rossini's opening seasons in Naples in 1815 and in Paris in 1824, and it would also play in November 1822 during the preparations for the Congress of Verona. Its designation *farsa* is unduly limiting; *dramma semiserio* would be a more accurate description of a romantic melodrama which is only occasionally comic. The libretto again derives from an earlier model, Palomba's libretto for Paisiello's *L'inganno felice* (Naples, 1798) reshaped for Rossini by Giuseppe Foppa. Set in a seaside mining community, the drama is concerned with the discovery and rehabilitation of Isabella, Duke Bertrando's wronged and, so he thinks, long-dead wife. The villains of the piece, basses in an opera which asks for three basses in a cast of five, are Ormondo, a confidant of the Duke, and his henchman, Batone. It was Ormondo who years before had attempted to dispose of Isabella after she had refused his sexual advances. Floated out to sea, she survived long enough to be rescued by Tarabotta, the respected leader of the mining community (the third bass: Filippo Galli's part in the Venetian production). The arrival of the Duke, Ormondo, and Batone in the village where Isabella now mysteriously resides triggers an action which culminates in a spaciously conceived dénouement in which Tarabotta and the Duke (now no longer estranged from Isabella) set a night-time trap for Ormondo and Batone amid the mines and mining-galleries. Like the opera's overture, where formal ideas begin to settle and where for the first time Rossini tries out an embryonic crescendo, this final scene tentatively tests out structural ideas which Rossini was to stabilize and develop with remarkable speed over the months which followed. It is a movement rich in tension and mystery with moments of special eloquence, not least the entry of the Duke (Ex.4) where both the vocal writing and orchestral colouring predict that most exquiste of night-time trysts, the Trio in Act 2 of *Le Comte Ory*.

Ex.4

Even more commanding in its melodic reach is Isabella's music. Her cavatina, 'Perchè dal tuo seno', has a quality of chastened sadness about it, and it is Isabella's anguished pleading which gives dramatic presence to the Trio, partially borrowed from *L'equivoco stravagante*, 'Quel sembiante, quello sguardo'. Her second aria, 'Al più dolce e caro oggetto', has a complex history,[4] but its quality is unmistakable; its range, both vocal and emotional, is remarkable. The *buffo* elements in the opera are reserved for the villains, and for Tarabotto himself when he and Batone try unsuccessfully to find out what the other knows about the girl in their F major duet 'Va taluno mormorando'. This is an excellent early example of the conspiratorial buffo duet in which words are subject to manic repetition and where the music reproduces the gossipy lunacy ('Oh, che ciarle, che pazzie') with repetitions and alliterations of its own. After numbers like these, it is not difficult to see why *L'inganno felice* was such a success; there is something in it for everyone. What's more, it is the most precisely crafted of all the *farse* before *Il Signor Bruschino*; among the early one-acters *L'inganno felice* is the one in which Rossini is most obviously emulating the clarity and expressive elegance of the music of Cimarosa, Mozart, and Paisiello.

Incongruously, the overture to *L'inganno felice* was pressed into service for Rossini's next opera, *Ciro in Babilonia*. This is Rossini's version of Belshazzar's Feast and his first attempt to write a semi-sacred piece designed to skirt round the regulations governing the use of theatres during Lent. The feast itself gives individuality to a libretto which in most respects conforms closely to a series of melodramatic plot and character archetypes which we shall encounter in several operas up to and including *Ermione*, where a tyrannic king will again threaten a grieving woman and use her young son as a helpless pawn in an ugly game of sexual politics. In *Ermione* it is Pyrrhus (Pirro) who is the tyrant; in *Ciro in Babilonia* it is Belshazzar (Baldassarre) himself, a difficult part, written for Ivanoff's teacher, Eliodoro Bianchi, in which megalomaniac fury is often expressed in writing which taxes the singer, dissipates the tension, and leaves the audience untouched. Rossini has a long way to travel to the declamatory simplicity of the best of Pyrrhus's part. Predictably, Rossini is more at home in the choruses – one of which sketches out for us the shape of Almaviva's 'Ecco ridente' – and in the writing for Amira, wife of the Persian king, Ciro, whose attempts to release his wife and son from captivity result in his own imprisonment and Belshazzar's gloating pursuit of Amira. The young Rossini would have little difficulty in writing Amira's two sweet-sounding, sweetly accompa-

---

[4] See Gossett, pp.172–80.

nied arias, 'Vorrei veder lo sposo'[5] and her prayer, 'Deh, per me non v'affligate'. What is more interesting is the opera's penultimate scene where Ciro, condemned to death and on his way to a public execution, takes leave of his family. It is a scene ('Ti abbraccio, ti stringo') of unusual though not surprising eloquence. Just as in later years the scene of the apple in *Guillaume Tell* would draw from Rossini writing inspired in part by his own familial affections and preoccupations, so here one senses that the subject has touched him deeply. Drawing on material first used in *Demetrio e Polibio*, he assembles a scene which alone should have denied the work its status as *fiasco*. The banquet scene in which Amira is prepared for marriage to Belshazzar is also strikingly handled, Rossini's first essay in stylized storm music driving home the fact that, in every sense, the writing is on the wall for the tyrant king. 'God has numbered the days of your kingdom,' Belshazzar is told by the prophet Daniel, 'and brought it to an end; you have been weighed in the balance and found wanting, and your kingdom has been divided and given to the Medes and the Persians.' In Rossini's *azione sacra*, the prophet has his own brief scene in which to deliver the message to an astounded assembly. Certainly, there are many striking moments in this score which suggest that it deserves better than to be remembered as the work in which Ferrara's *seconda donna*, Anna Savinelli, inspired Rossini to write an *aria del sorbetto* ('Chi disprezza gli infelici') on a single repeated B flat – though it was with such tales of youthful bravado that Rossini was later able to brush aside the disappointments of the early years in which flawed but potentially productive pieces were so easily assigned to near oblivion.

La scala di seta – La pietra del paragone – L'occasione fa il ladro – Il Signor Bruschino

The next nine months, from the spring of 1812 to February 1813, would bring about a substantial change in Rossini's handling of musical forms. The principal work of this period of transition is *La pietra del paragone*, a full-dress *melodramma giocoso* written for La

---

[5] Reused in Act 2 of *Mosè in Egitto* for Amaltea.

Scala, Milan, in September, 1812, though Rossini consolidated and effectively concluded his career in *farsa* with three engaging one-acters: *La scala di seta*, *L'occasione fa il ladro*, and, finest of all perhaps, *Il Signor Bruschino*. The first of these, *La scala di seta*, is based on a libretto derived from F.-A.-E. Planard's *L'échelle de soie* for an opera (Paris 1808) by the French composer Pierre Gaveaux whose principal claim to fame must be his *fait historique, Léonore* (Paris 1798) in which Gaveaux himself sang the role of Florestan. Rossini's *farsa comica* is a diverting piece, freshly and fluently written, memorable more for Rossini's skill in ordering the comic mechanism (the rhythmic ordering, above all) than for anything especially striking in theme or harmony. It is a legitimate response to Planard's entertainment which offers us a variation on the familiar story of the secret marriage. In this instance, Giulia is secretly married to Dorvil in spite of her guardian's wish that she should marry Dorvil's friend, a young army officer called Blansac. The only way out of Giulia's dilemma is for her to encourage Blansac and her cousin Lucilla to fall in love, a ruse which is eventually brought to fruition after a bevy of overheard conversations, whispered meetings, and an elaborate use of closets, screens, and the eponymous silken ladder. As befits farce, the characters in *La scala di seta* have minimal interior lives. There is little that is remarkable or touching about the delayed *cavatinas* of either Giulia or Dorvil. In a work notable for the sharpness of its rhythms, Lucilla's blithe and folksy 'Sento talor nell'anima', later redrafted as the gipsy chorus at the start of *Il turco in Italia*, is the more typical piece. If Rossini is interested in anyone, it is in the woozy old retainer, the opera's *basso buffo*, Germano. His duet with Giulia, 'Io so c'hai buon core', effectively launches the plot, and in a memorable scene, 'Amore dolcemente', it is Germano, baffled, tired, and a little drunk, who drifts the music into somnolence before Blansac arrives to trigger the elaborately plotted dénouement.

Rossini's next opera, *La pietra del paragone*, was first seen at La Scala, Milan, on 26 September, 1812. The libretto, by La Scala's resident librettist Luigi Romanelli, is cornucopian. Dramatically, it suffers from some otiose manoeuverings of plot but it proved to be a generally splendid vehicle for the 20-year-old Rossini. It allowed him space to show off to one of Italy's smartest audiences his skills as a wit, a man of sensibility, and a purveyor in music of the bustling, vituperative worlds of the fashionable society, the theatre, and the press. The story is set in the country house of the wealthy young Count Asdrubale. Amid elegant apartments, rustic arbours, and forest vistas, a house party is in progress. The guests include the heroine of the piece, the lovely and demure Marchesina Clarice (Marcolini's role), her frustrated admirer, the poet Giocondo, and a notable quartet of bores and imposters: the poetaster, Pacuvio, his escort, Donna Fulvia, and the journalist, Macrobio – 'incompetent, presumptuous, and venal' – with the Baroness Aspasia. Count Asdrubale is much taken with Clarice, and she with him; but she fears that in such company her affection for him will be thought mercenary and insincere. Happily for her, Asdrubale and his servant, Fabrizio, decide to test the guests' sincerity by announcing that Asdrubale has lost all his money, Asdrubale himself turning up in the guise of a foreign potentate to slap the famous seals ('Sigillara . . .') on the Count's possessions. Clarice, needless to say, remains loyal, but in an epilogue to the original plot she, too, is given the chance to test Asdrubale's good faith. Dressed, at Marcolini's particular request, as a Captain of the Hussars, she poses as Clarice's brother who has come to take her away from these 'ill-starr'd shores'. Asdrubale's response, 'Lasciami, amico, a qual destino in preda', is desperate enough to convince Clarice of the real depth of his feelings. Interestingly, the romantic lead, Asdrubale himself, is given not to a tenor but to a bass, Filippo Galli at the Milanese *prima*, with the tenor, the sympathetic Giocondo, reduced to the level of a carefully sketched *comprimario*.

La pietra del paragone is full of highlights, Rossini filling out Romanelli's spacious blueprint with music of unflagging vitality and endless invention. The first act is launched by a brilliant, large-scale ensemble for Asdrubale's guests during which Pacuvio's celebrated ditty 'Ombretta sdegnosa/Del Missipipì' is hinted at before it is winningly unfurled (Ex.5).

There are sober-minded souls who will think this trivial, with its jaunty folk rhythms and love of verbal nonsense; but, adapting Johnson on Garrick, we may safely say that the piece has contributed to the gaiety of nations and added to the public stock of harmless pleasure. As such it is quintessential Rossini. More sophisticated is Macrobio's long *buffo* piece on the power of the press, a disquisition by Italy's equivalent of Sheridan's Mr Puff. Stendhal, who knew a thing or two about journalists, describes Macrobio as 'an intriguer and a coward, and above all a *braggart*, spiteful but by no means

Ex.5

Allegretto
PACUVIO

Om bret - ta sde - gno - sa del Mis-si-si-pi pi pi pi

pi del Mis-si-si-pi Non far___ la - ri - tro - sa no

no ma re-staun po qui qui qui qui qui ma re-staun po qui.

foolish'.[1] The aria may lack the economy of Figaro's famous *cavatina*, but it has pace, variety, and a quality of bravura which very adequately conveys the time-honoured practices of media hacks. Rossini's inventive first act also contains moments of great lyric charm (Clarice's horn-accompanied echo duet with Count Asdrubale is the obvious highlight) and culminates in a finale of great reach and energy, the finest he ever wrote, avers Stendhal. Fulvia and Aspasia launch this superb movement by announcing the Count's sudden loss ('Oh, caso orribile!') with all the frenetic sweetness of the girls in *Così fan tutte*.

The second act begins with an ensemble built on the kind of subject Haydn liked to use in his more joky slow movements. There is also a richly-scored hunting chorus and a storm (the same storm that passes over Naples in Rossini's next opera and over Seville in *Il barbiere)* which catches the hapless Pacuvio out in the forest. Like Beethoven before him, Rossini uses the storm to effect a magical transition to pastoral quiet and a song, in this instance Giocondo's plaint to Clarice's beauty, 'Quell'alme pupille/Io serbo nel seno'. The Count's deception is eventually revealed. Donna Fulvia is entirely undismayed and reveals as much in a very brilliant *aria del sorbetto*. Macrobio is less fortunate. He is confronted by the Count and Giocondo and proves himself a veritable Aguecheek in the duel which follows, a fine Trio which Rossini liked well enough to offer to the Neapolitans in 1816 as part of *La gazzetta*. Clarice's additional appearance dressed as her soldier-brother, a re-run of Marcolini's

[6] VdR, p.93

travesti appearance as a boy soldier at the end of *L'equivoco stravagante*, was thought by Stendhal to be *de trop*, but it makes a generous end to an opera which, played with a full text, will always make a rich and diverting evening's entertainment.

L'occasione fa il ladro, written for the San Moisè, Venice, two months later, is shorter but it, too, has an added confidence and scope which must be derived in part from the experience of writing *La pietra del paragone* for Milan. It opens in a hostelry near Naples. A storm is raging, borrowed, it is true, from *La pietra del paragone* but now skilfully adapted as an allegro movement which, prefaced by a slow introduction, allows Rossini to dispense entirely with a formal overture. As the storm music dies away, we discover Don Parmenione, someone later described in an engaging short aria by his manservant, Martino, as an insolvent, egocentric, two-faced, wine-bibbing, womanizing man of the world. Also sheltering from the storm is Count Alberto, on his way to Naples to take delivery of his bride-to-be, Berenice, whom he has never met but whose portrait has been sent to him by the girl's obliging uncle. The part is nicely written for a well groomed *tenore di grazia*, though, with Don Parmenione and Martino in the company, his *cavatina* quickly becomes a drinking song. The plot thickens, and the opera gets its subtitle, *Il cambio della valigia*, when Alberto's comatose servant collects the wrong suitcase. Whilst Alberto is travelling to Naples with Don Parmenione's dirty washing, Parmenione and Martino are busy sifting through the Count's belongings. When money, papers, and the portrait of the beautiful Berenice are found there, Parmenione instantly resolves to make his way to Don Eusebio's house with every intention of passing himself off as Berenice's aristocratic husband-to-be. The scene ends with a sizzling *stretta*, rich in buzzing onomatopoeia, as Parmenione, and Rossini, whirl us off into a further hour of amorous intrigue.

Berenice's *cavatina* is typical early Rossini, simple and melodious, but equipped with a nagging chromatic tick which perfectly suggests a well-to-do young girl who fancies herself wronged by life. Resorting to the oldest ruse in the book, Berenice decides to test her lover's credibility by exchanging clothes with her servant, Ernestina. Two duets follow. First, Parmenione's encounter (Ex.6) with the elegantly attired Ernestina.

Where Parmenione stutters nervously in front of someone whom he takes to be a lady of quality, Alberto treats the maid-servant, the

Ex.6

disguised Berenice, with proper aristocratic condescension, a quality defined by Rossini in writing (Ex.7) whose elegance Donizetti will one day seek to emulate.

Ex.7

An ensemble develops which in a two-act opera would be the Act 1 finale: a moment of stasis as identities are pondered and emotions contained, followed by one of those Gadarene *stretti* during which the characters hurtle through what Rossini's librettist calls 'the dark and hideous vortex of misunderstanding'. In the opera's second half Berenice's lightening cross-examination of Parmenione is exceedingly brilliant and has the merit of unmasking the old adventurer; and such is the Count's attachment to the 'maid', he is happy to strike a bargain with Parmenione and allow him the 'lady' instead. At which point Rossini begins to build a substantial finale, launched with hushed accompanied recitative, in which Berenice imposes herself on the rival lovers with an unforseen authority. Touched by Alberto's sincerity but angered by the continuing confusion over his identity, she leads the ensemble through a slowly expanding series of movements to a *cabaletta* of considerable virulence. This emergence of Berenice as a decisive force both dramatically and musically interestingly confirms Rossini's growing predilection for showpiece solos as part of final movements.

Apart from *Adina* (1818), *Il Signor Bruschino*, written for Venice in January 1813, is the last of the Rossini *farse*, though the tradition it so robustly exploits is sustained in parts of Verdi's *Falstaff* and in Puccini's one-act comic masterpiece, *Gianni Schicchi* (14 Dec, 1918, New York). Foppa's libretto is again derived from a French source, *Le fils par hazard* (1809) by A. de Chazet and E.-T. Maurice Ourry. Three of the eight characters are stock figures: the two lovers, Sofia and Florville, and Sofia's guardian, Gaudenzio. Three more are peripheral; though two, the innkeeper, Filiberto, and the Commissioner of Police, are crucial witnesses to the astonishing act of impersonation which is the key to the plot. At the heart of the drama, giving it its special character and focus, are the Bruschinos, Signor Bruschino and his feckless, much talked of, and largely absent son. Young Bruschino is contracted to Sofia, though none of the parties has ever met. On his way to Gaudenzio's house, he has run up a huge bill at the local pub, has been detained by Filiberto, and has written a letter of apology to Gaudenzio. But it is Florville, posing as Bruschino, who presents the letter. By the time Bruschino-*padre* arrives everyone is convinced that Florville is the younger Bruschino, and Signor Bruschino is accounted a boor and a wretch when he vehemently denies the fact. Indeed, not only is he thought boorish to the point of insanity, his apoplectic behaviour brings him close to being so in reality.

From Bruschino's first fraught confrontation with Florville, the music has a toughness and angularity about it which must have shocked some contemporary ears. The *ostinato* figure underpinning Buschino's protestations in the Trio 'Per un figlia già pentito', is quite literally that: obstinate, bullish, grotesque, with Bruschino's grunts and groans, the cries of an exasperated animal, built by Rossini into a bizarre sonic mix. Later, as evidence piles on evidence, Bruschino is no more than a bear at the stake. The central movement, 'Ho la testa, o è andata via?', contains some of Rossini's most radical writing. At the height of his bemusement (Ex.8) Bruschino's vocal line advances in disjunct octave leaps, the orchestra cackles poisonously below, and Sofia's rejoinder – sensuous in G minor with upward-curving fifths and minor sixths – at once intensifies the mockery and points the pathos and the cruelty.

This mixing of sentiment and burlesque is typical of the score. Even Gaudenzio's big, free-wheeling *cavatina*, 'Nel teatro nel gran'

Ex.8

mondo', is darkened by an *a piacere* passage in which he bemoans his lack of success. The lie of the phrasing and the sombre harmonic movement create the impression of a man at odds with the world, like Verdi's Falstaff outside the Garter Inn in Act 3 or, grim irony, like Rossini himself in the gloom of the Florence years. There is sentiment and burlesque in the lovers' music, too. The love duet – by no means *de rigueur* in Rossinian comedy – derives from *Demetrio e Polibio* (Ex.1) but the most interesting writing comes during an interlude in the gulling of Bruschino. Sofia's 'Ah donate il caro sposo' is notable both for the expressive intricacy of the preceding recitative and for the use of the cor anglais. The instrument's plaintive colour is exactly right in this tense, edgy context. But, then, most of Rossini's effects in *Il Signor Bruschino* are nicely calculated, however bizarre. When young Bruschino finally appears at the end of the opera his plea for forgiveness is cast in the form of a quick, nervous minor key march, with the crucial word 'pentito' quickly robbed of its first syllable and turned into a gibbering act of childish self-abasement. At the end of the opera, Bruschino is able, briefly, to turn the tables on Gaudenzio by obliging him to accept Florville, the son of his old enemy, as Sofia's husband. Like Falstaff, Bruschino may have been duped, driven, and humiliated, but in the end the tables are turned, a fact which gives added piquancy and resonance to this rumbustious and often disturbing comedy.

20

Overtures

A remarkable feature of *Il Signor Bruschino* is its overture, a form with which Rossini had begun to experiment as early as 1806. From *Demetrio e Polibio* onwards, it was Rossini's habit, though not his invariable practice, to preface his operas with an overture. One of the most imposing of all his openings, the 'Scene of Shadows' in *Mosè in Egitto*, memorably banishes the form, neither inviting nor permitting any kind of intrusive preface. Indeed, in his Naples years Rossini often abandoned the earlier archetype or freely adapted it to include marches and choral movements: the lament for the fall of Troy heard off-stage before the curtain's rise in *Ermione* is an obvious and striking example. At other periods in his life, Rossini would assemble overtures imaginatively and pragmatically, as we have seen in the case of *L'occasione fa il ladro*, or cryptically, as he was to do to Berlioz's intense annoyance, in *Le Comte Ory*. And, of course, overtures were occasionally adapted and re-routed, to the great joy of the anti-Rossini brigade who – taking industry and indecision as an axiom of greatness – are fond of pointing to the fact that whereas Beethoven wrote four overtures for one opera, Rossini was capable of using one overture for three operas and would have probably used it for a fourth had the need arisen. Curiously, Beethoven's eventual solution to the *Fidelio* problem is a very Rossinian one: the rejection of symphonically conceived, thematically linked overtures and the substitution of a buoyant curtain-raiser, the kind of overture which Roncaglia in his book on Rossini aptly calls 'a musical visiting-card'. Simple practicality often resulted in overtures being written or substituted at the last minute. Overtures could be sight-read if necessary, singers' parts could not. And Rossini, like Beethoven, sometimes missed the first-night deadline. (The E major *Fidelio* Overture was first heard at the opera's second performance.) In fact, the overture to *Il barbiere di Siviglia*, first written for *Aureliano in*

Palmira and later re-used in slightly modified form for *Elisabetta, regina d'Inghilterra*, is curiously unrepresentative in two ways. In the first place music from the overture, including the whole of the *Andante maestoso*, recurs in the main body of the opera, a practice Rossini later criticized[1] even though he himself had adopted it in a number of operas. In the second place, no other Rossini overture was so obviously and extensively redeployed. Not that redeployment is unthinkable if an overture is intended to be no more than a curtain-raiser and when the music itself is in no sense programmatic. The *Andante maestoso* of the *Aureliano in Palmira* overture is sufficiently neutral to serve its several appointed functions, though the minor key wit of the first allegro subject (perhaps it is mere familiarity which prompts the idea) seems curiously well suited to its eventual resting-place as part of the overture to *Il barbiere di Siviglia*. Occasionally, overtures are not transferred by Rossini but elements within them are – *Il turco in Italia*, *Sigismondo*, and *Otello* all have material in common – a process begun in the years 1810–12[2] and made increasingly easy by Rossini's evolution of a method which confers autonomy on individual units within the structure.

In its stabilized form, the Rossini overture involves a slow introduction, first and second subjects, a recapitulation, and a coda. The whole thing is a functionally elegant scaling down of a classical sonata-form movement which Rossini proceeds to transform by the outstanding quality of his invention. George Bernard Shaw, no Rossini lover, commended the irresistible piquancy of the allegro subjects; but there is also the subtle drive of the rhythms, and the brilliance of the orchestration, not to mention the majesty and elegiac beauty of the melodies which Rossini often wrote for solo wind instruments in the central movement of the slow introduction. First subjects tend to be presented by the strings, though in *L'italiana in Algeri* it is the woodwinds which dazzlingly launch both the first subject and (their more usual function) the second subject, too. The

[1] See p.106 above.
[2] The first theme of the Sinfonia *al Conventello* (1806–7) is re-used in *Il Signor Bruschino*; the second theme of the Overture in D (1808) is re-used in *L'inganno felice*.

second subject will normally be in the dominant,[3] or in the relative major where the first subject is in the minor as it is in *Il barbiere di Siviglia* and *La gazza ladra*. This basic groundplan takes no account, however, of the variant procedures which exist within the structures. There is the skill with which Rossini shapes and times the leads towards the release of the *Allegro* (the launch of the *Allegro* in *La scala di seta* is a typical piece of harmonic dissimulation). There is also the complex interplay of rhythm, phrase-length, and harmony in the first subject groupings of the more mature overtures, the length of transitions between subjects, varying from the nugatory to the large scale, the variety of modulations Rossini introduces into his codas, and the simple skill with which some overtures are stopped. The overture to *La scala di seta*, one of the quickest and most brilliant, and distinguished throughout by glorious *concertante* wind writing, slaloms to a halt with all the grace of a downhill ski champion.

Three other aspects of the Rossini overture deserve notice: the quality and variety of the *incipits*, the crescendo, and the orchestration. Chorley noted that every great Rossini overture begins in a different way. The range of ideas is certainly astonishing. There is the awesome quiet at the start of *L'inganno felice*, the helter-skelter of *La scala di seta*, the side-drum's call to arms before the *marziale* of *La gazza ladra*, and the unforgettable colloquy for solo cellos at the start of *Guillaume Tell*. *L'italiana in Algeri* begins with a Haydn-esque preface which has suggested to one writer the movements of a guilty husband creeping home in the early hours of the morning and knocking over the grandfather clock. *Semiramide*, one of the finest of the overtures to exploit the full archetype, begins with a crescendo. One of the most extraordinary is *Il Signor Bruschino* itself. The start is quick, not slow, aggressive and not reflective, remote from the tonic, and brazen enough to reduce the motivating figure (a figure which boorishly recurs throughout the overture) to a skeletal form which the violins tap out with their bows against the metal shades of the candle-holders on their music-stands, a mildly anarchic

[3] In the Overture in E flat (1809), which later serves in modified form as the overture to *La cambiale di matrimonio*, the second subject, with attendant horn subject in triplets, is in the tonic. Having turned up in the wrong clothes, it eventually turns up in the right ones, but without horn subject. Yet such is the vitality and charm of the piece, we are powerless to complain about this youthful indiscretion.

gesture in 1813, and a further example of Rossini's inadvertently writing what he once wryly called 'the music of the future'.

The celebrated crescendo, first tentatively employed in *L'inganno felice*, takes some of its features from standard classical practice. The crescendo at the start of the development of the first movement of Beethoven's *Pastoral* Symphony, with its overlapping rhythmic (8 × 3) and harmonic (12 × 2) movement in the 24-bar period, is an example of one basic structural principle used by Rossini. In addition, Rossini tends to stabilize the harmony by an arrested, tonic-dominant oscillation. Hypnotized by this and by the sudden drop to *piano* or *pianissimo*, the audience is able to register Rossini's skilful structuring of the crescendo, dynamically and instrumentally, as wind and percussion instruments, often in extreme or unusual registers, are progressively added to the texture, yet added in a way which preserves the clarity and brilliance of Rossini's orchestral palette. In *L'italiana in Algeri* the crescendo is launched by strings and oboes, the violins exploiting the close-to-the-bridge, icy *sul ponticello* sound, an effect which makes for a remarkable conjunction of rhythmic fire and sonic ice. G.B. Shaw's talk of the 'textures thickening and warming until finally the big drum and the trombones [are] in full play'[4] reflects an experience of thickened late-nineteenth-century texts and an over-exposure to brass band transcriptions of the music. Properly judged, the use of something like the snare-drum in the crescendo of *La gazza ladra* is a colouristic effect to which only the very finest orchestrators could lay claim.

Rossini's ear was an extraordinarily fine one as the texts of the evolving Critical Edition clearly reveal. 'Music that is speedy must strip', wrote Richard Capell, and Rossini's invariably does in the earlier works when he exploits colour, tonal volumes, and the amusing incongruities of instrumental register with a skill which Stravinsky was to revive and reappropriate in his own neoclassical phase. As good an example as any also comes from *L'italiana in Algeri*. Initially, the second subject is given out (bar 82, G major) by the oboe, but it is recapitulated (bar 196, C major) by, of all things, piccolo and bassoon, greeting the world – like Paganini and Rossini in the Roman carnival of 1821 – with all the wit and physical incongruity of a pair of music-hall comedians. Rossini's inventive genius in pieces like this never ceases to astound.

[4] G.B. Shaw, *The Illustrated London News*, 5 March, 1892.

21

Tancredi: heroic comedy and the forming of a method

Interest in *Tancredi,* the *melodramma eroico* first seen in Venice in February 1813, has centred in more recent times on the opera's significance as a staging-post in the evolution of Rossini's formal procedures and on the problem of how the opera should end. Before we address these questions, though, it is important to define the work's particular aesthetic appeal. Commentators from Stendhal to Gossett have stressed its pristine beauty, what Stendhal calls its 'candeur virginale'. *Tancredi* is a limpid, lyrical, predominantly major-key work. Only Amenaide's prison scene is cast in the minor (in Rossini's key of darkness and incarceration, C minor) though the aria itself is in the major. Like her E major prayer before Tancredi's battle with Orbazzano and Tancredi's own 'Ah! che scordar non so' whose introduction contains a melody of Verdian amplitude, this is music, seemingly simple on the page, which a great singer can transmute into sublime song. The poet and critic, Giuseppe Carpani (1752–1825) put it well when he observed that *Tancredi* is 'cantilena and always cantilena, beautiful cantilena, new cantilena, magic cantilena, rare cantilena'.

Not that everything is quite such plain sailing as Carpani implies. Gaetano Rossi's libretto both simplifies and obfuscates Voltaire's *Tancrède* (1760). In Voltaire's play the lovers meet only once, and in public; in Rossi's careless adaptation there are recitatives, *scenas*, and duets sufficient for them to dictate their entire life histories, even though the plot's credibility stands or falls by the fact that they must be unable to communicate the simplest piece of intelligence. Ten years later working under Rossini's watchful eye at Castenaso, Rossi would have a harder time of it drafting *Semiramide, Tancredi's* sequel and the consummation of the methods it propounds.

Given the state of Rossi's libretto, some pre-history is important. At the centre of the drama are two warring families in the eleventh-century city state of Syracuse. Like the Montagues and

Capulets, the houses of Argirio and Orbazzano are constantly feuding. When the Orbazzani gain the upper hand, Argirio's wife and his daughter, Amenaide, are exiled to the court of the Byzantine Emperor. There Amenaide is wooed by the powerful Saracen leader, Solamir, but falls in love with another Sicilian exile, Tancredi. On her deathbed, Amenaide's mother gives her blessing to a marriage with Tancredi. Events at home, however, are not so propitious. Harrassed by Solamir and ineptly led by Orbazzano, the Syracusans put Argirio at the head of their army. The Saracens are driven back, but Argirio is shrewd enough to realise that Syracuse cannot survive whilst it remains divided against itself. As a gesture of reconciliation, he offers Amenaide's hand in marriage to Orbazzano, simultaneously agreeing to seize the Tancredi family estates and condemning Tancredi to death in his absence. As the opera starts, Amenaide, who is largely ignorant of these preceding events, has sent an anonymous note to Tancredi, urging him to return to Syracuse.

Such a pre-history might well lead to a drama which is explicitly tragic; but this is not a tradition to which Rossini was heir, nor is it one to which he would have been naturally sympathetic. In the opera's opening scene knights sing of 'peace, honour, faith, and love'. These abstract nouns embody the great classical virtues which bind communities and demand the sublimation of the individual will in disinterested acts of love and duty. In *Tancredi* Rossini accepts their moral and social premises but evokes them in a new populist manner and in larger, more continuous forms. In the process Rossini becomes what Julian Budden has called 'the reluctant architect of Italian romantic opera',[1] the purveyor of forms which Verdi will democratize, develop, and endow with a new kind of psychological realism.

The populist element in Rossini's art can be seen in the presentation of Tancredi himself, an old-fashioned *travesti* role which became one of the great dramatic vehicles for coloratura contraltos of the early *ottocento*. Tancredi arrives by boat to the accompaniment of a limpid barcarolle and greets his homeland in a recitative guaranteed to stir any Italian audience of the day. Out of the recitative, the *cavatina* 'Tu che accendi questo' shyly emerges only to be decisively trumped by the *cabaletta* 'Di tanti palpiti'. Whatever its intrinsic merit, this buoyant plea for mercy after much painful

[1] Budden, *The Operas of Verdi*, I, p.8.

love-longing, is wonderfully unaffected. In the morning-time of his art, Rossini seems to lack all artifice. The music's character derives from folk-song and like many of the most memorable folk-songs it is full of simple harmonic surprises, not least the sly upwards elision to A flat on the word 'pascerò' (Ex.9).

Ex.9

It is a characteristic gesture (the move to the flattened third is always a happy hunting-ground for Rossini locally or in larger harmonic structures) and one which nicely conveys the youthful, irresponsible Tancredi, his adolescent charm and unpredictability. As Rossini conceives Tancredi, he is closer to Cherubino than to Lohengrin.[2] It is the music of and by a man full of romantic yearning but a man blessed with energy, grace, and charm.

If 'Di tanti palpiti' establishes Tancredi's youthful insouciance, other numbers underline his sensibility and his sense of chivalric purpose. The Act 1 and Act 2 duets are of importance here, despite their being dramatically repetitive. In *Semiramide* the cues will be better judged, justifying the symmetry of a major duet for the lovers in each act. In *Tancredi* it is the beauty of the writing and the final unveiling of Rossini's three- or four-part duet structure which is of special interest. The Act 1 duet, 'L'aura che intorno spira', outlines the form: an initial statement by Amenaide, spaciously built in semibreves and minims, answered by Tancredi (*Allegro giusto*, 4/4, B flat); a lyric central section (*Andante*, 2/4, E flat) with voices in thirds and sixths; a freely modulating transition, and a *cabaletta* (*Allegro*, 4/4, B flat). Musically, the Act 2 duet, 'Lasciami! non

---

[2] It may have been Wagner's sense of outrage at a medieval knight being given the music of a street-vendor which prompted him to parody 'Di tanti palpiti' in the Tailors' Song in Act 3 of *Die Meistersinger*.

t'ascolto', is even finer. There is a stronger sense of confrontation and a richer use of quasi-canon and expressive trills in the central movement (*Andantino*, 3/4, G [mediant] major). In the Ferrara edition, which is clearly concerned to tighten the opera's dramatic argument, the duet is brought forward, supplanting 'L'aura che intorno spira' and introducing a not entirely plausible note of confrontation into the lovers' first encounter.

The Act 1 finale, in which Amenaide is wrongly accused of communicating by letter with the enemy Solamir, provides an expanded version of a similar structure, a four-part movement for principals and chorus, prefaced here by a wedding chorus. (Amenaide is now promised in marriage to Orbazzano.) Gossett identifies this as a 'pure' example of the form,[3] though in making the point it is necessary to stress that there are significant shortenings and expansions of the model by Rossini in his later works. This Act 1 finale is launched by a slow D major sextet in which communal feelings of shock and horror are duly expressed. A quick movement follows, launched in the key of the dominant with an important motif (Ex.10) to which Rossini later returns.

Ex.10

---

[3] Gosset, *Grove* 6, Vol. 16, p.230; see also Gossett's 'The *candeur virginale* of *Tancredi*', MT, cxii (1971), p.326.

Amenaide pleads first with her father, then with Tancredi and Orbazzano, all of whom reject her, precipitating a freely modulating passage in which she attemps to re-affirm her innocence. The third section, a Quartet (*Andante*, 2/4, B flat) consolidates the situation after which the chorus, which is poorly used elsewhere in the work (the 'Reign of Terror' chorus in Act 2 is anything but) launches the final quick, or 'kinetic', section. Suffering from a growing and understandable paranoia, Amenaide renews her plea in an increasingly fraught intervention based on Ex.10. Isaura stands by her but her enemies are reduced to a few lapidary utterances whilst the chorus bays for blood.

The *stretta* is arrived at via the dominant of the relative minor, as is the recapitulation in the *stretta* itself. It is a neat, unobtrusive device which points underlying tensions and gives the music variety of perspective whilst at the same time retaining the stability of the larger structure. There are also frequent shifts of harmony within the *stretta* itself; by the time we reach the ominous 'Suon di morta gela il core', we have already passed through B minor, G major, and arrived in E minor. Once established, these same structural and harmonic procedures are used in the Act 1 finales of works belonging both to the *opera seria* and *opera buffa* genres. The harmonic structuring of the *stretta* at the end of Act 1 of *Il barbiere di Siviglia* is in some respects identical to that in *Tancredi*, though something like the Act 1 finale of *Semiramide* is longer, more minor key, and with a *stretta* in a retarding 3/4 rhythm. It will be argued, no doubt, that Rossini unthinkingly or cynically muddles the *serio* and *buffo* worlds. On the surface this is so. But such an argument overlooks the overlaps which exist between the genres. The sentiment that the world is a mad and dangerous place is as germane to the finale of *Tancredi* as it is to *Il barbiere di Siviglia*. Rossini's sense of the unstoppable whirl of human endeavour, something induced in part perhaps by his sense of the often frantic and disordered state in which Europe found itself in these years, becomes one of the central images of his art. It is the image of a vortex into which we are all either willingly or unwittingly drawn, and it remains as potent in our own times as it was in 1813. If the form has limitations, they are the more obvious ones: a stereotyped view of human affairs, and a tendency, in the slow, non-kinetic sections to halt the action as a matter of course where the demands of the drama may be otherwise. But these are problems for those composers – Donizetti, Bellini, Verdi – who might wish to redeploy the forms; Rossini's deployment of forms he himself perfected is frequently and self-evidently successful.

There is, though, a more serious overlap, or ambiguity, in the status of the *serio* and *buffo* texts which Rossini set; and it is an ambiguity which affects our perception of the variant endings provided by Rossini for *Tancredi* in February and March 1813. As Rossi and Rossini first conceived it, the opera ended happily. After the defeat of Orbazzano and Tancredi's reluctant but successful intervention on the Syracusan side, the Saracens are defeated and Amenaide's innocence and good faith finally established. To repeated cries of 'felicità!' the opera ends with a vaudeville finale, charming but of no great distinction. In Voltaire, and in Lechi's revised Ferrara text, Tancredi is mortally wounded and dies accepting Amenaide's pleas of innocence and vows of love. In addition to this, the Ferrara revision brings forward Voltaire's Act IV, iv., the lovers' only encounter in the original drama, and shapes it into Tancredi's fine 'Perchè turba la calma', sung to Amenaide before his departure to fight the Saracens. It is the finale itself, though, which raises the more significant problem. The idea of Rossini's operas belonging to an eighteenth-century tradition of heroic comedy has already been touched on in connection with the character of Schiller's *Wilhelm Tell*.[4] In *Feeling and Form*, Langer prefaces her comments on Schiller's play with a more general comment on the genre which is relevant to the case of *Tancredi*.

> These stately Gallic classics are really heroic comedies. They are classed as tragedies because of their sublime tone, which is associated, in our European tradition, with tragic action . . . But there is no question of how the heroes will meet circumstances; they will meet them rationally; reason, the highest virtue of the human soul, will be victorious. This reason does not grow, through inner struggles against passional obstacles, from an original spark to full enlightenment, as 'the tragic rhythm of action' would demand, but is perfect from the outset.[5]

Tragic and even gruesome endings were not entirely unknown in the music-dramas of Rossini's day, despite the reasonable objections (unfashionable to twentieth-century taste) of the great eighteenth-

[4] See p.76.
[5] Langer, op.cit., pp.337–8.

century moralists.[6] It is, however, 'heroic comedy' which Rossini and his sophisticated young librettist are providing in the Ferrara revision. Bruno Cagli has described the Ferrara ending as a serene leave-taking, a tableau reminiscent of a marble bas-relief. It is well put. But how is it achieved?

After the battle, Tancredi is brought in, mortally wounded. First, we hear a plaintive A minor chorus, 'Muore il prode', 24 bars long, with not a note wasted. It crops up again as a prisoners' plea for clemency to the compromised Queen Zenobia in *Aureliano in Palmira*, a plausible new context, and a perfectly good resting place for a marvellous small invention which Rossini no doubt thought lost to the world when the Ferrara finale of *Tancredi* proved so unacceptable to contemporary taste. A string-accompanied recitative follows, finely written (Lechi's response to Voltaire's phrasing and prosody is sensitive) and expressively set. Finally, there is the death itself, curiously nominated as a *cavatina finale*. It begins and movingly ends in C major. Broken string phrases set the scene, ominously overhung by the sound of two clarinets. Later, voices and strings alternate but never merge. This is not a dialogue like that in the slow movement of Beethoven's G major Piano Concerto where an angry mood is assuaged by an emollient solo voice. Here the solo voice is grievingly alone, the strings enacting the role of solicitous bystanders awaiting the inevitable end. With a fading shudder of tone, the opera ends.

Perhaps Lechi and Rossini should have re-drafted the whole drama. Had they done so Rossini might have changed the course of Italian opera even more radically than he was already doing. But this was not practicable. Despite its stylistic oddity, the Ferrara ending is a sobering and finely judged resolution to this sad, touching, exquisitely imagined heroic idyll.

---

[6] Samuel Johnson's celebrated remarks on Nahum Tate's revision of Shakespeare's *King Lear* put the matter well. 'A play in which the wicked prosper, and the virtuous miscarry, may doubtless be good, because it is a just representation of the common events of human life: but since all reasonable beings naturally love justice, I cannot easily be persuaded, that the observation of justice makes a play worse . . .'

22

L'italiana in Algeri: formal mastery in the comic style

Produced in Venice in May 1813 to a libretto by Anelli previously used by Luigi Mosca, *L'italiana in Algeri* was the first full manifestation of Rossini's comic genius. Stendhal thought it 'perfection in the *opera buffa* style'.[1] It was, he argued, an opera so rich in enchantment and sensual delight that critical judgment is actively suspended, a work of pure escapism 'gay as our world is not'. This last point is an interesting one which might well be both sustained and contradicted by something like the great Act 1 finale where the characters are nonplussed and frozen in time before being released into a rising tide (the image of shipwreck is there in the text) of rhythm and melody which finally engulfs them. Rossini's world is, indeed, irrepressibly gay; but his great first act finales, like the uproarious galley scene at the end of Act 2 of Shakespeare's *Antony and Cleopatra*, provide images of human vitality and riotous hedonism alongside images of vanity, instability, and the vulnerability of powerful men. The lascivious, posturing Mustafà of Rossini's opera is no Napoleon and is temperamentally far removed from the sanctimonious (if slightly tipsy) Octavius Caesar of Shakespeare's drama; but he is as perplexed and vulnerable as any of the world's power-brokers. Stendhal is right to stress the vitality of *L'italiana in Algeri* and the delirium it induced in its first, and subsequent, audiences; but the music's appeal rests in some measure on our awareness of the thinness of the ice on which we skate. Nor does it need Rossini's sly allusion to the 'Marseillaise' before Isabella's 'Pensa alla patria' for us to be reminded once again that in 1813 Europe was itself, militarily and politically, a madcap place.

That *L'italiana in Algeri* is Rossini's first fully-fledged comic masterpiece is due in no small measure to the fine formal ordering of the score and to Rossini's increasingly sophisticated sense of the interplay of musical styles, qualities which stand out even more

[1] VdR, Ch.3, *passim*.

clearly if Rossini's treatment of Anelli's text is set side by side with Mosca's which is long on bustle and charm but short on stylistic self-awareness and formal control. Take, for instance, the two composers' setting of the duet 'Ai capricci della sorte' in Act 1 of the opera. The revelation by Haly, the Algerian pirate king, that Mustafà is in search of a pretty Italian girl, has Taddeo, Isabella's ageing admirer, beside himself with jealousy. Isabella's response is a waspish rebuke, beginning with some capricious remarks about fortune, the comic counterpart of that cruel fate she has only recently apostrophized in her cavatina 'Cruda sorte!'. From the outset, Rossini's shaping of the duet is masterly. We tend to take formal *incipits* for granted, but where Mosca's is breathless and dynamically bland, Rossini's opening bars (Ex.11) have both economy and wit.

Ex.11

There are details here whose absence would render the music commonplace but which are happily grist to the mill of a Haydn or a Rossini: the silent upbeat in bar 1, the thinning out and fragmenting of dynamics, texture, and rhythm in bar 2, the bassoon's comically forceful entry in bar 3, the skittish violin figure (fig. *a*) which will later take on the function of an important motor-rhythm, and the deliberately narrow, petulant-sounding intervals of the vocal line itself. Out of such detail is great comedy made. Anelli's libretto determines the shape of the vocal exposition, Isabella and Taddeo establishing their respective positions in formal stanzas. Strings and winds are discreetly supportive during these exchanges but in the repartee which follows it is fig. *a* which carries the drama forward until, in a simple stroke of comic genius – theatrical and musical elements perfectly aligned – Isabella silences Taddeo's grumblings by recapitulating the opening theme (Ex.11 bars 6 ff.). Though her language is far from elegant – 'Go to the devil, and good riddance!' – it is the fact of the musical recapitulation which gives her riposte its authority: verbal abuse endowed by the formal recapitulation with all the authority of an axiomatic utterance. It is a brilliant tactic, by Isabella and by Rossini. There is no such equivalent in Mosca's score. Recapitulation might imply imminent closure; in fact, the music continues towards a second bridge, a simple arching transition on the first violins which drops us down into B flat major as self-doubts begin to cloud the minds of the antagonists. The timing is exquisite; with the mood newly relaxed, and fig. *a* now playing the role of an amused spectator, Isabella and Taddeo contemplate the dangers facing them in overlapping soliloquies. The transition to the *stretta* is clear enough in the libretto but in his search for novel effects Mosca unsettles the linking stichomythia ('Donna Isabella? Messer Taddeo . . .' etc) where Rossini, with an Olympian simplicity of means, treats the stichomythia as a cat-and-mouse exchange linked by suave violin sextuplets before the coda's launch, *Allegro vivace* in G major. This final movement has a military feel about it – love as a battleground: an old conceit – with skirling winds and mock-heroic gestures which digress into coloratura display. During Isabella's big cadential flourishes it is almost impossible for poor Taddeo to get a word in edgeways. Having been silenced by an act of recapitulation earlier in the duet, he now finds coloratura rhetoric barring his path. It is Rossini's special merit that his best jokes are the musical ones.

It would be wrong to suggest that Rossini parodies the *opera seria* manner in *L'italiana in Algeri*; rather, he allows his heroine to deploy it as a powerful strategic weapon in her politico-sexual armoury. What is more, the heroic style is carefully balanced by much lighter, cat-like writing. 'Cruda sorte!', whose structure is not dissimilar to that of Rosina's *cavatina* in *Il barbiere di Siviglia*, follows heroic posturing with the lightening 'Già so per pratica', a movement specially drafted for Rossini's setting of Anelli's libretto. These additions to Anelli's libretto are of obvious interest for the light they throw on Rossini's needs and preoccupations. Most obviously, verses are expanded or modified and new alliterative and onomatopoeic effects added when characters are *in extremis*, as they are, for instance, in the Act 1 finale. But there are also omissions. There is no love duet for Isabella and Lindoro in the Rossini version. It is a deletion which is as much to do with Rossini's dislike of duets written for the male and female voices as for evidence of that absence of heart which Verdi's wife, Giuseppina Strepponi, fancied she detected in Rossini's psychopathology. In this score, passion is communicated by indirection, most obviously in the rapt and sensuous 'Per lui che adoro'[2] in Act 2 where Isabella expresses her feelings in the knowledge that she has a hidden audience crouching nearby: the besotted Mustafà and her two outraged admirers, Taddeo, and Lindoro, the real object of her affections. Above all, it is the Act 1 finale – and within it two great recognition scenes – which convey Isabella's passion for Lindoro and its comic correlative, her contempt for Mustafà.

The tonal structure of the finale need not detain us, though it is representative of Rossini's method: a C major movement framing episodes in keys a minor third away, the flattened mediant, E flat major, and the flattened submediant, A flat major. Of special interest, however, is a freely modulating episode which grows out of a delectably scored minuet-like *andantino* in the dominant G major. Mustafà's wife, Elvira, her confidante, Zulma, and Lindoro steal in to take their leave of Mustafà who has granted Lindoro his freedom provided he takes Elvira away with him. It is at this point that Lindoro and Isabella recognize one another. It is a truism that in the hands of a master a recognition scene can be a thing of special potency. Here Rossini demonstrates his mastery by dropping us quietly into the minor and a series of modulations (Ex.12a) of hypnotic simplicity.

[2] For details of variant versions and substitute arias written for Isabella and Lindoro during seasons in Venice (1813), Vicenza (1813), Milan (1814), and Naples (1815) see Appendices I–IV of the Critical Edition, ed. Azio Corghi, Pesaro, 1981. The Ricordi vocal score, Milan, 1982, also prints the appendices, as well as an English translation of the Critical Edition's most important background notes.

Ex.12a

The text is no more than nine lines of stereotyped exclamation, and musically the passage is little more than a transition back to the local home key of E flat major; yet the transition stands at the very heart of the opera, the lovers' supressed ardour touchingly juxtaposed with Mustafà's bumbling expression of earthbound bemusement (Ex.12b).

Ex.12b

At moments like this Rossini, like Mozart before him, shames his more long-winded successors by his simplicity of means.

Mustafà, arrogant and domineering, has been caricatured at the opera's outset, rendered ridiculous in the *Introduzione* ('Delle donne l'arroganza', *Andantino*, 4/4, E major) by grotesque intervals and elaborate coloratura. But Rossini's musical characterization in the lead towards the Act 1 finale is carefully balanced. When Mustafà is finally convinced that his wife is off his hands, he contemplates new erotic adverures ('Già d'insolito ardoro nel petto', *Allegro*, 4/4, B flat major) in terms robust enough to predict Sir John Falstaff's 'Va, vecchio John!' in Verdi's opera. Mustafà's meeting with Isabella, the first of the recognition scenes in the Act 1 finale, is an essay, not in comic pathos, but in burlesque. And it is prefaced by a chorus which appears to allude to Figaro's 'Non più andrai, farfallone amoroso' from Mozart's *Le nozze di Figaro*. This is not the only arcane reference in the score's choral writing; as has already been mentioned, the 'Marseillaise' crops up in a later number. The Mozart allusion comes as the second tenors intone the name 'Mustafà' and whilst the first tenors and the basses declare Mustafà to be 'the scourge of women'. If the quotation is deliberate – and Rossini must have envied Mozart a number he could have well written himself – it is a masterstroke of comic prolepsis. In the Mozart, Figaro tells Cherubino that his philandering days are over, which is precisely the situation towards which Mustafà is unwittingly heading. What's more, Da Ponte's Italian text provides Rossini with a ready-made ambiguity; for depending on the sense in which we take the word 'farfallone' we have either an amorous butterfly (Cherubino) or an amorous blunderer, which is as apt a description of Mustafà as any we are likely to find. The reference, inspired by Rossini's favourite composer, is one of his most sophisticated small jokes. At Isabella's entry the music stops and the strings make a furtive step-by-step ascent from C to E flat as if following Isabella's gaze as it travels upwards towards Mustafà's face. A slow round begins with the words 'O che muso' – 'My god, what a mug!' – a line which Conchita Supervia made as memorable as Edith Evans's exclamation about the handbag in Wilde's *The Importance of Being Earnest*. What follows wonderfully imitates the furtive co-existence of solemnity and barely suppressed laughter, with Rossini's wealth of comic detailing in the orchestra, and his sure formal patterning, greatly assisting any stage director sensitive enough to transfer the musical patterning into the visual medium.

This superb finale ends, as is well known, with Rossini's most uproarious *stretta*. Isabella's turning on Mustafà sends the whole company into a state of delirium, their heads full of the sounds of bells ('din din', the women), a hammer ('tac tac', Lindoro), crowing ('cra cra', Taddeo) and a cannon ('bum bum', Mustafà). The text was specially written for Rossini and makes a brilliant effect provided that the conductor observes Rossini's precise annotation of extreme dynamic levels as they are reproduced in the Corghi edition.

As is often the case with Rossini, the second act is not quite as full of good things as the first, though the second act of *L'italiana in*

Algeri has some memorable things in it: the investing of Taddeo in the spurious order of Kaimakan, the famous sneezing Quintet, and Mustafà's initiation into the order of the Pappataci, a nonsense word which implies not so much a cuckold as the kind of long-suffering husband immortalized by the hang-dog creature forever trailing after his formidable wife in Jacques Tati's *Les vacances de M. Hulot*. Such initiation ceremonies are a stock-in-trade of comedies derived from the Commedia dell'Arte tradition (one thinks of Molière's *Le bourgeois gentilhomme*). A satire on Masonry has been suggested here, too. Be that as it may, Mustafà is persuaded to do nothing but eat, drink, and sleep. The Act 2 finale promises well but is short-winded, with the Quintet and Isabella's *rondo*, 'Pensa alla patria', proving difficult acts to follow. In Naples in 1815 'Pensa alla patria' was banned, its fervent sentiments of which Rossini was later so proud, replaced by 'Sullo stil de' viaggiatori'. This is a big, striking number, carefully worked from materials which include the overture's second theme; but it lacks the glorious, long-breathed solemnity of the cantilena which is at the heart of the original and which must still strike Italian ears as eloquently as an Elgarian *nobilmente* strikes English ones.

L'italiana in Algeri is, then, a score of great richness and sophistication. Formally, it is an innovative piece; it is also a score notably free from any kind of self-borrowing. Some numbers – Haly's *aria del sorbetto* 'Le femmine d'Italia' – were farmed out, but such pieces, gracious and decorous in the Paisiello style, are a reminder of how fiercely the flame of Rossini's own comic invention burns in this remarkable piece which transcends Mosca's earlier effort as surely as *Il barbiere di Siviglia* was soon to transcend the Paisiello.

23

Milan and Venice (1813–14)

Aureliano in Palmira – Il turco in Italia – Sigismondo

The three operas Rossini wrote before his departure for Naples in 1815 include one of his comparatively rare failures, *Sigismondo,* and two operas, *Aureliano in Palmira* and *Il turco in Italia*, whose early lack of success must be attributed in part to their status as chamber opera.

In accepting the La Scala libretto for *Aureliano in Palmira*, Rossini was accepting a text which deals in imperial Roman history and the trading of empires for love. It is a stirring subject but neither Romani's verses nor Rosini's writing – touchingly *naif* but neither advancing nor even fully consolidating the achievements of *Tancredi* – allow it to be treated on a scale which subsequent generations would find plausible. The libretto is based on a modicum of historical fact. Lucius Domitius Aurelianus (*c.* A.D. 215–275) was a humble man who rose to supreme power after a brilliant military career. He did much to restore order both within and without the boundaries of the Roman Empire and did indeed tangle with the formidably expansionist Queen Zenobia whose conquests in Syria, Egypt, and Asia Minor were not taken lightly in Rome. It was also about this time that the Arsacids fell from power in Parthia, a line of feudal aristocrats who had probably been rather sterner than Rossini's Arsace, King of Persia (*sic*), a tender, sweet-natured, somewhat effete young man much taken with the beautiful Queen Zenobia. There is no evidence that such a trio of personalities ever met in real life. Arsace, the archetype of the youthful warrior, is a fictional figure and Aurelianus' magnanimity to the defeated lovers at the end of the opera, though rooted in the historical accounts of his sparing Zenobia, is another convenient fiction, a happy ending cloaked in the principles of the enlightenment.

The opera, lightly scored in Rossini's youthful neo-classical manner, derives some of its effectiveness from his use of specific vocal types. Aureliano, who offers Zenobia 'gloria e amor', is written for a tenor, an assertive, even strident presence whose first parley with Arsace is seen and heard against a backdrop of battlefield carnage with the river Euphrates adding enchantment to the more distant view. Celletti has suggested that Aurelianus is the opera's anti-hero; certainly, Rossini attempts to chart the twists and turns of Aurelianus's divided self. His *cavatina*, 'Caro patria! Il mondo trema', with its heroic horn obbligato, catches the man's stature and potential virulence. Queen Zenobia is transformed by Arsace from a warrior-queen who, like Mozart's Queen of the Night, uses her coloratura as a weapon, to someone much given to elegiac melody in the proto-Bellinian style of Arsace himself. And it is Arsace who determines the opera's prevailing colour and mood. This portrait of a youth at once comely and sad was created by Rossini for the great *castrato*, Velluti. Legend has it that Velluti over-decorated the music, but there is no firm evidence to support this. Some of the writing is intrinsically brilliant but much of it is quiet and subdued, ideally suited to the purity and homogeneity of the *castrato* voice. The world of Arsace and the tamed Zenobia is Arcadian, prelapsarian, a footnote to Rossini's sustained exploration of the heroic idyll which begins with *Demetrio e Polibio* and ends, in an epic configuration, with *Guillaume Tell*. The idyllic spirit is evident in the lovers' first duet and in their haunting nocturnal tryst, 'Mille sospiri, e lagrime'. Arsace himself has several other finely drawn moments, his prison scene (I, ix) and the scenes in Act 2 among the hills and woods of the Euphrates, scenes prefaced by the overture's slow introduction. This pastoral vigil is enchantingly written in a fresh, unsentimental style which Rossini seems to have learned in part from Haydn's two great oratorios, *The Creation* and *The Seasons*. As an image of rustic calm and continuity amid the carnage of imperial wars such scenes must have struck a responsive chord in the contemporary consciousness. The words of the shepherds' chorus – 'O care selve, o care/Stanza di libertà', the woods apostrophized as the source of true, inner freedom – are set by Rossini in a manner as clearly intended to rouse popular sentiment as Moses' hymn in the 1819 revision of *Mosè in Egitto* or the Prisoners' Chorus in Beethoven's *Fidelio*. The use of a solo violin is also unusually affecting. By contrast, the opera's military interludes are highly stylized, though Rossini does provide a host of small inventions within the military and political scenes, a fine short *cavatina* for the High Priest and an exquisite prisoners' plea to Zenobia salvaged from the Ferrara finale of *Tancredi*. What

Aureliano in Palmiro lacks in splendour, originality, and drive, it amply makes up for in sensibility and charm.

Il turco in Italia is also more a painting on ivory than on canvas. It was Rossini's first collaboration with the distinguished librettist Felice Romani then near the start of a career which, unlike Rossini's, would survive the onset of the full-blooded romantic style. A classicist by training, Romani was able to provide Rossini with a sophisticated text which mocked, rather than imitated or embodied, aspects of the *buffo* style and the Turkish vogue. It was an ideal text for Rossini with his instinct for detached observation and his dislike of all music which aims at gaudy description. Central to the project is the figure of the Poet who introduces himself in the first scene as a man in search of a subject for a *dramma buffo*. It is soon to hand in the form of some gypsies ('local colour!' he ironically remarks) and Geronio, the ageing husband of the lively Fiorilla. A classic *commedia dell'arte* entertainment is now in the offing with doting husband, flirtatious wife, and a pair of exotic lovers: the eponymous Turk, Selim, and the youthful Don Narciso. Nowadays we tend to think of a drama propelled into life by an on-stage surrogate dramatist as Pirandellian, but the idea pre-dates Pirandello, Romani, and Rossini. Da Ponte's Don Alfonso in Mozart's *Così fan tutte* is a variant of the same idea and Romani's libretto was itself based on a model from Mozart's time, Caterina Mazzola's *Il turco in Italia* successfully set first by Franz Seydelmann (1788, Dresden, and seen by Constanze Mozart in Vienna in 1789) and by Franz Süssmayr (1794, Prague). The Poet's enthusiasm for the puppets he is propelling into life and his quiet mockery of the sentimental expectations of *dramma buffo* are evidently shared with Rossini. When Selim is brought face to face with Zaida, the Turkish girl who has fled from his embraces, the Poet tells us – the music slipping blandly into F major with urbane bassoon counterpoints – that a chair will be necessary since heroines invariably faint at such a juncture. As Selim nervously awaits developments, the Poet slips out to fetch a chair. In the event, no one faints, leaving the Poet rueing his luck and deploring the plot's failure to comply with the usual rules.

One of the opera's finest numbers is the Trio 'Un marito – scimunito!' in which Geronio and Narciso strenuously question the roles they have been allotted by the Poet. The Trio begins, and wittily ends, with a broad-based theme in semibreves over which a second orchestral subject, at once delighted and resigned, is triggered into life (Ex.13).

Ex.13

What follows is finely honed. Skilfully varied *buffo* declamation, wry modulations, and the elegant interjection of phrases from the opera's overture sit cheek-by-jowl with a certain kind of serene, untroubled beauty. It is a juxtaposition which takes us closer to the spirit of Mozart than any alleged connection between the start of the Trio and the finale of Mozart's 'Jupiter' Symphony, K.551.

Like *L'italiana in Algeri*, the opera is distinguished by a memorable duet for the heroine and her aged admirer; yet if the situations are similar, the comedy itself derives from different sources. In 'Per piacere alla Signora' from *Il turco in Italia* the music first bustles and fizzes in the Mosca style. It is when a tone of tragic intensity is assumed by Fiorilla in the central *Andante* that the comedy is brought fully into focus. 'Voi, crudel, mi fate oltraggio!' she cries, accusing poor Geronio of being both cruel and outrageous in his treatment of her. The movement reaches a climax with Fiorilla's cry 'pietà, pietà!'. Maria Callas was invariably memorable at this point, weeping with tragi-comic intensity whilst the music resolved disarmingly back into G major. In the cabaletta Fiorilla addresses the audience, a sly and winning use of the form, again finely noted by Callas in a swift lightening of tone which transformed Fiorilla from a cavilling hussy into a sophisticated woman of the world.

Act 2 of *Il turco in Italia* has a duet, notable for its brilliant end, in which the two basses, Geronio and Selim, come to the verge of blows when Geronio refuses to sell his wife. There is also Fiorilla's enchanting ditty 'Se il zefiro si posa', a further reminder of Rossini's mastery of a folk style which is spry, piquant, local. The weakness of the act as it has come down to us is the slowing of the action for a pair of dramatically uninteresting tenor arias: an aria for Narciso written during the first season for Giovanni David, and an aria for Selim's henchman, Albazar, which is not by Rossini. The very end of the opera is also by someone other than Rossini. Gossett suggests that the standby composer who also wrote the recitatives and Geronio's *cavatina* with its gentle, elegant oboe part may have been Vicenzo Lavigna, Verdi's counterpoint teacher and, according to Verdi, 'a man who didn't care for any music but Paisiello's'.[1]

The undoubted highlight of Act 2, and the opera's real climax before its somewhat bathetic close, is the great Quintet ('Oh, guardate che accidente', *Andante*, 4/4, E flat) in which Geronio, having being lured to a masked ball, is presented with a pair of Selims and a pair of Fiorillas. Like parties in the plays of Harold Pinter, this is funny, up to a point. That the whole thing *is* a game, albeit a somewhat menacing one, is insisted upon by the featherlight canonic *allegro* ('Questo vecchio maledetto'), the quintessence of the spirit of play, which flourishes briefly before the Quintet spins deliriously to its conclusion ('Egli è un pazzo', *Allegro*, 3/8). Yet the Quintet begins with Geronio searching for Fiorilla, continues with his bemused mutterings beneath the lovers' complacent asides in the unaccompanied quartet, and ends in a sinister bout of hide-and-seek ('Egli è un pazzo') which leaves Geronio breathlessly attesting his sanity. It is an enigmatic movement, unstoppably brilliant, very funny, and rather chilling; and as such it is not untypical of this elegant, ambiguous, occasionally underrated score.

[1] Rossini did, however, manage to write an overture for *Il turco in Italia*, a charming and ebullient piece, partially redeployed in *Sigismondo* and *Otello*; it is notable for the lengthy, very powerful transition passage to the second subject.

Rossini's last pre-Naples score, *Sigismondo*, has suffered greater and perhaps understandable neglect. A *dramma* in two acts, it concerns Sigismondo, King of Poland, who on the advice of his chief minister, Ladislao, has expelled his wife Aldimira from the court. Striken by remorse, he has further reason to rue his decision when Aldimira's father, the King of Bohemia, makes war on Poland. After a series of powerful confrontations, Sigismondo is obliged to restore a triumphant Aldimira to her throne. On paper it is not a score which advances urgent arguments for revival, though without revival revaluation is to some extent hampered. The casting involves a *travesti* contralto, Sigismondo himself (Marcolini's role), a bass, Ulderico (sung by Luciano Bianchi, Rossini's first Obrazzano), and a tenor as Ladislao. The solo writing is often difficult, and busily written. Rossini's own inclination was to unpick some of those moments which pleased him most and redeploy them in works as different and as distant as *Elisabetta, regina d'Inghilterra, Torvaldo e Dorliska, Il barbiere di Siviglia,* and *Adina.* The introductory chorus to *Sigismondo's* Act 2 is re-used as part of the *Introduzione* to Act 1 of *Il barbiere di Siviglia*, a most prestigious posting, and it is in *Sigismondo*, in the duet 'Perchè obbedir disdegni', that we first encounter the figure which launches the crescendo movement in Don Basilio's famous calumny aria.

24

Arrival in Naples (1814–16)

Elisabetta, regina d'Inghilterra – La gazzetta – Otello

> *Elisabetta* offered all the great emotional tension and drama of the *opera seria* without exacting the usual toll of weariness and boredom.[1]

So wrote Stendhal after the glittering *prima* of Rossini's first Neapolitan opera. It was an important occasion for Rossini, and for Colbran whose own future career was to be much affected by the events of 1815. The version of the Elizabeth and Leicester story set by Rossini has its origins in the writings of an English lady novelist popular in the 1780s, Sophia Lee. Her novel *The Recess; or, a Tale of Other Times* had been turned into a stage drama in 1814 by Carlo Federici and it was on Federici's play that the Tuscan-born librettist Giovanni Federico Schmidt (*c.* 1771- *c.* 1840) based his libretto. The principal virtue of the libretto, which not for the first time Rossini appears to have modified as he went along, is the comparative simplicity and clarity of its situations. Leicester, the Queen's favourite nobleman, has returned in triumph from the Scottish wars; there are, however, hostages in his baggage-train, among them a girl, Matilde, whom Leicester has secretly married. Unbeknown to Leicester at the time, Matilde was no sweet country girl but the daughter of Mary, Queen of Scots. Unwisely, Leicester confides his dilemma to the unreliable Norfolk who stirs a hornets' nest of emotional intrigue by communicating the fact to the Queen. But his unwelcome intelligence brings him no recompense, and in a fit of pique he attempts to assassinate the Queen during a secret visit made by her to the cell of the condemned Leicester. His attempt is foiled by Matilde and her brother; Leicester is restored to favour; and the Queen vows to renounce all passions except those which will enhance both her glory and her capacity for mercy. Readers of Scott will recognise a similarity to *Kenilworth* (1821) which *Elisabetta*

[1] VdR, p.161.

pre-dates. Fourteen years later the Neapolitans would be presented with a comparable piece, Donizetti's *Elisabetta al castello di Kenilworth*, loosely derived from Scribe and Scott by one of Rossini's Neapolitan collaborators, A.L. Tottola. In neither opera does Amy Robsart, Leicester's wife, meet with the grim end accorded to her by Scott.

Rossini's cast for *Elisabetta* was superb. Not only was there Colbran as the Queen, there was Nozzari as Leicester, and García as the villainous Norfolk. In other circumstances we might have expected a baritone Norfolk, but Naples was prodigally stocked with fine tenors, a fact which has helped make the Neapolitan *opere serie* difficult to cast in later times. In the event, neither tenor is given wholly memorable music. Norfolk's finest moments are the revelation of Leicester's duplicity in Act 1 (accompanied recitative with *tremolo* strings and scurrying pizzicati) and the subsequent duet with Elisabetta where Rossini's skills in *opera buffa* lend an insinuating, conspiratorial colour to the music. Norfolk's long *scena* in Act 2 is fussily written and rather dull. Leicester's prison scene which follows this is more interesting. Melodramatic and rambling though it is by the end, the scene is expressively introduced and the dream sequence with its fractured vocal line and choiring wind obbligatos is plausible provided we put from our mind the comparable scene in Beethoven's *Fidelio* staged in Vienna the year before.

By contrast, the role of Elisabetta is brilliantly and fluently written, evidently tailored to show off Colbran's declamatory powers and her brilliant coloratura technique. In later years Rossini's heroines were not always accorded brilliant showpieces at either end of the opera; here, though, Elisabetta is richly provided with an entrance aria and a showpiece finale, the latter admirably blending cool display with an extraordinary inwardness in the lyric sections, the exfoliations of the vocal line creeping over the orchestra's slender trellising with magical effect. The entrance aria is Rossini at his most winning, though it is also a good (and no doubt to anti-Rossinians, a controversial) example of his adaptive techniques. Sections of the aria ('Questo cor ben lo comprende', *Moderato*, 4/4, F major) would be used four months later in Rome in Rosina's *cavatina*, 'Una voce poco fa'. Both heroines are blithe and vital creatures. As such, the music is apt to both, though in re-casting Elisabetta's music for Rosina Rossini gives it more point; a natural consequence of any successful act of revision, it might be argued, but a consequence which on this occasion usefully accords with Rosina's more shrewish character. The sharper pointing can be seen at the outset (Ex.14) where Elisabetta's line, if left undecorated, is a good deal more placid.

Ex.14

Later, Elisabetta's line is more florid and free-wheeling (Ex.15a), whilst the adaptation for Rosina is tauter and simpler with a sharper sense of timing and a productive tension between syllabic and melismatic writing which allows for an altogether deadlier kind of rhetoric (Ex.15b). The pity of it is that all too many sopranos ignore the rhetoric of the revision, failing to time Rosina's preliminary 'ma' or articulate the subsequent repeated Bs in a way which adequately sets off the malice and whimsicality of the semiquaver figure which is now deliberately isolated in a way it is not in the looser vocal construction of the original.

In spite of the brilliance of Elisabetta's role, Matilde is not neglected. The highly charged duet with her husband ('Incauta! che festi', *Allegro agitato*, 4/4, F minor) was prized at the *prima* and her *cavatina* is notable for the quality of its orchestral accompaniment. Rossini's concern for details of orchestral colour is a feature of the

Ex.15

a) ELISABETTA

ques-to cor___ ben lo___ com-pren - do pal - pi - tan - te dal___ di -

b) ROSINA

ma se mi toc - ca-no dov'è il mio de - bo-le sa-rò u-na vi - pe - ra___

score, prompted to some extent by the knowledge that in Naples he was writing for a first-rate orchestra. One thinks of the mellow sonorities of the horns before the sudden chill of the strings under-pinning Leicester's 'Il gelo della morte' in the Act 1 finale. This finale is, in all respects, first-rate theatre. Leicester and his wife are summoned to public audience with the Queen who proceeds with a kind of manic irony to heap praises on the bewildered Leicester. She even offers him her hand as consort in a terrible moment before the mask is finally dropped. Stendhal saw the finale as a grim showcase of primary impulses: '*jealousy*, which is tormenting Elisabetta to the very brink of madness; *despair* growing ever blacker in Leicester; and *love*, unbelievably sad and touching in his young wife.'[2]

Stendhal also reports, and the report has a plausible ring about it, that it was Rossini who proposed Leicester's intrusion into the Act 2 duet between the Queen and Matilde. This is the scene in which Elisabetta tries to persuade Matilde to renounce her husband, a tolerable duet which turns into a fine Trio, with its sinister annuncia-tory drum roll. There is also some quietly impressive scene-setting in the opera, notably in Act 2 where there is a beautiful *sotto voce* chorus for the populace and soldiers as they glumly ponder the fate of their hero, Leicester. Earlier, there are some brilliant, dancing choruses, freshly voiced, and there are dance rhythms in the *cabaletta* of the Leicester-Matilde duet in Act 1 suggesting that for all the grandeur of the occasion of his Neapolitan debut Rossini was still young and unspoiled, a 23-year-old phenomenon as yet unencum-bered by the art he served.

To show off his paces as a composer of *opera buffa* to the sceptical Neapolitans, Rossini followed up the revival of *L'italiana*

[2] VdR, p.160.

in Algeri (autumn, 1815) with *La gazzetta,* a featherweight *opera buffa* written, after the Rome *prima* of *Il barbiere di Siviglia,* for Naples's Teatro dei Fiorentini in September 1816. With its whirl-wind plot and re-cycled music, *La gazzetta* is one of those eminently revivable operas which have been given short shrift by most of Rossini's biographers. True, the opera sets some pre-conditions for revival. As there is a good deal of *secco* recitative, some of it in Neapolitan dialect, the opera ought, ideally, to be heard in the language of the audience, suitably adapted. It also needs a fine *buffo* actor in the role of Don Pomponio. The part was written for Carlo Casaccia of whom Stendhal wrote: ' "If you have ever laughed in your life", I might say to some clumsy English squire, whose solemn head is all one whirl of earnest arguments concerning the *Utility of Foreign Bible Societies* and the *Immortality of the French Nation,* "go to Naples and see Casaccia".'[3]

In the opera, which derives from Goldoni's *Il matrimonio per concorso,* the ambitious, fantastical Don Pomponio Storione adver-tises for a husband for his flirtatious daughter, Lisetta. In fact, Lisetta has fallen in love with Filippo who owns the hotel in which they are staying. Meanwhile, the wealthy and feckless Alberto has turned up at the hotel in search of a wife; and to confuse matters still further, a second father, Anselmo, arrives to stay with his daughter Doralice in whom an old roué called Monsù Traversen takes a salacious interest. With an itinerant busybody, Madama La Rose, fluttering on the periphery of the action and Rossini dispatching the plot lines in rapid recitatives, the whole thing is very lively and local, helped out by some fizzing short numbers and one or two longer ones: none of them newly written but all of impeccable pedigree, including the Quintet from *Il turco in Italia* (having disguised himself as a quaker in Act 1 of *La gazzetta,* Filippo now turns up disguised as a Turk) and the Trio from *La pietra del paragone* in which Don Pomponio is drawn into a duel in identical manner to the unfortunate Macrobio in the earlier opera. Even the texts are the same, though in *La gazzetta* the use of dialect involves the librettist in some redrafting. Macrobio's reflections on the danger of swords to life and limb – 'Sol due colpi in mezzo al petto/E finisco di tremar' – becomes in Don Pomponio's version 'Se sfonnassero lo pietto/E fenesco de tremmà'. Other music to be transferred includes the Fiorilla/Geronio duet

[3] ibid., p.457.

from *Il turco in Italia* and Fiorilla's alternative *cavatina* 'Presto amiche' which is given to Lisetta as a deft vaudeville number, 'Presto, dice'.[4] It should be added that *La gazzetta* gets off to an excellent start. The opening scene with its chorus of travellers and whirling disagreements about who should have the newspaper first is wonderfully bright and breezy, and it, in turn, is prefaced by one of Rossini's finest overtures, better known to the world at large as the overture to *La Cenerentola*.

Rossini's choice of subject for his third Neapolitan opera, staged at the Teatro del Fondo during the rebuilding of the Teatro San Carlo in 1816, is a somewhat curious one. With the benefit of Verdi and of hindsight, it is possible to see Shakespeare's *Othello* as a fit subject for translation into music-drama, but no such precedent existed in 1816, though precedents did exist for the musical treatment of other Shakespeare plays: *The Merry Wives of Windsor, A Midsummer Night's Dream, Romeo and Juliet, The Tempest*, and even the egregious *Cymbeline* (Rodolphe Kreutzer's *Imogène*, 1796, Paris). *Othello's* status as full-blown tragedy (something Rossini was happy to back away from in the notorious Rome revision of 1820) was a clear disincentive to composers of the eighteenth and early nineteenth centuries. The great Shakesperian tragedies would begin to infiltrate operatic life in the middle years of the nineteenth century, but in 1816 *Othello* must have seemed a bold choice – and perhaps for this reason the kind of 'informed' literary gesture which Berio di Salsa, the librettist and a leading Neapolitan dilettante, might fancy making to an astounded public. If the choice was in any sense Berio's, then all we can say is that he bungled his chance. His handling of the main body of Shakespeare's play is inept. The plot is reduced to the formula of a tetchy father, a love-lorn daughter, an heroic lover, and a scheming rival, the characters tied to Shakespeare's play by little more than their names. Shakespeare's language is ignored, his plot is changed, the location is modified, and the critical confrontations down-graded or dissipated. There are also some strange omissions. Desdemona has no entrance aria (though singers soon found appropriate cues and substitutes) and there is no

---

[4] This version of Fiorilla's *cavatina* is found in the version of *Il turco in Italia* reproduced in the Kalmus Vocal Scores series which omits Fiorilla's 'Non si dà follia maggiore'.

love duet.[5] And yet Act 3 – a distillation of Shakespeare's Act IV, iii and Act V – is something of a triumph, as different in atmosphere and intent from what has gone before as is the Lechi/Rossini transcription of Voltaire for the revised ending of *Tancredi*. In the absence of letters and working notes, we can only guess from the evidence of the music itself that Act 3 is very much Rossini's achievement. Here, finally, we have the imaginative model of how *Othello* might be subsumed into music-drama, a model which Verdi not only acknowledged but partially imitated.

The earlier acts of *Otello* are further complicated by the super-fluity of great tenors in Barbaia's company. Though singers like Malibran did later revert to the older *travesti* tradition (she sang Otello to Schroeder-Devrient's Desdemona in 1831), the roles of Otello, Rodrigo, and Iago were tenor roles. The first Otello was Nozzari. He may have refused to black his face but the power of the assumption, even in Berio's compromised version, seems to have impressed observers. Stendhal who knew Kean's Othello, spoke of Nozzari's magnificent stature, of grandeur tinged with melancholy; and Kean himself is said to have admired García's playing of the role in New York in the 1820s. The elevation of Rodrigo to a position of importance second only to that of Otello and Desdemona clearly reflects local, Neapolitan conditions. Written for Giovanni David, the role is filled with fierce and florid writing. His Act 2 aria, 'Ah, come mai non senti', a number which reveals Rodrigo's angry despair in the wake of the revelation that Otello and Desdemona are secretly married, is a brilliant showpiece with an unusually high tessitura and a fiendishly difficult high-lying *cabaletta*.[6] Listening to the opera's first two acts, one senses that the fires often burn brightest when the tenors are locked in vocal combat, notably in the Act 2 confrontation between Otello and Rodrigo, a superb piece of C major *scontro* with searingly highly declamatory lines, plunging basses, and visceral high Cs from both singers. Rossini was to repeat the formula, including its extension into a fraught Trio (Desdemo-

---

[5] See Stendhal's remark, VdR, p.210, 'The theme of serious love is as foreign to Rossini as it is to Walter Scott'.

[6] Part of this *cabaletta* and part of the Otello/Iago duet in the same act were joined by a certain G. Berthold to the 'Katte-Cavatine' of the Danish composer C.E.F. Weyse (1774–1842) to make the famous 'Cat Duet' or *Duetto buffo di due gatti* which is often wrongly attributed to Rossini. See Edward J. Crafts, 'A Tale of Two Cats', BdCRdS, 1975, No.3, p.5.

na's entry, *molto agitato*, nervously syncopated, C minor) in *La donna del lago*.

The Act 1 finale is also powerfully shaped along the lines of the *Tancredi* formula; but what redeems *Otello* is not its often ungainly bending of Shakespeare's play to formalized acts of confrontation. It is redeemed by Rossini's treatment of the character of Desdemona. Neither Rossini's Desdemona nor Verdi's is, in all respects, the same as Shakespeare's. Just as Shakespeare's Iago is turned by Boito and Verdi into a suave Machiavel, so his homely, often down-to-earth girl who entreats Othello to care for his gloves and feed on nourishing dishes is turned into a sweet, saintly, suffering thing. García, it is said, advised his pupils to study great paintings of Mary Magdalene and the Pietàs of the old masters to catch her special character and significance. Something of this is glimpsed in the earlier acts, in Desdemona's Act 1 duet with Emilia where the balletic 'Quanto son fieri i palpiti' gives ecstatic expression to the idea of love's pain and in the finale to Act 2, an E minor/E major sequence of great expressive and dramatic tension which a singer like Malibran must have gloried in. But it is Act 3 which co-ordinates and crowns these moments. Indeed, if 'Quanto son fieri i palpiti' expresses the pain of love, going on to spell out that 'the joy lasts but a moment; the pain stays for ever', its corollary comes near the start of Act 3 in the opera's most famous invention when the conversation of Desdemona and Emilia is interrupted by the song of a distant gondolier (Ex.16).

The words are taken from lines 121–3 of Canto V of Dante's *Inferno*. 'There is no greater woe,' says the poet, 'than to recall past happiness in time of distress.'[7] The interlude, precursor of the sailor's song in *Tristan und Isolde* and the shepherd boy's song in *Tosca*, casts its shadow over all that follows. Rossini tells us that the idea (which alone justifies the retention of the action in Venice) was his own. Berio, ever the cultural snob, appears to have objected on the grounds that no gondolier would sing Dante. The melody, it seems, is also Rossini's, and like the 'Willow Song' which soon follows

---

[7] Parodied by Donizetti in his opera *La romanziera e l'uomo nero* (1831, Naples) as 'There is no greater woe than to have an empty belly and to make love in time of distress'. Earlier, in *Le convenienze teatrali* (1827, Naples) Donizetti had used the 'Willow Song' from *Otello* as the subject for Mamm'Agata's catastrophic audition scene.

Ex.16

(Ex.17), it confirms the sharpness and sensitivity of his ear for the individual line and chromatic harmonies of folk song. The 'Willow Song', which begins in the same key as the gondolier's refrain, G minor, is scored for harp, strings, and wind. It is a wonderful invention, less highly individualized than Verdi's, but touching and memorable in equal measure.

Ex.17

Taking its cue from a line in the Shakespeare, the third stanza fails to resolve, and Desdemona's sudden access of self-doubt is intensified by the sound of the rising storm outside. The song resumes but the line is spare and unvarnished and there are broken exchanges with the clarinet before the song reaches its impassioned close on an unresolved cadence.

In *Othello* this scene is not followed by the murder of Desdemona. Berio and Rossini solve the problem – and sustain the act's remarkable seamless structure – by the introduction of a prayer, 'Deh, calma, o Ciel, nel sonno' (*Larghetto*, 6/8, A flat major), a procedure also adopted by Boito and Verdi. Verdi uses muted strings for his accompaniment, Rossini uses solo winds. Each is affecting in its way. The entry of Otello into the bedchamber is, it must be said, somewhat incongruous; Julian Budden has likened it to 'a gesture from one of Haydn's more humorous symphonies'.[8] We must await Assur's mad scene in *Semiramide* if we wish to hear writing for double-basses of Verdian intensity. Otello is given a good deal of expressive and dramatic licence in the recitatives which follow. A storm plays about the murder scene as it will in Verdi's *Rigoletto* but the dramatic thrust of the scene, if not its forward impetus, is to some extent compromised by the duet for Desdemona and Otello ('Non arrestare il colpo'). It has the feel of a set piece about it, and it has been further criticized for using a subsidiary figure from Don Basilio's Calumny aria. Calumny is not, I suppose, wholly irrelevant at this point in the story, but it is unlikely that Rossini used the idea emblematically. In fact, as Philip Gossett reports, Rossini noticed the incongruity and carefully pasted out the passage in the autograph, replacing it with an alterative which retains the harmonies whilst

[8] Budden, *The Operas of Verdi*, III, p.394.

modifying the melody and rhythm.[9] The murder of Desdemona – explicit and onstage – is both horrible and stirring and the aftermath is suitably bleak before the festive entry of the Doge, Rodrigo (Berio's conflation of Roderigo and Cassio, still alive), and Desdemona's father, Emilio. Otello's suicide is abrupt and rather perfunctory. 'This Otello is too patently shallow', wrote Stendhal, 'to convince me beyond reasonable doubt that it is not simple vanity which makes him seize the dagger'.[10] But Otello is not the key to Rossini's opera. At the work's centre stands Desdemona, one of the most strikingly imagined heroines of the *ottocento*, a heroine who does not deserve the near-oblivion which time and Verdi have imposed upon her.

[9] See Gossett, pp.315–16. The original version is misleadingly reproduced by Joseph Kerman as evidence of Rossinian irresponsibility in a dismissive passage on Rossini's *Otello* in *Opera as Drama*, New York, 2/1956, pp.144–5.

[10] VdR, p.211.

25

Il barbiere di Siviglia
and the transformation of a tradition

Il barbiere di Siviglia was not, in its earliest years, Rossini's best-liked opera. Its arrival at classic status came rather later, at a time, ironically, when Rossini's general stock was beginning to fall. Nowadays we accept its status but tend to overlook its radical impact at the time. In 1816 Rossini's Figaro shocked and stirred a largely unsuspecting public. Here, in its newest manifestation in Figaro's 'Largo al factotum', was the embodiment of the old-driving force itself, the libidinous *élan vital* which underpins much that is innovative and youthful in human affairs. In his book on Rossini, Lord Derwent spends no more than a couple of pages on *Il barbiere di Siviglia*. A good wine, he suggests, needs no bush, though before moving on he notes among other things the opera's 'nervous outburst of vitality',[1] a quality which must have commended the opera both to Beethoven, whose early enthusiasm for it seems entirely plausible in view of his own achievement in something like the Eighth Symphony, and to Verdi who was to be the opera's best and shrewdest advocate in the later years of the century.

This radical, vitalizing quality extends beyond the immediate impact of Figaro's famous *cavatina* to other elements – to Rossini's ear for vocal and instrumental timbres of a peculiar astringency and brilliance, to his control of form and the controlled explosions within the forms which are so much a feature of this opera, to his quick, intelligent word-setting, and to what Verdi calls 'the abundance of true musical ideas'.[2] If *Il barbiere di Siviglia* falters, as Mozart's *Le nozze di Figaro* almost does and Verdi's *Falstaff* does

[1] Lord Derwent, *Rossini and Some Forgotten Nightingales*, London, 1934, p.141. The English writer, Thomas Love Peacock (1785–1866) wrote of the first London performances of *Il barbiere di Siviglia:* 'We saw at once that there was a great revolution in dramatic music. Rossini burst on the stage like a torrent . . .' (*Works*, IX, London, 1924–34, p.244).

[2] Verdi, letter to Camille Bellaigue, 1898, *I coppialettere di G. Verdi*, Milan, 1913, p.415.

not, it is in its final half-hour. Berta's *aria del sorbetto*, the rapid dispatch of the various intrigues in *secco* recitative, the Count's redundant aria, 'Cessa di più resistere', soon to be re-used in *La Cenerentola*, and the cosy vaudeville finale all suggest not so much laziness as lack of time or simple impatience. By the middle of Act 2 the piece, musically and theatrically speaking, is in the bag and although one of the score's most masterly numbers, the Trio for Almaviva, Rosina, and Figaro is yet to come, the opera never quite regains the impulse achieved by the peremptory dismissal of Don Basilio to his sick-bed and the unmasking of the lovers which follows.

We must assume that Rossini had pondered the idea of the opera for some time. Beaumarchais was evidently a kindred spirit though choices were circumscribed. *Le mariage de Figaro* was out of the question; to the young Rossini's enlightened perception Mozart's *Le nozze di Figaro* was already *hors concours*. Paisiello, by contrast, was fair game. His setting of *Le barbier de Séville* had been prepared for the St Petersburg Court in 1782. Rossini was not himself averse to playing the role of court composer; in old age he wrote his *Petite messe solennelle* in a context, if not a style, which is distinctly courtly; but Paisiello's opera, for all its charm and accomplishment, was too placid, too settled in its ways to accord with the 24-year-old Rossini's concept of the play's explosive possibilities. Comparing Rossini's setting of the play with Paisiello's is an unnerving experience; for whatever generous protestations of respect were made in the libretto's *Avvertimento al pubblico*, Rossini's attitude to the music of his distinguished predecessor is that of a cat to a cornered mouse. The mouse may be allowed a few brief independent flurries (Rossini made no attempt to emulate the wonderful Trio for Bartolo and his sneezing, yawning servants, Wakeful and Youthful) but it is soon scotched and dispatched. The scotching of Paisiello is seen in a number of places. In both operas Count Almaviva's appearance as Don Basilio's assistant is characterized by a monotonous nasal whine but Rossini's setting is made funnier by excruciating violin colours and by the lightning *parlando* interludes which remind us of the multiple perspectives from which this drama of disguises and deceptions can be viewed. Cruellest cut of all, is Rossini's deliberately or inadvertently launching his own self-evidently superior setting of Basilio's calumny speech with a repeated-note figure which occurs midway through Paisiello's piece.

Crucially, Paisiello's version lacks the energy which informs Beaumarchais's and Rossini's recreation of the comic archetype. Beaumarchais's Figaro is, if anything, made even more vital by Rossini and Sterbini. In the opera he is less a man of the world, more a resourceful servant, closer to the archetypes we find in *commedia dell'arte* or such characters as Molière's Scapin or Dickens's Sam Weller, than to Beaumarchais's occasionally more urbane refugee from the sordid world of literary endeavour. Beaumarchais's darker *arrière-pensées* are systematically excluded from Sterbini's text, making the operatic Figaro a creature of motion, impulse, and concentrated energy. Which is why the portrait retains its vitality and its power of contemporary appeal. In the late 1970s, the Fiat car company based a famous television commercial on a voiceless, electronically revamped version of Figaro's *cavatina*. As Peter Conrad has noted:

> Figaro himself is an apt patron saint for Fiat's new car. In that opening aria he brags of his ubiquity and utility as a factotum for the whole city of Seville: he's as manoeuvrable, as adventurous and as speedy as the car. His aria also lightly converts technical difficulty into display, and implies that robots are – like him – not mechanical genii, but larky, embullient show-offs.[3]

Beaumarchais's play does, of course, provide its own energy and some specifically musical cues. When Figaro describes Bartolo as 'a stoutish, shortish, oldish, greyish, cunning, smarmy, posing, nosing, peeping, prying, creeping, whining, snivelling sort of man', Beaumarchais is indulging his own kind of dizzying verbal *stretta*. In Basilio's calumny speech Beaumarchais actually invokes the dynamic extremes which Rossini deploys in his mature comic movements: *piano, piano – pianissimo – rinforzando* – the *crescendo* itself. Paisiello's setting notes the devices but mutes them. There is none of Rossini's sly and senuous word-pointing, no chilling, buzzing string sonorities in the Paisiello. And Paisiello's *crescendo* is neither as well orchestrated, as well timed, nor as powerful as Rossini's which is crowned with formidable force by the bass drum on the phrase 'colpo di cannone'.

The forms now evolved by Rossini for deployment in *opera*

[3] Conrad, *Television: the medium and and its manners,* London, 1982, p.110.

buffa are used in *Il barbiere di Siviglia* both to contain the comedy and to furnish the characters with constraints which they either cling to or iconoclastically reject. The first act begins and ends with carefully formulated structures. The *introduzione*, which redeploys music first used in *Aureliano in Palmira* and *Sigismondo*, is a tripartite structure with the Count's *cavatina*, 'Ecco ridente in cielo' (*Largo*, 2/4, C major), as its centrepiece and the noisy paying off of the musicians as its *stretta*. The Act 1 finale has one of the finest of all Rossini's moments of frozen stasis ('Fredda ed immobile') and a *stretta* in which the Rossini train sways over the points more agreeably than in any other opera. There is, though, a disturbing rumbustiousness about the finale's first ten minutes. The annunciatory and motivating figure (Ex.18) is Beethovenian in its abruptness and thrust.

Ex.18

What follows – the Count's drunken entry, his confrontation with Bartolo, the appearance of Rosina, the incident of the letter – is rowdily disruptive, with frequent changes of musical pace and direction. There are also surprising touches: the sly pathos of Rosina's 'sempre un' istoria', and the magical transition for soloists and orchestra after the soldiers' arrival, a transition which drops us down into a sudden crazed *vivace*, a dazzling canonic passage in which the characters, locked by the situation into frenzied imitation, protest vehemently to the officer about each other's behaviour.

Much of the score's effectiveness in such moments can be put down to what Verdi calls Rossini's 'accuracy of declamation'. This is strikingly evident in Rosina's *cavatina*, 'Una voce poco fa' (*Andante*, 3/4, E major). As we have already seen (Exx. 14a and 14b) a fluent coloratura number has been transformed by Rossini into a keenly pointed, sharply observed portrait in words and music of this charming, vixenish creature. We hear this later in Rosina's duet with Figaro ('Dunque io son', *Allegro*, 4/4, G major), Sterbini's text brilliantly set by Rossini over an accompaniment of exceptional fleetness and wit. The earlier duet, between Figaro and the Count ('All' idea di quel metallo', *Allegro maestoso*, 4/4, G major), is more complex. As the plot to insinuate the Count into Bartolo's house is hatched, Rossini resorts to a complex multi-sectioned structure with a variety of comic devices from the mock-solemn to the farcical, bound together by recurring orchestral figures and the repetition of the choric, exclamatory, self-congratulatory refrain 'Che invenzione prelibata!', 'What a delicious idea!'. There is also a memorable short insert, Figaro's cameo portrait of a pathetically drunken man, and the famous *stretta* (the only part of the scene set by Paisiello) in which Figaro tells the Count how to identify his shop in Seville.

In the theatre the opera's comic thrust is a very obvious one. As Rodney Milnes has noted: 'The whole joyous point [of *Il barbiere di Siviglia*] is that all the characters are opportunist monsters; this is why, gazing into the proscenium mirror, we all love it so much.'[4] But the opera is also rich in specifically musical jokes, and not merely jokes at the expense of Bartolo's old-fashioned musical tastes or *opera seria* itself, both of which Rossini introduces into the singing scene. One of the best of the Beaumarchais-derived jokes comes near the start of the opera, though it is a pity that Sterbini's rather laconic *secco* recitative over-shortens Beaumarchais's build-up to the moment. In the opera it is not entirely clear when Figaro urges the Count to serenade Rosina beneath her balcony that the Count is extremely nervous both about the words he will sing and his guitar technique. What follows, however, vividly characterizes the Count's difficulties. Sterbini's verses are deliberately awkward and irregular, and Rossini's music, though miraculously capable of *bel canto* transformation, is also awkward in key, *tessitura*, and phrasing. Where Paisiello and his librettist give us a perfectly manicured *Canzone*

---

[4] Rodney Milnes, 'Barber black sheep', *Spectator*, 30 March, 1985, p.31.

(Ex.19a), Rossini's number (19b) is almost a parody of the form, a minor key *aubade* which is eloquent in spite of itself.

Ex.19

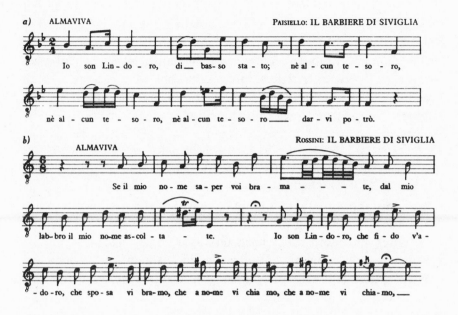

Twice in the opera, comedy derives from formal musical man-oeuvres. Dr Bartolo's *cavatina* ('A un dottor della mia sorte', *Andante maestoso*, 4/4, E flat major) is given dignity and pride by its principal motivating figure which returns with smug inevitability after a central *allegro* vivace, one of the fastest pieces of *buffo* patter ever written and cast in, of all things, sonata form. Cavilling, correct, sharp-eared, and a worthy adversary for all-comers, Dr Bartolo is characterized by Rossini in a way which suggests, if not Padre Mattei himself, then comparable academic figures who had haunted his teenage years in Bologna.

The second example is the Act 2 Trio, 'Ah! qual colpo' (*Andante maestoso*, 4/4, F major) in which Almaviva and Rosina bill and coo, to Figaro's despair, after their misunderstandings have been sorted out. This Trio is funny at several levels. Figaro's mockery is conveyed by a simple echo effect (first worked out, in this instance, in the innocuous context of the cantata *Egle ed Irene*), an effect familiar from orchestral writing where instrumental echoes are used to punctuate, round out or mock the vocal line at phrase ends. At this level the comedy is broad and obvious. But there is, as Philip Gossett has pointed out,[5] the more arcane comedy of the lovers' fatal delay being occasioned by the music's irksome compliance with the formal demands of *cabaletta* and cadence repeats.

The Trio, as we have seen, is a redeeming feature of the rather weak final movement of the opera, though we should not neglect to note the placing of the storm music close to Rosina's assumption of the infidelity of 'Lindoro', a move which heightens the sense of crisis in an effective way. Act 2 also contains one of the score's finest inventions, the unannounced arrival of Don Basilio who is rapidly frightened and bribed back to his sick bed having been convinced by the assembled company that he is suffering from scarlet fever. The farewell to Basilio (Ex.20) takes fresh impetus from the transition itself, G major arrived at after 'presto a letto' via the leading-note of the tonic E flat. The twice-stated opening phrase (a), with its descending motion and snapping cadence, is urgent and dismissive whereas the answering phrase (b) – disingenuously soothing and later taken up by all four characters as a choric refrain – has the simple charm of a lullaby. Whilst we enjoy the music's symmetry, energy, grace, and wit, poor Basilio is trapped between the two opposing but conjunct forces.

Ex.20

The Quintet over, Rossini, ever the master of mimetic movement, gives us one of his frothiest allegros for the shaving sequence, beautifully crossed by a level crotchet motion as the lovers furtively plot. Bartolo's unmasking of the lovers ('Bricconi! birbanti!', *Allegro*, 3/8, E flat major) undoes all this. As the characters hector and rage, the woodwinds give out a simple syncopated figure (Ex.21) which it is difficult not to identify with Rossini himself, ever the

[5] Gossett, *Grove 6*, Vol.16, p.233.

Ex.21

detached and amused observer of a world full of intrigue, folly, and a strange disruptive energy.

Whilst *Il barbiere di Siviglia* was being planned, Rossini and Sterbini were rushing out a not entirely satisfactory *dramma semi-serio* in two acts, *Torvaldo e Dorliska*. Sterbini's rather dim little drama generates no real dramatic momentum much before Act 2 and Rossini seems to have settled for a routine of rather long set-piece arias and duets. The story concerns the exceptionally unpleasant Duke of Ordow, Galli's role in the *prima* in Rome, and his designs on Dorliska, the wife of the young knight, Torvaldo. Before the opera begins, the Duke has ambushed Torvaldo and Dorliska. Dorliska has escaped (but takes refuge in the nearest habitation which turns out to be the Duke's castle) and Torvaldo has been left for dead. When we first encounter him, he has recovered sufficiently to don a disguise and visit the castle bearing a letter which he claims has been given to him by a dying knight for delivery to Dorliska. Unfortunately, at their first encounter (Sterbini's Act 1 finale) Dorliska betrays both herself and her husband by immediately and obviously recognizing him. With both hero and heroine now in the villain's grasp, Act 2 turns the opera into a rescue drama in which the rescue is largely engineered by the *buffo*, Giorgio, the Duke's steward but no friend of the monster. It is Giorgio who gives the opera its tentative status as *opera semiseria*. His pleasantries apart, the score is mainly notable for some incidental beauties in the solo numbers, though there is an elaborately worked confrontation between Dorliska and the Duke which carries a considerable dramatic charge as well as some memorable detail, and the prison duet for Torvaldo and Dorliska further develops aspects of the character of Dorliska first glimpsed in Act 1. Only the Duke's music has real power; indeed, Rossini was later to plunder his Act 2 aria 'Ah, quel voce d'intorno rimbomba' for parts of the vengeance duet in *Otello*.

26

La Cenerentola: an essay in comic pathos

The alacrity with which Rossini accepted the suggestion of an opera on the Cinderella story, and the speed, precision, and care with which he wrote the opera all point to a happy congruence of events in his creative life. It is a brilliant and witty piece, but a moving one, too, the *comédie larmoyante* element made the more effective by the restrained manner with which it is touched into the larger drama.

The Cinderella story, which Rossini must have known as a child and later through Pavesi's *Agatina* (1814, Milan), is one of the oldest and most frequently adapted fairy-tales. Specialists in folklore have identified over three hundred known variants of which there are probably three principal archetypes, each with its own social and psychological emphasis. The most familiar is the version which has come down to us from the seventeenth-century French writer, Charles Perrault. This is the version with the cruel stepmother, the fairy godmother, the pumpkin coach drawn by mice, and the famous slipper. It is a very feminine version of the tale, with a high element of romantic fantasy, the kind of thing which would have suited Weber or Berlioz better than Rossini. Two other variants are more male-orientated. Instead of a stepmother there is a father or stepfather who makes emotional demands, love tests and the like, on a favourite daughter. Again, it is not a version which would immediately attract Rossini. Sexually and psychologically disturbing, its most famous embodiment in literature is probably in Shakespeare's *King Lear*. The third variant, the one favoured by the witty, rational, humanistic Rossini, is stripped of fantasy and magic. The brutal, bullying stepfather is no more than an impoverished aristocrat; the ugly sisters become gossiping snobs. It is a version which suited Jane Austen as well as Rossini. Her last and in many ways her most haunting novel, *Persuasion*, presents Anne Elliot as a Cinderella figure, a girl who is the butt of uncaring female relatives and a snobbish father. This essentially rational, satirical version of the story is nicely adjacent to the well-known *opera buffa* formula of lovers, accomplices, and foolish guardians; but it is *buffo* comedy crossed with sentiment and pathos and a certain residual cruelty, a curious blend of the aristocratic and the bourgeois, the urbane and the homely.

These pathetic and moralizing elements are endemic in Rossini's immediate sources. His own opera is subtitled *La bontà in trionfo*; Pavesi's *Agatina* is subtitled *La virtù premiata*. Links can be traced back through Italian operatic history nearly sixty years to stage versions of such morally improving works as Samuel Richardson's *Pamela*. Not everyone approved of Rossini's tangling with this tradition. Stendhal was not at all taken with the idea of a dowdy girl crouching by a hearth; he found much of *La Cenerentola* touched with 'a servant's hall vulgarity'.[1] Rossini is, however, more sensitive than his urbane biographer. The very name Cenerentola suggests (in Italian and in the German Aschenputtel) ashes and expiation. And how better to express the solitary, expiatory mood in restrained but romantic terms than in the sad minor key folk-song which Rossini provides for his heroine? Cenerentola's song, which crops up several times in the opera, is a wonderful example of the art which disguises art. But, equally, how typical it is of Rossini to hold sentimentality at bay by allowing the song to be cruelly mocked by the ugly sisters, Clorinda and Tisbe, at its first reprise (Ex.22).

The ugly sisters resemble Baronessa Aspasia and Donna Fulvia, the unlovely pair of snobs in *La pietra del paragone*. Their prim interruption of the ballad and their high, obsessive calling of Cenerentola's name in the midst of her first encounter with Prince Ramiro remind us how aptly Rossini deploys vocal texture: Cenerentola's velvety contralto persistently thrown into acrid relief by the bright bird-like sounds of her querulous soprano rivals. Cenerentola's first encounter with Prince Ramiro, who has exchanged clothes and outward rank with his servant, Dandini, is an excellent example of Rossini's mastery of the deftly characterized, dramatically evolving ensemble. The sisters' off-stage calling introduces a further tension and instability into a duet which has begun conventionally enough but which has already gone awry at Cenerentola's gabbled and nonsensical 'Quel ch'è padre, non è padre', Rossini using comic

---

[1] VdR, p.246. For Stendhal's essay on *La Cenerentola* see Chapter XX, *passim*.

Ex.22

patter and a sinking tonality to convey to us Cenerentola's pathetically confused state of mind.

More arresting still is the scene ('Signor, una parola', Quintet, *Allegro*, 4/4, C major) in which Cenerentola's double-dealing stepfather, Don Magnifico, attempts to ignore her plea for an hour at the Prince's ball. Caught between the need to be obsequious ('Serenissima!') and ruthless ('Ma vattene' 'Get out of here'), Magnifico informs Ramiro and Dandini that the girl is a mere kitchen-wench, a 'servaccia ignorantissima'. 'A servant?' the visitors incredulously ask, and as the music moves forward the woodwinds add their own wry comment, as much as to say 'You must be joking!'. It is a harder, brittler world than that of, say, Mozart's *Le nozze di Figaro* and, in some ways, a more painful one. The sequence ends squarely in the tonic which is immediately supplanted by a bold summons in E flat major at the entry of Ramiro's tutor and moral guide, Alidoro. Alidoro has a list of eligible maidens in Magnifico's household and it includes three names. Magnifico blusters briefly and then, with Cenerentola standing near him, announces that the third sister is dead. In a naive aside, Cenerentola denies the fact but Magnifico, warming to his morbid lie, repeats it with a chilling assumption of sincerity, 'Your Highness, your Highness . . . dead', the orchestra producing shocked judders of sound and then (Ex.23) a plaintive descent to one of the opera's most charged silences.

Ex.23

At which point, having reduced his audience to numbed disbelief, Rossini launches into one of those ensembles in which the characters attempt to work out, with dispassionate concern, who precisely is duping whom. The *stretta*, which restores the C major tonality, is unusually brilliant. It is a scene which tells us a good deal about a sensibility which marries an almost morbid sensitivity to suffering with a notable capacity for detachment.

Not everything in *La Cenerentola* is quite as radical as this. Away from the drama's critical moments, Don Magnifico is expansively even loosely drawn. His *cavatina* describes a rather odd dream (a premonition of wealth, Magnifico thinks) which involves, among other things, a donkey which sprouts wings and ends up on top of a church spire. Like Macrobio's *cavatina* in *La pietra del paragone*, it gives Rossini scope for a lot of declamatory patter, urbane wind writing, sudden rumbustious tuttis, stalking pizzicati and that specially manic form of verbal and musical onomatopoeia of which he remained so fond. He also makes a good deal of Magnifico's role as Barone di Monte Fiascone, literally Baron Mount-Flagon. In a bibulous scene which predicts some of the carousings in *Le Comte Ory*, Don Ramiro installs Magnifico as 'Superintendant of the Wine Glass'.

Magnifico's real problem, however, is not his daughter or his drinking habits but Ramiro's servant, Dandini. In his essay on the opera, Stendhal spends a good deal of time extolling the merits of the great *buffo cantante*, Luigi Paccini. Stendhal's point is that no Magnifico could ever survive alongside Paccini's Dandini; which is presumably how Rossini wanted it to be. The scene in which Dandini reveals who he really is to an astounded Don Magnifico must rank as a highpoint in this, or any other comic opera we care to nominate; not least for the deft way in which Rossini transforms the broken phrases of Dandini's 'Un segreto d'importanza' into the seamless flow of Magnifico's outraged 'Di quest'ingiuria, di quest'affronto', the *stretta* in quick 6/8 time in which the poor duped man flushes into delirium. In some ways, Dandini is rather sinister, not merely because of his capacity to outwit his rivals in the time-honoured traditions of the Brighella figure of *commedia dell'arte* but because throughout *La Cenerentola* he seems to be manipulating the drama, pulling the strings of the puppets, not unlike the Poet in *Il turco in Italia*. His entrance aria is a parody of *opera seria* magniloquence and includes a passage which Rognoni suggests would make an excellent parody of Verdi but which must, for chronology's sake, be seen as Rossini mocking what are, in retrospect, would-be Verdian elements in his own evolving method. In the great Act 1 finale it is Dandini who unfreezes the characters who have been rendered immobile by the appearance of the strange lady at the Prince's ball. It is Dandini, too, who with his master launches the Act 1 finale with that most brilliantly conspiratorial of all Rossini duets, 'Zitto, zitto; piano, piano' (Ex.24)

Ex.24

Even Stendhal approved of this number, relishing what in a vaguely mixed metaphor he calls 'the bounding floodtide of fantasy'. For Dandini, as for Rossini himself in certain moods, all the world's a game, a festive comedy. Whilst Cenerentola sighs and dreams, the milling majority live out their extraordinary pantomimic existences: 'one man grumbles and complains, another shouts and raves; that one fumes, this one whines; we'll all end up as lunatics'.

The end of *La Cenerentola* is very grand and the heroine's big scene can, in the right hands, be both touching and imposing. As we have seen in Chapter 5, part of the music was borrowed, perhaps at Righetti-Giorgi's request, from the Count's big aria at the end of *Il barbiere di Siviglia*. It was a potentially perilous act of self-borrowing but the newer context is certainly the more productive one. In a sense, though, Cenerentola's intervention in the great Act 2 Sextet ('Siete voi?', *Maestoso*, 4/4, E flat major) is the more memorable. Her gesture of forgiveness is not perhaps as moving as the Countess's in *Le nozze di Figaro* or as sublime as Cordelia's in the parallel but very different context of *King Lear*, but it is an affecting one, a characteristic moment in what is one of Rossini's richest and most humane scores.

27

La gazza ladra and the semiseria style

La Cenerentola and Rossini's next opera, *La gazza ladra*, share some common ground since both operas belong to that *semiseria* genre for which Rossini had developed a special affection and skill. Gherardini's libretto for *La gazza ladra* derives from a real-life event in which a French peasant girl was convicted and hung for thefts later discovered to have been the work of a thieving magpie. The event had stimulated a substantial body of fiction, including a roughed-out text which was eventually taken up by the Parisian theatre-manager Louis Caigniez, 'the Racine of the boulevards', for his *mélodrame historique* or *drame larmoyante, La pie voleuse*.[1] As a drama, it is unusually rich in incident and character, centered on a country community, subject to the king, but dominated by the bustling, sadistic mayor, the 'Podestà del villaggio'. Like Dickens's *The Pickwick Papers*, which also marries high-spirited adventure with prison scenes of unusual grimness, the drama furnishes us with an array of characters, sympathetically, sentimentally, or quirkily drawn. There is the genial, wine-bibbing landowner, Fabrizio Vingradito, his wife, Lucia, and their son, Giannetto, recently returned from the wars and shortly to marry the charming and demure servant-girl, Ninetta, the heroine of the drama and another variant of the Cinderella archetype. Ninetta is herself surrounded by a bevy of minor characters, including the servant boy, Pippo (a *travesti* role) and the pedlar, Isacco, a clear model for Trabuco in Verdi's *La forza del destino*. His whining, nasal, and largely monotone *cavatina* provoked Stendhal into inveighing against Polish Jews in terms which nowadays would have him locked up. There is also the striking figure of Ninetta's father, Fernando Villabella, an army deserter through no fault of his own. One wonders what memories of Giuseppe Rossini's plight in 1800 were stirred by the presence in Gherardini's story of this man,

---

[1] A musical after-play by Isaac Pocock, *The Maid and the Magpie*, was staged at the Drury Lane Theatre, London, in the same year, 1815.

downtrodden, but a powerful, looming presence, and a compassionate father.

On the surface at least, *La gazza ladra* seems to border on
verismo. Ninetta is precisely the kind of sweet, wronged woman we
might expect to find in one of Puccini's operas. Indeed, *La gazza
ladra* owed some revivals in the 1940s and '50s to a shortened and
sweetened version of Rossini's score edited by Riccardo Zandonai, a
verismo composer whose tastes turned back at the end of his life
towards neoclassicism. Rossini's setting does have its romantic or
neoromantic elements. In Act 1, with the Ninetta and her father
standing before him, the Mayor receives a letter which provides a full
description of the deserter. As he has left his spectacles behind, the
Mayor asks Ninetta to read the description, which she does, changing it as she reads. (Interestingly, there is a similar episode in *Boris
Godunov* which may or may not owe something to Pushkin's having
seen *La gazza ladra* during its early progress through Europe.)
Rossini sets the reading as melodrama, the words spoken over a
simmering orchestral accompaniment.

In many other respects, though, *La gazza ladra* is an opera
formulated on classical lines. There are no flights of musico-
ornithological fancy for the eponymous magpie, nor are Rossini's
own forms in duets, trios, and the like sacrificed to short-term
considerations of realism. With the Mayor imminent, Ninetta and
her father still have their *cabaletta*; an expression as much of
Rossini's instinct for order as for any lazy compliance with the forms
he had himself initiated. It is through the more abstract musical
elements, above all, through the rhythms of the music, that feelings
of ecstasy, liberation, confusion, or entanglement are expressed.
When the kindly jailer, Antonio, tries to part Ninetta and Giannetto
lest the Mayor should discover his having allowed Ninetta a few
moments outside her cell, the situation is identical to that in which
Figaro is reduced to sly mockery of the dallying lovers in Act 2 of *Il
barbiere di Siviglia*. Not only is the scene from *La gazza ladra* bereft
of comedy, the very motion of the rhythms and the grimly militaristic
ostinato which underpins the lovers' voices strikingly illustrates
Rossini's formal command of rhythm. Rossini's musical portrait of
the Mayor is similarly controlled. The impression created in his
cavatina, very much a *buffo* piece, is modified in the great Trio which
follows the letter-reading ('O nume benefico', *Maestoso*, 3/4, F
major). Later, in the prison scene in Act 2 there is the dazzling 'Udrai

la sentenza' as the Mayor is called away to the tribunal. It is a *stretta* underpinned, ambiguously, by the overture's gamesome second subject, the snare-drum shedding its colour over a character and a scene which is both brilliant and threatening.

The forms now developed by Rossini allow him to set Gherardini's text in a manner big enough to match the expectations of La Scala, Milan, and the magnificent scenery provided by Sanquirico. One thinks of the tribunal scene with its powerful choral and orchestral writing or the long Act 1 finale which embraces the Mayor's harrying of Ninetta, Isacco's testimony, and Ninetta's commital. Roncaglia suggests that Ninetta is rather pallidly drawn, but this is surely to miss the artlessness of the girl. Her *cavatina* is wonderfully fresh-faced, with its unencumbered, rhythmically spontaneous *cabaletta*. There is the major key pathos of her response to Isacco's revelations in the Act 1 finale ('Mi sento opprimere', *Andantino*, 6/8, A flat major) and the exquisite prison duet ('E ben per mia memoria', *Andantino pastoso*, 12/16, G major) in which Pippo adds his own touching rejoinder (Ex.25)

Ex.25

There is also Ninetta's prayer at the start of the final scene, framed by an eerily scored march to the scaffold ('Infelice, sventurata . . . Deh tu reggi in tal momento', *Moderato*, 4/4, C minor; *Andantino*, 3/4, C major). Though the role of Ninetta attracted singers like Colbran and Pasta it is not in that sense a star part. Malibran was, by all accounts, a memorable Ninetta. Like her Zerlina, her Ninetta was deliberately and bewitchingly rustic, the realistic and idealistic elements, peasant girl and Arcadian shepherdess, fused in a way which must have struck Rossini as the ideal embodiment of his musical and dramatic vision.

It can be said with more justice that Giannetto is too slightly drawn. The libretto itself was criticized on these grounds by the prize-jury in 1816; but Giannetto has his moments, not least the despairing cry when it seems that Ninetta has, indeed, stolen the family silver (Ex.26).

Ex.26

GIANNETTO

(Ed __ io ____ la cre de - - a l'i - stes-sa o - ne - stà!)

It is, however, Ninetta's relationship with her father which is more fully noted. Like Verdi, Rossini was easily stirred by the emotion of parental love. It is the old father, Polidoro, who more or less single-handedly renders the rather chilly *Zelmira* humane; and in *La gazza ladra* it is Fernando who gives the opera some of its fundamental power and appeal. His Act 1 duet with Ninetta, the Trio already cited, and his intervention in the trial scene are pointers to the kind of thing we shall hear in middle-period Verdi. Unfortunately, opera house economics and the fickleness of singers have often led to the omission or replacement of Fernando's solo scene before the trial. The E flat major aria 'Accusato di furto' was often replaced by another piece, 'Oh colpo impensato', in Rossini's day.

La gazza ladra enabled Rossini to deploy a range of idioms and colours. The unbuttoned mood of the pastoral jollifications looks forward to the variety of choral and dance movements in Rossini's next opera, *Armida*, and his last opera, *Guillaume Tell*. There is also evidence of a growing range and added care in the orchestral writing. The reprise of Ninetta's march to the execution place creates a complex ensemble as the procession winds through the village: *fortissimo* strings and snare-drum, woodwinds and pizzicato strings, horns and clarinets, *smorzando*. The discovery of the magpie's nest of treasures and Ninetta's last-minute reprieve makes for a jubilant close. It may not be as stirring as the end of Beethoven's *Fidelio* but it brings to a triumphant conclusion an opera which can equally well be said to celebrate the power of human affection and the resilience and vitality of the human spirit in a disordered world.

28

Armida and the new romanticism

By the autumn of 1817, Naples had a new Teatro San Carlo and a rather different resident composer from the one who had given it *Elisabetta* and *Otello*. Stylistically speaking, the 25-year-old Rossini was beginning to put on weight. This added girth and power, much in evidence in *La gazza ladra* and to some extent consolidated in *Armida*, can be attributed in part to the natural processes of maturation. But by this stage in Rossini's career we have to reckon with other influences, too: with ever headier and more *outré* expressions of Romanticism in Europe at large,[1] and with the increasingly direct influence of Colbran and Barbaia on Rossini's work within Naples itself. Colbran's influence is evident in Rossini's enriched, dramatically enhanced, coloratura writing. Nor is it mere prurience which leads one to ask whether, before his twenty-fifth year and before the increasing closeness of his relationship with Colbran, Rossini would have been capable of writing music as impassioned and as implicitly erotic as much of the writing in *Armida* undoubtedly is. Even if we stop short of casting Colbran too obviously in the role of Rossini's Mathilde Wesendonk, there is no doubting a darker, more sensual quality in the writing here. There is also a new wilfulness in something like the *marziale* near the end of Act 1, a movement which would not sound amiss in Verdi's *Il trovatore*. In *Armida*, Rossini's music loses some of its innocence. Stendhal's famous phrase, *candeur virginale*, is not one which will often spring to mind in these later Neapolitan years.

The tale of Armida's enslavement of the Christian knight, Rinaldo, taken from Tasso's *Gerusalemme liberata*, had been set many times before. Its potential as spectacle must have attracted Barbaia who would have been looking for the grandest possible opening for his newly built theatre; and he must have prevailed with Rossini. To judge from letters Rossini wrote in later years, he was

[1] See Appendix A, 1816–21.

temperamentally averse to subjects which touched on the bizarre or the diabolic. Spontaneity and naturalism were ever his watchwords, he told Count Carlo Dona in 1853. *Armida* does not disprove the truth of the existence of these general predilections; but it does indicate that in the heyday of his career Rossini was not averse to experiment where it was persuasively propounded. Barbaia engaged as librettist Giovanni Schmidt. His text is a workmanlike one. He clearly knows his Tasso (quotations from the original are embedded in the libretto) and he gives an adequate form to the drama. The shape of Act 1 – where we might guess at interventions by Rossini himself – is especially interesting. It is a tripartite structure whose first two movements juxtapose the brilliant, daylit world of chivalric endeavour with the gloomier, more sensual world of Armida and whose third movement dramatically interlocks them. Act 2 has a more fluid, almost baroque feel to it; but Act 3 re-engages the Christian-pagan, light-and-dark, naif and sentimental oppositions. Characteristically, though, Rossini does not resolve these. The opera does not end in some minor key Faustian descent into the abysss nor in a hymn to reason, nor in erotic apotheosis. It may be less than a day's march from Rossini's sensuous vocal writing to 'O sink hernieder', but Rinaldo is no Tristan, and though Armida is one of the first of the great nineteenth-century operatic *femmes fatales*, Rossini is not interested in her immortal soul. As D.H. Lawrence noted, Italian opera runs on impulse and does not worry about the ultimate.

Rinaldo and the Paladin knights are first revealed to us in the overture's D minor *maestoso*, a march subject which unexpectedly recurs within twenty-seven bars of the start of the *allegro*. The Paladins' moral fervour, the daylit brilliance of their world, is clearly characterized in Goffredo's brief *cavatina*, an heroic annunciation of the funeral rites of the dead Duke Dudone. In fact, the succession to Dudone proves to be a controversial issue; it recurs throughout the first act, in the finale and in the big three-part aria for Gernando ('Non soffriro l'offesa', *Allegro*, 4/4, A major). Gernando is Rinaldo's jealous rival and one of six roles, not all of them major, requiring a tenor. It is the voice-type which gives to the chivalric world of Armida its peculiar *tinta*; it is also a voice-type for which Rossini writes with increasing assurance.

It is into this world that Armida insinuates herself. She has no entrance aria, but is immediately and strikingly characterized in the

great Quartet 'Sventurata! or che mi resta?' (*Allegro*, 4/4, E major).
On the page (Ex.27) the music looks merely florid. But as Maria
Callas memorably demonstrated in performances in Florence in
1952, and as Colbran must have done in Naples in 1817, this is
music in which the *bel canto* style is precisely and powerfully used to
convey the impression of Armida – part woman, part sorceress –
caught in the toils of her own fantasy.

Ex.27

The Paladin knights are intimidated by Armida, their consciences
stirred by her emotional blackmailing. In a famous phrase (Ex.28)
which Rossini may have owed in part to his Neapolitan predecessor
Giuseppe Giordani (1753–98), Goffredo, already overwhelmed by
Armida, asks what is to be done, though it is inevitable that her
disingenuous request for a troupe of choicest knights to help restore
her to her throne will be granted.

Ex.28

At the centre of Act 1 is the first, and more famous, of the love duets
Rossini writes for Armida and Rinaldo, 'Amor, possente nome!'
(*Allegro giusto*, 4/4, E flat major). For the modern tenor it must be a
tantalising piece, its elegant lines and heart-easing modulations coup-
led with some exceptionally difficult internal embellishment (Ex.29).
It is a classic Rossini duet which defines personalities and situations by sensuous invention and formal patterning. The lyric section in G
major, 'Vacilla a quegli accenti', is no mere essay in swooning thirds

Ex.29

and sixths. The quasi-canonic writing takes on a mimetic function, suggesting Rinaldo's dangerous proximity to, yet life-saving distance from, Armida's finely-spun web of sexual allure. Even where the voices merge, Rossini makes distinctions, Armida's line rising in a conventional triplet motion whilst on the words 'no, no, non ha', Rinaldo's drifts helplessly down in chromatic steps from G to E before being drawn up again into the triplet motion of Armida's line.

The effect of this first love duet is sustained beyond its end. Ostensibly, the start of the Act 1 finale returns us to the world of martial endeavour. Jealous of Rinaldo's political success, Gernando challenges Rinaldo to a duel and is killed. 'Che terribile momento!' reflect Armida and Rinaldo; but, insidiously, the contemplative moment seems to be more an extension of the love duet than a genuine reflection of the breach of chivalric decorum that has lead to Gernando's death. Goffredo is sent for, and in a second duet within the finale's structure, Armida expresses her disquiet at a lover who is so exposed to mortal danger. 'Duty, is Rinaldo's answer, but the A flat lullaby is delusive; as the music sinks towards E flat minor their disquiet is a shared disquiet. It is at this point, Rossini's music seems to suggest, that Rinaldo is really lost. In the after-shock of the confrontation with Gernando, he allows himself to slip into a child-like acquiescence with Armida's emotional demands. Goffredo returns and challenges Rinaldo; but both Rinaldo and Armida are now determined – as the somewhat arcane imagery indicates – to seize the goddess Fortune's proffered forelock. As has already been noted, the *stretta* has a martial, wilful gait which is Verdian in its raw power.

In Act 2 Rossini enters a ghastly, Fury-infested forest, a Weberish world which pre-dates *Der Freischütz* by three and a half years.

Never before has Rossini resorted so promiscuously to the use of diminished harmonies, nor has he written for brass quite so robustly. The first chorus, in A minor, is imposing; the second, 'Di ferro e fiamma cinti' (*Allegro moderato*, 4/4, C minor), is even more so. Here the declamatory choral writing, chilling trombones and bright trumpets powerfully embody the Furies' fretful assertion of vanished power in what is a defiant narrative of their Fall. After this hellish brew, the mood switches for the most languorous of the duets between Rinaldo and Armida ('Dove son io?', *Andante maestoso*, 3/4, A major). A solo cello accompanies the duet, Rossini now wonderfully acclimatized to writing for the blend of male and female voices. 'Dove son io?', built out of four short lines of stichomythia and a pair of two-line stanzas, is music, vocally speaking, of great erotic allure; but in the classically-derived world of *Armida* erotic consummation is sublimated into scenic transformation, the music welling from E flat to E as a great palace swims into view. After which, passion is further sublimated in choral tributes and ritual dance. This is Rossini's first full ballet. In the lovely E flat Andante the solo cello and solo horn are again prominent. Armida's culminatory *Tema con variazioni*, 'D'amore al dolce impero' (*Andante grazioso*, 3/4, F major) reworks the idea of *carpe diem*. It is a virtuoso display piece and is the blandest of the music Rossini writes for Armida; it remains, however, stylistically apt to its somewhat baroque context.

Act 3 re-establishes the tension between the two opposed worlds. Ubaldo and Carlo, the two knights dispatched to rescue Rinaldo, survey the innocent-seeming rural scene in a trudging F major pastoral duet in 6/8 time, though fear soon sweeps over them. There is a final sybaritic idyll for Armida and Rinaldo, 'Soavi catene' (*Andante grazioso*, 3/8, E major) where the two voices and a solo violin do indeed conjure sweet chains of sound. But at the heart of the act is the famous moment when Rinaldo sees his besotted image reflected in the adamantine shield which Ubaldo and Carlo hold up before him. The Trio for three tenors which follows ('In quale aspetto imbelle', *Maestoso*, 3/4, C major) is often spoken of. It is a brilliant realization of the moment, a thrilling sound concept in itself.

For the finale – Rinaldo's parting from Armida, her despair, and final furious arousal – Rossini is obliged to return to the richer palatte of some earlier scenes. Armida's 'Se al mio crudel tormento' returns us to the musical language of the Act 1 Quartet. The parting of the lovers is imaginatively handled, the harmonies changing beneath eighteen bars of a single repeated F sharp, dropping us down into Armida's 'Dove so: io?' and a brief perception of her as a defeated, grieving woman, like Niobe, all tears (Ex.30)

Ex.30

del — mio tro - var si — può più a - tro - ce — sta - to!

A curious piece of allegory follows. Armida is confronted by the spirits of Vengeance and Love. Love is banished but briefly restored in a passage illumined by touching flute descants before the Furies are summonded in a passage notable for more diminished harmonies and the bass's ominous descents in semitones. The opera ends, though, in the tonic major as Armida mounts her dragon-drawn chariot and prepares to ride off in what we must assume is a fatal pursuit.

29

Mosè in Egitto (1818–19) and Moïse et Pharaon (1827)

In its original form, *Mosè in Egitto* is an *azione tragico-sacra*, a biblical drama suitable for staging during Lent; and if that sounds unduly forbidding, it should be noted at once that Rossini and his librettist, Andrea Leone Tottola, have grafted on to the Old Testament narrative a love story taken from a drama of the 1760s. Thus a young Jewish girl, Elcia, falls in love with the Pharaoh's son, Osiride. Elcia and Osiride, Aida and Radames: it is a similar tale of disputed homelands, of the tension between love and duty, and the counterpointing of the bonds of family and the bonds of country.

For much of its length, *Mosè in Egitto* has a guileless beauty about it, apt to the theme of young love and young nationhood, qualities which are not so much sacrificed (much of the best music is preserved) as choked and smothered in the grandiose revision prepared for Paris in 1827 by an older composer writing for an alien audience and a sophisticated metropolitan culture. Wherever we turn in *Mosè in Egitto* – whether it is to the lovely F major Quintet in Act 1, to the famous Quartet 'Mi manca la voce' in Act 2, or to Moses' yet more celebrated Prayer in Act 3 – we hear melodies, effortlessly graceful as only Rossini could make them, wafted over harp and strings, and, in the Quintet, wonderfully irradiated by characteristically atmospheric writing for the horn. The first two acts of the original score are also notable for a memorable sequence of duets. The most memorable is perhaps the woodland vigil for the lovers in Act 2, 'Quale assalto! qual cimento!' (*Andante*, 2/4, G major) where Elcia's finely drifted line and Osiride's *parlando* response is evidence of the flexibility and ease with which Rossini deploys the forms he has perfected. It was a duet, Stendhal tells us, which Colbran and Nozzari made much of. There is also an earlier duet for the lovers in Act 1, an exquisite short number for Elcia and her confidant, Amenosi, within the Act 1 finale, and a duet for Osiride and his father, 'Parlar, speigar non posso' (*Moderato*, 4/4, A major) which brings to the fore the brilliant, gamesome quality of this ill-fated young man.

Ill-fated, because in the dramatically sterner 1818–19 version, Osiride is struck dead before the second act is over. This is no way to treat one's romantic lead; but *Mosè in Egitto* is not only a love story. What distinguishes the opera is the seriousness and sensitivity with which Rossini addresses the all-pervading Old Testament theme. As Stendhal's graphic reports make clear,[1] the opening is one of the most striking Rossini, or anyone else, ever conceived. There is no overture, simply three summoning Cs followed by a charged transition[2] to the C minor semiquaver figurations which will insinuate themselves beneath the broken utterances of the Egyptians whom Moses has plunged into darkness and dismay (Ex.31).

Ex.31

Rossini follows this 75-bar prelude with Moses's solemn invocation 'Eterno! immenso! incomprensibil Dio!' (Ex.32), a dramatic

---

[1] VdR, pp.319–20, quoted p.40 above.

[2] The falling, repeated B flat-A flat in bars 10–11 curiously predicts the Rhinegold motif in Wagner's *Der Ring des Nibelungen*. It is a coincidence, no doubt, though Wagner's admiration for this 'Scene of the Shadows' is well known.

recitative accompanied with hieratic spareness by trombones, horns, and woodwinds.

Ex.32

The model here may have been the 'Tuba mirum' from Mozart's *Requiem*, K.626, just as the brilliant C major transformation which follows – Moses restoring light to Egypt – suggests a debt to the first scene of one of Rossini's favourite works, Haydn's *The Creation*. Whatever the models, Rossini's scene works in its own right, grave and blazing by turns.

Neither Pharaoh nor his wife, Amaltea, who is sympathetic to the Israelite cause, is strongly characterized by Tottola or Rossini. The aria Rossini eventually wrote for Pharaoh, 'Cade del ciglio il velo', is rather less good than the aria originally supplied by Carafa, and Amaltea's 'La pace mia smarrita', touching though it is, rather obviously betrays its origins in a much earlier *azione tragico-sacra*, *Ciro in Babilonia*.[3] Yet the drama does not require strong peripheral characters. The situations are strong and simple (though much less so in the Paris rewrite) and the drama's central crisis – the death of Osiride – is splendidly engineered by both Tottola and Rossini. Named as co-ruler by his father, Osiride proves to be what we have always suspected, a nasty piece of work, and less wise, politically, than his vacillating father. The crisis grows in swift and vivid recitatives towards a fine confrontation between Osiride, Mosè, and the forlorn and emotionally riven Elcia. Her 'Porgi la destra amata' is a tender expiatory piece, the ornamentation, evidently written with Colbran in mind, capable of achieving great poignancy. Osiride's insolent and dangerous challenges to Mosè are met by a fatal

[3] 'Vorrei veder lo sposo'.

shaft of lightning. It is a notable *coup de théâtre.* The aftermath, Pharaoh's lament for his dead son, provides another example of Rossini's telling use of grotesque orchestral colours: the eerie *pizzicato strappato,* an effect worthy of Berlioz. In the wake of Osiride's death, Elcia becomes febrile, a nascent Lucia. Her twice-repeated cries 'È spento il caro bene/l'oggetto del tuo amor' are magnificent. The breaking up of this scene is one of the major crimes of the Paris revision.

Act 3 provides a coda to these traumatic events. Having travelled to the edge of the Red Sea, the Israelites can go no further. It is at this point that Moses leads them into the great prayer, 'Dal tuo stellato soglio'. The melody (Ex.33) is a remarkably simple one.

Ex.33

It is first stated in G minor, answered in the relative major, B flat and re-stated in the minor. In the reprise of the choral response to the third stanza it switches to G major, the opera's second transforming blaze from minor to major.

For Paris in 1827, Rossini revised the story, re-named many of the characters, juggled the best of the extant music into new positions, and added a limited amount of material which was either newly written or new to the subject. Three numbers are entirely new: the *Scène et Quatuor,* 'Dieu de la paix', in the new, grandiose Act 1; the big Act 4 *Scène et Air* for Anaide (=Elcia), 'Quelle horrible destinée', and the concluding, and rarely performed, 'Cantique', 'Chantons, bénissons le Seigneur'. The overture, introduction, and Act 3 ballet all draw on material from *Armida,* though the ballet is substantially new. It would be churlish to deny that the new Act 1 has its splendours, notably in the choral writing; but to anyone familiar with the economy and integrity of the original, it is so much musical rodomontade. It is also difficult to be at all sanguine about the cynical scissors-and-paste editing of the extant music. The new Act 1 inherits the lovers' A major duet from Act 1 of *Mosè in Egitto* and the earlier Act 1's finale: now used to bring about the plague of darkness rather than, as before, to reciprocate it with fire and hailstones. Act

2 of *Moïse et Pharaon* incorporates Act 1 of *Mosè in Egitto* from Ex.31 to the end of the Quintet; it also takes in the duet for Pharaoh and Osiride (=Aménofis) and the original Act 2 finale, omitting the death of Osiride/Aménofis and turning Elcia's 'Porgi la destra amata' into an appeal by Pharaoh's wife (=Sinaide) to her love-lorn son. Act 3 of the revision finds a place for the quartet 'Mi manca la voce' and the ballet. By the start of Act 4 Rossini and his librettists had still not used the lovers' central G major duet from Act 2 of *Mosè in Egitto*. In *Mosè in Egitto* the Prince is already dead by the time we reach the banks of the Red Sea. Here he is still alive, allowing Rossini, like Puccini in the last act of *Manon Lescaut,* to give us a love duet amid the desert wastes. It is an awkward transplant. The music suggests young love in a woodland setting; here the love is old, the landscape barren. To this, Rossini adds the *Scène et Air*, 'Quelle horrible destinée', a grand E minor/E major piece full of powerfully swerving harmonies at the end of which Anaide has taken the tribe's advice and become a born-again Israelite.

All of which rather upstages the famous prayer, dramatically and harmonically. It is often said that there is no evidence of long-term harmonic thinking in Rossini's operas. In some measure, this is true; but such a view neglects to note the unassuming skill with which Rossini deploys primary keys and colours. In *Mosè in Egitto*, as in the majority of Rossini operas, major keys predominate. There is a fondness in this score for the keys of F, G, and A, with E and E flat added for ceremonious music and the key of C held more or less skilfully in reserve. By chance or design, *Mosè in Egitto* begins and ends in C major, with the minor key highpoints – the C minor Scene of the Shadows, the C minor close to Act 1 and the G minor of Moses's prayer – placed strategically within the structure. By contrast, the 1827 revision is quite indiscriminate. It begins in D major and ends somewhat indeterminately in C major (or F major if we include the 'Cantique'). The new Act 1 finale ends in C minor, anticipating and undermining the C minor of the Scene of the Shadows which is now poorly placed at the start of Act 2. Throughout *Moïse et Pharaon* Rossini seems impervious to the effect of such juxtapositions. In the revised Act 4, the prayer competes not only with 'Quelle horrible destinée' but with the G major tonality of the transplanted duet. Even the end is unsatisfying, fading out in the revision into one of those night-and-silence closes which will become familiar in the nineteenth century. *Mosè in Egitto* is the source of the slow melody which accompanies the Egyptians' watery demise (a glorious melody underpinned with simple mastery by quiet brass chords and timpani rolls). In the original the melody is framed, and the opera itself optimistically rounded out, by a buoyant orchestral *stretta.*   Stendhal once observed of Rossini 'he creates without knowing how'; and there is Rossini's own remark 'I had facility, and lots of instinct'. *Moïse et Pharaon*, which seems to look forward to the operas of Meyerbeer and Saint-Saëns, suggests a diminution of that instinct. *Mosè in Egitto*, by contrast, has integrity born of instinct and sensibility. As music-drama it looks back to the worlds of Gluck and Monteverdi. Seen and heard in a theatre apt to its intimate scale, *Mosè in Egitto* will always make a special impact.

30

Ermione and other operas

Adelaide di Borgogna — *Adina* — *Ricciardo e Zoraide* – *Ermione* – *Eduardo e Cristina*

Tucked in between the three formidable offerings of 1817 and *Mosè in Egitto* written during Lent 1818, is *Adelaide di Borgogna* commissioned by Rome's Teatro Argentina where eighteen months before *Il barbiere di Siviglia* had received its stormy *prima*. It is a serious two act *dramma* to a libretto by Giovanni Schmidt set in tenth-century Italy. Lotario, King of Italy, has been murdered by Berengario. Lotario's widow, Adelaide, has survived but is under siege in the fortress of Canossa waiting a promised intervention by the German King Otto I (Ottone) who has a long-standing treaty with the peoples of Italy. It is a rather dry subject set in a grey world of feudal militarism; yet despite evidence of haste in the composition, the piece has an unignorable presence. As militarism is the order of the day, Rossini does not neglect what one contemporary called 'the timpani, big drum, and march tunes'; it is militarism, though, seen through a humane or patriotic perspective. There is a noble opening chorus, 'Misera patria oppressa' complemented in Act 2 by a chorus in honour of Italy. The opera's first concerted number is a Trio in which Adelaide rejects Berengario's sly suggestion that his son, Adalberto, should marry Adelaide in return for her restoration to Lotario's throne. Though the son later emerges as an attractive and plausible character, the villainous Berengario is poorly characterized; Rossini's sympathies, it is very clear, are all with Adelaide. In this Trio – the placidly beautiful vocal line heard over *sostenuto* violas and plucked strings – in her *cavatina* and in the Act 2 Quartet, Adelaide is given music of nobility and presence. At the end of the opera, with Berengario's army routed and Berengario and his son rounded up, Adelaide celebrates in a charming aria, 'Cingi la benda candida', notable for the sensuousness of the woodwind writing.

The role of Ottone is written for a *travesti* contralto. Again one is struck by Rossini's attention to accompanying orchestral colours. Ottone's *cavatina* is prefaced and infiltrated by an obbligato cor anglais; and in the scene in which Adalberto comes with treacherous peace terms, Rossini again favours the combination of cantabile lines and crepuscular counterpointing (here in the lower woodwinds) underpinned by pizzicato strings. Ottone is eventually lured into the fortress at Canossa though it makes a rather tame Act 1 finale. The situation contrived by Schmidt is lacking in plausible tensions and in the *stretta* Rossini can be heard cranking a rather wheezy engine. Act 2 begins *in medias res*. Berengario has the fortress under siege, Ottone has fled, Adelaide is distraught, and Adalberto is brought forward, first in the duet 'Della tua patria', later, after his father's defeat and capture, in his aria 'Grida natura' where he contemplates his own yearning for Adelaide and his mother's insistence that she be exchanged for the captive Berengario. The plot is eventually wound up in a flurry of exchanges of prisoners, with Adelaide's *scena* and *aria* topped by a showy rondo finale for the victorious Ottone. It would be idle to pretend that *Adelaide di Borgogna* is a masterpiece or that it should be expensively revived; but it is a coherent piece, taxing and rewarding in places for Ottone, Adelaide, and Adalberto, and not without distinguishing touches in the orchestration.

During the summer of 1818 Rossini wrote the last of his one-act *farse, Adina*, a curious private commission from a Portuguese patron set to a libretto (derived from Romani's *Il Califfo e la schiava*) by Rossini's friend the Marchese Gheraldo Bevilacqua-Aldobrandini. The plot rings minor changes on the familiar seraglio story. The Calif of Baghdad plans to marry the beautiful young slave-girl Adina. She, for reasons which are not immediately evident, is not unsympathetic to the Calif, but the reappearance of her one-time love, Selimo, places her in a dilemma. Aided by his servant, Mustafà, who doubles as a gardener in the royal palace, Selimo persuades Adina to elope with him; which is just as well, for it turns out that in reality Adina is the Calif's long-lost daughter. Abductions from seraglios being, in the nature of things, problematic, the plan goes awry and in a vivid little scene among the fishermen of the Tigris the escape party is arrested. Selim is sentenced to death and Adina faints away; but a medallion round her neck happily reveals her true identity to the Calif. The opera is certainly stageable and has been revived in recent times. It is a small-scale affair, a pen-and-ink sketch rather than a full-scale drawing, notable for the tender, elaborate music provided for Adina (the only woman in an otherwise exclusively male cast) for the crystal-clear orchestration, and for a mood which is prevailingly sad. It is a work that is more or less free of the sadistic ravings and quasi-oriental tintinnabulations which beset operas in this genre, even Mozart's. There is a touching duet, which may or may not be by Rossini, for Adina and her father, and a tender air with cor anglais for Selim taken from *Sigismondo*. Once, after Adina's swoon, Rossini makes us catch our breath with a lovely, brief E major chorus, slow and *sotto voce*. There is a whirring *stretta* after the lovers' arrest and a jubilant end after the recognition scene which is written, aptly enough, over a crescendo. Otherwise, the score is a rather quiet affair written, one senses, away from the bustle and stir of the theatre in the privacy of Rossini's home in Bologna. As far as we know, Rossini never heard the piece (it had its *prima* in Lisbon in 1826) though some of the music would have been heard by him in earlier contexts. Nor could he be cajoled into writing an overture for it. Practical as ever, he declined to do so on the eminently reasonable ground that no overture was specified in the contract.

Rossini returned to the real theatrical world in Naples in the autumn of 1818 to write *Ricciardo e Zoraide*. Like *Ermione*, which was to follow in March 1819, this is an important transitional work in which forms are stabilised, content consciously enriched, and theatrical devices – notably the stage band – newly deployed. If *Ricciardo e Zoraide* is the less interesting of the two pieces, it is because its subject is less surely focused than that of *Ermione*. Berio's libretto is an exotic blockbuster set amid Asian potentates, Christian knights, and African emissaries. Its theme is private grief, private envy, love and hate set in the context of public power wielded by a ruthless and besotted tyrant. There is nothing new in all this. Ricciardo, a Christian knight adept at disguise and conceived in Rossini's most brilliant style for Giovanni David, is in love with Zoraide. She in turn is the object of the affections of King Agorante who has taken her father, Ircano, prisoner. Oddly, Berio keeps Ircano, his *basso primo*, out of the drama for the best part of an act and a half; by contrast, Zomira, Agorante's jealous wife, is promptly and powerfully built into the drama. Told in any detail, the story would read like a Marlowe epic rewritten by the Marx brothers; it is Rossini's music which boldly informs and sustains the bald dramatic archetypes. Agorante, a trial run for Pirro in *Ermione*, is given powerful, posturing music, cast in traditional moulds, but Zoraide, Colbran's role, is given music of continuing variety and interest beginning with the *duetto* 'Che orribile istante' (*Allegro vivace*, 3/8,

A major). There are new colours in the confrontation with Zomira which soon follows ('Invan tu fingi ingrata', *Allegro giusto*, 4/4, E major), in the imaginatively conceived Trio, 'Cruda sorte' (a four-part, C major/A flat major structure with chorus), and in the Act 2 duet with Ricciardo, music of considerable sweep and power (Ex.34).

Ex.34

The opera not only fills out the older forms. Accompanied recitatives are increasingly important. Rossini had experimented in this area as early as *Ciro in Babilonia* but now recitatives are notable for the eloquence of their phrasing and for the care with which harmonic and orchestral detail is applied. The chorus is also power-fully and touchingly used, with the extensive use of a stage band further complicating and enhancing the scale of the drama. The opera's grandest chorus is 'Qual giorno, ahimè, d'orror!', a C minor *Maestoso con banda* in Act 2; but there is also the touching off-stage chorus, 'Il tuo pianto, i tuoi sospiri' (partly reused in the duet 'Li marinari' from *Les soirées musicales*), an essay in Rossinian pathos which might be compared with the off-stage Gondolier's song in *Otello*. Earlier, the Act 1 Trio is lightened by a chorus of young girls, an A flat *Andante* in 12/8 accompanied by the orchestral oboe and an off-stage *banda* of clarinets, bassoons, and harp. The use of stage band and chorus also extends, in a radical development of a method hinted at in *Armida*, to the overture, a piece which substitutes a freely assembled group of movements for the familiar archetype. Most imposing is the C major *marziale*, recapitulated within the overture as a choral movement which also serves as part of the *introduzione* of the opera itself. There is also a variation movement, *Andante*

grazioso in F major, apt to this rambling tale of foreign adventure, in which horn and clarinet are treated soloistically. Yet most remarkable of all in some respects is the overture's C minor *Largo* preface. Anyone innocent of its origins might think it the work of Schumann, so sweetly and solemnly blended is the writing for *sostenuto* strings, flutes, clarinets, and horns. By 1818, romantic and tramontane tendencies are plain for all to hear in Rossini's music.

These tendencies will be further developed in *La donna del lago*. Meanwhile, Rossini applied many of the stylistic features developed in *Ricciardo e Zoraide* to a wholly worthy subject: a transcription, adequately handled by Tottola, of Racine's *Andromaque*. The result was *Ermione*, the late Neapolitan work which least deserved its rapid fall from the repertoire. The choice of subject was an informed and serious one. *Andromaque* was Racine's first great success, a play which treats familiar plot and character archetypes with pace, lucidity, and power. There are four principal characters: Pyrrhus (Pirro), Orestes (Oreste), Hermione (Ermione), and Andromache herself (Andromaca). Rossini's decision to place Hermione at the centre of the drama is significant and sensible for it is Pyrrhus and Hermione who motivate the drama—Pyrrhus courting and blackmailing Andromache, Hector's widow and mother of the child, Astyanax; Hermione herself, loved by Orestes, infatuated with Pyrrhus. Hermione venerates Pyrrhus, despises him, yields to him, and in a fit of passion prompted by the announcement of his betrothal to Andromache, commissions his murder by Orestes. In such a context Andromache is important but, to some extent, peripheral. Rossini characterizes her well in her Act 1 *cavatina*; the *cabaletta* suggests that she, too, has an element of wildness in her nature, but the E flat *Andantino* with its *sostenuto* viola writing and rapt cantabile is Bellini-like in its regality. Andromache's love is directed towards the memory of her dead husband, and to her son. In Act 2 she yields to Pyrrhus (in the C major duet 'Ombra del caro sposo'), planning suicide when her son's safety is assured. Yet important as Andromache is, it is Hermione who towers over the action.

The opera begins gloomily in F minor. As in *Ricciardo e Zoraide*, the overture encloses a choral movement, a lament for the fall of Troy. This is not, however, an opera in which ensembles and choruses dominate; rather, Rossini exploits and extends solo arias and duets, movements well suited to the portrayal of characters as proud and self-absorbed as these. As in the case of the role of Armida, the coloratura style is deployed in a powerfully declamatory manner, the singers frequently instructed to colour and shade their music in specific ways. In her Act 1 duet with Pyrrhus, 'Non proseguir, comprendo', Hermione is directed to register irony, indignation, and anger within three lines. Typical of Rossini's expansion of, and experimentation with, closed formal units is Orestes' *cavatina*, 'Reggia aboritta'. Orestes is a sympathetic figure, but his passion for Hermione is ruthlessly exploited by her and he will end up deranged, and a murderer. The *cavatina*, which turns, interestingly, into a duet with his confidant, Pilades, begins as an *Allegro e recitativo*, a curiously effective conjunction of forms. The key is E flat major, but at the start of the lyric *Andantino* the music moves immediately towards the tonic minor (Ex.35).

Ex.35

The relationship between Orestes and Hermione briefly flowers as Pyrrhus's stratagems drive Hermione into bold retaliatory gestures of her own. 'Amarti?' demands Hermione, to which Orestes despairingly responds in phrases, harmonically tense, charged with feeling. It is here that, musically and dramatically, a larger ensemble is called for, an ensemble which Pyrrhus will dominate, shamelessly exploiting Hermione's love for him and Andromache's love for her son. The climax comes in a great declamatory outburst in which repeated Ds are underpinned by massive orchestral chording. The writing, which looks forward to Verdi's Otello as much as it glances back to Rossini's, vividly conveys the proud singleness of the man, a man imprisoned by his own obsessive passion.

Act 2 is very much Hermione's act. Its critical, tragic scenes derive from the final scene of Act 4 and Act 5 of Racine's play. Wracked by jealousy and by anger at Pyrrhus's treatment of her, Ermione commissions his murder. Her mood is such that a hushed *sotto voce* phrase will be translated within five bars into fierce runs triggered by the leap of a 10th, massively supported in the orchestra. Equally, there are moments of dignified repose – 'Amata, l'amai' which seems unusually close in melodic contour to Annius's 'Tu fosti tradito' from Act 2 of Mozart's *La clemenza di Tito* – or simpler, frailer phrases which, sung by a Colbran or a Callas, can lay bare the soul of this woman whose compassionate self is stained by an evil intent. Here, for once, Rossini is trading in tragedy; as he does so, the structure of the first of Hermione's grand *scene* is hugely expanded.[1] This *Gran scena* is separated from the *Scena, duetto*, and *finale* by a brief duet for Fenicio and Pilade, a simple breathing space before the finale which begins *agitato* in C minor, moves through powerful, sequential writing for Hermione and reaches its climax in the horrifying entry of the blood-bespattered Orestes (Ex.36), one of the most powerful of all moments in opera of the early *ottocento*.

At the end, Orestes is dragged senseless away, whilst Hermione swoons into insensibility, an on-stage representation of a death which in Racine is described by Pylades in rather bloodier detail. Revival of this remarkable score is long overdue.

Exhausted, perhaps, by the *Ermione* experience, Rossini travelled to Venice for one his most factitious triumphs, the April *prima* of *Eduardo e Cristina*, a pastiche assembled around a libretto originally prepared in Naples in 1810 for Pavesi. The plot concerns

---

[1] The *scena*, at the end of which Orestes is dispatched to assassinate Pyrrhus ('Se a me, nemiche stelle', *stretta* in E major) is in seven sections, including two recitatives, a sung transition, and three solo movements for Hermione, in addition to the two-part *cabaletta*-cum-*stretta*.

Ex.36

the secret marriage of Cristina to Eduardo, a gallant Swedish soldier (there is already a child by the marriage), the King's opposition, Eduardo's imprisonment, and his release when Sweden is threatened by foreign armies. In his haste, Rossini took over numbers from *Adelaide di Borgogna, Ricciardo e Zoraide*, and *Ermione*. Some new numbers were written, notably a chorus, 'Nel misero tuo stato', later re-cycled as the march which prefaces the Countess's 'En proie à la tristesse' in *Le Comte Ory*, but for the most part this is instant opera, as tasteless as dried packet-soup, and a comparable commercial success.

31

Rossini and Scott: La donna del lago

As the first fully-fledged opera to be derived from the works of Sir Walter Scott,[1] *La donna del lago* is something of a trail-blazer. The poet Leopardi thought it 'a stupendous thing' and Halévy vowed to read its first act through once more before he died. For over fifty years it was revived, adapted, and cannibalized. Even today it has a tentative hold on the repertoire, though the intimate scale of much of the music – its lyric-idyllic style – is ill-suited to larger houses, however grand the piece can be made to seem scenically. The work's other principal limitation is its sometimes static second act. Chorley thought the act little more than a 'concert in costume'. Indeed, some of the revivals and adaptations supervised or sanctioned by Rossini in later years were clearly aimed at shoring up the structure of a work whose end does not entirely bear out the high promise of its remarkable beginning.

Scott's poem had been published in 1810 before his emergence as something of a cult figure in European romanticism. Like much of his work, the poem is set in a romanticized past in which romance, chivalry, and prowess in arms are primary concerns. His central character is Scotland's King James V, a mysterious figure identified throughout the poem as James Fitz-James (Uberto in Tottola's unimaginative transcription). As a young boy, James had been held prisoner by Archibald Douglas. He had escaped, and Douglas had fled the land, returning later under the protection of the formidable tribal chieftain, Roderick Dhu (Rodrigo). As an earnest of his gratitude to Roderick, Douglas has promised him the hand of his daughter Ellen (Elena); but Ellen is in love with the young warrior, Malcolm Graeme, a love which threatens to breach the rebel alliance. Rossini had first encountered the poem in French transla-

[1] For comments on *The Knight of Snowdown* (1811, London) by Morton and Bishop, a 'musical drama' based on *The Lady of the Lake*, see Jerome Mitchell, *The Walter Scott Operas*, Alabama, 1977, p.10. Mitchell also has chapters on *La donna del lago*, *Ivanhoé*, and *Robert Bruce*.

tion and must have been struck by its suitability. It has a strong narrative line, strikingly contrasted characters, and promising ambient detail: picturesque loch and mountain settings, and numerous cues for chorus and folk-song in the romantic manner. Scott's own narrative is carried forward in rhyming octosyllabic couplets, helpfully offset by ballads, choruses, and laments. Schubert, who was blessed with a better poet-translator than Rossini, adapted some of these, including Ellen's 'Ave Maria' which became one of his most popular songs. Not all Scott's cues are neglected by Tottola. James's 'Aurora, ah! sorgerai' near the start of the final scene was probably suggested by Scott's 'Lay of the Imprisoned Huntsman' (VI, xxiv). After the triumph of the Gondolier's Song in *Otello* this must have been a temptation for Rossini. What is remarkable about the song (Tottola's text unhelpfully ignores Scott) is its use of the theme of Elena's *cavatina* (Ex.37) which has run through the first movement of the opera as a *leitmotif*.

The sweep of the opera's opening movement, which closely follows the form and content of Scott's poem, is its most remarkable feature, clearly demonstrating Rossini's evolved and evolving ideas about the structure of music-drama. Having built choruses into formal overtures in *Ricciardo e Zoraide* and *Ermione*, Rossini now reduces the orchestral preamble to a mere sixteen bars before switching into an ebullient chorus of countryfolk assembled near Loch Katrine. The visual perspectives on stage are complemented by the stereophonic deployment of on-stage horns and the sound of a distant hunt. Out of this essay in the sonic and pictoral picturesque, Ellen emerges, singing her folk-*cavatina* from a skiff on Loch Katrine. In Scott's poem she is a creature of classical loveliness:

> And ne'er did Grecian chisel trace
> A Nymph, a Naiad, or a Grace,
> Of finer form, or lovelier face!
>
> (I.xviii)

These qualities are echoed in the melody Rossini has contrived for Ellen (Ex.37).

The meeting of Fitz-James/Uberto and Ellen is charged but decorous, Rossini using arioso and accompanied recitative in a manner which hints at what Wagner will one day do when a warrior comes to the hearth of a strangely beautiful girl. In Elena's quietly modulated utterances – 'Amico asilo/Tu sia la mia dimora' is a notable small

Ex.37

example – Sieglinde's mood might be distantly descried. Recitative and arioso give way to tentative song in the duet 'Scendi nel piccolo legno' (*Andantino moderato*, 6/8, G major) in which the *cavatina* melody, Ex.37, remains prominent. A magnificent hunting chorus at once breaches and intensifies this tentative idyll, the huntsmen searching, as they do in Scott, for the lost huntsman, Fitz-James. The writing for male chorus, horns, and orchestra has a remarkable drive, thrust, and colour. The scene now shifts, though the music-drama is continuous, to a nearby cottage. Again it is fine accompanied recitative which carries the drama forward as Fitz-James becomes conscious of the fact that the cottage, its walls imposingly hung with armour, is Douglas's. A chorus of women, Ellen's companions, break up this second and more expansive duet movement, the music moving through stages which would have served as fully self-contained musical units in earlier operas. The music of Ellen and Fitz-James/Uberto is as brilliant as it is restrained, and as expressive as it is decorous; but the drama's underlying impulse is now a strong one. Not surprisingly, the forty-minute exposition culminates in a sudden outflow of energy, the *cabaletta* visceral with driving rhythms and squared-off periods in the manner of the young Verdi.

After this remarkable opening, the first act tends to fall back into a sequence of entrance arias. Malcolm Graeme is given a full-dress *scena e cavatina*, 'Elena, oh tu che chiamo' (*Andantino*, 6/8, E major) which depends for its dramatic effect on the skills of the singer. The undisputed object of Elena's affections, Malcolm, is a curiously passive lover; but he is under-characterized by Scott, too. Douglas's *cavatina*, a stern invocation to duty ('Taci, lo voglio', *Allegro maestoso*, 4/4, E flat major) is weakened by Tottola's ramshackle prosody and the rather florid writing for the bass. What, even before Act 2, is threatening to become a concert in costume is partially redeemed by Elena's duet with Malcolm, 'Vivere io non potrò' (*Moderato*, 4/4, A major), which returns to the sensuous, limpid style of Elena's earlier music, though where Elena and Fitz-James/Uberto rightly tended to set one another off, echoing rather than blending individual lines, Elena and Malcolm are soon locked in a more or less permanent musical embrace, the voices sensuous in thirds and sixths. There is no *cabaletta*. Instead, we have a warrior-chorus and Rodrigo's *cavatina*, 'Eccomi a voi miei prodi' (4/4, C major), an extraordinarily florid piece which sounds as though it was written for Giovanni David but which was, in fact, allocated to Nozzari whose fierce stage presence is required for Roderick Dhu. The F major *Andante* of this war-song is curious; so sensuous is it, we might think it out of character; but it works as a further affecting portrait of Elena, and it lies gloriously on the voice. The Act 1 finale re-engages the cross-currents in the drama. As Malcolm's rivalry with Rodrigo flares, news is brought of a military challenge to the rebels, news which allows Tottola and Rossini briefly to engage the poem's bardic theme in the famous war-hymn, the Chorus of the Bards (Ex.38). It was to become one of Rossini's most famous numbers, a favourite with patriots for the next fifty years.

Ex.38

The central achievement of Act 2 is the Trio, 'Alla ragion, deh rieda', another extended musical sequence which conflates with reasonable skill crucial events in Scott's poem: Fitz-James's later meeting with Ellen ('The Prophecy', IV, xvii-xix), Fitz-James's chance meeting with Roderick ('The Combat', *passim*), and their duel. The movement begins as a duet, but Rodrigo enters unnoticed in the cabaletta, the music becoming much more florid. The subsequent Trio contains one of Scott's finest moments, the sudden emergence from the heather of Roderick Dhu's warriors ('Da vostri aguate uscite', *Allegro vivace*, C minor). In the *cabaletta* Verdi might have better differentiated the antagonists. In Scott, Roderick is irascible and unstable, Fitz-James his rock-like adversary; in Rossini there seems to be little difference; perhaps Rossini was thinking of a later couplet – 'No tyrant he, though ire and pride/May lead his better mood aside' (VI.xxv) – though one rather doubts it.

The resolution of the crisis in the opera's final half-hour is uncertainly handled. In Rossini's time, and our own, reinforcements have been summoned: an aria from *Ermione*, the famous quartet from *Bianca e Falliero*, and so on. Fitz-James's plaint mentioned above reminds us of the opera's remarkable opening scenes and Elena's celebrated *rondo*, 'Tanti affetti in tal momento' reminds us of Rossini's continuing capacity to write inexhaustibly brilliant coloratura. When Chorley heard Grisi in the role of Elena in London in 1847 he noted a grandeur of style, a finish, a 'triumphancy' in her singing of this showpiece ending which was full of power, beauty, and intentional challenge. Vocally, it is a royal conclusion; but in *Guillaume Tell* Rossini will find an altogether more sublime way of ending a work whose drama is rooted in a people and a landscape not wholly dissimilar to the one which we encounter in *La donna del lago.*

32

Final operas in Italy

Bianca e Falliero – Matilde di Shabran – Zelmira – Semiramide.

The outstanding works of Rossini's final years as an opera composer in Italy are *Maometto II*, to be discussed in the next chapter in the context of the transition from the Italian to the French style, and *Semiramide*. The remaining three operas do, however, merit serious consideration. *Bianca e Falliero* was written for La Scala, Milan in the autumn of 1819, a commission approved by Rossini in a letter to Romani written a full four months before the *prima*. Set in seventeenth-century Venice, the story charts the machinations of a brutal father, Contareno, who would rather have the brilliant young general, Falliero, compromised, arraigned, and executed than see him marry his daughter, Bianca, for whom Contareno plans a politically advantageous marriage. In Antoine-Vincent Arnault's French melodrama, *Blanche et Montcassin*, from which Romani took his libretto, Falliero comes to a grim end, much as Cavaradossi will later do in *Tosca*; but Rossini and Romani, politically prudent, opted for a happy end. The opera was a success with the Milanese in 1819 but a decade of adaptation and dismemberment, culminating in the notorious La Scala revival of 1831, wrecked its musical and structural integrity. The opera's dramatic high point – Capellio's intervention on the lovers' behalf in Act 2, leading to the theatrically thrilling Quartet 'Cielo, il mio labbro ispira' – survived as a noble torso, but the rest of the work slipped quickly from public view.[1]

The opera's difficulties are easy to rehearse: the technical complexity of the writing for the three principals, the use of a *travesti* hero (Falliero), and Rossini's re-use, in the final scene, of the finale of *La donna del lago*. Yet in a well-cast performance these objections wither away. The massiveness of some of the set pieces (such as Falliero's Act 2 *Scena, Cavatina,* and *Aria*) and the close gearing of the *bel canto* style to musical and psychological ends are, at times,

[1] The opera was restored to the stage in Pesaro in 1986 in a new edition by Gabriele Dotto derived from the autograph full score of 1819.

awe-inspiring. Amid a welter of vocal display, brilliantly varied and linked to polyphonic writing of great virtuosity, one is struck by the fierceness of much of the music and by scenes of erotic allure, rare in Rossini. There is grace and beauty in the Desdemona style about much of the writing for Bianca but the Act 1 duet with Falliero is elaborately and frankly sensual. Throughout the opera, one is bound to note Rossini's preoccupation with the idea of emotional excess. Indeed, Contareno's *cavatina* ('Pensa che omai resistere'), his great challenge to his daughter, must rank as one of the nastiest set pieces ever penned for a coloratura tenor, the music suggesting moods which are, by turn, vindictive, suave, and wilful.

Matilde di Shabran, hastily written for the Roman carnival in 1821, is the last of Rossini's Italian operas in the *semiseria* genre. Like so many stageable Rossini operas, it is beset with textual problems though an edition by Edilio Frassoni was successfully mounted in Genoa in 1974.[2] *Matilde di Shabran's* principal misfortune is its central character, the belligerent and allegedly woman-hating Duke Corradino who is far from being one of nature's gentlemen. 'Try my temper,' he says at one point,' and you'll end up bleeding at my feet.' Something of a recluse, Corradino has taken prisoner Eduardo (a *travesti* role), son of his old enemy Raimondo; but he has also unwittingly given houseroom to Matilde, orphaned daughter of one of his old comrades-in-arms. Matilde is one of Rossini's minxes and is well equipped to deal with our ranting anti-hero, whom she proceeds to cajole and hypnotize into helpless submission. Having achieved this worthy aim, she promptly deserts him for the handsome Eduardo, leaving Corradino to fend off the advances of the imposing Contessa D'Arco who has throughout presented herself as a rival for Corradino's hand. Though the story lacks some of the expected *semiseria* features, there is plenty to divert the attention: rowdy peasants, the unreliable itinerant poet, Isidoro who advertises himself as the 'new Anacreon', and Corradino's various minders and advisers. If the opera lacks a prison scene, it makes amends in the battlefield encounters and Corradino's attempt to murder Matilde by having her pushed into a ravine by the enterprising – though, as it turns out, squeamish – poet.

Matilde is given an array of moments which are touching and

---

[2] The only widely available vocal score, published by Kalmus, a reprint of a Carli/Launer edition of the 1820s, is often unreliable.

terrifying as well as comic. Her response to Corradino's pronounce-
ment of the death sentence, 'Perfida, invan tu piangi' is very much an
opera seria moment before the music races off, hinting – Rossini
need do no more – that we must not really expect this shrewish
charmer to be pitched over the cliff. The opera's finest single
movement comes in the latter half of Act 1, beginning with the
Contessa's 'Questa è la Dea?', a haughty attempt to disparage
Matilde. Their sparring is interrupted by Corradino whose abrupt
'Ehi! Donna?' is swiftly met by Matilde's aggressively feminist 'Uom,
che vuoi?'. The effect of Matilde's insults is electrifying. Horns croon
and Corradino with them. From now until the end of the act he is as
urbane as Count Ory. Rossini builds the moment into a brilliant
quintet, another glinting *buffo* essay on the subject of the fevers of
love. Settled once more into the role of the amused spectator, Rossini
disarms us as surely as Matilde, quite literally, disarms the battle-
clad Corradino. A love duet is launched, *alla breve*, with racing
triplets, and brilliant, flashing high Cs; but it lasts no more than a few
moments. Drums roll off-stage. Eduardo's father has come to fetch
his son and within moments Corradino's castle is on a war-footing.
The characters briefly gather their thoughts in the traditional slow
interlude, an unaccompanied septet in A flat, before the war-
machine, headed by the poet-turned-war correspondent, Isadoro,
swings into action in a style Offenbach must have envied. Though
there are weaknesses and inequalities in the shorter second act,
Rossini's touch uncertain in a piece like 'Ah, perchè, perchè la morte'
which was switched from father to son and back again in successive
editions, the situations are varied enough to carry this unignorably
entertaining piece on from the first act's exhilarating conclusion.

Entertaining as *Matilde di Shabran* undoubtedly is, there is,
equally, a residual sense of the comedy and the comic method being,
in some sense, *déjà entendu*. Although Rossini was to round his
Italian career generously out with *Semiramide*, a certain staleness is
evident in places in the operas of the period 1819–22, and nowhere
more so than in *Zelmira* where the *opera seria* method has become
strangely petrified. Chorley thought the story of *Zelmira* – a blood-
and-thunder, mists-of-time story reworked from an eighteenth-
century source by Tottola – to be both absurd and wearisome. The
libretto is certainly no masterpiece. Set on the Greek island of
Lesbos, it concerns Polidoro, the deposed king, the adventurer
Antenore, murderer of the usurper, Azor, and Antenore's principal

opponents: Zelmira, daughter of Polidoro, and her Trojan husband, the warrior, Ilo, the more florid of the principal tenor roles and sung in what was by all accounts a somewhat *dégagé* manner by Giovanni David. For most of the opera, Zelmira is the victim of various calumnies. At the outset it is put about that she has murdered Polidoro. (She has, in fact, taken him to a safe retreat.) Later, when Ilo returns in search of his son, he is about to be stabbed by a henchman of Antenore when Zelmira seizes the dagger. One of life's quick thinkers, Leucippo accuses Zelmira of an attempt on her husband's life. It is certainly a wearisome affair and Chorley was right to think it absurd when there is at least one occasion when Zelmira might have explained the situation to her despairing husband. The *dramma* conforms at the end to the traditions of the *lieto fine*; thus Zelmira and Polidoro survive their many vicissitudes, rescued from death at the end of the opera in scenes reminiscent of Nahum Tate's rewrite of Shakespeare's *King Lear*.

The score is sombre, at times bellicose, its tone fairly set in the striking D minor opening (there is no overture) with its disturbing sense of civil unrest. Recitatives have a serious, brooding quality and arias and duets conform, by and large, to the closed forms evolved in the earlier Neapolitan years and before. The writing for Zelmira is careful rather than inspired, reflecting a certain circumspection in Rossini's writing for Colbran in such a context. There are opportunities for a singer of presence, not least the gentle F minor plaint, accompanied by harp and cor anglais, 'Perchè mi guardi e piangi' during which Zelmira commits her son to safe-keeping. There is also the near-obligatory closing rondo, though it does not take wing as Elisabetta's, Cenerentola's or Elena's do. The prison scene near the opera's end is rich in incidental details, cues for longer things, but Rossini doesn't oblige. It took a younger *prima donna* Giuditta Pasta, to stir Rossini into providing music worthy of Zelmira in these final scenes. For the 1826 Paris revival he wrote a new *Andante*, rounded out with a cabaletta from *Ermione*, for the imprisoned Zelmira to sing as she watches over her ailing father. Curiously, this late Parisian addition joins hands with the one number which looks forward to the chaste declamation of the French style: the old king's gravely beautiful *cavatina*, 'Ah, già trascorse il di'. The principal melody (Ex.39a) naggingly predicts Donizetti's 'Una furtiva lagrima', whilst the *cavatina*'s brief central movement is a bass *cantilena* which in comparable circumstances — a father's plaint to his daughter in a time of stress – Verdi might have been proud to shape (Ex.39b).

Ex.39

If Zelmira proves to be something of a disappointment, *Semiramide* is quite the reverse. There is a sense in which *Semiramide* might be dubbed *Tancredi Revisited*. Ten years after the *prima* of *Tancredi*, almost to the day, La Fenice, Venice was witnessing a Rossini opera derived by Gaetano Rossi from a drama by Voltaire. The forms first fully essayed in *Tancredi* are here majestically redeployed; the virginal charm may have partially evaporated but there is ample compensation in the richness and reach of the vocal and orchestral writing and in the cogency of the dramatic structure itself. The scale of the writing is well illustrated by the celebrated overture, several of whose themes recur in the main body of the opera. In some respects, the *Semiramide* overture is the apotheosis of the archetype established in the pre-Naples years and outlined in Chapter 20. The quality of the thematic invention is exceptional and the scale of both the harmonic thinking and the orchestration invest it with a full-bodied character more usually associated with symphonic writing. Not for nothing was this a favourite *cavallo di battaglia* of Arturo Toscanini.

Voltaire's *Sémiramis* (1748) appropriated a legend which was already familiar in opera houses. A semi-mythical figure, Semiramide had attracted Metastasio's attention and interest in the subject had remained high for the best part of a century. Portogallo's *La morte di Semiramide* (1801, Lisbon; rev. 1806, London) was a famous vehicle for Angelica Catalani and, interestingly, Rossi had worked the subject with the 27-year-old Meyerbeer four years previously. The story is a strong one, closely tied in with powerful myth and archetypes. Semiramide, in league with Prince Assur, has murdered her husband, King Ninus, and attempted to murder her son. The son has survived the attempt and, fifteen years later and no longer known to his mother or would-be stepfather, has become a brilliant young commander on the kingdom's furthest frontier. Now known as Arsace, he returns to Babylon on a military summons (the Queen is shortly to nominate her new consort) bringing with him a casket containing a sword and scrolls which were the property of his late father. It is a fateful return. Smitten by the glamorous young warrior, Semiramide announces that she will take, not Assur, but Arsace as consort. A crisis of complex proportions is thus precipitated, to which are added grumbling interventions from the tomb of Ninus. Like old Hamlet, Ninus speaks from beyond the grave laying on Arsace the responsibility for avenging his as yet unexplained death.

The strategic planning of *Semiramide* is impressive. Like *Tancredi*, it opens with a movement which consolidates the drama's pre-history. *Semiramide's* opening is, however, both longer (700 bars to *Tancredi's* 400), more forward-moving, and containing its own natural points of climax. The structure is continuous and tonally coherent, an F major movement encapsulating sections in C major and A flat major (Rossini's fondness for major keys a minor third apart again in evidence) with a natural point of culmination in the thunderclap which greets Semiramide's first approach to Ninus's tomb. It is a movement which begins in gloom and unease. The opening pages – the High Priest, Oroe, before the altar of Baal – are scored for high winds, solemn brass, and double-basses whose colouristic possibilities will again be imaginatively exploited later in the opera. The Act 1 finale has a similar scope: a 900-bar, six-movement structure, two of them in the minor, with a broad C major context. In the first episode, a slow section in E flat, allegiance is sworn to Semiramide, the overture's solemn horn subject (Ex.40) recapitulated and then redeployed in unaccompanied choral form.

The two minor key episodes which follow Semiramide's catastrophic announcement of her decision to make Arsace her consort are particularly impressive. 'Quel mesto gemito', Semiramide's stunned response to the rumblings from Ninus's tomb, deploys a sombre ostinato similar to that which Verdi will later use in the 'Miserere'

Ex.40

from *Il trovatore*. The later episode in which the Ghost of Ninus addresses Arsace, is equally powerful, restless in F minor. Chorley noted that the terror is told as much in the rhythm as in the declamation.

If there are signs of the petrification of forms in the opera, they mostly affect Arsace's role. Like Tancredi, he is omitted from the opening scene, arriving from afar for his cavatina ('Ah, quel giorno ognor rammento', *Andantino*, 6/8, E major). It is fuller than Tancredi's but the cabaletta lacks individuality. Julian Budden's phrase, 'sexless musico-heroics',[3] is not entirely unjust. In Act 2, isolated by the revelation of his mother's complicity, his formal aria ('In sì barbara sciagura', *Andante sostenuto, 6/8*, E flat major) is met by a fierce response from the chorus. Within moments Arsace is brandishing his sword and swearing fraternity and vengeance like a figure in David's painting *The Oath of the Horatii*; yet his thoughts turn back to his mother in a touching eleven-bar transition, Rossini softening the outline of the character in chromatic writing which gives the portrait a certain *sfumato* quality before the onset of the brightly-lit *cabaletta*.

Semiramide is finely integrated into the drama, entering, like Armida, in an expository quartet. Her *cavatina*, when it arrives later in the first act, is the score's most dazzling number ('Bel raggio lusinghier', *Andante grazioso*, 6/8, A major), a brilliant show-piece but a love song, too, irradiating Semiramide's personality. In *Tancredi* the libretto vitiates the credibility of the duets which are central to each act. In *Semiramide* the situations are much stronger. The Act 1 duet is a duet of mutual misunderstanding, the Queen seeking Arsace's love, Arsace seeking ratification of his love for Princess Azema. It is one of Rossini's loveliest duets ('Serbami ognor sì fido', *Andantino*, 6/8, E flat). The use of the overture's *crescendo* subject as

[3] Budden, *The Operas of Verdi*, I, p. 16.

234

a transition within the cabaletta proves abortive as the reprise – Rossini at his sensuous, languorous best – dissipates the accumulating energies; the coda, by contrast, is gloriously shaped with augmented rhythms in the voice part and seething figurations beneath. The Act 2 confrontation between Arsace and Semiramide, the equivalent of the famous closet scene in Shakespeare's *Hamlet*, is very fine. It is a scene in which Ninus is also tacitly present; he is even accorded a brief theme (Ex.41)

Ex.41

The truth revealed, Semiramide offers her life to her son ('Ebben . . . a te, ferisci', *Allegro Agitato*, 4/4, E minor/major) but Arsace's response is generous. However hateful Semiramide is in the sight of heaven, she is his mother. Semiramide perceives her son's tears and the music drops serenely into G major for the lyric *Andante*. Faced with scenes like this, it is difficult to understand how *Semiramide* has come to be thought of as a chilly *bel canto* showpiece or that Gustav Kobbé could write, in the opera's centennial year, '*Semiramide* seems to have had its day'.

It is a token of the richness of Rossini's invention that there is a further full-length portrait to be noted: the role of the accomplice and would-be usurper, Assur, the last of the great bass roles to be written by Rossini for Filippo Galli. Two scenes in particular merit notice. At the start of Act 2 Assur and Semiramide row, like the Macbeths, over events which are beginning to overshadow them. In the duet's *Andantino* Assur reminds Semiramide of 'the night of death' in phrases which are at once suave and terrific. Semiramide responds in the minor, Assur murmuring 'Rammenta!', 'Remember!', like a ghost in the cellarage before the voices eventually come together in 10ths. The second scene, near the opera's end, is Assur's mad scene. Here colours implicit in the opera's very first scene – colours derived from flutes, low strings, and, beneath all, the basses – are broodingly mixed. It is Assur's intention to murder Arsace but near the tomb of Ninus he is overcome by terrible visions. The scene is powerfully written, full of fractured declamation and fraught rhythms; even the transition to the *cabaletta* brings its rich cargo of effects as Rossini charts Assur's hazy return to consciousness before the stirring *marziale* conveys to us the resolve of the newly-restored man. It is difficult to believe that this remarkable and original scene was not, in some sense, a model or inspiration for the Banquet Scene in Verdi's *Macbeth*.

For once, then, Rossini's inspiration appears to grow towards the opera's end. The Act 2 finale follows Assur's mad scene. It is set in the depths of the Ninus monument. Arsace on his still unspecified mission of revenge, is joined by Assur and Semiramide, who fears for her son's life. Her prayer, 'Al mio pregar t'arrendi' (*Andante*, 3/8, A flat major) is not the sweetest Rossini wrote; perhaps it has about it the feel of Claudius's line in *Hamlet* 'My words fly up, my thoughts remain below'. As the characters circle one another in the gloom Rossini writes a stylized Trio; it is said that this was an afterthought but it is a useful still point before the dénouement and as a metaphor of a community of fatally interlocked interests it is not ineffective.

Unlike *Tancredi*, *Semiramide* should not raise major questions about its ending. There is evidence that Rossini thought the end – the death of Semiramide, Arsace's grief at her hapless killing, his attempted suicide, and acclamation as king – too swift. For the Paris revivals of 1825–6 he extended Semiramide's death throes. Stage decorum required that she die behind the tomb of Ninus but there is no denying her tragic status. I can find no authority for the happy ending – 'Arsace stabs Semiramide instead of Assur' becoming simply 'Arsace stabs Assur' – proposed in the libretto of the distinguished gramophone recording of the opera in which Joan Sutherland sings the title role. Like Iago, Assur seems sullenly to survive.

33

Maometto II and Le siège de Corinthe

The Venetian *prima* of *Semiramide* was accompanied by a revision and revival of *Maometto II*, a grand and innovative piece which had been coolly received by the Neapolitans in December, 1820. In the Naples version of the opera and in *Le siège de Corinthe*, the 1826 Parisian revision of *Maometto II*, the heroine kills herself on stage; in Venice, with due regard for both the law and the profits, Rossini provided a happy ending set to old music, 'Tanti affetti' from the finale of *La donna del lago*. An overture was added, using the old Rossini archetype and drawing on material from the opera itself, and there were some further additions borrowed from *Ermione* and *Bianca e Falliero*. These further instances of Rossini's artistic pragmatism should not, however, blind us to the fact that in its original form and in its Paris revision, *Maometto II* is one of Rossini's most substantial undertakings despite an undistinguished libretto adapted by Cesare della Valle from his own verse drama, *Anna Erizo* (1820), a drama which may, in turn, owe something to Byron's poem, *The Siege of Corinth* (1816), which explores a different siege but similar subject.

In the original version of *Maometto II*, Venetian forces are at bay in their colonial fortress on Euboea or Negroponte as it was called at the time of the drama's action in 1476. The aggressor is the Islamic warrior, Mahomet II, the man who reversed the tide of history by terrorizing the Graeco-Roman world in the middle years of the fifteenth century. Della Valle's plot is sadly predictable. Anna, daughter of the Venetian commander, Erisso, once loved a man who is now revealed to have been the disguised and peripatetic Mahomet. The inner lives of the characters caught in this dilemma are never explored but the passions which are aroused emerge in Rossini's opera to be patriotic and familial rather than erotic. In the Paris revision, contemporary concern with the cause of Greek Independence is exploited, most notably in the blessing of the Greek banners, a new composition; and Anna's somewhat peripheral suitor is rendered more ardent and more plausible as the tenor (Néoclès) than as the *travesti* contralto (Calbo). But though the balance of interests is altered in the Paris revision, the familial element is by no means written out.

What is lost in the Paris revision is something of the architectural grandeur of the original piece: two ninety-minute acts composed for Naples in a handful of long, interlocking musical units. There were precedents for structuring on this scale in some of the contemporary music conducted by Rossini at this time – in Haydn's *The Seasons* and Spontini's *Fernand Cortez* – but Rossini's development of large forms is self-evidently generated from within, a token of a serious and sustained interest in the problems of structure which is to culminate in the massive achievement of *Guillaume Tell*. True, the second act of *Maometto II* is a sustained essay in writing for the all-dominant Colbran. It culminates in an unbroken series of movements – two Trios, a *Scena con coro* and a four-movement second finale – all of which feature the heroine. But the first act has no such prop to support it. As Rossini conceives the act, it becomes a massive exposition cast in five interlocking movements, respectively 325, 115, 867, 362, and 855 bars long. The longest movement, the third, is quippingly designated by Rossini as a *Terzettone*: an outsize *Terzetto*, a monstrously large *Terzettino*. So massive is its scope, it is able to withstand intrusive cannon fire, the temporary departure of two principals, an outbreak of popular dismay, and a prayer (in F sharp minor, later transferred to Act 3 of *Le siège de Corinthe*) before it resumes its majestic course. Indeed, the *Terzettone* never properly ends. Conceived in E major, it has important episodes in B major and G major, the latter acting as the dominant of the stirring Islamic war-song which follows it. In the Paris revision this huge movement is reduced from 867 bars to 365, gaining in pace and concentration and bequeathing one of its finest numbers to a later act, but losing something in dramatic sweep.

Within the *Terzettone's* huge structure, Rossini establishes a father-daughter relationship, strongly felt, eloquently delineated. It is not a huge jump from Erisso addressing Anna (Ex. 42a) to Verdi's Rigoletto or Germont-*père*; and Rossini knew quite as well as Verdi how to affect us with the teasing repetition of rhythmic-melodic fragments as trivial as they are emotionally charged (Ex. 42b).

Even the long duet between Anna and Maometto in Act 2 ('Anna, tu piangi', *Allegro giusto*, 4/4, C major) has a father-daughter

Ex.42

feel to it, with Rossini, more a master of *agape* than *eros*, sculpting for us one of his most classically serene melodies in the *Larghetto*, 'Lieta innocente un giorno' (6/8, A flat major).

The theme of familial love and familial loyalty is further emphasised by della Valle's preoccupation with Anna's relationship to her dead mother before whose tomb much of the action takes place. Indeed, it is a measure of the importance of this theme (made clearer in the theatre where the tomb is physically present) and of the care Rossini now lavishes on the writing of accompanied recitatives that one of the opera's most striking moments, Anna's consecration of her soul to her mother's spirit before Mahomet's fateful entry, is cast in recitative (Ex. 43).

Maometto II is a rich score orchestrally. As always with Rossini,

Ex. 43

percussion is daringly and imaginatively used; but in *Maometto II* we are also aware of the rich and diverse use of the expanded brass choir of four horns, three trombones, two trumpets, and serpentone. Sometimes the brass is used, as it is at the start of the opera, to establish a particular, darkened mood. At other times, at the launch of the *Terzettone*, for instance, brass and timpani are used in a declamatory role of their own. Even where the brass is being used in a formal, ceremonial role, the deployment is carefully plotted. In the opening scene, where Venetian defeatism is transformed by Calbo into a spirit of burgeoning determination, the brass writing is central to Rossini's strategy; though, typically, it is the rhythm – a robust patriotic march quarried brilliantly out of the subdued marching 3/4 of the first chorus – which both determines and underwrites the mood of the music-drama. The chorus of Muslim warriors which follows the *Terzettone* ('Dal ferro, dal fuoco', *Allegro vivace*, 2/4, C major) is also interesting; with its asymmetical rhythms, powerful unisons, and exotic use of percussion it stands somewhere between the Overture to *Il Signor Bruschino* and the Anvil Chorus in Verdi's *Il trovatore*. And Verdi or Tchaikovsky would have been hard pressed to provide finer-grained orchestration – light percussion and high woodwinds imaginatively deployed – than that provided by Rossini in the Moslem women's 'gather ye rosebuds' chorus ('È follia sul fior degli anni', *Vivace*, 3/8, A major) at the start of Act 2.

The decision to adapt *Maometto II* for performance at the Paris Opéra confirmed Rossini's faith in the work, though the contemporary appeal of the adapted libretto and Rossini's awareness, through works like Spontini's *Fernand Cortez*, of the kind of thing the Opéra was traditionally used to, are clear additional factors. Certainly, by 1826 Rossini was sufficiently familiar with French theatre and with French prosody to undertake the task, though in setting French texts for *Le siège de Corinthe* and *Moïse et Pharaon* he was occasionally obliged to ignore the high-flown literary style – the rhetoric and the clever verse rhythms – foisted on him by librettists whose eyes were rather too firmly fixed on the opinions of the Parisian literary press.

Faced with the task of writing for a bigger theatre, and in the French manner but for a cosmopolitan audience, Rossini revealed himself to be both shrewd and workmanlike. By further emphasising the role of the orchestra and chorus, and by scaling down the huge musical structures of *Maometto II*, Rossini conventionalizes the piece but makes it more stageworthy. The *travesti* role of the warrior-lover, Calbo, is offered in a new alternative for tenor (Adolph Nourrit's role at the *première*) and some of Calbo's more otiose solo writing is deleted. Throughout the opera, vocal lines are chastened where in *Maometto II* they were unduly florid. In the theatre it is the choruses, hymns, and prayers – either newly composed or newly placed – which make the greatest impact, not least the chaste but sensuous *Hymne*. 'Divin prophète' (*Adagio*, 3/4, C major) which prefaces the Act 2 finale which is itself the one newly composed longer structure in *Le siège de Corinthe*. It is a movement notable, above all, for yet another Trio, led by Mahomet with a vocal line which admirably demonstrates Rossini's great skill in marrying Italianate songfulness with declamatory eloquence (Ex. 44).

Ex. 44

241

The third and final act of *Le siège de Corinthe* is no longer a glorification of the sacrifice of a single woman. Pamyre's supreme act of self-sacrifice is now placed firmly within a context of national fervour and national suffering occasioned by the hell that is war. The act's opening scene, prayer and air, and its scene and trio, are quarried from Act 2 of *Maometto II* but the blessing of the Greek banners (Hiéros and Chorus, 'Quel nuage sanglant', 4/4, F minor/major) is new. Pamyre's F sharp minor prayer, 'Juste ciel, ah! ta clémence' is from *Maometto* II, Act 1, but Rossini's depiction of the sack of Corinth is a skilful reworking of fragments gathered from the original finale, with the orchestra alone drawing the drama to a close as it had done several years previously in *Mosè in Egitto*. Like the Venice *Maometto II*, *Le siège de Corinthe* has an overture. The Paris overture begins – curiously for a man little given to direct plagiarism – with a slow *marcia religiosa* taken from Mayr's *Atalia* which Rossini had conducted in Naples in 1822. Structurally the overture breaks no new ground, and it also goes in for some self-borrowing (the *allegro assai*'s subject in the key of the dominant is Ex. 50a from Rossini's Neapolitan *Messa di Gloria*) but it has a gravity and fiery abruptness which adequately prepares us for the fervent and noble work which follows.

34

Il viaggio a Reims and Le Comte Ory

Written in honour of the Coronation of Charles X in 1825, *Il viaggio a Reims* was a sumptuous enough musical banquet temporarily to still gossips and malcontents in the Parisian musical world who thought Rossini remiss in not bringing forward a new composition sooner. But though it was a considerable success at the time of its *première*, its subsequent career was a chequered one. Sections which were soon to form part of *Le Comte Ory* were worked over, submitted as copy to Troupenas, and subsequently lost. The autograph of the remainder survived more by luck than by good management. Inherited by Olympe Pélissier and bequeathed by her to Rossini's doctor, Vio Bonato, it was not formally identified and catalogued until 1977, since when its fortunes have undergone a renaissance. An edition has been prepared for the *Edizione critica delle opere di Gioachino Rossini* by Janet Johnson,[1] and it was on the basis of this that the work was heard for the first time in nearly 160 years at the 1984 Pesaro Festival in performances conducted by Claudio Abbado.

As we have already noted, *Il viaggio a Reims* served several causes. Ostensibly, it was an act of homage to Charles X. But it was also a showcase for an exceptionally brilliant troupe of international singers, an entertainment, a piece of national and international razzmatazz, and – last, but by no means least in view of its partial transformation into *Le Comte Ory* – an elaborate appropriation of and satire on Mme de Staël's *Corinne*. This is Rossini at his most urbane, guying the Romantically decadent, pseudo-heroic elements in de Staël's work in his deftest, wittiest style whilst at the same time treating the heroine's more affective utterances in his own most affecting manner.

The work's subtitle, *L'albergo del giglio d'oro*, refers to the Inn

---

[1] The background to this is given in Janet Johnson's 'A lost Rossini opera recovered: *Il viaggio a Reims*, BdCRdS, 1983, p.5.

of the Golden Fleur-de-lis at Plombières where the resident staff, marshalled by Madama Cortese (*prima donna soprano*, sung originally by Ester Mombelli) are preparing their international clientele for a journey to the coronation at Reims. The principal guest, Pasta's role, is Corinna, a celebrated Roman improvising poetess or *improvisatrice*. In her entourage there is an orphaned Greek girl, symbol of Corinna's philhellenic and humanitarian sympathies at a time of crisis for the cause of Greek Independence, as well as Don Profondo, a lover of antiquities (*primo buffo cantante e basso*), and the 'colonnello Inglese', Lord Sidney (*primo basso cantante*). Both men have big scenes. Milord Sidney's elaborate *opera seria* tribute to Corinna with its dazzling flute obbligato did not find its way into *Le Comte Ory*, but Don Profondo's witty disquisition on foreign characters, a strophic song written in a downward spiral of keys a major or minor third apart, turns up again – the climax now less well placed in relation to the new text – when Robert explores the Formoutiers cellars in *Le Comte Ory*. The galant young French officer, Il Cavalier Belfiore, the *primo tenore*, and the vivacious young Contessa di Folleville (another *prima donna soprano*, Cinti's role) complete the group. The Contessa is a widow, despite her years, and so is the Marchesa Melibea (*prima donna contralto*); the Polish widow of an Italian general, she helps make a formidable triangle with the Conte di Libenskof (another *primo tenore*), a jealous Russian much in love with the Marchesa, and a Spanish naval officer, Don Alvaro (*secondo basso cantante*). The mutual antagonisms between the various characters help energize Balocchi's plot, though in the great *Sestetto* amorous jousting is quickly abandoned when national and international solidarity are called for.

The *Sestetto* – the Act 1 finale in all but name and a number not reused in *Le Comte Ory* – is one of Rossini's finest, late operatic inventions. It is launched in bullish style (*Allegro giusto*, 4/4, C major) by the *primo basso comico*, the German Barone di Trombonok. Trombonok, a retired major of no party, is a passionate lover of music and proponent of the virtues of harmony in all its manifestations. Harmony is a thing apt to any international gathering but the Barone is surrounded by hysterical women (notably the Contessa di Folleville who fears that a precious bonnet has been ruined in a stage-coach accident, the mock-heroic text far funnier than its replacement in *Le Comte Ory*) and by jealous rivals. As the first movement of the *Sestetto* majestically unfolds, so the rivalries of

Alvaro and Libenskof become more explicit as they are joined by Melibea and Madama Cortese. The second movement – a movement of stasis, reflection, and ironic comment – is superb ('Non pavento alcun periglio', *Andante*, 2/4, A flat major/minor). Here, Rossini's fully matured craftsmanship is well revealed: his mastery of the elegantly shaped and finely elaborated melodic line; his skill in deploying canon and the interplay of duple and triple time, finely meshed; his gift for the introduction of dramatic asides as economical as they are unexpected. Above all, there is his marvellous ear for the texture of vocal ensembles which are as limpidly clear as they are richly stored.

At the end of the second movement, before the explosively brilliant *stretta*, we do not expect a second slow movement; but this is what we are given when the lovers' tiffs are superseded by the *improvisatrice*'s wafted F major song ('Arpa gentil, che fida', *Andantino*, 6/8). Vocally intricate, but spiritually tender, the improvisation elaborates folksong into high art without sacrificing that simplicity of utterance which makes Corinna's references to the Brotherhood of Man and the cause of the Greeks seem so touching and yet so lofty. But if the F major Improvisation is a tribute to the visionary power of de Staël's novel, elsewhere in *Il viaggio a Reims*, Rossini and Balocchi openly parody the Romantic excesses of *Corinne* with its sentimental valuations of antiquity, and its pseudo-heroic language. In another number excluded from *Le Comte Ory*, the duet between Libenskof and Melibea ('D'alma celeste, Oh Dio!', *Allegro moderato*, 4/4, C major) the recitative is rich in de Staël-like rhetoric, Melibea accusing the Count of failing to appreciate 'the sacred and ardent passion of a great soul', an accusation which the Count greets with bemusement at Melibea's linguistic excesses and which Rossini subverts by writing music of peerless clarity and charm, the cabaletta smiling back to the unclouded world of *Tancredi*.

Il viaggo a Reims is a series of treats for the musical gourmet which rises to great heights in the *Sestetto* and in the stupendous *Gran pezzo concertato a 14 voci* which must be heard in its original form; the slimmed down version in *Le Comte Ory* is, from the sonic point of view, a pale shadow of the original. In contrast to these formidable musical structures, the finale itself is a good deal more informal. Festivities are announced in Paris; the guests, it now seems, must be re-routed; but before they leave they agree to provide a spectacular evening of dance and song for the residents of Plombières.

There is a ballet in a lavish garden setting, and toasts in the form of national songs provided by the principal guests. The Barone sings the German national anthem to Haydn's famous tune, Melibea sings an italianate polonaise, and Lord Sidney, thinking himself unmusical, also resorts to his national anthem: a wonderfully grandiloquent version of 'God Save the King' whose second verse is rudely interrupted by the Barone's cries of 'Basta! basta!' With everyone enjoying themselves rather as they will one day do in Act 2 of Strauss's *Die Fledermaus*, Corinna is summoned for a second improvisation ('All'ombra amena'), richly elaborated in A major and F sharp minor. At the end of the improvisation portraits of the French royal family appear, with emblems, palms, and crowns, the whole thing brilliantly lit and, at the *première*, dazzlingly refracted by the imaginative use of water displays. It makes a triumphant end to one of the oddest and most exhilarating entertainments ever to issue from the pen of an opera composer.

**Details of numbers adapated from *Il viaggio a Reims* for
*Le Comte Ory***

Il viaggio a Reims		*Le Comte Ory*
No.1 Introduction, 'Presto, presto', G major, 558 mm.	=	No.2 Introduction, 'Jouvencelles, venez vite', G major, 625 mm.
No.2 Recit. and Aria, Contessa, 'Partir, o ciel! desio', E flat major, 246 mm.		No.5 Air, Comtesse, 'En proie à la tristesse', E flat major, 227 mm.
No.5 Recit. and Duet, Corinna, Cavaliere, 'Nel suo divin sembiante', A major, 324 mm.		No.8, Comtesse, Ory, 'Ah quel respect, madame', A major, 281 mm.
No.6 Aria, Don Profondo, 'Medaglie incomparabili', E flat major, 309 mm.		No.10, Air, Raimbaud 'Dans ce lieu solitaire', E flat major, 292 mm.
No.7 *Gran pezzo concertato a 14 voci*, 'Ah! a tal colpo inaspettato', A major, 450 mm.		No.6 Finale I, 'Ciel! ô terreur, ô peine extrême!', A major, 449 mm.

There is reason to believe that Count Ory was an historical figure (descendants of the Ory family exist to this day) but the opera's hero first surfaces in a late-eighteenth-century ballad, adapted as a one-act entertainment in 1817 by Scribe and Delestre-Poirson. Their play provided the basis for the opera's second act in which Count Ory, disguising himself as a Mother Superior and his followers as nuns, gains access to the Castle de Formoutiers in a vain attempt to woo and win the Countess during her brother's absence on a Crusade. As this was too short for a full evening's entertainment, Scribe and Delestre-Poirson added a prefatory act in which the characters are introduced and Ory tries a similar ploy, disguising himself as a hermit who dispenses advice to the spiritually anguished. True, the situations are repetitive, but Act 2 is stronger than Act 1; in the theatre, the opera evolves towards its best moments. There are few funnier scenes in opera than the nuns' carousings, their drinking song (they have discovered the absent Count's splendid cellar) turning into sanctimonious prayer whenever the Countess or her companion appear; and there are few more exquisite episodes than the nocturnal Trio, 'A la faveur de cette nuit obscure'.

Le Comte Ory's origin in *Il viaggio a Reims* does, however, add to our pleasure, confirming our sense of the work's sensibility, sophistication and capacity for irony. The greatest weight of direct borrowing is in Act 1, which helps explain the librettists' difficulties in keeping pace with Rossini's composition processes. Apart from the exposition, there is the Countess's *cavatina*, tautened and enriched orchestrally, and the whole of the Act 1 finale, marvellously racy music in the manner of *Il barbiere* at its best, prefaced by a slimmed-down seven-voice version of the *Gran pezzo concertato*. And there are refinements within the borrowings. The Countess's cavatina is now prefaced by a memorable 28-bar prelude taken from *Bianca e Falliero*, and the Count's 'Que les destins prospères' – the *tenore di grazia* bowing into French comic opera in a 'way Auber and Offenbach will want to emulate – is the more delicious for the ironically heightened language ('Que les *destins* . . .) of a text which will later introduce a strophic drinking song with words

> Dans ce lieu solitaire
> propice au doux mystère

more usually associated with pallid heroines lingering by moonlit fountains. Musically, memories of Belfiore's absurd attempts to woo

Corinna (*Il viaggio a Reims*, No.5) heighten our enjoyment as Ory, unavailingly disguised, tries to woo the Countess (*Le Comte Ory*, No.8). The opening of the duet is tender but insinuating, gracious yet questioning, and the *cabaletta* is pure burlesque, rhythmically flat-footed in a way comically alien to a score whose orchestral writing is often airily free of any need slavishly to underpin vocal lines. There are innumerable other delights in this inexhaustible score: Ory's prankish high Cs and the amusing mannerism of the voice's sudden rise by an octave or a major sixth, an aspiring note wittily contradicted in the *cabaletta* of the Act 2 Trio where the Countess's placid exposition is met by Ory's aspiring rise to the tonic A and ignominious descent by semitones in the next five bars, Rossini's urbanely phrased vocal line perfectly conveying the sense of a man whose fortunes are sinking fast. There is also Ory's page, Isolier, a precursor of Oscar in Verdi's *Un ballo in maschera*, whose recognition duet with the Count, 'Une dame de haut parage', is one of the highlights in Act 1 which does not derive from *Il viaggio a Reims*. If a false note is struck anywhere in the opera it is in the *Prélude*,[2] an enigmatic A-B-A piece in B minor/D major which proposes in skeletal form one of the Act 2 drinking songs. 'Mewings which slow down and gradually fade away like a death-rattle' was Berlioz's frustrated description of its end. The composer of *Les péchés de vieillesse* is clearly at work in this *Prélude blagueur*.

The opera culminates in its glorious Act 2 Trio. Rarely, if ever, did Rossini write more sensuously for winds and muted strings; the sound worlds of Mozart and Berlioz are here at once celebrated and anticipated in music which remains quintessential Rossini. Nor is the Trio mere ravishment for the ear; Ory's comic courtship of the Comtesse and Isolier is shaped in a very Rossinian way, for whilst the Trio has a delightfully improvised feel about it, the forms are faultlessly deployed. The *tempo di mezzo* is skilfully used, as is the recapitulation which signals a new-found ease in the exchanges; what had begun for the Countess as an ordeal has become a delicious game. Chorley summed up the appeal of *Le Comte Ory* well when he commended 'a felicitous curiousness in the modulations . . . a crispness of finish, a resolution to make effects by disappointing the ear

---

[2] A new piece. There is no known overture to *Il viaggio a Reims;* the overture which is sometimes associated with that work is a later *pot-pourri* more closely connected to *Le siège de Corinthe*.

which not only bespeaks the master's familiarity with great music of the greatest classical writers, but also a wondrous tact in conforming to the taste of the new public whom he was to fascinate'.[3] On another occasion he added: 'There is not a bad melody, there is not an ugly bar in *Le Comte Ory*'.[4]

---

[3] Chorley, op.cit., p.338.
[4] ibid., p.363.

35

Guillaume Tell

As we have seen in Chapter 10, Schiller's *Wilhelm Tell* is not a revolutionary work in content or intention. It is a tale of country men and women stirred by tyranny to acts of simple courage, its mood at once idyllic and heroic. As such it was a subject well suited to Rossini's temperament and experience, and may well have had the additional merit of meeting Rossini's instinct for a great summarizing subject which would satisfyingly round out nearly twenty years of sustained creative endeavour. As music-drama, *Guillaume Tell* is faithful in most essentials to the original: grandly mapped by Jouy, refined by Bis and Marrast, and evidently supervised and shaped by Rossini himself at critical points.

There are, of course, changes and contrivances, and one or two *mauvais quarts d'heure* which Schiller did not initiate. These occur principally in the first act which Rossini treats with a spaciousness suggested by Schiller but not enacted by him in his play. Within a dozen pages of the start of *Wilhelm Tell*, Schiller has implanted two central images: the grandeur and harmony of nature, and the disruptive and unpredictable nature of politicized man. The play begins with a *ranz-des-vaches*[1] passed between fisherboy, shepherd, and hunter, heard against an imposing background of mountain, pasture, and lake. As a storm begins to gather over the lake, a fugitive rushes in (Schiller's Konrad Baumgarten, Rossini's Leuthold). He has killed a soldier of the occupying Austrian forces. Horsemen arrive but are too late; spurning the vacillations of fisherboy, shepherd, and hunter and the dangers of the storm-stirred lake, Tell has rowed Baumgarten to safety, to the fury of the Austrians who order the slaughter of animals and the razing of the village to the ground. Most of this is in *Guillaume Tell* but at much greater length, Rossini initiating over an hour's music from the fisherboy's song to the act's genuinely terrific final *stretta*.

[1] A traditional melody played on the alpenhorn or, as in this instance, sung by Swiss herdsmen.

This leisureliness is doubtless deliberate. 'A man like Rossini,' notes Berlioz in his essay on the opera, 'always gets what he wants from his poet.'[2] In the first act of *Guillaume Tell* Rossini consciously celebrates the spaciousness and ease of the bucolic life, something which begins before the curtain rises in the famous overture, a four movement programmatic piece, formally different from anything we have encountered in the familiar Rossini archetype. Of the four movements only the second, the storm, is less than remarkable. The opening colloquy for five solo cellos is a rare inspiration evoking, Berlioz eloquently suggests, 'the calm of profound solitude, the solemn silence of nature when the elements and the human passions are at rest'.[3] The pastoral scene which follows the storm is also memorable. The *ranz-des-vaches*, which will reappear in many guises (see Ex.48), gives Rossini material for the finest of all his many cor anglais solos, to which he adds a skirling *al fresco* flute and pin-pricks of triangle tone which evoke the bells of the mountain sheep. It is a subtler sound than Mahler's grumbling cowbells and it too will recur in the opera's peroration. Act 1 itself consists of choruses and more choruses, dances, and some intermittent drama. The dances are exceptionally piquant and have won fame independently of the opera; the choruses are less distinguished, their lack of intrinsic variety highlighted by Rossini's decision to put one of the most congenial into the minor key. Even the fisherboy's song, oddly accompanied by two harps, lacks the freshness of Rossini's best folk-song writing. In terms of plot, the act's principal function is to bring Arnold Melcthal into the drama. He has lost his heart to the Hapsburg Princess Mathilde (Schiller's Berta von Bruneck, radically redrawn) and it is Tell's task to convince him of his duty to his wounded country. Much of what they have to say to one another is dully written – Berlioz has two pages on Rossini's mindless use of repeated notes on the dominant – but we nod off at our peril for *Guillaume Tell* is rich in sudden illuminating strokes of genius, not least among which is a melody (Ex.45) whose ardour must alone convince us that events will be dire indeed if they are to lure Arnold away from his beloved.

[2] Hector Berlioz, '*Guillaume Tell* de Rossini', *Gazette musicale de Paris*, I (1834), 326–7, 336–9, 341–3, 349–51. Reprinted in English translation in *Source Readings in Music History*, ed. O. Strunk, New York, 1950, p.809.
[3] Strunk, op. cit., p.810.

Ex.45

ARNOLD
(aside)

O   Ma - thil - de,   i - do - - le de mon â - - me,

Whatever its *longueurs*, Act 1 has the undeniable merit of establishing the scale of the drama. Act 2, by contrast, is generally acknowledged to be a thing of genius. It was not mere sycophancy which prompted Donizetti to remark that the opera's first and last acts were written by Rossini, the second by God. It is sometimes said that this act is the one which is closest to Schiller. In some respects it is, though there are some incidental changes (in Schiller old Melcthal is blinded, in Rossini he is murdered) and one major innovation. The innovation in the opera is Tell's presence during the oath-swearing of the Swiss confederates on the Rütli heights. In Schiller, Tell makes it clear to Stauffacher that he is not a man for counsels and congregations – 'When you need action, call on me, I'll be there', is his boast (I, iii) – and he is absent from the oath-swearing. It has been suggested that Schiller wished to avoid any sense of the rising being inspired by one man; yet Rossini avoids the trap equally well. Rossini's Tell is very much *primus inter pares*, a father (the Scene of the Apple is central to Rossini's purpose), and a nature-lover. If there is a rabble-rouser in Rossini it is Arnold, hot-headed and eloquent: a useful contrast vocally – tenor to baritone – and temperamentally to Tell himself.

Act 2 begins with a hunting chorus crossed by an evening song for the workers in mountains and fields which ends with an exquisite *smorzando* passage in consecutive fifths and octaves. Mathilde and Arnold dominate the act's first movement. In Mathilde's *Scène et Aria*, 'Sombre forêt', pulses quicken in the preceding recitative. The aria itself retains much of the old sweetness remembered from *Tancredi* days but the line is longer now, linked by a chain of finely judged modulations and elegant phrase shapes. Rossini prefaces each stanza with a soft drum roll, one of the most affecting small instrumental gestures in all opera. If this, and the duet which follows ('Oui vous l'arrachez à mon âme', *Agitato*, 4/4, C major) are memorable musically, what follows is memorable both as music and drama. In the great Trio, 'Quand l'Helvétie est un champ de supplices' (*Allegro maestoso*, 4/4, A major), news is broken to Arnold by

Tell and Walter Furst that his father has been murdered. When we think of *Guillaume Tell* as, in some sense, a drama of paternity, we think of Tell's 'Sois immobile'; but Arnold's response to a tragedy which is actual rather than potential is quite as moving (Ex.46).

Ex.46

The Trio builds gloriously, for though Tell and Furst will be happy to see Arnold's grief act as a whetstone to his sword, it will be crucial that any act of vengeance should be sublimated within the communal cause, not an individual act. From this point, Rossini further builds the tension with the massing of the men of Unterwalden, Uri, and Schwyz. Each group is separately characterized, our sense of the rootedness of these so-called rebels clearly communicated in the idyllic music ('En ces temps de malheurs', *Andantino*, 6/8, A flat major) which Rossini writes for the men of Schwyz. In a difficult *Allegro vivace* ('Guillaume, tu le vois'), Rossini adds the loftiest of all his many conspiratorial ensembles before Tell addresses the assembled group. At the great oath-taking, 'Jurons, jurons par nos dangers', the trumpets sound, but there is no baying *stretta*. Day breaks, the drum again quietly rolls, and the cry 'Aux armes!' is three times repeated before the orchestra adds a torrential sixteen-bar coda. It is a thing of great economy and huge power. 'Ah, it is sublime,' cries Berlioz at this point in his essay. 'Let us take breath.'

It is sometimes said that the opera falls away from this point, but there is no reason to agree with such a judgement. The centres of interest become more diffused but the drama stays majestically on course. The parting of Matilde and Arnold at the start of Act 3 and Arnold's visit to his father's deserted cottage at the start of Act 4 are memorable scenes at the periphery of the drama. The Act 3 scene really belongs to Mathilde. In it we hear still the sweet dazzlement of Cinti-Damoreau's voice and technique. 'Sur la rive étrangère', tense and plaintive, calm and sweet in E minor and E major, is especially memorable. Arnold's Act 4 aria 'Asile héréditaire' (*Andantino*, 6/8, E flat major), one of the most testing in the tenor repertory, is justifiably famous. Berlioz thought it the finest single thing in the score. It is another filial lament written with great finish and beauty, and its *cabaletta* provides all the *slancio* and fire which we were rightly denied at the end of Act 2.

The central event between these two scenes is the arrest of Tell and Gesler's sadistic testing of Tell's bowmanship. Again, the build-up is leisurely. Rossini takes his time over the enforced festivities

Ex.47

during which a reluctant populace celebrates one hundred years of Austrian rule. There is a suitably brutal chorus for Gesler's men and the famous unaccompanied 'Choeur tyrolien' in which tenors and basses give out the rhythm for the voices above. Two moments catch the attention before we reach the heart of the scene of the apple: Tell's remark to Gesler 'Ah! tu n'as pas d'enfant!' and his kneeling to him, 'Gesler . . . je fléchis le genou devant toi'. Tell's address to his son, Jemmy, before the shooting, 'Sois immobile', stands at the heart of the opera and is one of the most personal of all Rossini's musical utterances (Ex.47). A solo cello is used at the outset as it might be in a Bach Passion but the minor-major oscillations and the lie of the line itself are fashioned in Rossini's own special way. Verdi would follow Rossini's cues when it came to portraying another grieving father, Rigoletto.

The declamatory power of the music, which Wagner noted, movingly culminates in Tell's cry 'Jemmy, Jemmy, songe à ta mère!' Can there be any doubt that the power of the music owes something to Rossini's own recent loss – to his mother's death and father's grief – and to the stirring in him of strong familial affections? He confessed as much to Wagner and the music bears eloquent testimony to the fact.

Towards the end of the opera, Mathilde takes a more active interest. Her rescue of Jemmy from Gesler and her decision to join the Swiss cause prompts a Trio, 'Je rends à votre amour' (*Andantino*, 3/8 A flat major), touching in the way that the Michaela sub-plot in *Carmen* is.[4] With Tell still in danger and another storm rising, Tell's wife leads the prayer 'Toi qui du faible es l'espérance'. A prayer is not uncommon at this point in a Rossini opera and some have also been storm-girt, as Desdemona's was. But this prayer is larger-scale. Beginning tensely in E minor, it graduates to the status of duet and then choral ensemble. The murder of Gesler, meanwhile, is rather perfunctorily treated; where Schiller agonizes over the ethics of assassination in a 'just' cause, Rossini treats the murder as a self-evident

---

[4] Rossini wrote a generous letter of introduction for Bizet to Felice Romani in December, 1857. Bizet greatly admired Rossini's music and was clearly influenced by it at several stages in his career. On 31 December 1858, he wrote to Hector Gruyer 'When I hear *Le nozze di Figaro* or the second act of *Guillaume Tell*, I am completely happy. I experience a sense of perfect well-being and satisfaction, I forget everything. Oh, how lucky one is to be thus favoured!'.

necessity. After this, the confederates gather, the skies clear, and the glorious landscape is again seen in all its splendour. Moved by the scene before him, Arnold addresses his dead father, 'Ah, father why are you not here in this moment of joy for all Helvetia?' The line is not in Schiller, but it is not surprising to find it in Rossini. This touching tribute over, Rossini's hymn to nature and liberty steals forth, the *ranz-des-vaches* (Ex.48) stealing softly in on the horns with a numinous beauty which Wagner would match but not surpass.

Ex.48

Thus as the music swells out, moving majestically from key to key, the last of Rossini's heroic idylls reaches its appointed end and with it the end of his own career as an opera composer. Coming to *Guillaume Tell* at the end of a full survey of Rossini's huge operatic output, it is difficult not to be moved by the sounding of these last great C major chords. As Rossini himself wrote in 1868 in a letter to Tito Ricordi, 'Let dear Giulio [Tito's son] study *with kindness* my first work, *Demetrio e Polibio* and *Guillaume Tell*. He will see that I was not idle!'[5] It is a modest summary of an operatic career which is by any standards a dazzlingly inventive, formally innovative and, in the end, musically majestic achievement.

[5] LdR, pp. 321–3; Rognoni, pp.328–9.

36

Sacred music

Messa di Gloria (1820) – Stabat mater (1832/41) – Petite messe solennelle (1864)

Opera composers of the classical and post-classical periods are often thought, in Anglo-Saxon countries in particular, to write sacred music which is self-evidently, even shamelessly operatic, the term being loosely used in this context to imply glib, worldly, or hedonistic. Mozart, Berlioz, and Verdi have all had this charge preferred against them, as has Rossini. For what, the argument goes, could this unschooled, cynical, *bon viveur* know of the traditions of church music or the solemn ritual of the Mass? The answer is, a considerable amount. There are, it is true, movements in Rossini's sacred works which are as sensuous as a Rubens Madonna. There is the sweet, swaggering 'Cuius animam' from the *Stabat mater* to reckon with and the worldly *opera seria* heroism of the tenor's contribution to the otherwise darkly impressive 'Qui tollis' from the *Messa di Gloria*; but as early as 1820 Rossini concluded his *Messa di Gloria* with a fugal subject (Ex.49) notable for its breadth and self-contained energy, a subject, what is more, capable of a witty and effective inversion which even Padre Mattei might have wondered at.[1]

Ex.49

In glo-ri-a De - i Pa - tris, A - - - - - - men.

As his punning preface to the *Petite messe solennelle* makes clear, Rossini was intelligently aware of the fact that composers of sacred

---

[1] Rossini as contrapuntalist or pragmatist? The fugue may be the work of Pietro Raimondi (1786–1853), an unsuccessful opera composer but superb contrapuntalist, resident in Naples at the time.

music could all too easily be joined to the devil's party without their knowing it; but his own sacred music, and in particular the *Petite messe solennelle*, often points aspects of Rossini's style and personality which mythology has obscured. We glimpse here a darker, more troubled side to his nature as well as a compensatory love of the older, pre-classical choral disciplines, themselves complemented by Rossini's acute and delighted sense of new possibilities in matters of texture and harmony. The *Messe*, a singular achievement at a time when choral music was becoming ever more bloated, looks back to Palestrina and forward to the sacred music of such composers as Fauré and Poulenc.

The *Messa di Gloria*, first heard in Naples on 24 March, 1820, is a nine movement setting of the Mass's 'Kyrie' and 'Gloria'. Some movements are for soloist and orchestra: the A major 'Laudamus' for soprano, and two movements with important obbligato wind parts, the tenor's F major 'Gratias', eloquently accompanied by the cor anglais, and the bass's E flat major 'Quoniam' which has an elaborate part for clarinet, an instrument Rossini often features soloistically in his Naples years. There is also a sensuous duet in G flat major for two tenors ('Christe eleison') and an E flat major Trio for two sopranos and bass ('Domine Deus'). In three of the movements, choral and orchestral forces are grandly deployed in a way which looks forward to the choral writing of Berlioz and Verdi. The 'Kyrie', in E flat major, starts boldly in A flat minor and is richly scored for the larger instrumental and vocal forces Rossini was deploying in his later Neapolitan works. By contrast, the E minor choral sections of the 'Qui tollis' belong to a style evolved by Rossini in the Scene of the Shadows in *Mosè in Egitto* with its winding ostinatos and hushed choral entries. The jauntiest movement, aptly enough, is the 'Gloria' itself, a movement which sent the Neapolitans into paroxysms of delight. It is built on two figures, an impish pizzicato (Ex.50a) and a swirling second theme (Ex.50b) which follows it in a brilliant ritornello, joyously crowned by soloists and chorus. Beethoven was to do much the same kind of thing in the presentation of the Joy theme in the last movement of his Ninth Symphony. Contemporary writers saw Rossini's two themes as characterizing the earthly and the spiritual, shepherds and angels, overlaying the 'Gloria' with the spirit of a hymn to Christ's Nativity. Whatever emblems one cares to attach, it is gloriously affirmative music which confirms the truth of Théophile Gautier's assertion that Italian

Ex. 50

sacred music is by nature 'heureux, souriant, presque gai, toujours en fête'.[2]

Gautier made these remarks after hearing Rossini's *Stabat mater* in Paris in 1842 and was one of several writers and musicians who wrote eloquently about the new work. Gautier also praised Rossini's melody as being 'noble, simple et sévère' and 'pleine d'élan et d'effusion'. Perhaps it is unnecessarily defensive to argue that the appeal of the *Stabat mater* rests as much in the variety, sweep, and richness of the setting as in the justice of this or that detail; but there is a sense in which the work's appeal is a sensuous one. Heine, in a famous encomium which Weinstock prints in full,[3] commends Rossini's 'eternal grace', his 'irresistible tenderness'; so glorious were the sounds which issued from the Théâtre-Italien, 'it seemed like a vestibule of Heaven'.

The *a cappella* movements – the 'Eja, Mater' with its recitatives for solo bass, and the 'Quando corpus morietur' much admired by Wagner in later years – place Rossini within the vanguard of those romantic composers who wished to appropriate pre-classical choral styles and procedures. (Mendelssohn's famous performance of Bach's *St Matthew Passion* had been given in Berlin in 1829.) What is notable here, given the 'operatic' charge that is levelled against the work, is the music's shape and sombre mood, quite different from anything we will find in the unaccompanied ensembles in the operas. Having parodied the *a cappella* style in *Le Comte Ory* ('Noble châtelaine . . .') Rossini now addresses it with true gravity. Further evidence of his seriousness of purpose comes in the

[2] *Resumé des opinions de la presse sur la* Stabat Mater *de Rossini*, published by the Escudier brothers, Paris, 1842, p.63. Ex.50a is later reused, in a more martial context, at the end of Act 2 of *Le siège de Corinthe*.

[3] Heine, *Sämtliche Werke* VII, p.217; Weinstock pp.218–20.

big double fugue, written in 1841, with which Rossini concludes the work. Its first subject, 'In sempiterna saecula, Amen', is a splendid inspiration, answered and freely imitated by the second fugue on the word 'Amen'. The recollection of the work's gloomy opening phrases shortly before the end is an additional stroke of imagination, commended by an admiring Adolphe Adam in 1842 and by many others since.

Other movements have the power to thrill, disarm, and delight, the would-be profanities kept always in check. A tragic rhythm underwrites the gloriously phrased soprano solos in the 'Quis est homo', the bass's dramatic entry instantly dispels the rather jaunty mood of the 'Sancta Mater', and even the 'Cuius animam' (a movement, formally, which is quite unoperatic) ends quietly. The Victorians tired of the 'Inflammatus' (Bernard Shaw dubbed it the 'spavined *cheval de bataille* of obsolete prima donnas') but it is a powerful movement, Rossini's 'Dies Irae'. With the exception of the concluding fugue, the 1841 additions, Nos 2–4, are simpler, more melodic, more soloistic. In some respects, the *Stabat mater*'s most impressive movement is its first. Gloriously laid out for the voices, it begins with the cellos' and bassoons' gloomy ascent and a broken pizzicato over which 'dum pendebat Filius' will, at the end, exhaustedly sound. Written in the wake of *Guillaume Tell*, this fine G minor movement is as impressive in the particularity of its detailing as it is in the effective shape of the whole.

The *Petite messe solennelle*, by contrast, is sometimes said to be a rather esoteric piece, a point which may or may not be made the more plausible by Robert Craft's testimony that W.H. Auden would sing extracts from the *Messe* when drunk. Scored for twelve voices, two pianos, and harmonium, the *Messe* is certainly a good deal sparer than the *Stabat mater*. It is also more disturbing. In the 'Kyrie eleison' Rossini's music movingly charts a sense of bewilderment which the prayer in some sense attempts to articulate. The tonality, free-ranging and often unsettling in its fluidity, is predominantly minor key, with Rossini's fondness for keys a minor third apart, here A minor and C minor, very much in evidence. Even more unsettling than the tonal orientations, is the actual sound of the music: harmony notes sustained by the eerie-sounding harmonium, whilst the pianos sketch out skeletal, asymmetrical ostinato figures which will later accompany the voices without in any real sense sustaining them. The choir's entry is a tautly worked contrapuntal fabric, as the realization of the moment of Incarnation will later be, the voices bunched anxiously together before perspectives expand and we are dropped into the major and a sweet, burgeoning melody which Fauré would have been proud to own. In the 'Kyrie' the melody does not reverse the anxious mood; the tonal orientation is still minorwards and remains so for the 'Christe eleison', a C minor unaccompanied choral meditation, conceived in the Palestrina style and beautifully achieved in its own right (Ex.51).

Ex.51

The 'Kyrie' is recapitulated in C minor but the melodic subject brings us finally to A major where, in principle, the music remains. By the end of the 'Kyrie' we have adjusted to the pianos' angular rhythms and to the wheezing harmonium; but Rossini has already drawn us into a world which is a good deal stranger and more emotionally complex than we had probably bargained for at the outset.

By contrast, the 'Gloria', with its trinity of F major flourishes, is splendidly affirmative. The key changes are rich, exotic even, but the mood in which the solo voices praise, bless, and adore is one of settled calm. In the 'Gratias', three of the soloists work together independent of the chorus. Again it is a movement of great economy, the bass giving out the principal subject and then wittily underwriting the contralto's statement with a three-note, syncopated figure, the tenor illuminating the word 'gloriam' with a single high A late in the movement. Occasionally, solo numbers loosen the work's structure, blurring the distinction between Mass and Cantata; the insertion of the Latin hymn, 'O salutaris', as a post-Communion prayer is perhaps *de trop* after the soprano's 'Crucifixus' which is the work's principal point of meditation, though the sweetness of the writing is tempered, as it is in *La charité* (1844, Paris) by dissonances in the piano writing. The solo and duet writing in the *Messe* is, none the less, distinguished. The 'Qui tollis' clearly owes its inspiration to Rossini's artistic love-affair with the Marchisio sisters. This is music of tragic eloquence, long-breathed and given a kind of rapt, gloomy beauty which the creator of Senta's music might well have wondered at. The A flat 'Crucifixus' is a strange piece. To Rognoni it is a Blues number, a not entirely fanciful view. The piano's rhythm is lazily syncopated and the drop back to a B natural in the reiterated cry of 'Crucifixus' in bar 4 establishes the minor third's melancholy presence, something which Rossini develops midway through the movement in an agonizing sequence of rising minor thirds – C sharp, E natural, G, and B flat – during a further fourfold repetition of 'Crucifixus'.

The 'Crucifixus' inhabits a similar world to the 'Prélude religieux' for piano or harmonium solo, written to accompany the Offertory within the Eucharist itself. As has often been pointed out, the movement owes a good deal to Rossini's study of Bach's *The Well-tempered Clavier*, though both the phrasing and the use of chromatic harmony provide a foretaste of what, in the context of César Franck's music, we shall come to know as a state of serene anxiety.

For the concluding double fugues of both the 'Gloria' and the 'Credo' Rossini reverts to a freely varied version of the *stile antico*, familiar from the writing of Italian composers back to Palestrina. The final movement of the 'Gloria', the 'Cum sancto spiritu' is based on a buoyant figure which Haydn might have dreamt up. It is vital,

though, that Rossini's music is not sung with inflated forces since the
fugal subjects, and the freely modulating *smorzando* and homo-
phonic writing, must be sung with accuracy and sensibility. The
'Sanctus' is set *a cappella*; and it is a two-bar unaccompanied call of
'Dona nobis pacem' which comes as balm, *sotto voce* and *legato*, to
the restless melancholy of the concluding 'Agnus Dei'. The movement begins with a melancholy little E minor figure (Ex.52) and a
syncopated ostinato, both of which might have been written by
Schubert in his late, tragic vein.

Ex.52

The vocal line of the 'Agnus Dei' – lyrical, long-breathed, and rising
to great heights of declamation in the climactic cries of 'miserere'
– is Rossini's last gift to the contralto, Barbara Marchisio. At its
climax, the music switches as electrifyingly as Moses' prayer had
done into the major. But the irksome little E minor figure returns as
surely as does the Scherzo's goblin theme (E.M. Forster's famous
metaphor) in the finale of Beethoven's Fifth Symphony. The goblins'
return was for Forster an earnest of Beethoven's honesty, allowing us
to trust him when he says other things; and much the same thing
might be said about the end of Rossini's *Messe*. It is a work which
expresses the hopes, joys, and fears of a man for whom honest doubt,
and with it a certain brooding melancholy, is an integral part of a
faith tenaciously felt.

37

Vocal and piano music

Early songs – Giovanna d'Arco – Les soirées musicales – Péchés de vieillesse

Rossini's output of songs and vocal ensembles during his years as an opera composer is a modest one. The charming folk-song about a love-lorn boy and his girl who works at the mill, 'Se il vuol la molinara', has been attributed to 1801 but the finished composition is probably rather later. A number of songs were written in Naples in 1821, including the enchantingly sly 'La pastorella' about a girl three times betrayed and the brilliant Spanish song, 'En medio a mis dolores'. There were also some occasional pieces which have already been mentioned, including the Carnival song concocted by Rossini and Paganini in Rome in 1821 ('Siamo ciechi, siamo nati') and 'Addio ai viennesi' written for Rossini's departure from Vienna in 1822 and later adapted for use in other cities. Occasionally, a chamber work would be conceived and later used in operatic form, as is the case with 'Amore mi assisti', written c. 1814/15 for soprano, tenor, and piano. It recurs in *Torvaldo e Dorliska* (26 Dec, 1815, Rome) as the *duettino* for Torvaldo and Dorliska, 'Quest' ultimo addio'.

After 1829, Rossini's urge to compose was channelled into smaller forms. Abandoning all plans to write an opera on the subject of Faust or Joan of Arc, he contented himself in 1832 with a twenty-minute cantata, a *gran scena* for soprano and piano, entitled *Giovanna d'Arco*, a work in which full-scale drama is distilled into private soliloquy in a manner often favoured by poets of the period where theatrical forms were unavailable or uncongenial. At the outset, Joan waits, like the poet at the start of Mahler's 'Abschied'. Nothing stirs as she contemplates her imminent departure except the wind-ruffled waters and her inner sense of her own destiny. In the central lyrical section, Joan sentimentally contemplates her mother's sorrow and sense of loss upon discovering her daughter's departure. Both the *maestoso*, Joan's vision, and the *cabaletta*, the anticipation of battle, are boldly, elaborately written in a style Rossini now handles with disarming ease.

Rossini's principal achievement in Paris in the early 1830s was the writing of a group of pieces – eight chamber arias and four chamber duets, all with piano accompaniment – which were to be gathered together and published by Troupenas in 1835 under the title *Les soirées musicales*. The first three songs to texts by Metastasio provide a somewhat muted preface to the collection; the second song in particular sets a text, 'Mi lagnerò tacendo' which Rossini returned to with an obsessive, even morbid, regularity. It is the more brilliant and extrovert songs which have caught the imagination of the public at large and composers as various as Liszt, Respighi, and Britten whose dazzling orchestration of some of the pieces in his *Soirées musicales* and *Matinées musicales* would surely have delighted Rossini. The set takes wing with 'L'orgia', a flamboyant waltz-song about the joys of wine, women, and song. The dances which follow – waltz, boléro, yodelling *tirolese*, barcarolle, and tarantella – are uninhibitedly popular. But if the rhythmic basis of the pieces is frankly demotic, the writing is full of courtly sophistication. The piano writing, as we would expect of Rossini, is wonderfully urbane, harmonies and phrasing often slyly redirecting our attention away from routine expectation back to what Rossini has actually provided for us. Thus there is a polish and detachment about the piano accompaniments which skilfully sets off vocal writing which is, by turns, sensual, sly, and brilliant. The heroines of operas and operettas by composers like Bizet, Heuberger, Johann Strauss, Suppé, and Zeller won't sound so different in the years ahead. The duets are equally charming, especially the Venetian dialect song, 'La regata veneziana', in which two coquettish girls urge a pair of gondoliers to put their backs into their punting. A grimmer maritime note is struck in 'Li marinari', a long duet for tenor and bass partially derived from music originally written for *Ricciardo e Zoraide*. Its brooding mood and lyrical-declamatory style attracted the attention of the young Wagner who orchestrated the duet in 1838.

Rossini's return to composition in 1857 was marked by the presentation to Olympe on 15 April of his *Musique anodine*. No doubt his having resumed work again was a sufficient reason for celebration; but the music reveals the scars of his illness and evidence of the obsessive and morbid states already referred to. The *Musique anodine* consists of six separate settings of the Metastasio text used for the second of *Les soirées musicales* and for numerous brief albumleaf compositions during the otherwise largely silent years between 1835 and 1857.

> Mi lagnerò tacendo
> Della mia sorte amara;
> Ma ch'io non t'ami, o cara,
> Non lo sperar da me.
>
> Crudel! in che t'offesi?
> Farmi penar così, perchè?[1]

The melodically appealing first setting is for contralto, Rossini's favourite voice type, and there is a declamatory fifth setting for mezzo-soprano. The soprano has the third and fourth settings, the latter in 3/4 time. The baritone has the second, its melody's upward curve curiously predicting Verdi's 'Celeste Aida', and the sixth, which is the most congenial of the set. What makes this multiple setting the more curious is that there are many other songs by Rossini which use the same text, sometimes as an archetype disguised by new words, sometimes as an archetype with a new French or Italian text set beneath Metastasio's original text. Songs which come into this general category include 'Aragonese', 'I gondolieri', 'La fioraia fiorentina', a touching song of a Florentine flower-girl's beggar mother, and a Rossinian *Kindertotenlied*, 'Le dodo des enfants', in which a mother sings a lullaby to her baby son, 'ephemeral rose', who is near to death. A song which is to all appearances similarly bleak is 'Un sou', a 'Complainte à deux voix' for tenor and baritone in which two beggars, father and son, bewail their misfortune. Their dog, Medor, has died and they are offering his leash, their last possession, for a sou. How seriously we are meant to take this song, a possible companion to the Rossini/Paganini song of 1821, is open to question. Rossini's humour in his last years could be of the graveyard variety and there were those among Rossini's friends who would have given rather more than a sou to have Mme Rossini's dog – variously described as moth-eaten, nauseous, and a fetid carcass – put away with Medor for good.

The vocal items in the *Péchés de vieillesse* are not numerically

---

[1] I will complain in silence/Over my bitter fate;/But that I cease to love you, dear,/Do not expect it of me./Cruel one, how have I offended you?/Why do you make me suffer so?

preponderant nor, on balance, are they as distinguished a group as the pieces for solo piano. But there are some nice reminders of the variety of Rossini's musical skills, ranging from the *a cappella* 'Cantemus Domino' ('There's a waste of time!!!' notes Rossini at the end of the autograph score) to the diverting Offenbach-like 'Chanson du bébé' with its delighted regressions to nonesense words, 'Atchi!' 'Papa', 'Pipi', 'Caca'. There is also a splendid hunting chorus 'Choeur de chasseurs démocrates'. 'La nuit de Noël' for baritone solo, four-part vocal octet, piano and harmonium is as worthy of attention as much of the incidental music we hear at Christmas, as is the brilliant four-part chorus, 'Toast pour le nouvel an' in which Rossini manages the dizzying feat of celebrating both champagne and the blessed Virgin in the same song. And occasionally, amid these festive and discursive pieces, we encounter a genuinely great song. 'L'ultimo ricordo' is a song in which a dying man presses into his wife's hand a faded flower which she carried on their wedding day. The song's mood resembles that of the 'Agnus Dei' of the *Petite messe solennelle*. A swaying ostinato and rich, often noticeably chromatic texturing underpin a vocal line of chiselled beauty which itself rises to a declamatory climax similar to that in the 'Agnus Dei' or Tell's 'Sois immobile'. As in 'Sois immobile', the plea is made personal, but on this occasion Rossini goes a stage further. By deleting the poet's 'Elvira' and substituting his own wife's name – 'This faded flower/I leave to you, Olympe, as gift' – he turns the song into his own private *Liebestod*. Equally remarkable, with its despairing final cry of 'Ma mère, adieu!' is 'Adieux à la vie', an 'Elégie sur une seule note '. In *Ciro in Babilonia* the 20-year-old Rossini's writing the voice part of an aria on a single note is little more than a cruel prank; here the effect is utterly different. Supported by another impassioned piano part, the monotone declamation can, in a skilled performance, give the song a haunted, despairing character as shifts of key, volume, and pace articulate the text's changing perspectives.

It is difficult to understand why such songs do not appear more frequently in recitals of chanson and lieder; and it is equally difficult to understand why Rossini's substantial body of piano music, dating from the years 1857–68, has been neglected by all but a handful of pianists.[2] In his last years, it was Rossini's charming habit to sign

---

[2] The death of the brilliant young Italian pianist, Dino Ciani, in March 1974 was a great loss. A pupil of Cortot who was himself a pupil of Rossini's

many of his letters 'G. Rossini, pianist of the fourth class'. Perhaps Saint-Saëns was less than just when he talked of Rossini' 'scribbling' these late pieces (the autographs are often beautiful calligraphic specimens) but most contemporary witnesses seem to agree with him when he writes that Rossini played the piano 'to perfection'.[3] By all accounts, Rossini's playing was precise without being dry, light-toned and sparely pedalled yet capable of considerable sensuous beauty, the hands gliding effortlessly across the keyboard. There is evidence of the neoclassical brilliance of his playing in pieces like the 'Prélude pétulant rococo' and 'Gymnastique d'écartement' and it needs a fleet yet resilient touch to do justice to 'Un reveil en sursaut' which rouses 'Un profond sommeil' out of its Lisztian slumbers. In his earliest years Rossini had delighted in eighteenth-century Italian keyboard music (Clementi, by then domiciled in England, was a great hero). Later J.S. Bach's music was to leave its mark, clarifying and energizing Rossini's own writing, and drawing from him a succession of wry tributes in pieces like the 'Prélude prétentieux' and the punningly named 'Prélude fugassé'. At the same time, Rossini had followed with interest the careers of Chopin and Mendelssohn, kindred spirits in many ways, and, of course, Liszt. Ever the detached observer, sympathetic though sometimes acerbic, Rossini appropriates and occasionally parodies their styles, hiding behind whimsical titles and defensive verbal epilogues lest we should be tempted to take his music too seriously. Thus we have a 'Thème naïf et variations idem', a 'Castor Oil Waltz', and a charmingly ruminative, rather Mendelssohnian piece entitled 'Ouf! les petits pois'. Once the victim is openly named in the 'Petite caprice (style Offenbach)', a number – part jest, part parody – said to have been Rossini's quiet retort to Offenbach's guying of the Trio from *Guillaume Tell* in Act 3 of *La belle Hélène*.[4] Marked *Allegretto grotesco* and fingered in a decidedly novel way, the piece tiptoes and occasionally dangerously blunders its way through a harmonic minefield. It has become familiar in Respighi's orchestration in *La boutique fantasque*; but

young house-pianist, Louis Diémer, Ciani stood in direct line of succession. He was a distinguished exponent of Rossini's music as he was of the music of Weber, Hummel, Chopin, Schumann, and Debussy. Happily, Ciani made a number of gramophone recordings of Rossini's piano music.

[3] Saint-Saëns, op.cit., p.265.
[4] 'Lorsque la Grèce est un champ de carnage'.

orchestration blunts the wit and makes the obviously empty formal manoeuvres seem less banal. Rossini's relations with Chopin, Schumann, and Mendelssohn seem more benign. 'Une caresse à ma femme', with its questioning Trio (*Allegretto moderatissimo*) and a first subject (Ex.53) of Eusebian wistfulness could almost be by Schumann.

Ex.53

Chopin may be gently chided in the title of the 'Prélude inoffensif' and made to wait upon tedious warming-up exercises in 'Mon prélude hygiénique du matin' but what follows pays generous tribute to a piano style noted for the elegance of its cantilenas, the brilliance of its sonorities, and the quiet beauty of its modulations. It is here that Rossini seems most at home. In the *Album de château*, he gives us specimens of the music of time past, time present, and time to come. 'Spécimen de l'ancien régime' is a delight with its fine-grained melodic sense, its charming Biedermeierish waltz, and an exquisite short *fugato* in the Bach style. By contrast, 'Spécimen de mon temps', though it has some coursing pages in the manner of Schumann, seems to be parodying the four-square, robustly stated melodies all too familiar from many operas of the period. Cruellest cut of all is 'Spécimen de l'avenir'. Rossini's own piano music looks forward – to Saint-Saëns's neoclassicism, and Satie's, and to composers who will come under the spell of the Chinese influence and dabble in whole tone scales – but this is a wicked parody of the Lisztian method. Elaborate harmonic blueprints are set down but, like the volcanic left hand runs, they seem to lead nowhere; a huge accompaniment is set in motion but remains bereft of any covering melody; when a theme does finally appear towards the end of the piece it is one of over-whelming banality. Of course, Rossini himself can be banal at times. If some of his pieces have a fault, it is that they are too long, as flatulent as the salon pieces they occasionally deride; but, ever the enigma, Rossini is as capable of appropriating Lisztian devices as he is of parodying them, drawing on a brooding, chromatic style for some of his gloomier compositions: 'Memento homo', 'Un cauche-mar', or 'Un rêve'.

For all their good humour, grace, and wit, there is a sense in which these late pieces are the work of a man of complex moods. Sometimes the humour seems morbid and coarse. The train-crash piece, 'Un petit train de plaisir comico-imitatif'[5] deploys the same joke as Lord Berners's 'Funeral March for a Rich Aunt', but in a grimmer context and in a less sanguine manner. And there is Rossini's own 'Marche et reminiscences pour mon dernier voyage' to reckon with. The march is a funeral march after the manner of Beethoven or Chopin but altogether more broken-winded. Between the march fragments are quotations from several of Rossini's best-known operas. We hear, among other things, a sad echo of 'Di tanti palpiti' from *Tancredi* and brief flurries from *La Cenerentola* and the overture to *Semiramide*. There is a snatch from the *Le Comte Ory*'s ironically sanctimonious chorus 'Noble châtelaine' after which the final *galop* from the overture to *Guillaume Tell* cuts a grotesque little caper. It is followed, in turn, by the melancholy strains of the Gondolier's song from *Otello* and – apt and nicely timed – the good night Quintet from *Il barbiere di Siviglia*. Rossini portrays himself in a theme marked '*grazioso e leggiero*', sustaining his public image as a graceful, irresponsible creature with all the insouciance of Verdi's Falstaff recalling his days as page to the Duke of Norfolk. But the march continues to its grim close, at which point Rossini adds a single word: *Requiem*. It is a gloomy end, though it is not beyond the bounds of possibility that Rossini, like the irrepressible Count Ory, will be carousing again the moment our back is turned.

[5] See pp.89–90.

Appendix A

Calendar

Year	Age	Life	Contemporary Events
1792		Gioachino Antonio Rossini born 29 Feb in Pesaro, only child of Giuseppe Rossini (33) and Anna Rossini (20). Rossini's parents had been married in Pesaro on 26 Sept, 1791.	Imprisonment of French Royal Family. Anfossi 64; Auber 10; F. Basili 25; Beethoven 21; Bishop 5; Boccherini 49; Boieldieu 16; Cannabich 60; Carafa 4; Cavos 16; Cherubini 31; Cimarosa 42; Clementi 40; C. Coccia 9; Colbran 7; Crotch 16; Czerny 1; Dalayrac 38; Dittersdorf 52; Dragonetti 28; Field 9; Fioravanti 27; F. Galli 8; M. García 17; Gazzaniga 48; Generali 18; Gossec 58; Grétry 51; Guglielmi 63; J. Haydn 59; Hérold 1; Hummel 13; Le Sueur 32; W. Linley 22; S. Mattei 42; Mayr 28; Méhul 28; Meyerbeer 6 months; Morlacchi 7; Nasolini 24; Paër 20; Paganini 9; Paisiello 51; Pavesi 13; Piccinni 64; I.J. Pleyel 34; Portogallo 24; P. Raimondi 5; Salieri 41; Schenk 38; Seyfried 15; Shield 43; Spohr 7; Spontini 17; C. Stamitz 46; Tadolini 2; Vaccai 1; Velluti 11; Viotti 36; Weber 5; Weigl 25; S. Wesley 26; Winter 37; Zelter 3; Zingarelli 39.
1793	1		Execution of Louis XVI, 21 Jan.
1794	2		Danton and Robespierre executed.
1795	3		Blake's *Songs of Experience*. Marshner born, 16 Aug;

Year	Age	Life	Contemporary Events
1796	4		Mercadante born, *c.* 17 Sept. Napoleon in Italy; Bologna and Ferrara occupied. G. Pacini born, 17 Feb; Berwald born, 23 July; Loewe born, 30 Nov.
1797	5	French troops enter Pesaro, 5 Feb; Giuseppe Rossini voted out of office of public *trombetta* in Dec.	Spread of revolutionary sentiment in Italy. Battle of Cape St Vincent. Schubert born, 31 Jan; Donizetti born, 29 Nov; Heine born, 13 Dec.
1798	6	Gioachino appears with band of Pesaro's Civil Guard, Apr.	French invasion of Papal States. Haydn's *The Creation*, 29 Apr, Vienna. Wordsworth's and Coleridge's *Lyrical Ballads*. Leopardi born 29 June; Cannabich (66) dies, 20 Jan.
1799	7	Increasing number of professional engagements for Anna Rossini as operatic soprano. Appears in Cimarosa's *I nemici generosi* in Ferrara.	French army suffers defeats in Italy; end of brief Parthenopaen Republic in Naples. Olympe Pélissier born, 9 May; Beaumarchais (67) dies, 18 May; Halévy born, 27 May; Dittersdorf (59) dies, 24 Oct.
1800	8	Giuseppe Rossini arrested and imprisoned; freed after defeat of Austrians at Marengo, 14 June.	Piccinni (72) dies, 7 May; V. Gabussi born.
1801	9	Giuseppe Rossini appointed 'Professore di corno di caccia' at Bologna Accademia. Rossini takes horn lessons from his father.	Resignation of Pitt. Haydn's *The Seasons*, 24 Apr, Vienna. Cimarosa (51) dies, 11 Jan; Lanner born, 12 Apr; C. Stamitz (56) dies, 9 Nov.
1802	10	Family moves to Lugo; Anna Rossini working with opera in Imola.	Peace of Amiens, Mar. De Staël's *Delphine*. Beethoven's Heiligenstadt Testament, 6 Oct.
1803	11	Rossini befriended by wealthy Malerbi family; access to Malerbi music library; takes singing lessons from Canon Giuseppe Malerbi. Anna Rossini in Mosca's *L'impresario burlato* in Imola.	Britain declares war on France. Adam born, 24 July; Lortzing born, 23 Oct; Berlioz born, 11 Dec.
1804	12	Rossini appears in public concert with Anna Rossini, Imola, 22 Apr; programme	Napoleon becomes Emperor of France, 28 May; crowned in Nôtre-Dame, 2 Dec. Schiller's

Year	Age	Life	Contemporary Events
		includes a cavatina in the *buffo* style by Rossini. Composes six *sonate a quattro* for Triossi at Conventello, Ravenna.	*Wilhelm Tell.* Glinka born, 1 June.
1805	13	Family moves to Bologna; Rossini appears as Adolfo in Paër's *Camilla* at Teatro del Corso. Private study with Padre Angelo Tesei.	Napoleon forms his Kingdom of Italy. Battles of Trafalgar (Oct) and Austerlitz (Nov). Beethoven's *Eroica* Symphony, 7 Apr, Vienna; Scott's *Lay of the Last Minstrel.* Boccherini (62) dies, 28 May. Schiller (45) dies, 9 May.
1806	14	Rossini enters Bologna's Liceo Musicale, Apr; studies singing, cello, piano; studies counterpoint with Mattei. Overture 'al Conventello'; possible work on numbers for *Demetrio e Polibio* for Mombelli family. Begins to work as continuo player in local opera houses.	Napoleon occupies Naples; Joseph Bonaparte becomes King of Naples. Deaths of Pitt (Jan) and Fox (Sept). Duprez born, 6 Dec.
1807	15	Colbran (22) makes her Bologna debut, 11 Apr. Rossini plays in Guglielmi's *La serva astuta* in Faenza. End of Anna Rossini's career.	French invasion of Spain and Portugal. De Staël's *Corinne.*
1808	16	Writes choral music for Ravenna and Bologna; *Il pianto d'Armonia sulla morte di Orfeo*, 11 Aug, Bologna; Overture in D.	Joseph Bonaparte enters Madrid; Murat new King of Naples. Mosca's *L'italiana in Algeri*, 16 Aug, Milan. Costa born, 4 Feb; Maria Malibran (*née* García) born, 24 March; Balfe born, 15 May.
1809	17	Overture in E flat. Plays in operas by Paër, Sarti, and Cimarosa.	Battle of Corunna, death of Sir John Moore. Barbaia moves to the Teatro San Carlo, Naples. Mendelssohn born, 3 Feb; J. Haydn (77) dies, 31 May.
1810	18	Abandons studies in Bologna. *La cambiale di matrimonio*, 3 Nov, Venice.	Siege of Lisbon. Isouard's *Cendrillon*, 22 Feb, Paris. Scott's *Lady of the Lake*; Crabbe's *The Borough.* Chopin born, *c.*1 Mar; Schumann born,

Year	Age	Life	Contemporary Events
			8 June; Nicolai born, 9 June; S.S. Wesley born, 14 Aug; Ivanoff born, 22 Oct.
1811	19	Prepares performance of Haydn's *The Seasons* in Bologna; Cantata *La morte di Didone* for Ester Mombelli; *L'equivoco stravagante*, 26 Oct, Bologna.	Jane Austen's *Sense and Sensibility*. A. Thomas born, 5 Aug; Liszt born, 22 Oct; Hiller born, 24 Oct.
1812	20	Writes five new operas: *L'inganno felice*, 8 Jan, Venice; *Ciro in Babilonia*, 14 Mar, Ferrara; *La scala di seta*, 9 May, Venice; *La pietra del paragone*, 26 Sept, Milan; *L'occasione fa il ladro*, 24 Nov, Venice.	Napoleon's invasion of Russia (June) and retreat from Moscow (Oct); Perceval murdered. Byron's *Childe Harold*, i and ii. Dickens born, 7 Feb; Flotow born, 27 Apr.
1813	21	*Il Signor Bruschino*, 13 Jan, Venice; *Tancredi*, 6 Feb, Venice; Ferrara revision of *Tancredi*, Mar; *L'italiana in Algeri*, 22 May, Venice. Opens new Teatro Rè with *Tancredi*, Milan, Dec; *Aureliano in Palmira*, 26 Dec, Milan.	Austrian advances in Italy; defeat of Napeoleon at Battle of Leipzig, Oct. Byron's *The Giaour*. Dargomïzhsky born, 14 Feb; Heller born, 15 May; Wagner born 22 May; Grétry (72) dies, 24 Sept; Verdi born, 9 Oct.
1814	22	Revival of *L'italiana in Algeri*, Teatro Rè, Milan, Apr; *Il turco in Italia*, 14 Aug, Milan; *Egle ed Irene*, Milan; *Sigismondo*, 26 Dec, Venice.	Napoleon abdicates, 6 Apr. Beethoven's *Fidelio*, 23 May, Vienna. Henselt born, 9 May.
1815	23	Murat in Bologna, Rossini's *Inno dell'Indipendenza*, 15 Apr. Austrians re-take Bologna. Contract with Barbaia at San Carlo, Naples. Travels to Naples; *Elisabetta*, 4 Oct, Naples; *Torvaldo e Dorliska*, 26 Dec, Rome; contract for *Il barbiere di Siviglia*, 15 Dec.	Congress of Vienna; Napoleon's return to France, Mar; Battle of Waterloo, 18 June; Quadruple Alliance of Austria, Great Britain, Prussia, Russia. Restoration of Louis XVIII. J.M.W. Turner's *The Founding of Carthage*.
1816	24	San Carlo, Naples gutted by fire, 13–14, Feb; rowdy *prima* of *Il barbiere di Siviglia* (*Almaviva*), 20 Feb, Rome; *Le nozze di Teti e di Peleo*, 24 Apr, Naples; *La gazzetta*, 24 Sept,	Byron leaves England, publishes *Childe Harold*, iii, and *Siege of Corinth*; Coleridge's *Kubla Khan*. Sterndale-Bennett born, 13 Apr; Paisiello (76) dies, 5 June.

Year	Age	Life	Contemporary Events
		Naples; *Otello*, 4 Dec, Naples. Travels to Rome.	
1817	25	*La Cenerentola*, 25 Jan, Rome; *La gazza ladra*, 31 May, Milan; *Armida*, 11 Nov, Naples; *Adelaide di Borgogna*, 27 Dec, Rome.	Revision of Spontini's *Fernand Cortez*, 8 May, Paris. Byron's *Tasso* and *Manfred*; Keats's *Poems*. Monsigny (87) dies, 14 Jan; Gade born, 22 Feb; Méhul (54) dies, 18 Oct. Mme de Staël (51) dies, 14 July; Jane Austen (41) dies, 18 July.
1818	26	First version of *Mosè in Egitto*, 5 Mar, Naples. Gala opening of new opera house in Pesaro with *La gazza ladra*, 10 June. Seriously ill with 'severe throat infection'. *Adina* commissioned. Begins negotiations with Opéra in Paris. *Ricciardo e Zoraide*, Naples, 3 Dec.	Congress of Aix-la-Chapelle. Byron's *Childe Harold*, iv; Mary Shelley's *Frankenstein*. Donizetti's debut as composer, *Enrico di Borgogna*, 14 Nov, Venice. C. Novello born, 10 June; Gounod born, 18 June; Godefroid born, 24 July; Golinelli born, 26 Oct. Karl Marx born, 5 May.
1819	27	*Omaggio umiliato*, 20 Feb, Naples. Revised *Mosè in Egitto*, Mar; *Ermione*, 27 Mar, Naples. *Eduardo e Cristina*, 24 Apr, Venice. Returns to Pesaro, 24 May; driven out by Bergami faction. *La donna del lago*, 24 Oct, Naples; *Bianca e Falliero*, 26 Dec, Milan.	Byron's *Don Juan*, i–ii; Goethe's *West-östlicher Divan*; Scott's *Bride of Lammermoor*; Schopenhauer's *Die Welt als Wille und Vorstellung*; Géricault's *The Raft of the Medusa*. Suppé born, 18 Apr; Offenbach born, 20 June. Ruskin born, 8 Feb.
1820	28	Conducts Italian *prima* of 2nd rev. of Spontini's *Fernand Cortez*. *Messa di Gloria*, 24 Mar, Naples. *Maometto II*, 3 Dec, Naples.	Risings against Bourbon rule in Naples, July; Ferdinand I summoned to Laibach, Dec. Death of King George III; trial of Queen Caroline. Scott's *Ivanhoe*. Vieuxtemps born, 17 Feb.
1821	29	*Matilde di Shabran*, 24 Feb, Rome, conducted by Paganini. Rossini and Paganini take part in Roman Carnival. Conducts Haydn's *The Creation*, Apr, Naples. Appearances outside Italy negotiated. *La riconoscenza* as part of gala evening in Rossini's honour, 27	Congress of Laibach, Jan; Austrians enter Naples, Mar; Ferdinand I returns, May. Outbreak of Greek Revolt, Feb. Napoleon (51) dies, 5 May. Weber's *Der Freischütz*, 18 June Berlin. Constable's *The Hay-wain*. Byron's *Don Juan*, iii–v; De Quincey's *Confessions of an*

Year	Age	Life	Contemporary Events
		Dec, San Carlo, Naples.	*English Opium Eater*; Shelley's *Adonais*. Keats (25) dies, 23 Feb; Baudelaire born, 9 Apr; Pauline Viardot (*née* García) born, 18 July.
1822	30	*Zelmira*, 16 Feb, Naples. Conducts Mayr's *Atalia*, Mar. Leaves Naples for season of his operas in Vienna. Marries Isabella Colbran at Castenaso, nr. Bologna, 16 Mar. Hears *Der Freischütz* in Vienna; hears *Eroica* Symphony and meets Beethoven. Vienna's Rossini season 13 Apr to 8 July. Works on *Semiramide* during Oct in Castenaso; travels to Congress of Verona, mid-Nov; writes two official cantatas. Revises *Maometto II* for new production, 26 Dec, Venice.	Castlereagh's suicide; Canning becomes British Foreign Secretary. Congress of Verona convened to deal with situations in Spain and Greece. Rogers's *Italy*, i. Raff born, 27 May; E.T.A. Hoffmann (46) dies, 25 June; Franck born, 10 Dec.
1823	31	*Semiramide*, 3 Feb, Venice. Spends spring and summer in Castenaso. Travels to Paris, Nov. Banquet in his honour, 16 Nov. Reaches London, 13 Dec. Travels to Brighton, 29 Dec. Received by King George IV.	War between France and Spain. Weber's *Euryanthe*, 25 Oct, Vienna. Byron's *Don Juan*, vi-xiv. Lalo born, 27 Jan.
1824	32	Season of Rossini operas at King's Theatre, London. Rossini fêted by the English aristocracy. Fails to write promised new opera; writes short cantata *Il pianto delle muse in morte di Lord Byron* and *Duo* for cello and double-bass. Visits Cambridge. Takes up residence in Paris; contract renegotiated after death of Louis XVIII.	Lord Byron (36) dies, 19 April; *Don Juan* xv-xvi. Meyerbeer's *Il crociato in Egitto*, 7 Mar, Venice; Beethoven's Ninth Symphony, 7 May, Vienna. Stendhal's *Vie de Rossini*. Louis XVIII (68) dies, 16 Sept. Smetana born, 2 Mar; Viotti (69) dies, 3 Mar; Reinecke born, 23 June; Bruckner born, 4 Sept; Cornelius born, 24 Dec. Géricault (32) dies, 26 Jan.
1825	33	Coronation of Charles X, June; *Il viaggio a Reims*, 19 June, Paris; additional charity performance 12 Sept. Supervises revivals of his own	Deaths of Ferdinand I (74), 4 Jan, and Tsar Alexander I (47), 1 Dec. Bellini's debut as opera composer, *Adelson e Salvini*, Naples. Salieri (74) dies, 7

Year	Age	Life	Contemporary Events
		works and Meyerbeer's *Il crociato in Egitto* at Théâtre-Italien.	May; S. Mattei (75) dies, 12 May; Winter (71) dies, 17 Oct; J. Strauss (ii) born, 25 Oct.
1826	34	Conducts charity concert for Greek patriots, 3 Apr. New opera, *Figlia dell'aria*, not forthcoming. *Le siège de Corinthe* (revision of *Maometto II*), 9 Oct, Paris.	Britain and Russia mediate in Greek-Turkish war. Cooper's *Last of the Mohicans*. Alboni born, 6 Mar; Weber (39) dies, 5 June; Foster born, 4 July.
1827	35	Anna Rossini (55) dies in Bologna; Giuseppe Rossini travels to Paris. *Moïse et Pharaon* (revision of *Mosè in Egitto*), 26 Mar, Paris. Stays with Aguado in villa near Paris; visits Dieppe; talks of return to Italy.	Battle of Navarino. Bellini's *Il pirata*, 27 Oct, Milan. Manzoni's *I promessi sposi*. Beethoven (56) dies, 26 March.
1828	36	*Le Comte Ory*, 20 Aug, Paris. Work on *Guillaume Tell*. Maria Malibran makes her Paris debut in *Semiramide*, 8 Apr.	Outbreak of Russo-Turkish war; Wellington becomes Prime Minister of Britain. Schubert (31) dies, 19 Nov; Ibsen born, 20 Mar; Tolstoy born, 9 Dec.
1829	37	Renews negotiations over contract, 10 Apr; threatens to suspend work on *Guillaume Tell*; contract signed by Charles X, 8 May. *Guillaume Tell*, 3 Aug, Paris. Leaves Paris for Bologna, 13 Aug; meets Bellini and attends performance of *Il pirata*, late Aug.	Mendelssohn conducts Bach's *St Matthew Passion* in Berlin. The London Protocol guarantees Greek autonomy. W. Shield (80) dies, 25 Jan; Gossec (95) dies, 16 Feb; A. Rubinstein born, 28 Nov.
1830	38	Spends winter and spring in Bologna and Castenaso. Writes to La Rochefoucauld about libretto for new opera, 4 May. Charles X deposed in July Revolution in Paris; Louis-Philippe succeeds to throne; Rossini's contract with Opéra invalidated. Leaves for Paris, 4 Sept.	Revolutionary movement throughout Europe after deposition of Charles X, Paris, July. Bellini's *I Capuleti ed i Montecchi*, 11 Mar, Venice; Donizetti's *Anna Bolena*, 26 Dec, Milan; Berlioz's *Symphonie fantastique*, 5 Dec, Paris. Goethe's *Wilhelm Meister*; Cobbett's *Rural Rides*. Portogallo (67) dies, 7 Feb; Goldmark born, 18 May.
1831	39	Visits Madrid with Aguado; conducts *Il barbiere di Siviglia*	Meyerbeer's *Robert le diable*, 21 Nov, Paris; Bellini's *Norma*,

Year	Age	Life	Contemporary Events
		in presence of King Ferdinand VII. *Stabat mater* commissioned by Fr. Manuel Fernández Varela.	26 Dec, Milan. Balzac's *La peau de chagrin*; Pushkin's *Boris Godunov*.
1832	40	Dines with Olympe Pélissier and Balzac, Jan. Completes *Stabat mater* (Nos 1, 5–9) with help of Giovanni Tadolini (Nos 2–4, 10–12 of original score). Cholera in Paris; travels with Aguado in southern and central France. Cantata *Giovanna d'Arco* dedicated to Olympe Pélissier. Revivals of Rossini's *Semiramide* and Donizetti's *Anna Bolena* at Théâtre-Italien.	Otto of Bavaria appointed King of Greece; British Reform Act passed. Chopin's first Paris recital, 26 Feb; Donizetti's *L'elisir d'amore*, 12 May, Milan. Goethe's *Faust* part 2. Goethe (82) dies, 22 March; Scott (61) dies 21 Sept. Manet born, 23 Jan. Clementi (80) dies, 10 March; M. García (57) dies, 9 June; Generali (58) dies, 3 Nov.
1833	41	Continues to fight legal case over contract; signs of deteriorating health. Continues to write occasional music (*Les soirées musicales*). *Stabat mater* receives *première* in Madrid, Good Friday.	Hérold (41) dies, 19 Jan; Brahms born, 7 May; F. Bache born, 14 Sept; Borodin born, 12 Nov; Barbara Marchisio born, 6 Dec.
1834	42	Tribunal finds in Rossini's favour, 21 Mar; government appeals against ruling, 23 May. Spends summer in Bologna and Castenaso; returns to Paris late Aug.	Peel becomes Prime Minister of Great Britain. Berlioz's *Harold in Italy*. Pushkin's *The Queen of Spades*. Ponchielli born, 31 Aug; Boieldieu (58) dies, 8 Oct.
1835	43	Théâtre-Italien, Paris stages first performances of Bellini's *I puritani*, 24 Jan, and Donizetti's *Marino Faliero*, 12 Mar. Rossini acts as honorary pall-bearer at Bellini's funeral in Les Invalides. Ministry of finance concedes Rossini's pension claim, 24 Dec. Troupenas publishes *Les soirées musicales*.	Halévy's *La juive*, 23 Feb, Paris; Donizetti's *Lucia di Lammermoor*, 26 Sept, Naples. Cui born, 18 Jan; Bellini (33) dies, 23 Sept; Saint-Saëns born, 9 Oct; Carlotta Marchisio born, 8 Dec.
1836	44	Declines invitation to write new opera for Kärntnertortheater, Vienna. Visits Belgium and the Rhineland with Lionel de Rothschild; meets	Meyerbeer's *Les Huguenots*, 29 Feb, Paris. Büchner's *Woyzeck*; Dickens's *The Pickwick Papers*; Gogol's *The Government Inspector*.

Year	Age	Life	Contemporary Events
		Mendelssohn. Returns to Paris after short stay in Bavaria and travels to Bologna.	V. Lavigna (60) dies, 14 Sept; Malibran (28) dies, 23 Sept.
1837	45	Olympe Pélissier moves to Bologna. Formal separation of Rossini and Isabella. Rossini and Olympe travel to Milan, Nov, for winter season. Meets Liszt who is working on second book of *Années de pèlerinage*. Liszt transcribes Rossini's *Les soirées musicales* for piano. Death of Varela; manuscript of *Stabat mater* sold, 1 Dec.	Berlioz's *Grande messe des morts*. Balakirev born, 2 Jan; Field (54) dies, 23 Jan; Zingarelli (85) dies, 5 May; Fioravanti (72) dies, 16 June; Le Sueur (77) dies, 6 Oct; S. Wesley (71) dies, 11 Oct. Pushkin (37) dies 10 Feb; Leopardi (38) dies, 14 June.
1838	46	Much affected by news of Severini's death in fire at Théâtre-Italien, Paris, 14/15 Jan. Returns to Bologna. Giuseppe Rossini not well, but celebrates 80th birthday, 3 Oct.	Bruch born, 6 Jan; Bizet born, 25 Oct.
1839	47	Increasingly serious attacks of urethritis and depressive cycles. Giuseppe Rossini (80) dies, 29 Apr. Visits Naples during summer on doctor's advice; stays with Barbaia. Returns to Bologna on 17 Sept.	Verdi's debut as composer, *Oberto*, 17 Nov, Milan; Berlioz's *Roméo et Juliette*. A Nourrit (37) dies, 8 Mar; Rheinberger born, 17 Mar; Mussorgsky born, 21 Mar; Paër (67) dies, 3 May. Cézanne born, 19 Jan.
1840	48	Takes up post as consultant to Liceo Musicale, Bologna. Urethritis remains chronic, new treatments complicate condition. Rossini's protégé, Ivanoff, presents *Rodolofo di Sterlinga*, an adaptation of *Guillaume Tell*, in Bologna.	Tchaikovsky born, 7 May; Paganini (57) dies, 27 May; Stainer born, 6 June. Monet born, 14 Nov.
1841	49	Travels to Venice to *prima* of *Clemenza di Valois* by his friend, Vincenzo Gabussi, 20 Feb. Takes waters at Porretta, June. Manuscript of *Stabat mater* sold to Aulagnier in Paris, 1 Sept; Rossini intervenes, cedes rights to Troupenas, and begins immediate work on replacing	Adam's *Giselle*, 28 June, Paris. Donizetti's *Maria Padilla*, 26 Dec, Milan. Chabrier born, 18 Jan; Dvořák born, 8 Sept; Barbaia (63) dies, 19 Oct.

Year	Age	Life	Contemporary Events
		movements originally assigned to Tadolini. Attempts to interest Donizetti in directorship of Liceo Musicale, Bologna.	
1842	50	*Première* of all-Rossini *Stabat mater*, Théâtre-Italien, Paris, 7 Jan; huge artistic and commercial success. Italian *prima*, Bologna, 18 Mar, cond. Donizetti. Efforts to interest Donizetti in Liceo directorship fail. Aguado (58) dies, Apr. Verdi visits Rossini in Bologna.	Verdi *Nabucco*, 9 Mar, Milan; Donizetti's *Linda di Chamounix*, 19 May, Vienna; Donizetti appointed Kapellmeister to Austrian Court. Stendhal (Henri Beyle) (59) dies, 22 Mar. Boito born, 24 Feb; Cherubini (81) dies, 15 Mar; Massenet born, 12 May; Sullivan born, 13 May.
1843	51	Visits Paris for treatment by surgeon, Jean Civiale, May to Sept. Cedes rights of incidental music to *Edipo a Colono* to Gabussi, 28 June. Hears Verdi's *Nabucco* in Bologna, Oct.	Wagner's *Der fliegende Holländer*, 2 Jan, Dresden; Donizetti's *Don Pasquale*, 3 Jan, Paris. Diémer born, 14 Feb; Patti born, 19 Feb; Lanner (42) dies, 14 April; Grieg born, 15 June. Henry James born, 15 April. Ruskin's *Modern Painters*.
1844	52	Visited by Troupenas. Visits Ferrrara to hear Donzelli in Mercadante's *Il bravo*. Adapts two choruses from *Edipo a Colono* and writes a third chorus for *Trois choeurs religieux*, 20 Nov, Paris.	Dickens visits Italy; *Pictures from Italy*. Heine's *Neue Gedichte*. Rimsky-Korsakov born, 18 Mar. Nietzsche born, 15 Oct.
1845	53	Isabella Colbran-Rossini seriously ill; Rossini visits her 7 Sept; she dies, aged 60, 7 Oct.	Wagner's *Tannhäuser*, 19 Oct. Dresden. Disraeli's *Sybil*; Engels's *The Condition of the Working Class in England*. Widor born, 21 Feb; Fauré born, 12 May; Mayr (82) dies, 2 Dec.
1846	54	Co-operates with Niedermeyer, Reyer, and Vaëz in *Robert Bruce*, pastiche based on *La donna del lago*; première 30 Dec, Paris Opéra; Rossini does not attend. Writes two cantatas in honour of newly elected Pope Pius IX. Marries Olympe	Repeal of Corn Laws in Britain. Berlioz's *La damnation de Faust*. Weigl (79) dies, 3 Feb. Tosti born, 9 Apr; Dragonetti (82) dies, 16 April; Gabussi (46) dies, 12 Sept. Thackeray's *Vanity Fair*.

Year	Age	Life	Contemporary Events
		Pélissier in Bologna, 16 Aug.	Mendelssohn (38) dies, 4 Nov.
1847	55	*Prima* of Cantata in honour of Pius IX, 1 Jan, Rome. Controversy in press concerning *Robert Bruce*. *Tantum ergo*, 28 Nov, Bologna.	
1848	56	Alarmed by revolutionary activity in Bologna and by demonstration outside his house 27 Apr; leaves for Florence 28 Apr. Writes a Choral March for Bologna's Guarda Civica but declines entreaties to return to Bologna and does not attend *prima* on 21 June. Takes up temporary residence in Florence.	Year of revolution in Europe. Sicilian revolt, 12 Jan; revolution in Paris, 22 Feb; Metternich resigns, 13 Mar; risings against Austrians in Milan and Venice; liberal constitutions granted in Papal States, Tuscany, Piedmont, Naples; Radetzky's victory at Custozza, 25 July; assassination of Count Rossi, 15 Nov. *Communist Manifesto* published, Feb. Duparc born, 21 Jan; Parry born, 27 Feb; Donizetti (50) dies, 8 Apr; Vaccai (58) dies, 6 Aug.
1849	57	Continues to run affairs from Florence; regular flow of letters to Bologna on domestic matters.	Republic proclaimed in Rome by Mazzini, 9 Feb; Austrian victory at Novara, 23 Mar; accession of Victor Emmanuel II; Pius IX restored, 4 July; Venice surrendered to Austrians, 28 Aug.
1850	58	*Inno alla Pace* written for the painter Vincenzo Rasori, 26 June. Returns to Bologna in Sept with police escort; spends winter attending to domestic and business affairs.	Louis-Philippe (76) dies, 26 Aug. Basili (83) dies, 25 Mar; Tomášek (75) dies, 3 Apr; Heuberger born, 18 June; Pavesi (71) dies, 28 July. Balzac (51) dies, 21 Aug.
1851	59	Principal possessions crated for dispatch to Florence; Rossini unnerved by continued political unrest in Bologna; returns to Florence 5 May; remaining possessions of Bologna palazzo sold by proxy in Nov.	Verdi's *Rigoletto*, 11 Mar, Venice. London's Great Exhibition opens in Paxton's new Crystal Palace, 1 May. Louis Napoleon's *coup d'état*, Paris, 2 Dec. Lortzing (49) dies, 21 Jan; Spontini (76) dies, 24 Jan; d'Indy born, 27 Mar. J.M.W. Turner (76) dies, 19 Dec.
1852	60	Health remains intermittently	Louis Napoleon takes title of

Year	Age	Life	Contemporary Events
		poor; severe depressions and talk of suicide. Corresponds with Ivanoff about Verdi's *Rigoletto*; makes new arr. of *Giovanna d'Arco*. Declines Donzelli's request for some new compositions, 30 Oct.	Napoleon III; launching of expansionist financial, commercial, and industrial policies of the Second Empire. Stanford born, 30 Sept.
1853	61	Buys property in Florence's Via Larga (now Via Cavour) for renovation. Attends performance of *Guglielmo Tell* staged in his honour in Pitti Palace, Apr. Letters reveal continued manic-depressive cycles.	Verdi's *Il trovatore*, 19 Jan, Rome; *La traviata*, 6 Mar, Venice. Liszt's B minor Sonata. P. Raimondi (66) dies, 30 Oct; Messager born, 30 Dec.
1854	62	Some private music-making though visitors report acute nervousness, depression, and insomnia. Takes waters, Lucca, June-July, to no avail.	Crimean War; Battle of Balaclava; Tennyson's 'The Charge of the Light Brigade'. M and L Escudier's *Rossini: sa vie et ses oeuvres*, Paris. Catalani born, 19 June; Janáček born, 3 July; Humperdinck born, 1 Sept.
1855	63	Departure from Italy. Leaves Florence 26 Apr; arrives in Paris late May. Spends July-Sept in Trouville, Normandy; meets Hiller. Takes up permanent residence in Paris during autumn.	Opening of the Bouffes-Parisiens at the Salle Marigny with Offenbach season, July. Début of Hortense Schneider in Offenbach's *Le violoneux*, 31 Aug. Chausson born, 20 Jan; G. Rossi (80) dies, 25 Jan. Bishop (68) dies, 30 Apr. Lyadov born, 11 May.
1856	64	Rents small villa in Passy. Visits Strasbourg in June; takes waters at Wildblad; received by Maximilian II of Bavaria in Kissingen.	Martucci born, 6 Jan; Sinding born, 11 Jan; Adam (52) dies, 3 May; Schumann (46) dies, 29 July; Taneyev born, 25 Nov. Heine (58) dies, 17 Feb.
1857	65	Writes his *Musique anodine* as gift for Olympe, 15 Apr. Beginning of new phase in Rossini's creative and social life. Moves to apartment in rue de la Chaussée d'Antin.	Indian Mutiny. Liszt's *Faust* and *Dante* symphonies; Baudelaire's *Les fleurs du mal*. Glinka (52) dies, 15 Feb; Elgar born, 2 June; Czerny (66) dies, 15 July.
1858	66	Acquires land for a new villa in Passy. Draws up will, 5 July nominating Olympe as principal beneficiary and, after	Assassination attempt on Napoleon III. Offenbach's *Orphée aux enfers*, 21 Oct, Paris. E. Smyth born, 22 Apr;

Year	Age	Life	Contemporary Events
		her death, the Comune of Pesaro for founding of a Liceo Musicale. Regular composition of the *Péchés de vieillesse*. First *samedi soir*, 18 Dec.	Leoncavallo born, 8 March; F.E. Bache (24) dies, 24 Aug; Puccini born, 23 Dec.
1859	67	French government committee of which Rossini was absentee president reports on standard musical pitch; $a' = 435$ enforced by law. Feb. Cornerstone of Passy villa laid, 10 Mar. Enthusiastically received at Conservatoire concert of his music, 17 Apr.	Spohr (75) dies, 22 Oct; L. Ricci (54) dies, 31 Dec.
1860	68	Wagner conducts concerts in Paris; visits Rossini, Mar. Debut of Marchisio sisters at Paris Opéra in new production of *Semiramide* in a French version by Méry and Carafa, 9 July. Receives visits by Moscheles and Hanslick.	Campaign for Italian unification by Garibaldi, Sicily and Naples, May. Wolf born, 13 Mar; Albéniz born, 29 May; G. Charpentier born, 25 June; Mahler born, 7 July; MacDowell born, 18 Dec. Chekhov born, 29 Jan; Schopenhauer (72) dies, 21 Sept.
1861	69	*Soirée* on Good Friday, 29 Mar, devoted to *Stabat mater*, with Marchisio sisters as soloists; orch. arr. for double string quartet. Declines commission for 1862 London Exhibition. *Chant des Titans*, 22 Dec, Paris. Attempts to promote performance of Raimondi's gargantuan *Putifar, Giuseppe, e Giacobbe* in London, unsuccessfully.	Start of American Civil War. Berlioz's *Les Troyens* accepted by Paris Opéra. Marschner (66) dies, 14 Dec.
1862	70	Sits for portrait by the Roman painter Guglielmo De Sanctis. Continues to compose prolifically for *samedi soirs* and to lead a full, if carefully regulated, social life.	Bismark becomes Minister-President of Prussia. Delius born, 29 Jan; Halévy (62) dies, 17 Mar; Debussy born, 22 Aug. Dostoevsky's *The House of the Dead*.
1863	71	*Soirée* on Good Friday includes movements from Pergolesi's and Rossini's *Stabat mater*. Begins work during summer on the *Petite messe solennelle*.	Cinti-Damoreau (62) dies, 25 Feb; Mascagni born, 7 Dec. Manet's *Le déjeuner sur l'herbe*; Delacroix (65) dies, 13 Aug.

Year	Age	Life	Contemporary Events
1864	72	*Première* of the *Petite messe solennelle* as part of the dedication of the chapel of the Countess Pillet-Will, Sunday, 14 Mar, Paris. Writes his touching 'Quelques mesures de chant funèbre' in response to Meyerbeer's death. Made *grand officier* of the Légion d'Honneur. Extensive celebrations of his name-day in Paris and Pesaro, Aug.	Offenbach's *La belle Hélène*, 17 Dec, Paris. Foster (37) dies, 13 Jan; d'Albert born, 10 Apr; Meyerbeer (72) dies, 2 May; R. Strauss born, 11 June.
1865	73	Visited by Weber's son, Mar. Encourages Costa with his oratorio, *Naaman*; tries to interest London hospital, through Costa, in cancer 'cure' of Bolognese surgeon.	Wagner's *Tristan und Isolde*, 10 June, Munich. Pasta (67) dies, 1 Apr; Magnard born, 9 June; Nielsen born, 9 June; Glazunov born, 10 Aug; Dukas born, 1 Oct; Sibelius born, 8 Dec.
1866	74	Liszt plays at *soirée*, Holy Saturday, 31 Mar. Rossini begins correspondence with Pope Pius IX in unsuccessful attempt to bring about revocation of Papal ban on women singers in church. Mild stroke or thrombosis, Dec.	Austro-Prussian war. A. Pacini (87) dies, 10 March; Busoni born, 1 April; Satie born, 17 May; Cilea born, 26 July. Dostoevsky's *Crime and Punishment*.
1867	75	Works on orchestration of *Petite messe solennelle*. Writes *Hymne à Napoléon III*, Palais de l'Industrie, Paris, 1 July.	Verdi's *Don Carlos*, 11 Mar, Paris. Granados born, 27 July; Giordano born, 28 Aug; Koechlin born, 27 Nov; G. Pacini (71) dies, 6 Dec. Ibsen's *Peer Gynt*. Baudelaire (46) dies, 31 Aug.
1868	76	'500th' performance of *Guillaume Tell* celebrated at Paris Opéra, 10 Feb. Becomes embroiled in controversy about funding of Italian musical academies. Receives letter early Aug. from composer of a new version of *Il barbiere di Siviglia*. Discusses his art and ideas in a letter to Filippo Filippi, 26 Aug. Last *samedi soir*, 26 Sept. Undergoes two operations for	Wagner's *Die Meistersinger*, 21 June, Munich. Berwald (71) dies, 3 Apr; Bantock born, 7 Aug. Albéniz aged 8; Auber 86; Balakirev 31; Balfe 60; Berlioz 64; Bizet 30; Boito 26; Borodin 35; Brahms 35; Bruch 30; Bruckner 44; Busoni 2; Catalani 14; Chabrier 27; Charpentier 8; Chausson 13; Cilea 2; Costa 60; Debussy 6; Delibes 32; Delius 6; Dukas 2;

Year	Age	Life	Contemporary Events

malignant rectal fistulas, early
Nov. Lingers in great pain for
over a week. Dies at 11.15 p.m.
on Friday, 13 November.
Gustave Doré makes deathbed
drawings next morning (see
plate 24). Funeral at Eglise de la
Trinité, Paris at noon on 21
Nov. attended by over 4,000
people; buried in the Cemetery
of Père-Lachaise.

[Olympe Rossini died on 22
Mar, 1878. Rossini's remains
were reinterred in the Church
of Santa Croce, Florence, 2
May, 1887. The monument for
the tomb was dedicated on 23
June, 1902.]

Duparc 20; Dvořák 27; Elgar
11; Fauré 23; Flotow 56;
Franck 45; Gade 5; Giordano
1; Glazunov 3; Goldmark 38;
Gounod 50; Granados 1; Grieg
25; Humperdinck 14; d'Indy
17; Janáček 14; Lalo 45;
Leoncavallo 10; Liszt 57;
Loewe 71; Lyadov 13;
Magnard 3; Mahler 8;
Mascagni 4; Massenet 26;
Mercadante 73; Messager 14;
Mussorgsky 29; Nielsen 3;
Offenbach 49; Parry 20;
Ponchielli 34; Puccini 9;
Rimsky-Korsakov 24; A.
Rubinstein 38; Saint-Saëns 33;
Satie 2; Sibelius 2; Smetana 44;
Stainer 28; Stanford 16; J.
Strauss, ii 43; R. Strauss 4;
Sullivan 26; Suppé 49;
Tchaikovsky 28; A. Thomas
57; Tosti 22; Verdi 55; Wagner
55; Widor 23; Wolf 8.

Appendix B

List of works

Editions
QR   *Quaderni rossiniana, a cura della Fondazione Rossini* (Pesaro, 1954–)
EC   *Edizione critica delle opere di Gioachino Rossini,* ed. Fondazione
      Rossini (Persaro, 1979–)
ERO *Early Romantic Opera* (Garland Publishing, New York, 1976–84).
      Eleven Rossini operas have been published in facsimile form from
      manuscript or contemporary printed editions, with introductions
      by Philip Gossett.

A limited number of operas are published in vocal score by Ricordi, Milan;
Otos, Florence; Kalmus, New York. Where editions are unedited photo-
graphic reprints of early nineteenth-century editions, they should be treated
with caution.

I Operas

Demetrio e Polibio, dramma serio, 2 acts; libretto by V. Viganò-Mombelli
    after Metastasio's *Demetrio.* Composed before 1808; *prima* Teatro Valle,
    Rome, 18 May, 1812.
La cambiale di matrimonio, farsa comica, 1 act; libretto by G. Rossi after
    C. Federici's play (1791), and G. Checcherini's libretto for Carlo Coccia's
    Il matrimonio per lettera di Cambio (1807). Teatro San Moisè, Venice,
    3 Nov, 1810.
L'equivoco stravagante, dramma giocoso, 2 acts; libretto by G. Gasparri.
    Teatro del Corso, Bologna, 26 Oct, 1811.
L'inganno felice, farsa, 1 act; libretto by G. Foppa after G. Palomba's
    libretto for Paisiello's *L'inganno felice* (1798, Naples). Teatro San Moisè,
    Venice, 8 Jan, 1812.
Ciro in Babilonia, ossia La caduta di Baldassare, dramma con cori, 2 acts;
    libretto by F. Aventi. Teatro Comunale, Ferrara, ?14 March, 1812.
La scala di seta, farsa comica, 1 act; libretto by G. Foppa after Planard's
    libretto for Gaveaux's *L'échelle de soie* (1808, Paris). Teatro San Moisè,
    Venice, 9 May, 1812.
La pietra del paragone, melodramma giocoso, 2 acts; libretto by L.
    Romanelli. Teatro alla Scala, Milan, 26 Sept, 1812.
L'occasione fa il ladro, burletta, 1 act; libretto by L. Prividali, Teatro San
    Moisè, Venice, 24 Nov, 1812. ECI/viii.
Il Signor Bruschino, ossia Il figlio per azzardo, farsa giocosa, 1 act; libretto
    by G. Foppa after A. de Chazet's and E.-T. Maurice Ourry's *Le fils par
    hazard* (1809). Teatro San Moisè, Venice, 27 Jan, 1813. ECI/ix.

Tancredi, melodramma eroico, 2 acts; libretto by G. Rossi after Voltaire's *Tancrède* (1760). Teatro La Fenice, Venice, 6 Feb, 1813. ECI/x.

L'italiana in Algeri, dramma giocoso, 2 acts; libretto substantially derived from A. Anelli's libretto for Mosca's *L'italiana in Algeri* (1808, Milan). Teatro San Benedetto, Venice, 22 May, 1813. ECI/xi.

Aureliano in Palmira, dramma serio, 2 acts; libretto by F. Romani after Gaetano Sertor's libretto for Anfossi's *Zenobia di Palmira* (1789). Teatro all Scala, Milan, 26 Dec, 1813.

Il turco in Italia, dramma buffo, 2 acts; libretto by F. Romani derived from C. Mazzolà's libretto for *Il turco in Italia* set by Seydelmann (Dresden, 1788) and Süssmayr (Prague, 1794). Teatro alla Scala, Milan, 14 Aug, 1814. ECI/xiii.

Sigismondo, dramma, 2 acts; libretto by G. Foppa. Teatro La Fenice, Venice, 26 Dec, 1814.

Elisabetta, regina d'Inghilterra, dramma, 2 acts; libretto by G. Schmidt after C. Federici's play (1814) based on S. Lee's *The Recess* (1783–5). Teatro San Carlo, Naples, 4 Oct, 1815. ERO, 2 vols.

Torvaldo e Dorliska, dramma semiserio, 2 acts; libretto by C. Sterbini. Teatro Valle, Rome, 26 Dec, 1815.

Il barbiere di Siviglia (originally *Almaviva, ossia L'inutile precauzione*), *commedia*, 2 acts. Libretto by C. Sterbini after Beaumarchais's *Le barbier de Séville* (1775) and G. Petrosellini's libretto for Paisiello's *Il barbiere di Siviglia* (1782, St Petersburg). Teatro Argentina, Rome, 20 Feb, 1816.

La gazzetta, dramma/opera buffa, 2 acts. Libretto by G. Palomba after Goldoni's *Il matrimonio per concorso* (1763). Teatro dei Fiorentini, Naples, 26 Sept, 1816.

Otello, ossia Il moro di Venezia, dramma, 3 acts; libretto by F. Berio di Salsa after Shakespeare's *Othello* (1604). Teatro del Fondo, Naples, 4 Dec, 1816. ERO, 2 vols. ECI/xix.

La Cenerentola, ossia La bontà in trionfo, dramma giocoso, 2 acts; libretto by J. Ferretti after Perrault's *Cendrillon* (1697) and libretti by C.-G. Etienne for Isouard's *Cendrillon* (1810, Paris) and by F. Romani for Pavesi's *Agatina, o La virtù premiata* (1814, Milan). Teatro Valle, Rome, 25 Jan, 1817. ECI/xx.

La gazza ladra, melodramma, 2 acts; libretto by G. Gherardini after d'Aubigny's and Caigniez's *La pie voleuse* (1815). Teatro alla Scala, Milan, 31 May, 1817. ECI/xxi.

Armida, dramma, 3 acts; libretto by G. Schmidt after Tasso's *Gerusalemme liberata* (1581/93). Teatro San Carlo, Naples, 11 Nov, 1817.

Adelaide di Borgogna, dramma, 2 acts; libretto by G. Schmidt. Teatro Argentina, Rome, 27 Dec, 1817.

Mosè in Egitto, azione tragico-sacra, 3 acts; libretto by A.L. Tottola after F. Ringhieri's *L'Osiride* (1760). Teatro San Carlo, Naples, 5 Mar, 1818 (Act 3, rev. March, 1819). ERO, 2 vols.

Adina, farsa, 1 act; libretto by G. Bevilacqua-Aldobrandini. Composed 1818; first performed Teatro de San Carlos, Lisbon, 22 June, 1826.

Ricciardo e Zoraide, dramma, 2 acts. Libretto by F. Berio di Salsa. Teatro San Carlo, Naples, 3 Dec, 1818. ERO, 2 vols.

Ermione, azione tragica, 2 acts; libretto by A.L. Tottola after Racine's *Andromaque* (1667). Teatro San Carlo, Naples, 27 Mar, 1819.

Eduardo e Cristina, dramma, 2 acts; libretto by G. Schmidt rev. by G. Bevilacqua-Aldobrandini and A.L. Tottola after libretto for Pavesi's *Odoardo e Cristina* (1810). Teatro San Benedetto, Venice, 24 Apr, 1819.

La donna del lago, melodramma, 2 acts; libretto by A.L. Tottola after Sir Walter Scott's *The Lady of the Lake* (1810). Teatro San Carlo, Naples, 24 Oct, 1819. ECI/xxix.

Bianca e Falliero, ossia Il consiglio dei tre; melodramma, 2 acts; libretto by F. Romani after A.-V. Arnault's *Blanche et Montcassin* (1798). Teatro alla Scala, Milan, 26 Dec, 1819. ECI/xxx.

Maometto II, dramma, 2 acts; libretto by C. della Valle after his *Anna Erizo* (1820). Teatro San Carlo, Naples, 3 Dec, 1820. ERO, 2 vols.

Matilde (di) Shabran, ossia Bellezza, e cuor di ferro, melodramma giocoso, 2 acts; libretto by G. Ferretti after F.-B. Hoffman's libretto for Méhul's *Euphrosine* (1790/1, Paris) and J.M. Boutet de Monvel's play *Mathilde* (1799). Teatro Apollo, Rome, 24 Feb, 1821.

Zelmira, dramma 2 acts; libretto by A.L. Tottola after Dormont de Belloy's *Zelmire* (1762). Teatro San Carlo, 16 Feb, 1822. ERO, 2 vols.

Semiramide, melodramma tragico, 2 acts; libretto by G. Rossi after Voltaire's *Sémiramis* (1748). Teatro La Fenice, Venice, 3 Feb, 1823. ERO, 2 vols.

Il viaggio a Reims, ossia L'albergo del giglio d'oro, dramma giocoso, 1 act; libretto by L. Balocchi derived in part from de Staël's *Corinne, ou l'Italie* (1807). Théâtre-Italien, Paris, 19 June, 1825.

Le siège de Corinthe [rev. of *Maometto II*], tragédie lyrique, 3 acts; libretto by L. Balocchi and A. Soumet after libretto for *Maometto II*. Opéra, Paris, 9 Oct, 1826. ERO, 1 vol.

Moïse et Pharaon, ou Le passage de la Mer Rouge [rev. of *Mosè in Egitto*], opéra, 4 acts; libretto by L. Balocchi and E. de Jouy after libretto for *Mosè in Egitto*. Opéra, Paris, 26 March, 1827. ERO, 1 vol.

Le Comte Ory, opéra/opéra comique, 2 acts; libretto by E. Scribe and C.G. Delestre-Poirson after their own play (1817). Opéra, Paris, 20 Aug, 1828. ERO, I vol.

Guillaume Tell, opéra, 4 acts; libretto by E. de Jouy, H.-L.-F. Bis *et al.* after Schiller's *Wilhelm Tell* (1804). Opéra, Paris, 3 Aug, 1829. ERO, 2 vols.

Works derived from Rossini operas with the composer's participation:

Ivanhoé, music adapted from several of Rossini's operas by A. Pacini; libretto by E. Deschamps and G.-G. de Wailly from Sir Walter Scott's *Ivanhoe* (1819). Théâtre de l'Odéon, Paris, 18 Sept, 1826.

Robert Bruce, adapted from *La donna del lago* and other Rossini operas by L.-A. Niedermeyer; libretto by A. Reyer and G. Vaëz. Opéra, Paris, 30 Dec, 1846.

II Incidental Music

Edipo a Colono, music for Sophocles' *Oedipus at Colonus* translated by Giambattista Giusti, for B, chorus, orch. Composed before 1817. ECII/i

III Religious Music

Compositions dating from 1802–9:
Kyrie a tre voci for 2 T, B, orch; *Gloria,* A, T, B, male chorus, orch; *Laudamus,* A, orch; *Gratias,* T, male chorus, orch; *Domine Deus,* 2 B, orch; *Qui tollis,* T, orch; *Laudamus* and *Qui tollis,* T, orch; *Quoniam,* T, orch; *Crucifixus,* S, A, orch; *Dixit,* 2 T, B, orch; *De torrente,* B, orch; *Gloria Patri; Sicut erat,* 2 T, B, orch; *Magnificat,* 2 T, B, orch. *Messa* (Bologna): Christe eleison, 2 T, B, orch; Benedicta et venerabilis, 2 T, B, orch; Qui tollis; Qui sedes, S, horn, orch. *Messa* (Ravenna): Kyrie, Gloria, Credo, solo male voices, male chorus, orch. *Messa:* Kyrie, Gloria, Credo, solo male voices, male chorus, orch. *Messa* (Rimini), S, A, T, B, orch.
Quoniam, B, orch. Sept, 1813.
Messa di Gloria, S, A, 2 T, B, chorus, orch. San Ferdinando, Naples, 24 Mar, 1820: ECIII/ii.
Preghiera: 'Deh tu pietoso cielo', S, piano. *c.*1820.
Tantum ergo. S, T, B, orch. 1824.
Stabat mater, 2 S, T, B, chorus, orch. 1st version, 1832, nos. 1, 5–9 by Rossini, nos. 2–4, 10–12 by Tadolini. Cappella di San Filippo El Real, Madrid, Good Friday (5 April) 1833. 2nd version, 1841, 10 nos. all by Rossini. Théâtre-Italian, Paris, 7 Jan, 1842.
Trois choeurs religieux: 1. La foi (P. Goubaux); 2. L'espérance (H. Lucas); 3. La charité (L. Colet), female voices, piano. Salle Troupenas, Paris, 20 Nov, 1844.
Tantum ergo, 2 T, B, orch. Chiesa di San Francesco dei Minori, Bologna, 28 Nov, 1847.
O salutaris hostia, S, A, T, B. Paris, 29 Nov, 1857.
Laus Deo, Mez, piano. Paris, 1861.
Petite messe solennelle, S, A, T, B, chorus of eight voices, two pianos, harmonium. Home of Countess Louise Pillet-Will, Paris, 14 Mar, 1864. 2nd version with orchestral accompaniment, 1867. Théâtre-Italien, Paris, 24 Feb, 1869. ECIII/iv.

IV Cantatas

Il pianto d'Armonia sulla morte di Orfeo (G. Ruggia), cantata, T, chorus, orch. Liceo Musicale, Bologna, 11 Aug, 1808.
La morte di Didone, cantata, S, chorus, orch. Composed 1811. Teatro San Benedetto, Venice, 2 May, 1818.
Dalle quete e pallid'ombre, cantata (P. Venanzio), S, B, piano. Venice, 1812.

Egle ed Irene, cantata, S, A, piano. Milan, 1814.

L'Aurora, cantata, A, T, B, piano. Rome, Nov 1815.

Le nozze di Teti e di Peleo (A.M. Ricci), cantata, 3 S, 2 T, chorus, orch. Teatro del Fondo, Naples, 24 April, 1816.

Omaggio umiliato (A. Niccolini), cantata, S, chorus, orch. Teatro San Carlo, Naples, 20 Feb, 1819.

Cantata (G. Genoino) for Francis I's visit, S, 2 T, chorus, orch. Teatro San Carlo, Naples, 9 May, 1819.

La riconoscenza (G. Genoino), cantata, S, A, T, B, chorus, orch. Teatro San Carlo, Naples, 27 Dec, 1821.

Giunone, cantata, S, chorus, orch. Naples, before 1822.

La Santa Alleanza (G. Rossi), cantata, 2 B, chorus, orch. Arena, Verona, 24 Nov, 1822.

Il vero omaggio (G. Rossi), cantata, S, 2 T, B, chorus, orch. Teatro Filarmonico, Verona, 3 Dec, 1822.

Omaggio pastorale, cantata, 3 female voices, orch. Treviso, ?1 April, 1823.

Il pianto delle muse in morte di Lord Byron, canzone, T, chorus, orch. Almack's Assembly Rooms, London, 9 June, 1824.

Cantata per il battesimo del figlio del banchiere Aguado, 6 solo voices, piano. Home of A.-M. Aguado, Paris, 16 July, 1827.

L'armonica cetra del nume, solo voices, chorus, piano. Home of Marchese Sampieri, Bologna, 2 April, 1830.

Giovanna d'Arco, cantata, S, piano. Paris, 1832. Rev. 1852. QRxi, 1–29.

Cantatina, S, A, T, three-voice male chorus, piano. July, 1832.

Cantata in onore del Sommo Pontefice Pio Nono (G. Marchetti), 4 solo voices, chorus, orch. Senate, Rome, 1 Jan, 1847.

V Choruses, Hymns

Inno dell'Indipendenza ('Sorgi, Italia, venuta è già l'ora') (G. Guisti), hymn. Teatro Contavalli, Bologna, 15 April, 1815.

De l'Italie et de la France, hymn, S, B, chorus, orch. Paris, 1825. QR ix, 62–95.

Santo Genio dell'Italia terra (G. Marchetti) for tercentenary of Tasso's birth, chorus, orch. Palazzo Carignano, 11 March, 1844 (closely derived from the Chorus of the Bards from *La donna del lago*.)

Su fratelli, letizia si canti (Canonico Golfieri) for Pope Pius IX, chorus, orch. Piazza Maggiore, Bologna, 23 July, 1846.

Segna Iddio ne'suoi confini (F. Martinelli), chorus, with acc. arr. for band by D. Liverani. Piazza Maggiore, Bologna, 21 June, 1848.

È foriera la Pace ai mortali (G. Arcangeli after Bacchilde), hymn, Bar, male voices, piano. Florence, 26 June, 1850. QR xii, 1–20.

Hymne à Napoléon III et à son Vaillant Peuple ('Dieu tout puissant') (E. Pacini), Bar, chorus, orch, military band. Palais de l'Industrie, 1 July, 1867. QR xii, 21–85.

VI Vocal Music[1]

Se il vuol la molinara, S, piano, 1801. ?Rev.
Dolce aurette che spirate, T, orch. 1810.
La mia pace io già perdei, T, orch. 1812.
Quai voce, quae note, S, piano, 1813.
Alla voce della gloria, B, orch. 1813.
Amore mi assisti, S, T, piano. *c.*1814.
Three pieces for Giuseppe Nicolini's *Quinto Fabio*, 1817. 1 *Coro e cavatina* 'Cara Patria, invitta Roma', S, chorus, orch. 2 *Aria* 'Guido Marte i nostri passi', T, chorus, orch. 3 (possibly not by Rossini) *Duet* 'Ah! per pietà t'arresta', 2 S, orch.
Il trovatore ('Chi m'ascolta il canto usato'), T, piano. Naples, 1818.
Il Carnevale di Venezia ('Siamo ciechi, siamo nati') (Rossini, Paganini, M. d'Azeglio, Lipparini) 2 T, 2 B, piano. Rome, 1821.
Beltà crudele ('Amori scendete propizi al mio core') (N. di Santo-Mango), S, piano. Naples, 1821.
La pastorella ('Odia la pastorella') (N. di Santo-Magno), S, piano. Naples, *c.*1821.
Canzonetta Spagnuola ('En medio a mis dolores' or 'Piangea un dì pensando') S, piano, Naples, 1821.
Infelice ch'io son, S, piano. Naples, 1821 (based on a theme taken from the prayer 'Nume, cui 'l sole è trono' from *Maometto II*).
Addio ai viennesi ('Da voi parto, amate sponde'), T, piano. Vienna, 1822. Adapted for use in other cities and known as *Addio di Rossini*.
Dall'Oriente l'astro del giorno, S, 2 T, B, piano. London, 1824 (From chorus in *Ermione*.)
Ridiamo, cantiamo, che tutto sen va, S, 2 T, B, piano. London, 1824. (From chorus in *Armida*.)
In giorno sì bello, 2 S, T, piano. London, 1824.
Tre Quartetti da Camera, Paris, 1827, 1 not traced. 2. 'In giorno si bello', 2 S, T, B, piano. 3 'Oh giorno sereno', S, A, T, B, piano.
Les adieux à Rome ('Rome pour la dernière fois') (C. Delavigne), T, piano/harp. Paris, 1827.
Orage et beau temps ('Sur les flots inconstants') (A. Betourne), T, B, piano. Paris, *c.*1829–30.
La passeggiata ('Or che di fiori adorno'), S, piano. Madrid, 1831. Also known as *Anacreontica*.
La dichiarazione ('Ch'io mai vi possa lasciar d'amare') (Metastasio), S, piano. Paris, *c.*1834. Also known as *La promessa*.
Les soirées musicales. Paris, *c.*1830–35.
   1 La promessa ('Ch'io mai vi possa lasciar d'amare') (Metastasio), S, piano. (Though identical textually with *La dichiarazione*, the setting is quite different musically.)

[1] See also section VIII.

2 Il rimprovero ('Mi lagnerò tacendo') (Metastasio), S, piano.
3 La partenza ('Ecco quel fiero istante') (Metastasio), S, piano.
4 L'orgia ('Amiamo, cantiamo') (C. Pepoli), S, piano.
5 L'invito ('Vieni o Ruggiero') (C. Pepoli), S, piano.
6 La pastorella dell'Alpi ('Son bella pastorella') (C. Pepoli), S, piano.
7 La gita in gondola ('Voli l'agile barchetta') (C. Pepoli), S, piano.
8 La danza ('Già la luna è in mezzo al mare') (C. Pepoli), T, piano.
9 La regata veneziana ('Voga o Tonio benedetto') (C. Pepoli), 2 S, piano.
10 La pesca ('Già la notte s'avvicina') (Metastasio), 2 S, piano.
11 La serenata (Mira, la bianca luna') (C. Pepoli), S, T, piano.
12 Li marinari ('Marinaro in guardia stà') (C. Pepoli), T, B, piano.

Deux nocturnes (Crével de Charlemagne), S, T, piano. 1 Adieu à l'Italie ('Je te quitte, belle Italie'). 2 Le départ ('Il faut partir'). Paris, 1836.

Nizza ('Mi lagnerò tacendo', 'Nizza, je puis sans peine') (Metastio, E. Deschamps), S, piano, Paris, 1836.

L'âme délaissée ('Mon bien aimé') (C. Delavigne), S, piano. 1844. Also published as *L'âme du Purgatoire* and in Italian as *L'abbandonata* ('Mio dolce amor').

Francesca da Rimini ('Farò come colui che piange e dice') (Dante), S, piano. Florence, 1848. Also known as *Recitativo ritmato*.

Mi lagnerò tacendo (Metastasio). Rossini made numerous settings of these lines, many of them as albumleaves. Sometimes a new text would be added: e.g. *La separazione* ('Muto rimase il labbro') (F. Ucceili), Paris, *c.*1858. See Chapter 37.

VII Instrumental[2]

Six *Sonate a quattro* in G, A, C, B flat, E flat, D, 2 violins, cello, double-bass. Ravenna, 1804. QRi, 1.

Overture *al conventello*, D, orch. *c.*1806. First theme reused in *Il Signor Bruschino*.

Five duets, E flat, E flat, B flat, E flat, E flat, 2 horns, *c.* 1806.

Overture, D, orch. 1808. Second theme reused in *L'inganno felice*. QR viii, 1–16.

Overture, E flat, orch. 1809. Reused with revisions in *La cambiale di matrimonio* and, in the revised version, in *Adelaide di Borgogna*.

Overture *obbligata a contrabasso*, D, orch, *c.*1807–10.

Variazioni a più istrumenti obbligati, F, 2 violins, viola, cello, clarinet in B flat. 1809. QRix, 1–44.

Variazioni di clarinetto, C, clarinet, orch. 1809. QR vi, 57–67.

Andante e Tema con variazioni, F, flute, clarinet, horn, bassoon. 1812. QRvi, 18–30.

[2] See also section VIII.

Andante e Tema con Variazioni per arpa e violino, F, harp, violin. Naples *c.* 1820. (Variations on 'Di tanti palpiti' from *Tancredi*.) QR vi, 1–8.

Passo doppio, military band. 1822. Lost, but mentioned in Radiciotti. Reused in final movement of the overture to *Guillaume Tell*.

Waltz, E flat, piano. Venice, 1823.

Serenata, E flat, 2 violins, viola, cello, flute, oboe, cor anglais. Paris, 1823. QR vi, 31–56.

Duetto, D, cello, double-bass. London, 1824.

Rendez-vous de chasse, D, 4 hunting horns, orch. Paris, 1828. QR ix, 45–61.

Fantasie, E flat, clarinet, piano, Paris, 1829.

Three Military Marches, G, E flat, E flat, military band. 1837 for marriage of Duc d'Orléans, Fontainebleau.

Scherzo, A minor, piano. 1843, rev. 1850.

Tema originale di Rossini variato per violino da Giovacchino Giovacchini, A, violin, piano. 1845.

March ('Pas-redoublé'), C, military band. 1852.

Thème de Rossini suivi de deux variations et coda par Moscheles Père, E, horn, piano. Paris, 1860.

La corona d'Italia, E flat, military band. Paris, 1868.

VIII Péchés de vieillesse (1857–68)

Vol.i Album italiano
1. I gondolieri, S, A, T, B, piano; QR vii, 1–15.
2. La lontananza (G. Torre), arietta, T, piano; QR iv, 12–18.
3. Bolero 'Tirana alla spagnola', 'Mi lagnerò tacendo', S, piano; QR iv, 30–43. Music identical with vol. xi, no.3.
4. L'ultimo ricordo (G. Redaelli), elegia, Bar, piano; QR iv, 19–24.
5. La fioraja fiorentina ('I più bei fior comprate'), arietta, S, piano; QR iv, 5–11. Theme first used for setting of 'Mi lagnerò tacendo', Florence, 1848.
6. Le gittane (G. Torre), S, A, piano.
7. Ave Maria ('A te, che benedetta'), aria on two notes, A, piano; QR iv, 51–9.
8-10. La regata veneziana, three canzonettas, Mez, piano.
   8. Anzoleta avanti la regata ('Là su la machina'). French version, barcarolle, 'Plus de vent perfide'.
   9. Anzoleta co passa la regata ('Ixe qua vardeli povereti').
   10. Anzoleta dopo la regata ('Ciapa un baso').
11. Il fanciullo smarrito ('Oh! chi avesse trovato un fanciulletto') (A. Castellani), T, piano.
12. La passeggiata, S, A, T, B, piano; QR vii, 16–34.

Vol. ii Album français
1. Toast pour le nouvel an ('En ce jour si doux') (?E Pacini), 2 S, 2 A, 2 T, 2 B; QR vii, 50–61.

2. Roméo ('Juliette chère idole') (E. Pacini), T, piano.

3. Pompadour, la grande coquette ('La perle des coquettes') (E. Pacini adapted from 'Mi lagnerò tacendo'), S, piano.

4. Un sou. Complainte à deux voix ('Pitié pour la misère') (?E. Pacini), T, Bar, piano; QR v, 58–68.

5. Chanson de Zora, La petite Bohémienne ('Gens de la plaine') (E. Deschamps), Mez, piano; QR v, 49–57.

6. La nuit de Noël ('Calme et sans voile') (E. Pacini), B solo, 2 S, 2 A, 2 T, 2 Bar, piano, harmonium; QR vii, 62–76. Italian version 'Tu che a salvarci'. Piano and harmonium accompaniment reused in vol.ix, no.6.

7. Le dodo des enfants ('Mon fils, rose éphémère') (E. Pacini). Mez, piano; QR v, 9–16.

8. Le Lazzarone. Chansonette de Cabaret ('Au bord des flots d'Azur') (E. Pacini), Bar, piano.

9. Adieux à la vie. Élégie sur une seule note ('Salut! dernière aurore') (E. Pacini adapted from 'Mi lagnerò tacendo'), Mez, piano; QR v, 75–80.

10. Soupirs et sourires, Nocturne ('Dans le sentier des Roses') (E. Pacini), S, T, piano. With Italian text as 'Il cipresso e la rosa' (G. Torre).

11. L'orphéline du Tyrol, Ballade élégie ('Seule, une pauvre enfant') (E. Pacini), Mez, piano; QR v, 31–6.

12. Choeur de chasseurs démocrates ('En chasse amis, en chasse') (E. Pacini), male chorus, tam-tam, 2 drums; QR vii, 35–49.

Vol.iii Morceaux réservés

1. Quelques mesures de chant funèbre: à mon pauvre ami Meyerbeer ('Pleure, pleure, muse sublime') (E. Pacini), male voices, drum; QR vii, 84–8.

2. L'Esule ('Qui sempre ride in cielo') (G. Torre), T, piano; QR iv, 25–9.

3. Les amants de Séville, Tirana pour deux voix ('Loin de votre Séville') (E. Pacini), A, T, piano; QR v, 37–48.

4. Ave Maria ('Ave Maria gratia plena'), chorus, organ; QR xi, 43–52.

5. L'amour à Pékin: mélodie sur la gamme chinoise ('Mon coeur blessé') (E. Pacini), A, piano; QR v, 81–9.

6. Le chant des Titans ('Guerre! Massacre! Carnage!') (E. Pacini adapted from 'Mi lagnerò tacendo'), 4 B in unison, piano, harmonium. Arr. for 4 B, orch; QR viii, 66–89.

7. Preghiera ('Tu che di verde il prato'), 4 T, 2 Bar, 2 B; QR vii, 89–95. With French text as 'Dieu créateur du monde'.

8. Au chevet d'un mourant, Élégie ('De la douleur naît l'espérance') (E. Pacini), S, piano. QR v, 17–24.

9. Le sylvain, ('Belles Nymphes blondes') (E. Pacini), T, piano; QR v, 1–8.

10. Cantemus Domino, imitazione ad otto voci reali, 2 S, 2 A, 2 T, B; QR xi, 53–7.

11. Ariette à l'ancienne ('Que le jour me dure') (J.-J. Rousseau), Mez, piano; QR v, 69–71.

12. Le départ des promis, Tyrolienne sentimentale ('L'honneur appelle') (E. Pacini), 2 S, 2 A, piano.

Vols iv–viii

These were regrouped by Rossini as 'A little of everything. A collection of 56 semi-comical piano pieces . . . dedicated to pianists of the fourth class to which I have the honour of belonging'.

Vol. iv Quatre mendiants et quatre hors d'oeuvres (QR xix)

Quatre mendiants: 1. Les figues sèches, D; 2. Les amandes, G; 3. Les raisins, C; 4. Les noisettes, B minor. Quatre hors d'oeuvres: 1. Les radis, A minor; 2. Les anchois, D; 3. Les cornichons, E; 4.Le beurre, B flat.

Vol. v Album pour les enfants adolescents

1. Première Communion, E flat, QR xv, 1–10; 2. Thème naïf et variations idem, G, QR xv, 11–20; 3. Saltarello à l'italienne, A flat, QR xv, 21–9; 4. Prélude moresque, E minor, QR xv, 30–40; 5. Valse lugubre, C. QR xv, 41–7; 6. Impromptu anodin, E flat, QR xv, 48–58; 7. L'innocence italienne; La candeur française, A minor, A major, QR ii, 19–29; 8. Prélude convulsif, C, QR xv, 59–71; 9. La lagune de Venise à l'expiration de l'année 1861!!! G flat, QR xv, 72–82; 10. Ouf! les petits pois, B, QR ii, 30–6; 11. Un sauté, D, QR xv, 83–92; 12. Hachis romantique, A minor, QR xv, 93–105.

Vol. vi Album pour les enfants dégourdis

1. Mon prélude hygiénique du matin, C, QR x, 28–37; 2. Prélude baroque, A minor, QR xvi, 1–15; 3. Memento homo, C minor, QR x, 87–93; 4. Assez de memento: dansons, F, QR x, 94–103; 5. La pesarese, B flat, QR x, 60–7; 6. Valse torturée, D, QR xvi, 16–28; 7. Une caresse à ma femme, G, QR ii, 37–41; 8. Barcarole, E flat, QR xvi, 29–37; 9. Un petit train de plaisir comico-imitatif, C. QR ii, 42–58; 10. Fausse couche de polka-mazurka, A flat, QR xvi, 38–45; 11. Étude asthmatique, E, QR xvi, 46–66; 12. Un enterrement en Carnaval, D, QR x, 68–86.

Vol. vii Album de chaumière

1.Gymnastique d'écartement, A flat, QR xiv, 1–17; 2. Prélude fugassé, E, QR xiv, 18–24; 3. Petite polka chinoise, B minor, QR xiv, 25–34; 4. Petite valse de boudoir, A flat, QR xiv, 35–42; 5. Prélude inoffensif, C, QR ii, 8–18; 6. Petite valse, 'L'huile de Ricin', E, QR xiv, 43–61; 7. Un profond sommeil; Un reveil en sursaut, B minor, D major, QR xiv, 62–90; 8. Plein-chant chinois, Scherzo, A minor, QR xiv, 91–103; 9. Un cauchemar, E, QR xiv, 104–25; 10. Valse boiteuse, D flat, QR xiv, 126–36; 11. Une pensée à Florence, A minor; QR xiv, 137–49; 12. Marche, C, QR xiv, 150–64.

Vol. viii Album de château

1. Spécimen de l'ancien régime, E flat, QR ii, 59–82; 2. Prélude pétulant-

rococo, G, QR xvii, 1–16; 3. Un regret; Un espoir, E, QR xvii, 17–32; 4. Boléro tartare, A minor, QR xvii, 33–59; 5. Prélude prétentieux, C minor, QR x, 1–10; 6. Spécimen de mon temps, A flat, QR x, 38–59; 7. Valse anti-dansante, F, QR xvii, 60–77; 8. Prélude semipastorale, A, QR xvii, 78–108; 9. Tarantelle pur sang (avec Traversée de la procession), B minor, QR ii, 83–101 (also for chorus, harmonium, and hand-bell *ad lib*); 10. Un rêve, B minor, QR x, 11–27; 11. Prélude soi-disant dramatique, F sharp, QR xvii, 109–31; 12. Spécimen de l'avenir, E flat, QR x, 104–25.

Vol. ix
Album for piano, violin, cello, harmonium, and horn 1. Mélodie candide, A, piano, QR xvi, 67–73; 2. Chansonette, E flat, piano, QR xvi, 87–94; 3. La savoie aimante, A minor, piano, QR xvi, 74–86; 4. Un mot à Paganini, élégie, D, violin, piano. 5. Impromptu tarantellisé, F, piano, QR xvi, 95–106; 6. Echantillon du chant de Noël à l'italienne, E flat, piano, QR ii, 102–7; 7. Marche et reminiscences pour mon dernier voyage, A flat, piano, QR ii, 108–16; 8. Prélude, thème et variations, E, horn, piano, QR iii, 1–17; 9. Prélude italien, A flat, piano, QR xvi, 107–19; 10. Une larme: thème et variations, A minor, cello, piano; 11. Echantillon de blague mélodique sur les noires de la main droite, G flat, piano; 12. Petite fanfare à quatre mains, E flat, piano 2 or 4 hands.

Vol. x Miscellanée pour piano
1. Prélude blagueur, A minor; QR xviii, 1–20; 2. Des tritons s'il vous plaît (montée-descente), C, QR xviii, 21–4; 3. Petite pensée, E flat, QR xviii, 25–8; 4. Une bagatelle, E flat, QR xviii, 29–30; 5. Mélodie italienne: une bagatelle ('In nomine Patris'), A flat, QR xviii, 31–2; 6. Petite caprice (style Offenbach), C, QR ii, 1–7.

Vol.xi Miscellanée de musique vocale
1. Ariette villageoise ('Que le jour me dure') (J.-J. Rousseau), S, piano; QR v, 72–4.
2. La chanson du bébé ('Maman, le gros Bébé t'appelle') (E. Pacini), Mez, piano; QR v, 25–30.
3. Amour sans espoir, Tirana all'espagnole rossinizé, ('Faut-il gémir d'amour sans retour') (E. Pacini). Music identical with vol.i, no.3.
4. A ma belle mère, Requiem eternam, A, piano; QR xi, 58–9.
5. O salutaris, de campagne, A, piano. (Essentially the same as the O salutaris from the *Petite messe solennelle*.)
6. Aragonese ('Mi lagnerò tacendo') (Metastasio), S, piano; QR iv, 44–50.
7. Arietta all'antica, dedotta dal O salutaris ostia ('Mi lagnerò tacendo') (Metastasio), S, piano, based on O salutaris hostia, 29 Nov, 1857; QR iv, 60–1.
8. Il candore in fuga, no text, 2 S, A, T, B.

9. Salve amabilis Maria, motet, S, A, T, B; QR vii, 77–83; also as Hymne à la musique ('Chantons! Toi par qui règne le Génie').
10. Giovanna d'Arco, cantata, 1832, arr. S, piano, strings. 1st ver. QR xi, 1–29; 2nd ver. QR xi, 30–42.

Vol.xii Quelques riens pour album
24 pieces for piano; ECVII/vii.

Vol. xiii Musique anodine
Prélude and six petites mélodies, settings of 'Mi lagnerò tacendo' (Metastasio): 1. A, piano; 2. Bar, piano; 3–4, S, piano; 5. Mez, piano; 6. Bar, piano; 15 April, 1857; QR iv, 62–88.

IX Other Late Works

Canone perpetuo per quattro soprani, 4 S, piano; also known as *Canone scherzosa a quattro soprani democratici*.
Canone antisavant for three voices, words by Rossini.
La vénitienne, Canzonetta, C, piano; QR xviii, 33–45.
Deux nouvelles compositions, S, piano: 1. *À Grenade* ('La nuit règne à Grenade') (E. Pacini); QR v, 90–7. 2. *La veuve andalouse* ('Toi pour jamais') (E. Pacini).
Une réjouissance, A minor, piano; QR xviii, 46–51.
Encore un peu de blague, C, piano; QR xviii, 52–4.
Tourniquet sur la gamme chromatique, ascendante et déscendante, C, piano; QR xviii, 55–62.
Ritournelle gothique, C, piano; QR xviii, 63.
Un rien (pour album) ('Ave Maria'), S, piano; QR xi, 60.
Sogna il guerrier (pour album) (Metastasio), Bar, piano.
Brindisi ('Del fanciullo il primo canto'), B, chorus.
Solo for Violoncello, A minor; QR vi, 9–17 [with added piano acc.]
Questo palpito soave, S, piano.
L'ultimo pensiero ('Patria, consorti, figli!') (L.F. Cerutti), Bar, piano.
Thème, E flat, piano.

X Vocal Exercises, Cadenzas

Gorgheggi e solfeggi, 1 voice, piano; 1822–7. Published in Paris with the remarks 'Vocalises et Solfèges pour rendre la Voix agile et pour apprendre à Chanter selon le Goût Moderne'.
15 petits exercices pour égaliser les sons, prolonger la respiration et donner de l'élasticité aux poumons, 1 voice, 1858 (Paris, 1880).
Petit gargouillement, 1 voice, piano, 1867.

Variants and cadenzas provided by Rossini for his operas are widely dispersed. Collections exist in Paris, Opéra (for *Il barbiere di Siviglia, Otello, La donna del lago* etc); Brussels, Fonds Michotte (for *Tancredi, Il barbiere di Siviglia* etc); Chicago, University Library (for *La Cenerentola, Matilde di Shabran* etc); Milan, Biblioteca del Conservatorio (for 'Una voce poco fa' from *Il barbiere di Siviglia*); New York, Pierpont Morgan Library (for *Tancredi* etc).

XI Works Spuriously Attributed to Rossini

Duetto buffo di due gatti, 2 voices, piano; QR iv, 1–4. [See p.179, n.6.]
Sinfonia di Odense, A, orch; QR viii, 17–65.

Appendix C

Personalia

Aguado, Alexandre-Marie (1784–1842). Parisian banker and from 1827 friend, financial adviser, and patron of Rossini. A naturalized Frenchman of Spanish origin, he was intermediary in the commissioning of the *Stabat mater* in Madrid in 1831.

Barbaia, Domenico (1778–1841) was the most astute and characterful impresario of his day. A self-educated entrepreneur who made several fortunes in military contracts, building, and gambling, he ran the royal theatres in Naples during the years 1809–24, 1827–31, 1836–40. An important figure in the careers of a number of composers, including Donizetti and Weber, Barbaia changed the course of Rossini's career when in 1815 he offered him a long-term contract with the Naples theatres. Lessee of two Viennese theatres from 1821–8, Barbaia also arranged Rossini's Viennese season of 1822. His mistress, Isabella Colbran, later became Rossini's first wife.

Bellini, Vincenzo (1801–35). Italian composer and, with Donizetti, Rossini's most important immediate successor. Encouraged by Rossini's approval of *Il pirata*, Bellini continued to receive support and advice from him in the years 1830–5. Rossini was an honorary pallbearer at his funeral and later helped settle the composer's estate.

Berlioz, Hector (1803–69) was the leading French composer of his age. His relations with Rossini were cool and equivocal but his essay on *Guillaume Tell*, which he proof-read for the publisher Troupenas, is both just and generous, one of the finest assessments of an opera ever written.

Bevilacqua-Aldobrandini, Gherardo. Bolognese aristocrat, patron of the Liceo Musicale, Bologna, and amateur librettist. He adapted a libretto by Romani for Rossini's *Adina* and contributed to the librettos for *Eduardo e Cristina* and *Semiramide*.

Boito, Arrigo (1842–1914). Composer, librettist, poet, and critic. Described by Rossini as 'my ardent colleague', the young Boito was a frequent caller on Rossini in Paris in the 1860s. Boito became involved in the Broglio affair of 1868, wittily denouncing the Minister of Public Education in an article in *Il pungolo*, to the delight of Verdi.

Carafa, Michele (1787–1872). Neapolitan prince, composer, and life-long friend of Rossini. He contributed arias to *Adelaide di Borgogna* and *Mosè in Egitto* and was a permanent fixture at Rossini's *samedi soirs* in Paris in the 1860s. Supervised a French version of *Semiramide* at the Paris Opéra in 1860 for which he wrote ballet music; the rights of this version were ceded to Carafa by Rossini.

Cinti-Damoreau, Laure (1801–63). French soprano who created principal roles in Rossini's five Paris operas between 1825–9. Notable for the beauty of her tone and the purity of her intonation, she was the finest French Rossini soprano of her day. She also performed and published authoritative cadenzas for important soprano arias in several of Rossini's earlier Italian operas.

Coccia, Carlo (1782–1873). Neapolitan composer, pupil of Paisiello. His first opera, *Il matrimonio per lettera di cambio* (1807, Rome) anticipates Rossini's opera on the subject by three years. Though he had success with *Clotilde* (1815, Venice), Coccia was driven from Italy by the Rossini craze only to find himself as conductor at the King's Theatre, London at the start of the 1824 Rossini season. Was invited in 1869, aged 87, to contribute to the abortive Rossini-Requiem.

Colbran, Isabella (1785–1845). Spanish soprano. Rossini's first wife and the singer for whom he wrote an important series of dramatically powerful *opera seria* roles for performance in Naples between 1815 and 1822, and Venice in 1823. Rossini first heard her in Bologna in 1807, the year after her Spanish stage debut. She retired in 1824 after appearing in poor voice as Zelmira in London. Her marriage to Rossini was not a success and they were legally separated in 1837.

Costa, Sir Michael (1808–84). Conductor and composer who occupied an important place in London musical life in the middle years of the nineteenth century. A naturalized Englishman of Neapolitan extraction, he was one of Rossini's several surrogate sons. Their correspondence is extensive and amusing, well detailed in matters concerning Costa's own work.

David(e), Giovanni (1790–1864). Italian tenor noted for the agility and range of his voice. He created principal roles in a number of Rossini's Neapolitan operas including Rodrigo in *Otello*, Oreste in *Ermione*, Uberto (James V) in *La donna del lago*.

Diémer, Louis (1843–1919). French pianist and composer. As a brilliantly gifted teenager Diémer was entrusted with the preparation and perform-ance of many piano pieces composed by Rossini for the *samedi soirs* between 1858 and 1868. A classically-inclined pianist noted for the purity and precision of his playing. Diémer's pupils included Cortot and Casadesus.

Donizetti, Gaetano (1797–1848). Italian composer, close follower of Rossi-ni, and, with Bellini, his most important immediate successor. Rossini championed Donizetti's music in Paris in the early 1830s and several years later attempted unsuccessfully to engage him as a teacher of composition of Bologna's Liceo Musicale. During the period of the negotiations Donizetti conducted the Italian *prima* of Rossini's *Stabat mater* in Bolog-na on 18 March, 1842.

Donzelli, Domenico (1790–1873). Italian tenor. Created roles in *Torvaldo e Dorliska* and *Il viaggio a Reims*, and was the first Pollione in Bellini's *Norma*. He retired in 1844. A close friend of Rossini for many years, he loaned his villa in Bologna to Rossini during the 1840s.

Doré, Gustave (1833–83). French painter and one of the most distinguished of all nineteenth-century book illustrators. Attended many of Rossini's *samedi soirs* where he sang chansons and arranged music-hall skits. Was present in Passy during Rossini's final illness and made his death-bed portrait (see plate 24).

Duprez, Gilbert-Louis (1806–96). French tenor and composer. Allegedly the first tenor to sing a top C as a chest note, he was not Rossini's favourite tenor, but the revival of the fortunes of *Guillaume Tell* in Paris in 1837 must be credited in substantial measure to Duprez's singing of Arnold in the new *tenore di forza* style.

Escudier, Marie (1819–80) and Léon (1821–81). French music publishers and founders in 1837 of *La France musicale* whose contributors included Adam, Balzac, Gautier, and Schumann. Passionate admirers of Rossini's music, the Escudier brothers successfully staged the première of the revised *Stabat mater* at the Théâtre-Italien, Paris in January, 1841.

Ferretti, Jacopo (1784–1852). Although Ferretti was professionally employed in administering the tobacco monopoly of the Papal States, he was one of the ablest Italian librettists of his day, writing over sixty texts between 1807 and 1846. Based in Rome, he worked on the text of Rossini's *Matilde di Shabran* (1821) but is best known for his re-shaping of extant texts for Rossini's *La Cenerentola* (1817).

Gabussi, Vincenzo (1800–46). Italian composer of largely unsuccessful operas, including *Clemenza di Valois* (1841, Venice) which Rossini travelled to hear. He rediscovered Rossini's incidental music to *Edipo a Colono* and was ceded publishing rights in the music in June, 1843.

Galli, Fillipo (1783–1853). The greatest Italian bass of his generation, Galli created eight major roles for Rossini and sang several more. Roles created by Galli include Tarabotto in *L'inganno felice*, Mustafà in *L'italiana in Algeri*, the title role in *Maometto II*, and Assur in *Semiramide*.

García, Manuel (1775–1832). Spanish tenor, composer and teacher. One of Rossini's closest associates, he created Norfolk in *Elisabetta, regina d'Inghilterra* and Almaviva at the chaotic *prima* of *Il barbiere di Siviglia*. He sang regularly in Paris and London between 1816 and 1825 and took the nucleus of an opera company to New York in 1825, staging Mozart's *Don Giovanni* and six operas by Rossini. He was father of Pauline Viardot, Maria Malibran, and Manuel García (author of *Traité complet de l'art du chant*, Paris, 1840), and was a teacher of Adolphe Nourrit.

Hérold, Ferdinand (1791–1833). French composer whose career as a composer of *opéra comique* stubbornly refused to flower during the period of Rossini's rise to fame. *Maestro al cembalo* at Théâtre-Italien, Paris from August 1815, and from 1826 principal coach at the Paris Opéra, he engaged a number of distinguished singers for the Théâtre-Italien, including Galli and Pasta, and was closely involved in the Paris production of *Mosè in Egitto* in 1822.

Hiller, Ferdinand (1811–85). German composer, conductor, teacher, and writer. Encouraged by Rossini in his earlier years, he met him again in Normandy in 1855. Rossini's reminiscences, as recorded by Hiller at this time, are a useful if not infallible source of information on Rossini's life and opinions.

Ivanoff, Nicholas (1810–80). Russian tenor who made his French debut as Giannetto in *La gazza ladra* in 1833. A protégé of Rossini more noted for the sweetness of his voice than for his stage presence, he sang in the Italian *prima* of the *Stabat mater*; he also staged *Guillaume Tell* as *Rodolfo di Sterlinga* in Bologna in 1841. At Rossini's request, Verdi wrote additional arias for Ivanoff's use in *Ernani* and *Attila*.

Lechi, Luigi (1786–1867). Member of distinguished Lechi family of Brescia with whom Rossini may have had extensive contact during the Napoleonic period. Educated in Milan and Pavia in literature, philosophy, and medicine, Lechi was a respected member of a group of northern Italian neoclassical writers and artists, and a friend of the poet Ugo Foscolo. In March 1813, Lechi drew on his first-hand knowledge of Voltaire's work to provide Rossini with revisions and a new 'tragic finale' for the Ferrara production of *Tancredi*. Lechi was friendly with the singer Adelaide Malanotte with whom he lived until her death in 1832.

Liszt, Franz (1811–86). Hungarian composer, pianist, and teacher. Met Rossini in Milan in 1837 and made piano transcriptions of *Les soirées musicales*. Attended Rossini's *samedi soirs* in Paris in the 1860s where he played his two *Légendes*. Rossini sought his advice during his approaches to Pope Pius IX on the matter of the papal ban on female singers in church.

Malerbi family. Well-to-do, music-loving family in Lugo. Rossini took lessons from Canon Giuseppe Malerbi and between 1802–4 made extensive use of the family's music library, in particular their editions of the works of Haydn and Mozart.

Malibran, Maria (1808–36). Spanish mezzo-soprano, daughter of Manuel García. She made her London debut as Rosina in *Il barbiere di Siviglia* in 1825 and her Paris debut in *Semiramide* in 1828. Brilliantly gifted, both as a singer and as an actress of great personal magnetism, she died from complications following a riding accident during a pregnancy in 1836. In later years, Rossini called her the 'only' interpreter of his music, comparable with Colbran but a unique phenomenon in her own right.

Marchisio, Barbara (1833–1919) and Carlotta (1835–72). Contralto and soprano respectively, the Marchisio sisters made their debuts at the Paris Opéra in *Semiramide* in July 1860 to the delight of Rossini who described them as 'possessors of that song which is sensed in the soul'. They sang for Rossini in private performances of *Stabat mater* in Paris and were the partial inspiration for Rossini's last major work, the *Petite messe solennel-*

le (1864). Barbara sang in Santa Croce, Florence at the re-burial ceremony in 1887. Her pupils included Toti dal Monte.

Marcolini, Maria (floruit *c.* 1805–18). Italian mezzo-soprano who created roles in *Ciro in Babilonia, La pietra del paragone, L'italiana in Algeri,* and *Sigismondo.* The most important female singer during Rossini's pre-Naples years, she exercised considerable influence over the writing of the roles which he created for her.

Mattei, Stanislao (1750–1825). Italian composer and teacher, a pupil of Padre Martini. He held a number of important academic posts in Bologna including that of professor of counterpoint and composition at the Liceo Musicale from 1804. He taught Rossini from 1806–10, and later taught Donizetti. His teaching seems to have aroused respect rather than enthusiasm or affection.

Mendelssohn, Felix (1809–47). German composer whose youthful brilliance and serious interest in the music of Bach aroused Rossini's particular interest. The two men met in Frankfurt in 1836.

Meyerbeer, Giacomo (1791–1864). German composer, follower, and later friend of Rossini. His early operatic successes were in Italy from 1817–24. Moved to Paris where Rossini's Théâtre-Italien staged *Il crociato in Egitto* in 1825. Auber's *La muette de Portici* (1828, Paris) and Rossini's *Guillaume Tell* crystallized his own ideas about writing for the Opéra. *Robert le diable* (1831) and *Les Huguenots* (1836) resulted; these may in turn have influenced Rossini in his decision to cease writing for the Opéra. In March 1864 Meyerbeer attended the *première* of Rossini's *Petite messe solennelle* and was much affected by it. He died six weeks later, moving Rossini to write his 'Quelques mesures de chant funèbre: à mon pauvre ami Meyerbeer' for male chorus and drum.

Michotte, Edmond (1830–1914). Wealthy amateur musician and sometime President of the Administrative Council of Belgium's Conservatoire Royal de Musique to which he left a valuable collection of Rossini scores, librettos, and other memorabilia. His accounts of an evening with Rossini in Passy in 1858 and of Rossini's meeting with Wagner in 1860 were published in Brussels and Paris over forty years later.

Mombelli, Domenico (1751–1835). Italian tenor who with his second wife, Vincenza, and two of their daughters, Ester and Marianna, formed a touring opera group. Rossini's *Demetrio e Polibio* was written piecemeal to a libretto provided by Vincenza (niece of Boccherini and sister of the choreographer Salvatore Viganò) and first performed by the Mombelli troupe in Rome in 1812.

Morandi, Rosa Morolli (1782–1824). Italian soprano and wife of the composer Giovanni Morandi (1777–1856). Friends of Giuseppe and Anna Rossini, the Morandis were instrumental in securing Rossini his first professional operatic commission, *La cambiale di matrimonio.* Rosa created the role of Fanny in the opera. She later created the role of Cristina in *Eduardo e Cristina.*

Nourrit, Adolphe (1802–39). French tenor who studied with García. He created leading tenor roles in four of Rossini's Paris operas including the title role in *Le Comte Ory* and Arnold in *Guillaume Tell*. A subtle and intelligent singer, he was well suited to the music Rossini wrote for him, though illness and depression brought on by overwork and rivalry with the tenor, Duprez, seriously distorted his career in the late 1830s. He committed suicide on 8 March, 1839 by throwing himself from the top floor of the Hotel Barbaia in Naples after a benefit concert.

Novello, Clara (1818–1908). English soprano, daughter of Vincent Novello. Admitted to the Institution de Musique Religieuse, Paris as a young girl in 1829; Rossini was on the adjudicating panel. She made her debut in Bologna in 1841 as Semiramide and was chosen by Rossini for the Italian *prima* of the *Stabat mater* the following March. The cadenza Rossini wrote for her at the close of the 'Sancta mater' is extant, and has been recorded.

Nozzari, Andrea (1775–1832). Italian tenor. A late developer, Nozzari was at the height of his powers in Rossini's Naples years. He possessed a powerful, somewhat baritonal tenor and was a commanding actor. He created many important roles for Rossini, among them Otello, Rinaldo in *Armida*, Osiride in *Mosè in Egitto*, Agorante in *Ricciardo e Zoriade*, Pirro in *Ermione*, Rodrigo in *La donna del lago*, Erisso in *Maometto II*, and Antenore in *Zelmira*.

Pacini, Giovanni (1796–1867). Italian composer, pupil of Mattei and one of Rossini's closest imitators. His father created the role of Don Geronio in *Il turco in Italia* and his son, Émilien, provided a number of short texts for Rossini in the 1860s. As a composer he lacked Rossini's care and control of form and detail, though *Saffo* (1840, Naples) reveals a continuing interest in evolving contemporary styles.

Paër, Ferdinando (1771–1839). Italian composer. Rossini made his stage debut in Paër's *Camilla* (1799, Vienna) in Bologna in 1805. Paër worked in Vienna, Prague, and Dresden before, under Napoleon's patronage, succeeding Spontini as Director of Paris's Théâtre-Italien in 1812. His co-directorship with Rossini from 1824 to 1827 was an uneasy one though a good deal less difficult than vituperative press reports would have us believe.

Paisiello, Giovanni (1740–1816). Influential Italian composer who enjoyed widespread international success in the late eighteenth and early nineteenth centuries. Paisiello's was the flag to which anti-Rossinians, in England as well as in Italy, invariably rallied. The rift between the two schools became irreconcilable after Rossini's *Il barbiere di Siviglia* which treats Beaumarchais's play with a disruptive energy entirely at odds with the urbanity and grace of Paisiello's famous setting of 1782.

Pasta, Giuditta (1797–1865). Italian soprano. From 1821 until the debut in Paris of Malibran in 1828 Pasta was unrivalled as an interpreter of such roles as Tancredi, Desdemona, and Semiramide in productions at the

Théâtre-Italien. Though she was not Rossini's favourite singer (the voice was sometimes uneven, the method idiosyncratic), she was a singing-actress of magnetism and great persuasive power. Stendhal devotes a chapter to her in his *Vie de Rossini*. She created roles for Rossini's immediate Italian successors including the title roles in Donizetti's *Anna Bolena* (March 1831, Milan) and Bellini's *Norma* (December 1831, Milan).

Patti, Adelina (1843–1919). Italian soprano of fame and distinction whose career began as a child prodigy in the USA in 1857–9 and lasted into the age of the gramophone. She made her Paris début in 1862 and sang at Rossini's *samedi soirs*. Trained, initially, by Maurice Strakosch, she was rebuked by Rossini for the over-elaborate use of ornament but she remained his devoted admirer. She was present at his villa in Passy at the time of his death, and sang at his funeral.

Pélissier, Olympe (1797–1878). Rossini's second wife whom he married in 1846 after the death of Isabella Colbran-Rossini. Courtesan, mistress of the painter Vernet, and partial model for Foedora in Balzac's *La peau de chagrin*, she became Rossini's close companion in Paris in the early 1830s. She moved to Bologna in 1837 and was responsible for Rossini's return to Paris in 1855. Her patient care for Rossini during years of often debilitating illness and her undoubted skills as a society hostess sustained Rossini in the latter half of his life; without her remarkable care, Rossini's return to active creative life in the late 1850s might never have come about.

Radiciotti, Giuseppe (1858–1931). Italian composer and musicologist whose scrupulous research procedures and fine critical and historical perceptions found their most complete expression in his three-volume study of Rossini's life and works published in 1927–9. A limited edition and one of the most beautifully designed and printed of all musical biographies, copies are, alas, rare.

Ricordi, Giovanni (1785–1853). Founder of the most famous of Italy's music publishing houses. His appointment as prompter and copyist at La Scala, Milan coincided with Rossini's arrival in the city in December, 1814. In 1825 he acquired the theatre's entire musical archives. Between 1846 and 1864 the firm published an extensive Rossini edition. Rossini expressed alarm at the publication of early works which had failed and been partially re-cycled in later ones, but he did not oppose the project. There is no evidence of his own editorial collaboration with the edition nor did he benefit financially until 1867 when a small sum was forthcoming under new copyright laws. In 1980 the Ricordi house began publication of the complete *L'edizione critica delle opere di Gioachino Rossini* in collaboration with the Fondazione Rossini, Pesaro.

Righetti-Giorgi, Geltrude (1793–1862). Italian contralto who created the roles of Rosina in *Il barbiere di Siviglia* and Cenerentola. Born and trained in Bologna, she appears to have been specially chosen by Rossini for these important Rome productions in 1816–17. She retired for reasons of health in 1822 and left an interesting memoir which details the fiasco of the first night of *Il barbiere di Siviglia*.

Romani, Felice (1788–1865). The most skilful and productive Italian librettist of his day who provided texts for Mayr, Rossini (notably *Il turco in Italia*), Donizetti, and Bellini. He also furnished Verdi with the text for his early *melodramma giocoso, Un giorno di regno*.

Rossi, Gaetano (1774–1855). Italian librettist working principally in Venice. He wrote over 120 librettos for composers ranging from Mayr (*Adelaide di Gueselino* 1799, Venice) to Donizetti (*Linda di Chamounix*, 1842, Vienna). His work could be careless and lacking in dramatic credibility as the libretto to *Tancredi* all too readily proves; but his libretto for *Semiramide* – a popular subject set by Rossi under Rossini's own close scrutiny – is eminently satisfactory.

Rossini, Anna (1771–1827). Rossini's mother. A talented but untrained soprano whose brief career as an opera singer gave the seven- to twelve-year-old Rossini first-hand experience of operatic life during his most impressionable years. Rossini remained deeply attached to her throughout his life.

Rossini, Giuseppe (1758–1839). Rossini's father. A professional horn and trumpet player. An over-zealous republican whose political enthusiasms landed him in trouble in the late 1790s, he remained close to his son throughout his life and was one of his early teachers. After his wife's death, he spent more time than he would have wished with Isabella Colbran-Rossini during her lonely and disaffected years in Bologna in the 1830s.

Rubini, Giovanni Battista (1794–1854). Italian tenor who completed a long apprenticeship under Barbaia in Naples after his debut there in *L'italiana in Algeri* in 1816. He reached a wider audience and was soon dubbed 'le roi des ténors' in Paris in 1825 where he appeared in productions of *La Cenerentola, Otello*, and *La donna del lago*. A consummate vocalist but a poor actor, he later inspired a number of roles whose technical and stylistic difficulties pose considerable problems for the modern interpreter.

Saint-Saëns, Camille (1835–1921). French composer and pianist. His account of Rossini's *samedi soirs* which he regularly attended are of considerable interest. His own music shares some of the stylistic and aesthetic priorities evident in Rossini's late works.

Sanquirico, Alessandro (1777–1849). Italian scene painter and designer whose stage designs for La Scala, Milan (1817 ff.) were widely admired and copied. His designs are notable for the fidelity, grandeur, and classical simplicity of their architectural impressions and the complementary beauty of his landscape evocations. See plates 7 and 8.

Schiller, Friedrich von (1759–1805). German dramatist, poet, aesthetician, and historian. His final play, *Wilhelm Tell* (1804), provided Rossini with a drama tailor-made to his musical, theatrical, aesthetic, and political needs.

Schmidt, Giovanni (*c*.1775–*c*,1840). Italian librettist who provided Rossini with texts for *Elisabetta, regina d'Inghilterra, Armida, Adelaide di Borgogna,* and *Eduardo e Cristina.* It is said that Rossini thought him an uncongenial and gloomy man.

Scott, Sir Walter (1771–1832). Scottish poet and novelist whose works were widely taken up by musicians in the new wave of Romantic feeling which followed the end of the Napoleonic wars. Rossini's *La donna del lago* is the first important operatic setting of a work by Scott.

Scribe, Eugène (1791–1861). French dramatist and librettist. The young Scribe wrote many *comédies-vaudevilles,* among them the delightful *Rossini à Paris, ou Le grand dîner* and the play on which *Le Comte Ory* was later to be based by Scribe himself. He also worked closely with Meyerbeer and provided texts for Auber, Bellini, Donizetti, Gounod, Offenbach, and Verdi.

Spontini, Gasparo (1774–1851). Italian composer who strongly influenced the course of serious French opera. The formal, ritualistic aspects of his writing and his use of multiple musical perspectives made their impression on Berlioz and Wagner, and on Rossini who conducted the revised *Fernand Cortez* in Naples in 1820.

Stendhal (Henri Beyle (1783–1842). French novelist and critic. A musician *manqué,* Stendhal was an early admirer of Mozart and a passionate follower of Italian opera. His *Vie de Rossini* often blurs fact and fantasy, is cavalier about detail, and reveals anti-Bourbon sentiments in its treatment of Colbran, but no other work evokes so vividly the world in which Rossini worked during his Naples years.

Sterbini, Cesare (1784–1831). A Roman civil servant with a sophisticated grasp of literary forms. He provided librettos for *Torvaldo e Dorliska* and *Il barbiere di Siviglia,* the latter a generally excellent adaptation of Beaumarchais's play well suited to the demands of Rossini's music with its energy, its irony, its highly developed sense of incongruity, and its skilful deployment of dramatic perspective.

Tadolini, Giovanni (*c*.1789–1872). Italian composer and teacher. He wrote and worked in Bologna and Paris. Returning to Paris as musical director of the Théâtre-Italien in 1829, he wrote six of the twelve movements for the first version of Rossini's *Stabat mater* (1832). The revised *Stabat mater* (1841) contains none of Tadolini's music.

Tottola, Andrea Leone (d.1831). Italian librettist, and official poet to the royal theatres in Naples. He provided Rossini with librettos for *Mosè in Egitto, Ermione, La donna del Lago,* and *Zelmira.* Though not a first-rate writer, he was more skilful and innovative than is often supposed; his first three Rossini librettos, drawn respectively from the Bible, Racine, and Scott, make sensible use of aptly chosen materials.

Troupenas, Eugène-Théodore (1799–1850). French music publisher whose career was effectively launched by his editions of Rossini's last four operas. On Rossini's advice he also published Auber's work from 1828 onwards. His proof-readers included Berlioz who read *Guillaume Tell* for the Troupenas edition.

Velluti, Giovanni Battista (1781–1861). Italian male soprano who, like Rossini, studied with Mattei in Bologna. Rossini wrote the role of Arsace in *Aureliano in Palmira* for him and he was later engaged for Rossini's cantata *Il vero omaggio* in Verona in 1822. The sound of the castrato voice – its purity, flexibility, and penetrating accent – was something Rossini never forgot.

Verdi, Giuseppe (1813–1901). Italian composer: Rossini's most distinguished successor. Relations between the two men were cordial rather than warm. Rossini commissioned and payed for two arias from Verdi for use by Ivanoff and he included music by Verdi in his *samedi soirs* in Paris (see plate 19). After Rossini's death Verdi attempted unsuccessfully to assemble a Requiem Mass in his honour written by a number of Italian composers. His own contribution, the 'Libera me', was later used in his own Manzoni Requiem Mass. In 1898, modestly overlooking the claims of *Falstaff*, Verdi declared *Il barbiere di Siviglia* to be the most beautiful *opera buffa* ever written.

Wagner, Richard (1813–83). German composer. As a young man Wagner orchestrated 'Li marinari' from *Les soirées musicales* and took a close interest in such works as *Mosè in Egitto*, *La donna del lago*, and *Guillaume Tell*. The composers' respective styles, Wagner's written excoriations in 1841, and Rossini's many alleged witticisms at Wagner's expense would seem to suggest an unbridgeable gulf between them but Rossini's influence on the young Wagner is perhaps greater than has yet been allowed and their meeting in Paris in 1860 was both cordial and of mutual interest.

Weber, Carl Maria von (1786–1826). German composer whose innovative and imaginative genius was a principal inspiration to the new Romantic German school. In the early 1820s Weber feared Rossini as a rival and envied his success, though the two men parted on amicable terms shortly before Weber's premature death. Rossini comes close to aspects of Weber's Romanticism in works like *Armida* and *La donna del lago*, both of which pre-date *Der Freischütz*, and in *Guillaume Tell*, but there is little evidence of direct mutual influence.

Appendix D

Select bibliography

Publications of the Fondazione Rossini, Pesaro

BdCRdS *Bollettino del Centro rossiniano di studi* (1955–60, 1967–)
EC *Edizione critica delle opere di Gioachino Rossini* (1979–)

Letters

A new edition of Rossini's letters is in preparation by the Fondazione Rossini. Mazzatinti's edition, published in 1890 and revised in 1892 and 1902, includes only a small proportion of the many thousands of letters written by and to Rossini during his Italian and French years, the letters themselves often tidied by Mazzatinti into grammatical respectability. Below are the principal sources extant at the time of the preparation of the present volume.

G. Mazzatinti: *Lettere inedite di Gioacchino Rossini* (Imola, 1890, rev. 2/1892 as *Lettere di G. Rossini*)
A. Allmayer: *Undici lettere di Gioachino Rossini publicate per la prima volta* (Siena, 1892)
G. Biagi: 'Undici lettere inedite di G. Rossini', *Onoranze fiorentine a Gioachino Rossini* (Florence, 1902), 101
R. De Rensis: 'Rossini intimo: lettere all'amico Santocanale', *Musica d'oggi*, xiii (1931), 343
F. Schlitzer: *Rossiniana: contributo all'epistolario di G. Rossini, Quaderni dell'Accademia chigiana*, xxxv (Siena, 1956)
F. Walker: 'Rossiniana in the Piancastelli Collection', *The Monthly Musical Record*, x (1960), 138, 203
F. Lippmann: 'Autographe Briefe Rossinis und Donizettis in der Bibliothek Massimo, Rome', *Analecta musicologica*, no.19 (1979), 330
J. Kallberg: 'Marketing Rossini: sei lettere di Troupenas ad Artaria', BdCRdS (1980), 41

Other Source Materials

G. Radiciotti: *Gioacchino Rossini: vita documentata, opere, ed influenza su l'arte* (Tivoli, 1927–9)

V. Viviani, ed.: I libretti di Rossini (Milan, 1965)

P. Gossett: 'Le fonti autografe delle opere teatrali di Rossini', *Nuova rivista musicale italiana*, ii (1968), 936

——: *The Operas of Rossini: Problems of Textual Criticism in Nineteenth Century Opera* (dissertation, Princeton Univ, 1970)

B. Cagli, P. Gossett, A. Zedda: 'Criteri per l'edizione critica delle opere di Gioachino Rossini', BdCRdS (1974), 1, 5.

Books, Articles, Memoirs by Contemporaries

Stendhal: *Rome, Naples, et Florence en 1817* (Paris, 1817; Eng. trans., 1959)

Guerre aux Rossinistes (Paris, 1821)

G. Righetti-Giorgi: *Cenni di una donna già cantante sopra il maestro Rossini* (Bologna, 1823; repr. in Rognoni, 3/1977)

Stendhal: *Vie de Rossini* (Paris, 1824; Eng. trans., 1956, 2/1970 with notes by R.N. Coe)

G. Carpani: *Le rossiniane ossia Lettere musico-teatrali* (Padua, 1824)

A. Wendt: *Rossinis Leben und Treiben* (Leipzig, 1824)

Edgcumbe, Earl of Mount: *Musical reminiscences of an old amateur* (London, 1824, rev. 1827, 1834)

H. Berton: *De la musique mécanique et de la musique philosophique*, (Paris, 1826)

J. Ebers: *Seven Years of the King's Theatre* (London, 1828)

J.-L. d'Ortigue: *De la guerre des dilettanti* (Paris, 1829)

P. Brighenti: *Della musica rossiniana e del suo autore* (Bologna, 1830, 2/1833)

A. Zanolini: *Biografia di Gioachino Rossini* (Paris, 1836, rev. Bologna, 1875)

M. and L. Escudier: *Rossini: sa vie et ses oeuvres* (Paris, 1854)

E. de Mirecourt: *Rossini, Offenbach* (Paris, 1855)

Castil-Blaze: *L'Opéra-Italien de 1548 à 1856* (Paris, 1856)

H.F. Chorley: Thirty Years' Musical Recollections (London, 1862, 2/1926)

E. Montazio: *Giovacchino Rossini* (Turin, 1862)

L. Escudier: *Mes souvenirs* (Paris, 1863–8)

A. Aulangier: *G. Rossini: sa vie et ses oeuvres* (Paris, 1864)

A. Azevedo: *G. Rossini: sa vie et ses oeuvres* (Paris, 1864)

G. Pacini: *Le mie memorie artistiche* (Florence, 1865, rev. 2/1872)

F. Hiller: 'Plaudereien mit Rossini (1856)', *Aus dem Tonleben unserer Zeit*, ii (Leipzig, 1868, 2/1871)

R. Wagner: 'Eine Erinnerung an Rossini', *Allgemeine Zeitung*, Augsburg, 17 Dec 1868; repr. *Gesammelte Schriften und Dichtungen*, viii, Leipzig, 1883; Eng. trans. *Richard Wagner's* Prose Works, ed. and trans. W.A. Ellis (London, 1894–9), iv, 269

H.S. Edwards: *The Life of Rossini* (London, 1869, rev. 2/1881 as *Rossini and his School*)

E. Hanslick: *Aus dem Concertsaal* (Vienna, 1870/R1971, 2/1896)

F. Mordani: *Della vita privata di G. Rossini: memorie inedite* (Imola, 1871)

A. Pougin: *Rossini: notes, impressions, souvenirs, commentaires* (Paris, 1871)

L.S. Silvestri: *Della vita e delle opere di Gioachino Rossini: notizie biografico-artistico-aneddotico-critiche* (Milan, 1874)

F. Hiller: *Felix Mendelssohn Bartholdy: Briefe und Erinnerungen* (Cologne, 1874)

G. De Sanctis: *Gioacchino Rossini: appunti di viaggio* (Rome, 1878)

G.L. Duprez: *Souvenirs d'un chanteur* (Paris, 1880)

E. Branca: *Felice Romani ed i più riputati maestri di musica del suo tempo* (Turin, Florence, Rome, 1882)

G. Dupré: *Ricordi autobiografici* (Florence, 1895, 2/1896 as *Pensieri sull'arte e ricordi autobiografici*)

A. Cametti: *Un poeta melodrammatico romano: appunti e notizie in gran parte inedite sopra Jacopo Ferretti e i musicisti del suo tempo* (Milan, 1898)

E. Michotte: *Souvenirs personnels: la visite de R. Wagner à Rossini Paris, 1860* (Paris, 1906, repr. in Rognoni, 3/1977; Eng. trans., ed. H. Weinstock, New York, 1968, 2/1982)

——: *Souvenirs: une soirée chez Rossini à Beau-Séjour (Passy) 1858*, (Brussels, c.1910; Eng. trans., ed. H. Weinstock, New York, 1968, 2/1982).

C. Saint-Saëns: *Ecole buissonnière* (Paris, 1913; Eng. trans., 1919, as *Musical Memories)*

General Literature

G.B. Shaw: 'Rossini Centenary', *The Illustrated London News*, 5 and 9 March, 1892.

L. Dauriac: *La psychologie dans l'opéra français: Auber, Rossini, Meyerbeer* (Paris, 1897)

——: *Rossini: biographie critique* (Paris, 1906)

E. Celani: 'Musica e musicisti in Roma (1750–1850)', *Rivista musicale italiana*, xxii (1915), 257–300

G. Fara: *Genio e ingegno musicale: Gioachino Rossini* (Turin, 1915)

A. Cametti: 'La musica teatrale a Roma cento anni fa', *Regia Accademia di Santa Cecilia: annuario* (Rome, 1915–30)

F. Vatielli: *Rossini a Bologna* (Bologna, 1918)

A. Casella: 'Some reasons why futurists may admire Rossini', *The Chesterian,* ii (London, 1920), 321

H.de Curzon: *Rossini* (Paris, 1920)

V. Cavazzocca Mazzanti: 'Rossini a Verona durante il Congresso del 1822',

Atti e memorie dell'Accademia di agricoltura, scienze e lettere di Verona, 4th ser. (Verona, 1922), 53–112

G. Radiciotti: *Anedotti rossiniana autentici* (Rome, 1929)

J.-G. Prod'homme: 'Rossini and his works in France', *The Musical Quarterly*, xvii (1931), 119

Lord Derwent: *Rossini and some Forgotten Nightingales* (London, 1934)

F. Toye: *Rossini: a study in tragi-comedy* (London, 1934, 2/1963)

H. Faller: *Die Gesangkoloratur in Rossinis Opern und ihre Ausführung* (Berlin, 1935)

E.J. Dent: 'Rossini' in *The Rise of Romantic Opera* (lect. Cornell Univ., 1937–8, London, 1976)

Rossiniana (Bologna, 1942)

A. Capri: 'Rossini e l'estetica teatrale della vocalità', *Rivista musicale italiana*, xlvi (1942), 353

A. Della Corte: 'Fra gorgheggi e melodie di Rossini', *Musica*, i (1942), 23

U. Rolandi: 'Librettistica rossinana', *Musica*, i (1942), 40

L. Ronga: 'Vicende del gusto rossiniano nell' ottocento', *Musica*, i (1942), 6

——: 'Svolgimento del gusto rossiniano al novecento', *Musica*, ii (1943), 184

G. Roncaglia: *Rossini l'olimpico* (Milan, 1946, 2/1953)

Rassegna musicale, xxiv/3 (1954), 209–303

M. Curtis: 'Bizet, Offenbach, and Rossini', The Musical Quarterly, xl (1954)

L. Rognoni: *Rossini* (Parma, 1956, 2/1968, 3/1977)

C. Vannini-Simoni: 'Rossini e Pacini', BdCRds (1956), II, no.6

F. Zagiba, ed.: *Chopin* (Vienna, 1956)

A. Bonaccorsi: 'Temporali dell 'Ottocento', BdCRdS (1958), III, no.5

W. Klefisch: 'Rossini und Schopenhauer', BdCRdS (1958), III, no.4

F. Schlitzer: *Rossini e Siena*, Quaderni dell 'Accademia chigiana, xxxix (Siena, 1958)

A. Toni, T, Serafin: *Stile, tradizioni e convenzioni del melodramma italiano del settecento e dell'ottocento* (Milan, 1958)

H. Rosenthal: *Two centuries of opera at Covent Garden* (London, 1958)

R. Bacchelli: *Rossini e Esperienze rossiniane* (Milan, 1959)

G. Meyerbeer: *Briefwechsel und Tagebucher* (ed. H. Becker), vol. 1 (Berlin, 1960)

E.N. McKay: 'Rossinis Einfluss auf Schubert', *Österreichische Musikzeitschrift*, xviii (1963), 17

R. Celletti: 'Vocalità rossiniana', *L'opera*, ii (Milan, 1966), 3

F.d'Amico: *L'opera teatrale di Gioacchino Rossini* (Rome, 1968)

G. Barblan: 'Rossini e il suo tempo', *Chigiana*, xxv (1968), 143

F. Bisogni: 'Rossini e Schubert', *Nuova rivista musicale italiana*, ii (1968), 920

A. Bonaccorsi, ed.: *Gioacchino Rossini* (Florence, 1968)

R. Celletti: 'Origini e sviluppi della coloratura rossiniana', *Nuova rivista musicale italiana*, ii (1968), 872

——: 'Il vocalismo italiano da Rossini a Donizetti: Parte I: Rossini', *Analecta musicologica*, 5 (1968), 267

M. Fabbri: 'Ignoti momenti rossiniani', *Chigiana*, xxv (1968), 265

E. Forbes: 'Sir Walter Scott and Opera', *Opera*, 19 no. 11 (1968), 872

P. Gossett: 'Rossini and Authenticity', *Musical Times*, cix (1968), 1006

P. Graves: 'Homage to Rossini', *Opera*, 19 no.11 (1968), 858

F. Lippmann: 'Per un'esegesi dello stile rossiniano', *Nuova rivista musicale italiana*, ii (1968), 813

——: 'Sull' estetica di Rossini', BdCRdS (1968), 4–6, 62

H. Weinstock: *Rossini: a Biography* (New York, 1968)

——: 'Rossini, Donizetti, Bellini, Verdi', *Opera*, 19 no.11 (1968), 865

F. Lippmann: 'Rossinis Gedanken über die Musik', *Die Musikforschung*, xxii (1969), 285

M. Aspinall: 'Musica proibita', *Records and Recording*, 14 no.2 (1970), 32

P. Gossett: 'Gioachino Rossini and the Conventions of Composition', *Acta musicologica*, xlii (1970), 48

J. Loschelder: 'L'infanzia di Gioacchino Rossini', BdCRdS (1972), 1, 45; 2, 33

——: 'Rossinis Bild und Zerbild in der Allgemeinen musikalischen Zeitung Leipzig', BdCRdS (1973), 1, 23; 2, 23 (1977); 3, 17

R. Risaliti: 'Rossini e Liszt', BdCRdS (1972), no.3, 40

A. Caswell: 'Vocal Embellishment in Rossini's Paris Operas: French Style of Italian?', BdCRdS (1975), no.1, p.5; no.2, p.5

——: 'Mme. Cinti-Damoreau and the Embellishment of Italian Opera in Paris: 1820–1845', *Journal of the American Musicological Society*, xxviii (1975), 459

J. Loschelder: 'Spontini und Rossini', BdCRdS (1975), 1, 65

E. Crafts: 'A Tale of the Cats', BdCRdS (1975), 3, 5

S. Alberici: 'Rossini e Pio IX', BdCRdS (1977), 5

——: 'Appunti sulle librettistica Rossiniana', BdCRdS (1978), 1–3, 45
Chigiana, xxxiv (1977)

P. Fabbri: 'Presenze rossiniane negli archivi ravennati: due inediti, un autografo ed altro', BdCRdS (1978), 5

F. Lippmann, ed: *Die stilistische Entwicklung der italienischen Musik zwischen 1770 und 1830 und ihre Beziehungen zum Norden* (Rome, 1978); *Analecta musicologica*, no.21 (1982)

P. Fabbri: 'Alla scuola dei Malerbi: altri autografi rossiniani', BdCRdS (1980), 5

P. Gossett: Rossini, *New Grove Dictionary of Music and Musicians*, Vol. 16 (London, 1980), 226; 2/1983 in *The New Grove Masters of Italian Opera*

B. Cagli: 'Rossini a Londra e al Théâtre-Italien di Parigi: documenti inediti dell'impresario G.B. Benelli, BdCRdS (1981), 1–3, 5

F. Lippmann: 'Rossini – und kein Ende', *Studi musicali*, x (1981), 279

W. Dean: 'Rossini's French Operas', 'Rossini's Italian Operas', *The New Oxford History of Music*, VIII, ed. Abraham (London 1982), 104, 403.

M. Ferrero: 'Per Rossini: un primo tentativo di iconografia scenografica', BdCRdS (1982), 1–3, 5

G. Landini: 'G.L. Duprez ovvero l'importanza di cantar Rossini', BdCRdS (1982), 1–3, 29

S. Henze-Döhring: 'La natura nelle opere di Rossini', BdCRdS (1983), 113

P. Fabbri: 'I Rossini, una famiglia in arte', BdCRdS (1983), 125

N. Till: *Rossini: his life and times* (London, 1983)

J. Rosselli: *The Opera Industry from Cimarosa to Verdi: The Role of the Impresario* (London, 1984)

V. Gui: 'Scritti Rossiniani', BdCRdS (1985), 19

E. Neill: 'Paganini e Rossini', BdCRdS (1986), 15

P. Fabbri: '*Minima rossiniana*: ancora sulle carriere dei Rossini', BdCRdS (1987), 5

G. J. Joerg: 'Rossini a Londra e la cantata *Il pianto delle Muse in morte di Lord Byron*', BdCRdS (1988), 47

F. Panzini: 'La casa natale di Rossini', BdCRdS (1988), 77

R. Celletti: *A History of Bel Canto* (London, 1991)

D. Kimbell: *Italian Opera* (London, 1991)

J. Rosselli: *Music and Musicians in Nineteenth-Century Italy* (London, 1991)

A. Kendall: *Gioacchino Rossini: The Reluctant Hero* (London, 1992)

R. Milnes: 'Rossini's *comédie humaine*', Opera 43 No.3 (1992), 272

Individual Works

Overtures

P. Gossett: 'The overtures of Rossini', *19th Century Music*, iii (1979–80), 3

——: 'Le sinfonie di Rossini', BdCRdS (1979), 1–3, 7

La cambiale di matrimonio

F. Cacaci: '*La cambiale di matrimonio da Federici a Rossi*, BdCRdS 1975, 1–2

L'equivoco stravagante

A. Damerini: 'La prima ripresa moderna di un'opera giovanile di Rossini' *Chigiana*, xxii (1965), 229

L'inganno felice
L'occasione fa il ladro

A. Melica: 'Due operine di Rossini', *Musicisti della scuola emilana*, Chigiana, xiii (1956), 59

G. C. Ballola: 'An Italian *jeu de l'amour et du hazard*', Pesaro Festival (1987), 14

La scala di seta

A. Wiklund: '*La scala di seta* in Stockholm', Pesaro Festival (1988), 13

F. Degrada: 'Rossini's *La scala di seta*, a Study', Pesaro Festival (1988), 29

Il Signor Bruschino

G. Radiciotti: 'Il *Signor Bruschino* e il *Tancredi* di G. Rossini', *Rivista Musicale Italiana*, Turin, 2, XXVII, 1920.

A. Gazzaniga: 'From *Le fils par hazard* to *Il Signor Bruschino*', Pesaro Festival (1988), 16

A. Zedda: '*Bruschino*: a farce to be taken seriously', Pesaro Festival (1988), 23

Tancredi

P. Gossett: 'The *candeur virginale* of *Tancredi*', *Musical Times*, cxii (1971), 326

P. Gossett: *The Tragic Finale of 'Tancredi'* (Pesaro, 1977)

D. Tortora: 'Fortuna dei "palpiti" rossiniani nella musica strumentale a stampa dell 'Ottocento', BdCRdS (1988), 5

L'italiana in Algeri

P. Gallarati: 'Dramma e ludus dall *'Italiana* al *Barbiere*', *Il melodrama italiano dell'ottocento: studi e ricerche per Massimo Mila* (Turin, 1977)

C. Questa: *Il ratto del serraglio: Euripide, Plauto, Mozart, Rossini* (Bologna, 1979)

Il turco in Italia

G. Gavazzeni: *'Il turco in Italia'*, *La rassegna musicale*, 1, 1959

G. C. Ballola: 'The (A)moral of the story', Pesaro Festival (1986), 16

Torvaldo e Dorliska

G. Ballola: 'Una *piece à sauvetage* da Salvare', BdCRdS (1971), 11

Il barbiere di Siviglia

A. Zedda: 'Appunti per una lettura filolgica del *Barbiere*', *L'opera*, ii (Milan, 1966), 13

——: 'In margine all 'edizione critica del *Barbiere di Siviglia*, BdCRdS (1970), 1, 3

——: 'Ancora sul belcanto, lo stile ed il *Barbiere*', *Rassegna musicale Curci* (1970), no.1

M. Tartak: 'The two *Barbieri*', *Music and Letters*, 1 (1969), 453

J. Stone: 'Creative malice – *Il barbiere* revisited', *Musical Times*, cxxxiii (February 1992), 63

La gazzetta

G. Saponaro: '*La gazzetta* di G. Rossini', *Autumno musicale napoletano*, III (Naples, 1960)

Otello

J. Klein: 'Verdi's *Otello* and Rossini's', *Music and Letters*, xlv (1964), 130

F. Tammaro: 'Ambivalenza dell '*Otello* rossiniano', *Il melodramma italiano dell'ottocento: studi e ricerche per Massimo Mila* (Turin, 1977)

F. D'Amico: 'The high C sharp on the coat-rack', Pesaro Festival (1988), 19

M. Collins: 'Toward a definitive *Otello*: evidence from the manuscripts', Pesaro Festival (1988), 35

La Cenerentola

P. Gossett, ed.: *La Cenerentola: riproduzione del autografo esistente presso l'Accademia filarmonica di Bologna* (Bolgna, 1969)

A. Zedda: 'Problemi testuali della *Cenerentola*', BdCRdS (1971), 29

La gazza ladra

G. Romagnoli: 'Gioacchino Rossini, Giulio Perticari e *La gazza ladra*', *Vita italiana*, iii (1897), 106

A. Melica: '*La gazza ladra* nella revisione di Zandonai', BdCRdS (1956), 3

P. Gossett: '*La gazza ladra*, notes towards a critical edition', BdCRdS (1972), 1, 12

R. Celletti: 'La vocalità rossiniana e *La gazza ladra*', BdCRdS (1973), 2, 5

Armida

L. Tozzi: '*Armida*, ou la couleur fantastique', BdCRdS (1975), 3, 27

Mosè in Egitto

P. Petrobelli: 'Balzac, Stendhal, e il *Mosè* di Rossini', *Annuario 1965–70* del Conservatorio G. B. Martini di Bologna, 1971

P. Isotta: 'Da *Mosè* a *Moïse*', BdCRdS (1971), 87

——: 'I diamanti della corona: grammatica del Rossini napoletano', *Mosè in Egitto*, Opera: collana di guide musicali, iv (Turin, 1974)

M. Conati: 'Between Past and Future: the Dramatic World of Rossini in *Mosè in Egitto* and *Moïse et Pharaon*', *19th Century Music*, iv (1980–81), 32

Adina

G. Confalonieri: 'Avventure di una partitura rossiniana: l'*Adina* ovvero *Il califfo di Bagdad*', *Le celebrazioni del 1963 e alcune nuove indagine sulla musica italiana del XVIII e XIX secolo*, Chigiana, xx (1963), 206

Ricciardo e Zoraide

L. Tozzi: 'Sulle tracce di *un péché de jeunesse, Ricciardo e Zoraide*', BdCRdS (1974), 2–3, 9

F. Agostinelli and G. Gravagna: '*Ricciardo e Zoraide*: from autograph to critical edition', Pesaro Festival (1990), 31

P. Gossett: 'The coarse country girl and the golden lyre', Pesaro Festival (1990), 17

Ermione

G. Ballola: 'Lettura dell' *Ermione*', BdCRdS (1972), 3, 12

P. Gossett: '*Ermione*: Rossini's *tragédie lyrique*', Pesaro Festival (1987), 22

Eduardo e Cristina
M. Marino: 'Rossini e Pavesi: a proposito di un'aria dell'*Eduardo e Cristina*', BdCRdS (1986), 5

La donna del lago
A. Bonaccorsi: '*La donna del lago*', *La Rassegna Musicale* (1958), no.2
A. Melica: 'L'aria in rondò de *La donna del lago*', BdCRdS (1958), no.6
——: 'Appunti sullo Scott e la sua *Donna del lago*', *Annuario 1965—70 del Conservatorio di Musica G.B. Martini di Bologna*, 1971
P. Isotta: '*La donna del lago* e la drammaturgica di Rossini', BdCRdS (1970), 2, 45
J. Mitchell, '*La donna del lago*', *The Walter Scott Operas* (Alabama, 1977)

Bianca e Falliero
B. Cagli: 'Le fonti letterarie delle opere di Rossini', BdCRdS (1973), 1, 8
G. Dotto: 'Rossini's last Milanese opera', Pesaro Festival (1986), 12

Maometto II
B. Cagli: 'Le fonti letterarie dei libretti di Rossini', BdCRdS (1972), 2, 10

Matilde di Shabran
M. Tartak: 'Matilde and her cousins', BdCRdS (1973), 3, 13

Zelmira
A. Parente: 'La *Zelmira* di G. Rossini', *Annuario del Conservatorio di Musica S. Pietro a Majella*, Naples, 1965
A. Lanfranchi: 'Alcune note su *Zelmira*', BdCRdS (1981), 55

Semiramide
A. della Corte: 'La drammaturgica della *Semiramide* di Rossini', *La Rasegna Musicale*, 1938, no.1

Ugo re d'Italia (uncompleted)
A. Porter: 'A lost opera by Rossini', *Music and Letters* xlv (1964), 39

Il Viaggio a Reims
J. Johnson: 'A lost Rossini opera recovered: *Il viaggio a Reims*', BdCRdS (1983), 1–3, 5

Ivanhoé (adaptation)
J. Mitchell, 'Ivanhoe', *The Walter Scott Operas* (Alabama, 1977)

Moïse et Pharaon
H. Lacombe: 'Contributo allo studio delle fonti del *Moïse* di Rossini', BdCRdS (1989), 47

Le Comte Ory

E. Zanetti: '*Il Comte Ory*', *Rossiniana* (Bologna, 1942)

A. Porter: '*Le Comte Ory*', *Opera*, 5 (1954), 550

Guillaume Tell

V.-J. E. de Jouy: *Essai sur l'opéra franais* (Paris, 1823), ed. A. Gerhard, BdCRdS (1987), 61

H. Berlioz: '*Guillaume Tell*', *Gazette musicale*, i (1834), Oct-Nov, 326, 336, 341, 349; Eng. trans. in *Source Readings in Music History*, ed. O. Strunk (New York, 1950; 2/1981)

A. Cametti: 'Il *Guglielmo Tell* e le sue prime rappresentazioni in Italia', *Rivista musicale Italiana*, vi (1899), 580

V. Gui: 'Si naturale o la naturale a proposito del *Guglielmo Tell*', *Musica d'oggi*', xiii (1926)

A. Porter: '*William Tell*', *Opera*, 9 (1958), 146

B. Cagli: '*Guglielmo Tell, La Guida all 'Opera*, ed. G. Tomasi (Milan, 1971)

R. Kirby: 'Rossini's overture to *William Tell*', *Music and Letters*, xxxiii (1952), 132

A. Gerhard: 'Incantesimo o specchio dei costumi. Un'estetica dell'opera del librettista di *Guillaume Tell*', BdCRdS (1987), 45

Robert Bruce (adaptation)

J. Mitchell: 'Tales of a Grandfather', *The Walter Scott Operas* (Alabama, 1977)

Edipo a Colono

H. Prunieres: 'L'*Edipo a Colono* de Rossini', *La Revue Musicale*, xiv (1933), 32

N. Gallini: 'Importante inedito Rossiniano: la musica di scena dell' *Edipo a Colono* di Sofocle ritrovata nella sua integrità', *La Scala*, no.31 (1952), 19

A. Bonaccorsi: '*Edipo a Colono*', BdCRdS (1957), no.3.

Messa di Gloria

P. Gossett: 'Rossini in Naples: Some Major Works Recovered', *Musical Quarterly*, liv (1968), 316

F. Rimoli: 'Del sacro in Rossini: divagazioni soggettive sull'oggettività in musica', BdCRdS (1987), 25

Giovanna d'Arco

E. Valente: 'La cantata *Giovanna d'Arco*', BdCRdS (1970), 1

Stabat mater

J. d'Ortigue: *Le* Stabat *de Rossini* (Paris, 1841)

H. Valentino [pseud. of R. Wagner]: *Neue Zeitschrift für Musik*, 28 Dec. 1841; Eng. trans. W.A. Ellis, *Richard Wagner's Prose Works* (London, 1894–9), vii, 143

A. Aulangier: *Quelques observations sur la publication du 'Stabat Mater' de Rossini* (Paris, 1842)

J. Delaire: *Observations d'un amateur non dilettante au sujet du'Stabat Mater' de Rossini* (Paris, 1842)

E. Troupenas: *Resumé des opinions de la presse au sujet du 'Stabet Mater' de M. Rossini* (Paris, 1842)

H. Heine: *Sämtliche Werke*, VII, 217

M. Carner: 'The Mass from Rossini to Dvořák', *Major and Minor* (London, 1980), 122

F. Rimoli: 'Del sacro in Rossini: divagazioni soggettive sull'oggettività in musica', BdCRdS (1987), 25

M. Spada: 'Francesco Rangone e la *Narrazione* sullo *Stabat mater* a Bologna con altri documenti', BdCRdS (1989), 5

Petite messe solennelle

A. Ambros: 'Die *Messe solennelle* von Rossini', *Bunte Blätter*, i (Leipzig, 1872), 81

M. Carner: 'The Mass from Rossini to Dvořák', *Major and Minor* London 1980), 124

F. Rimoli: 'Del sacro in Rossini: divagazioni soggettive sull'oggettività in musica', BdCRdS (1987), 25

Péchés de vieillesse

G. Hirt: 'Di alcuni autografi di G. Rossini', *Rivista musicale italiana*, ii (1895), 23

S. Martinotti: 'I peccati del giovane e del vecchio Rossini', *Quadrivium*, xiv (1973), 249

P. Gossett: 'Rossini e i suoi *Péchés de viellesse*', *Nuova rivista musicale italiana*, xiv (1980), 7

Medical and Psychological

B. Riboli: 'Profilo medico-psicologico di G. Rossini', *La rassegna musicale*, 7–9 (1954), 292

——: 'Malattia di G. Rossini secondo una relazione medica del 1842', *Note e riviste di psichiatria*, 7 and 12 (1955), reprinted as pamphlet, Pesaro, 1956

D. Schwartz: 'Rossini: a Psychoanalytic Approach to the Great Renunciation', *Journal of the American Psychoanalytic Society*, xiii (1965), 551

A. Storr: 'Creativity and the Obsessional Character', *The Dynamics of Creation* (London, 1972)

Index